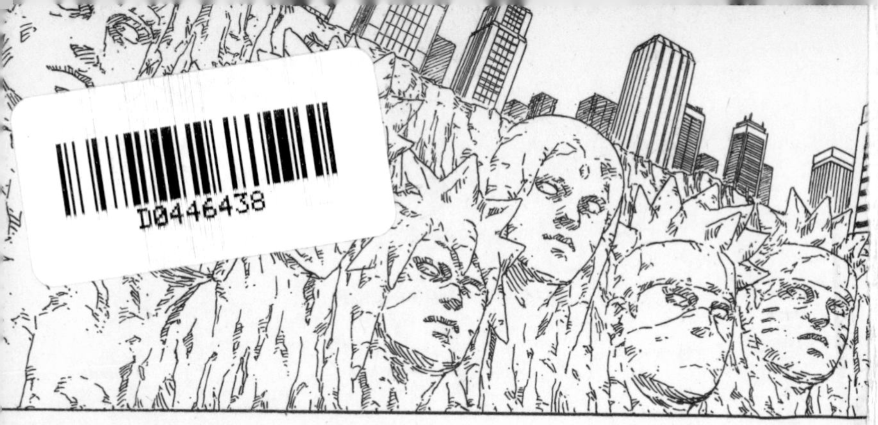

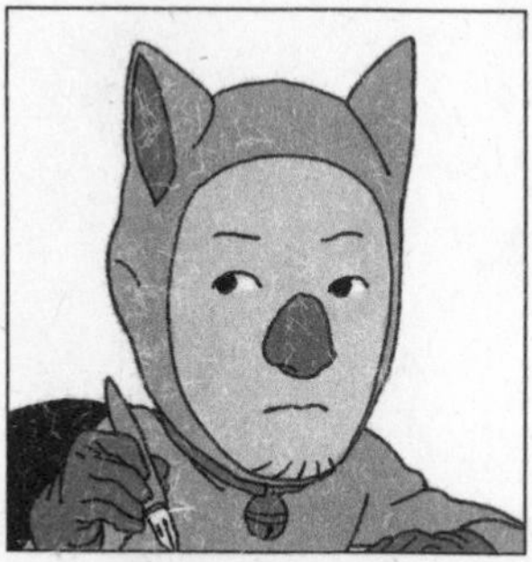

池本幹雄

"I'm short on time and this part's a pain to draw. Could you take it on, Mikio?" That's what Kishimoto-san used to say to me a lot while drawing *Naruto*. In the beginning, it would be a background character, people sitting in spectator seats, the bad guy's gaggle of minions and so on. At times, he would say, "You're the only one I can trust with this," and I would also get to draw Naruto's shadow doppelgangers, or even a large-sized main character that wasn't a doppelganger. And then, one day, circumstances led to me being entrusted with an entire manga. An honor that is more than I deserve!

–Mikio Ikemoto, 2016

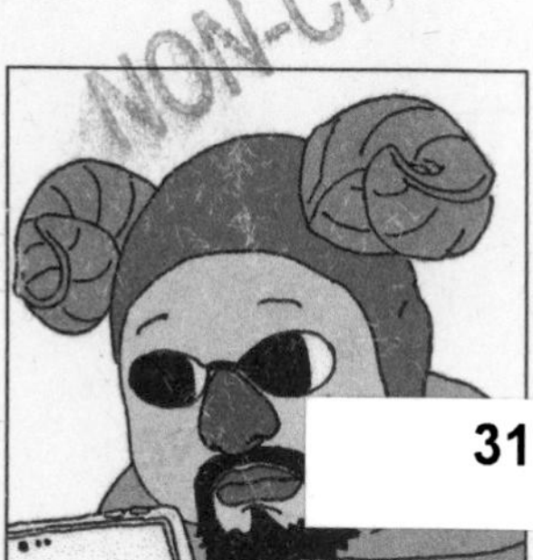

小太刀右京

I've loved ninja since I was a kid, and I had been creating lots of tabletop RPGs (RPGs that don't involve computers) with ninja characters when I was tapped to help with the *Boruto* film and the *Naruto* novel series world building, which then led to getting entrusted with the script

to deliver to all of you readers the many ideas and stories that Kishimoto Sensei has bequeathed to me. Thank you in advance!

–Ukyo Kodachi, 2016

BORUTO

-NARUTO NEXT GENERATIONS-

SHONEN JUMP MANGA EDITION

Creator/Supervisor MASASHI KISHIMOTO
Art by MIKIO IKEMOTO
Script by UKYO KODACHI

Translation: Mari Morimoto
Touch-up Art & Lettering: Snir Aharon
Design: Alice Lewis
Editor: Alexis Kirsch

BORUTO © 2016 by Masashi Kishimoto, Ukyo Kodachi, Mikio Ikemoto
All rights reserved.
First published in Japan in 2016 by SHUEISHA Inc., Tokyo.
English translation rights arranged by SHUEISHA Inc.

Printed in the U.S.A.

Published by VIZ Media, LLC
P.O. Box 77010
San Francisco, CA 94107

10 9 8 7 6 5 4 3
First printing, April 2017
Third printing, October 2017

viz.com

shonenjump.com

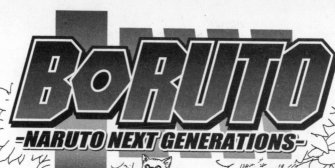

BORUTO

-NARUTO NEXT GENERATIONS-

VOLUME 1

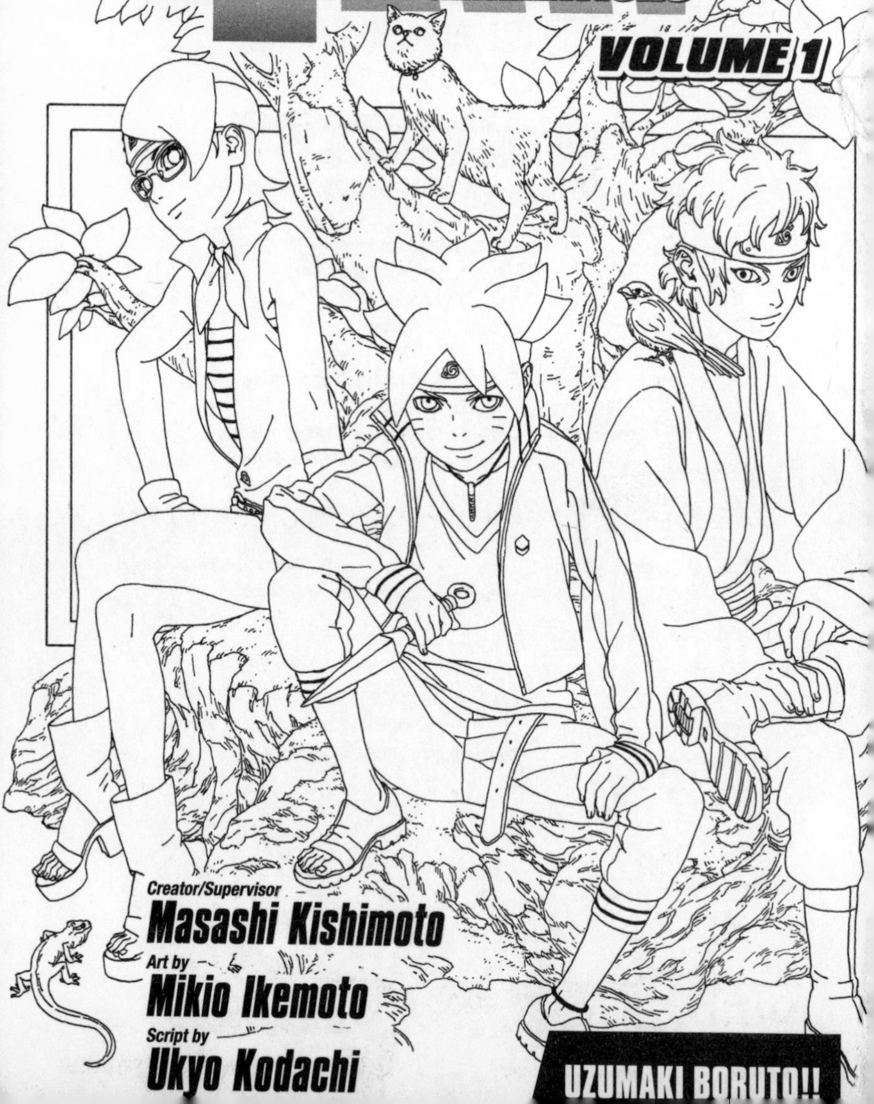

Creator/Supervisor
Masashi Kishimoto
Art by
Mikio Ikemoto
Script by
Ukyo Kodachi

UZUMAKI BORUTO!!

BORUTO

-NARUTO NEXT GENERATIONS-

VOLUME 1
 UZUMAKI BORUTO!!

CONTENTS

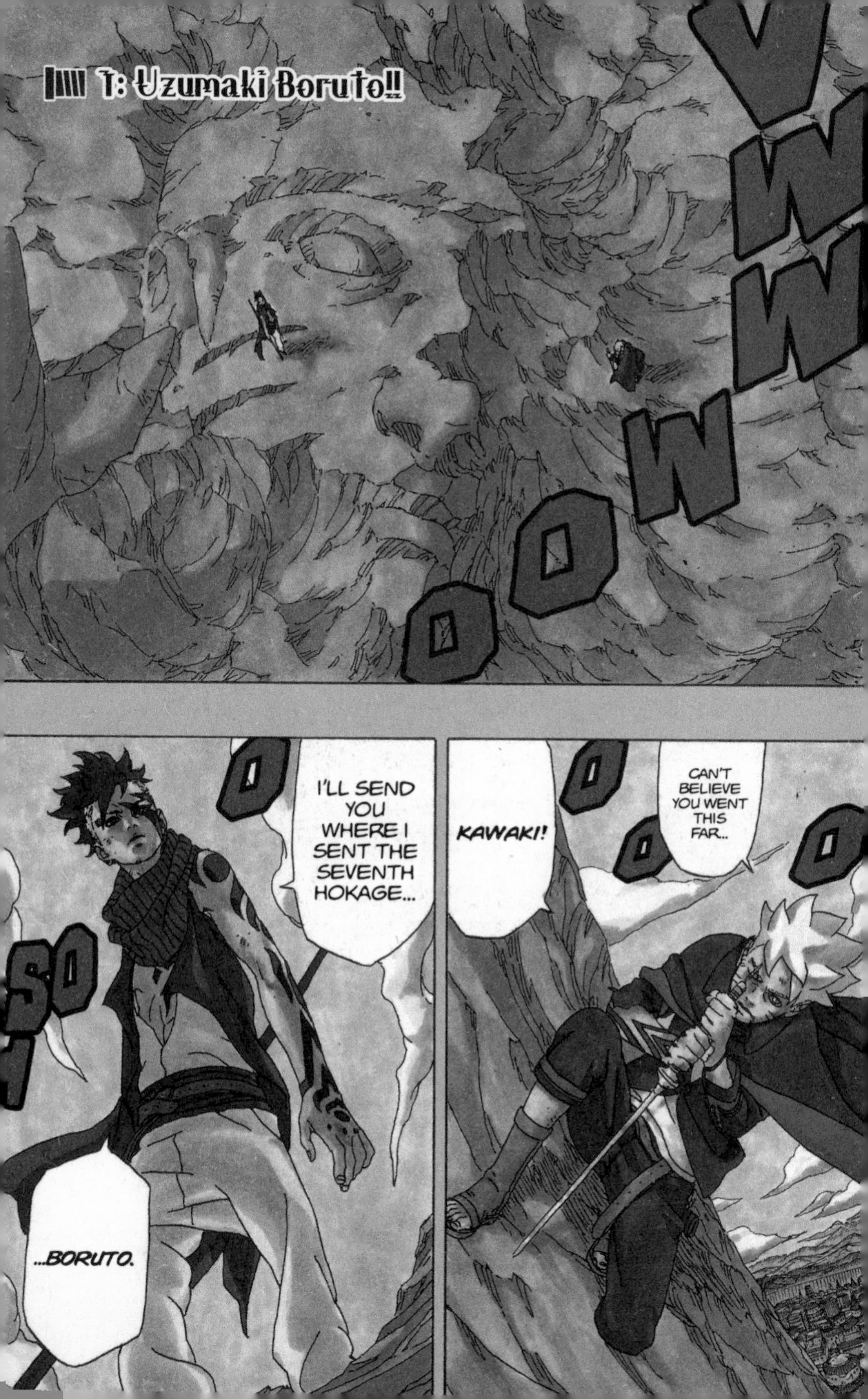
1: Uzumaki Boruto!!
CAN'T BELIEVE YOU WENT THIS FAR...
KAWAKI!
I'LL SEND YOU WHERE I SENT THE SEVENTH HOKAGE...
...BORUTO.

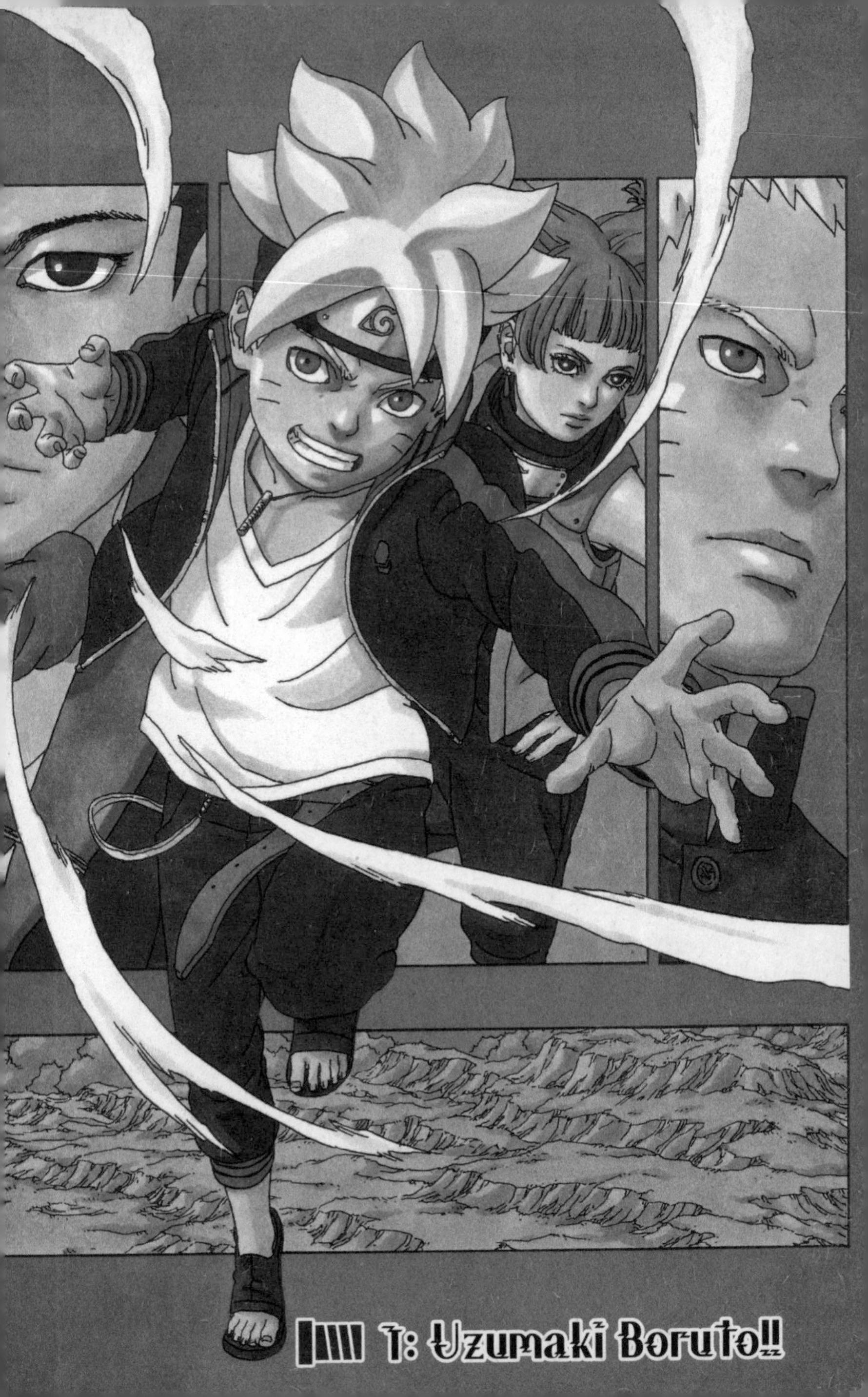
1: Uzumaki Boruto!!

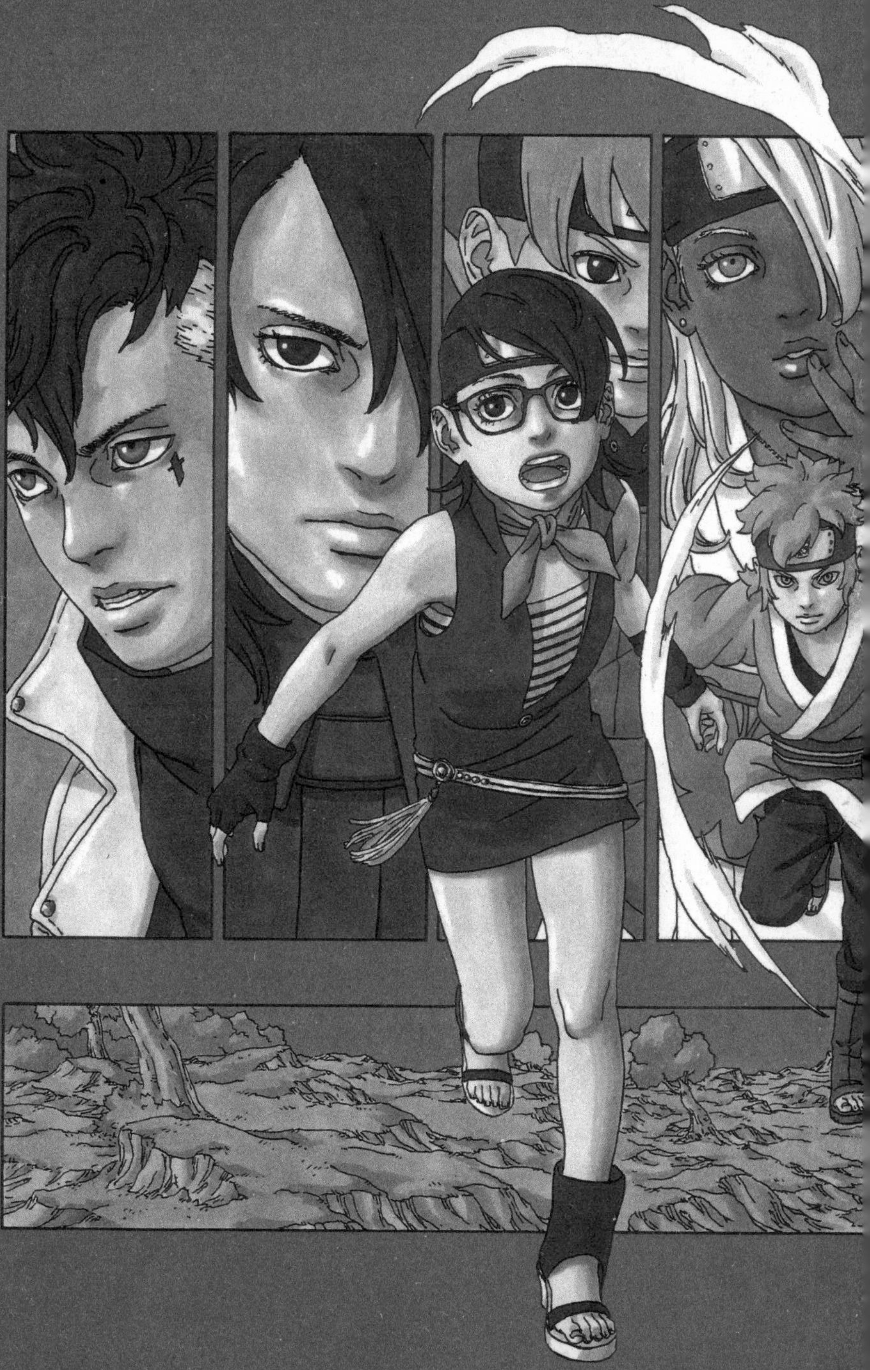

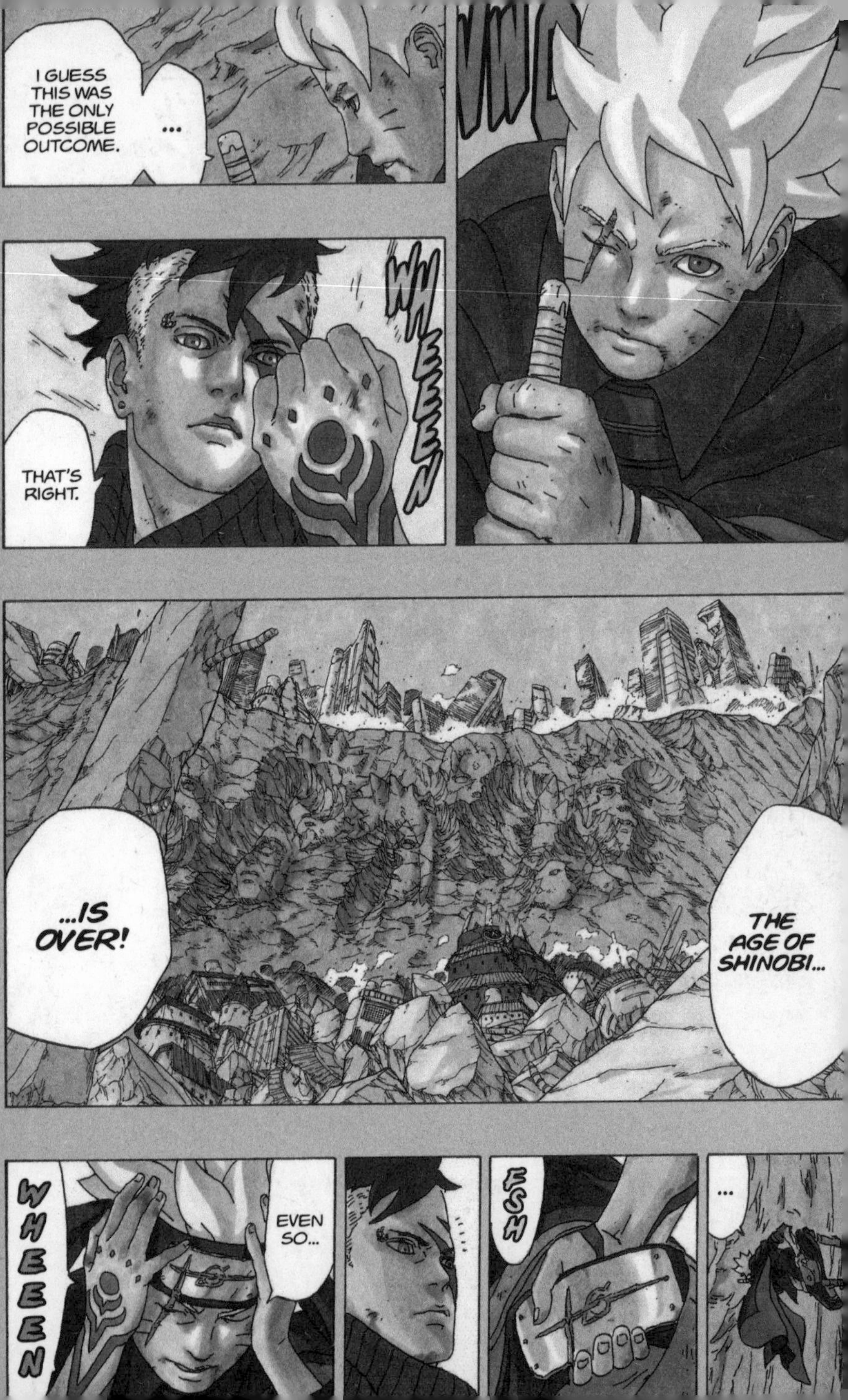
...
I GUESS THIS WAS THE ONLY POSSIBLE OUTCOME.
WHEEEEN
THAT'S RIGHT.
THE AGE OF SHINOBI...
...IS OVER!
...
FSH
EVEN SO...
WHEEEEN

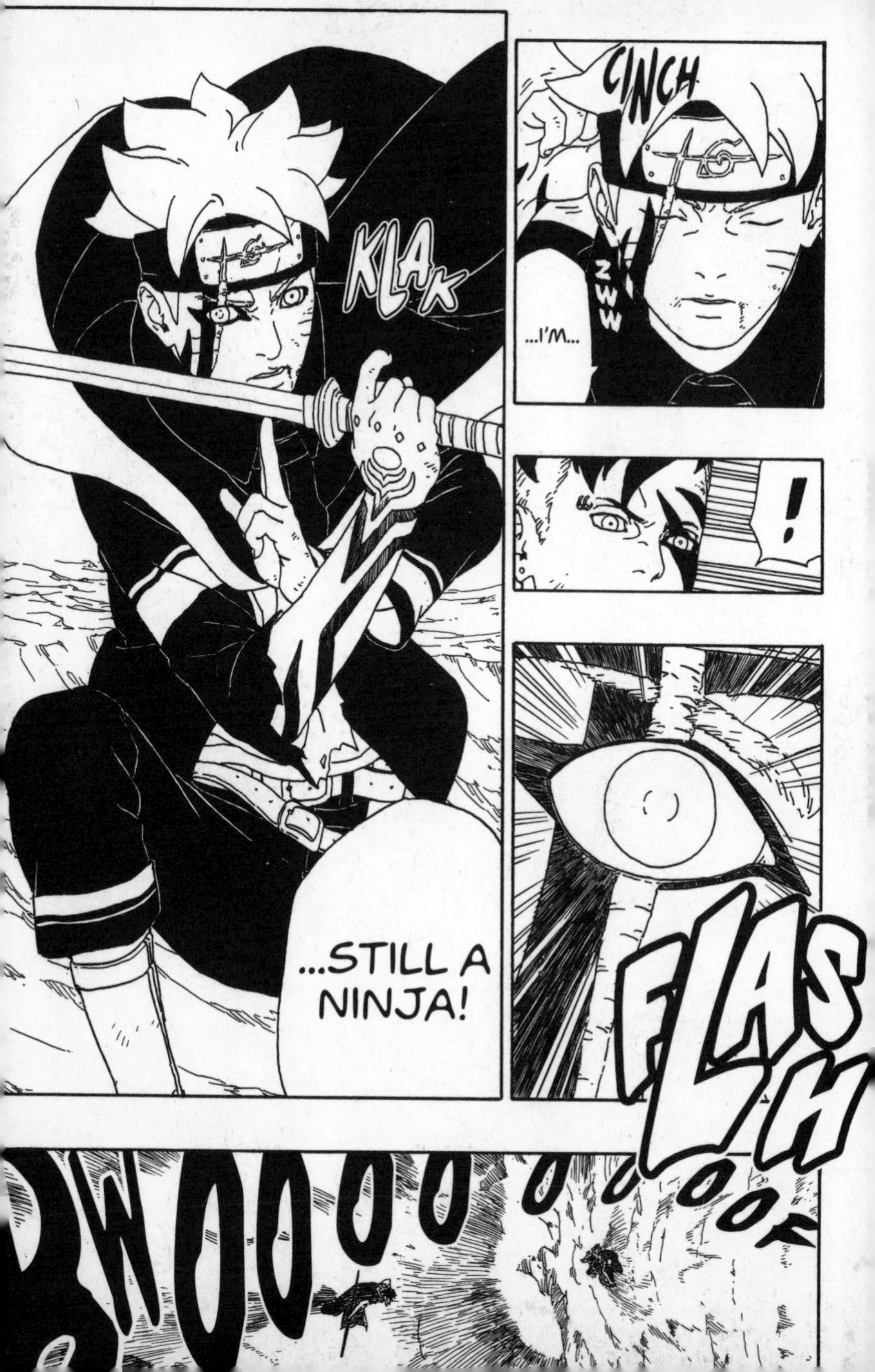
CINCH
ZWW
...I'M...
!
FLASH
KLAK
...STILL A NINJA!

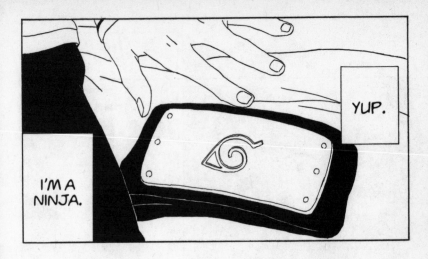

YUP.

I'M A
NINJA.

...I COULDN'T CARE LESS ABOUT BEING A NINJA.

BUT *BACK THEN...*

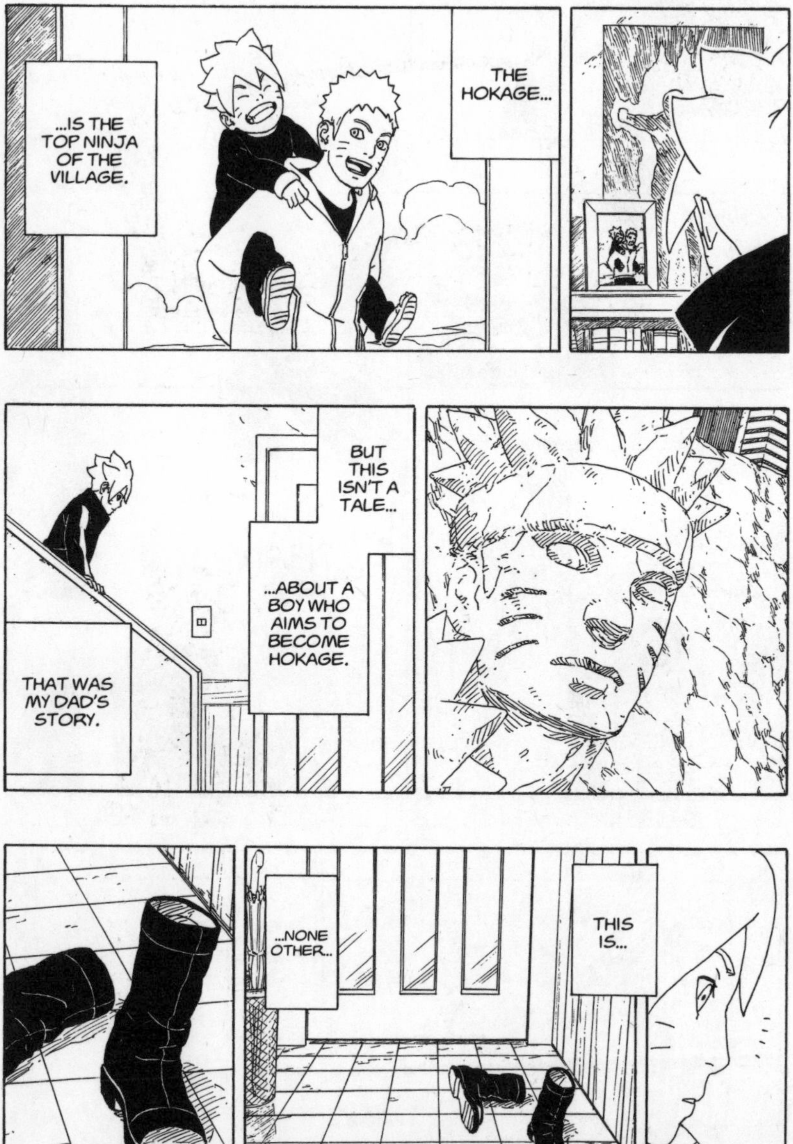
THE HOKAGE...
...IS THE TOP NINJA OF THE VILLAGE.
BUT THIS ISN'T A TALE...
...ABOUT A BOY WHO AIMS TO BECOME HOKAGE.
THAT WAS MY DAD'S STORY.
THIS IS...
...NONE OTHER...

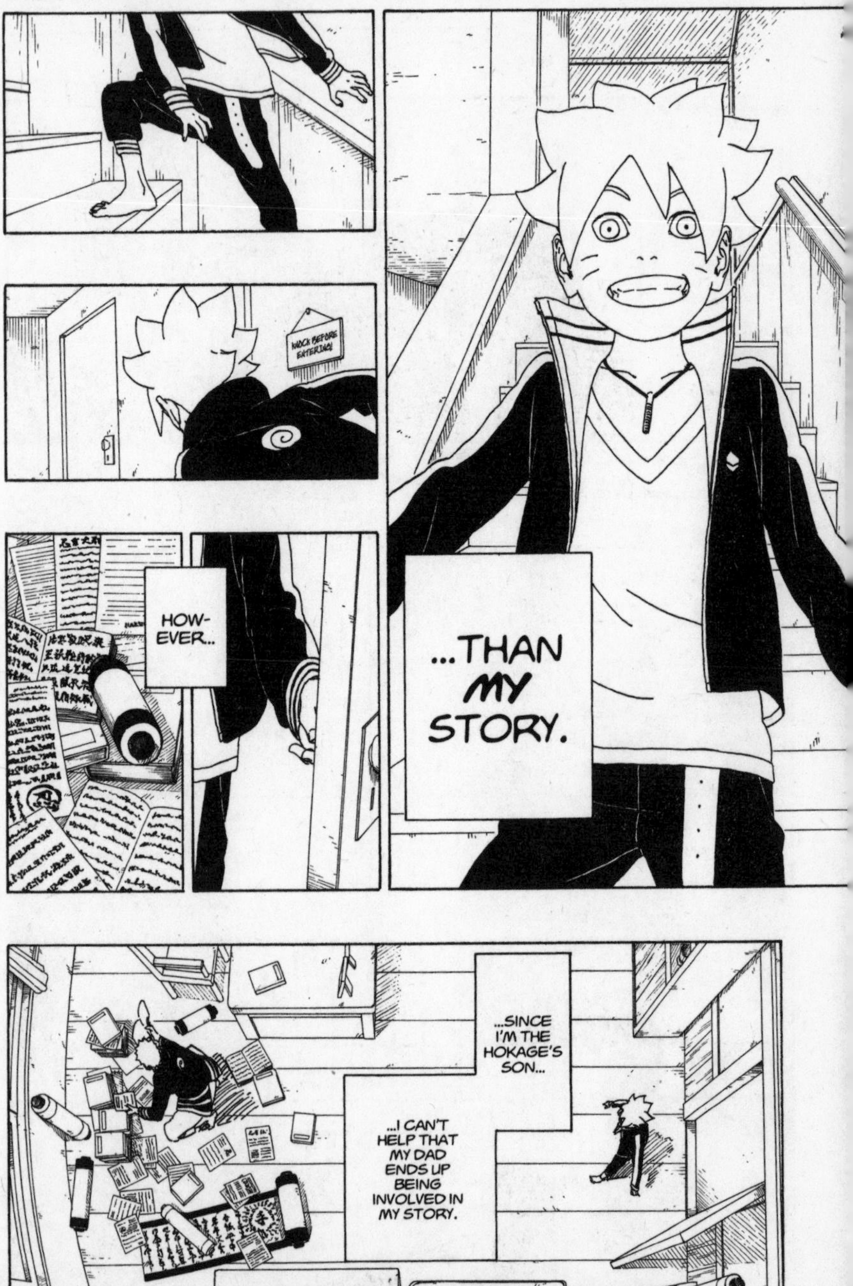
...THAN MY STORY.
KNOCK BEFORE ENTERING!
HOW-EVER..
...SINCE I'M THE HOKAGE'S SON...
...I CAN'T HELP THAT MY DAD ENDS UP BEING INVOLVED IN MY STORY.

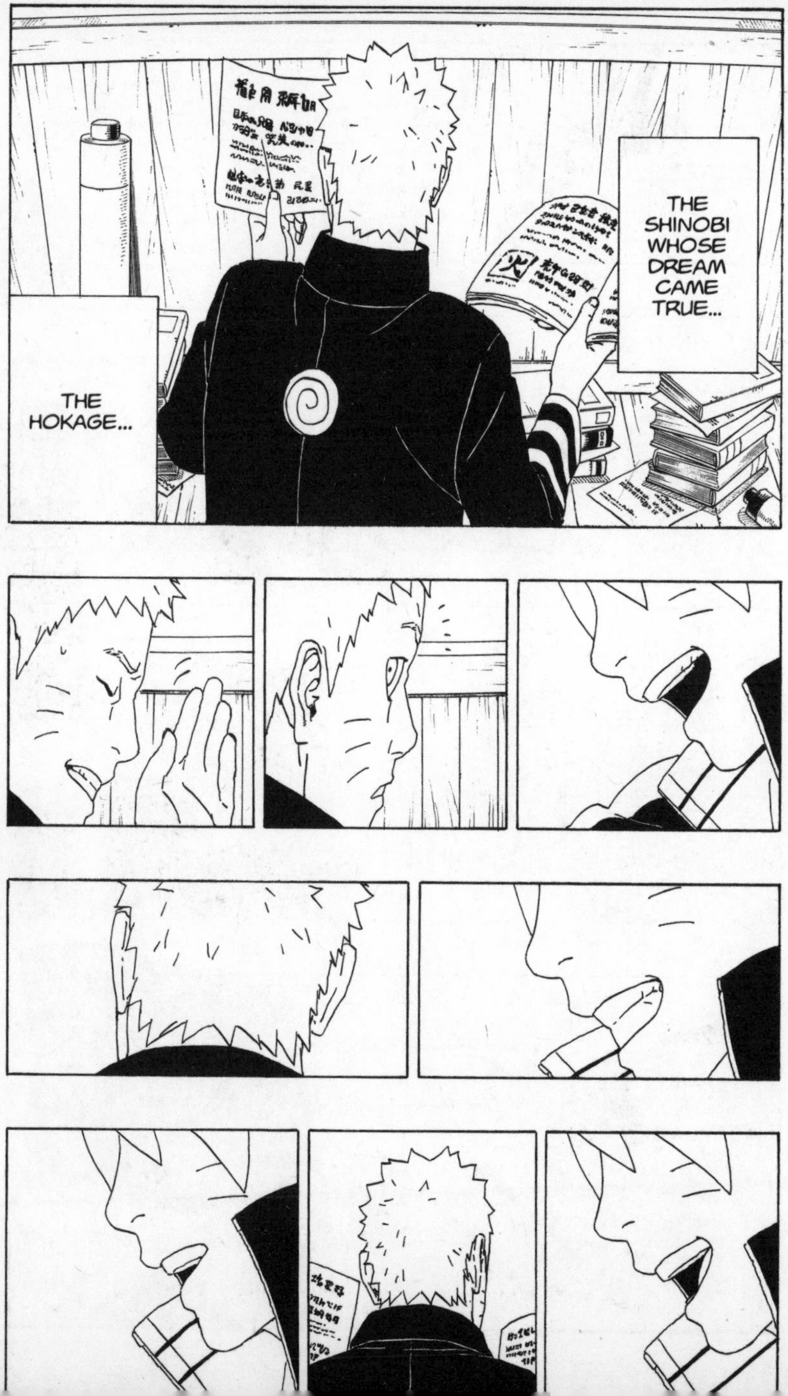
THE SHINOBI WHOSE DREAM CAME TRUE...
THE HOKAGE...

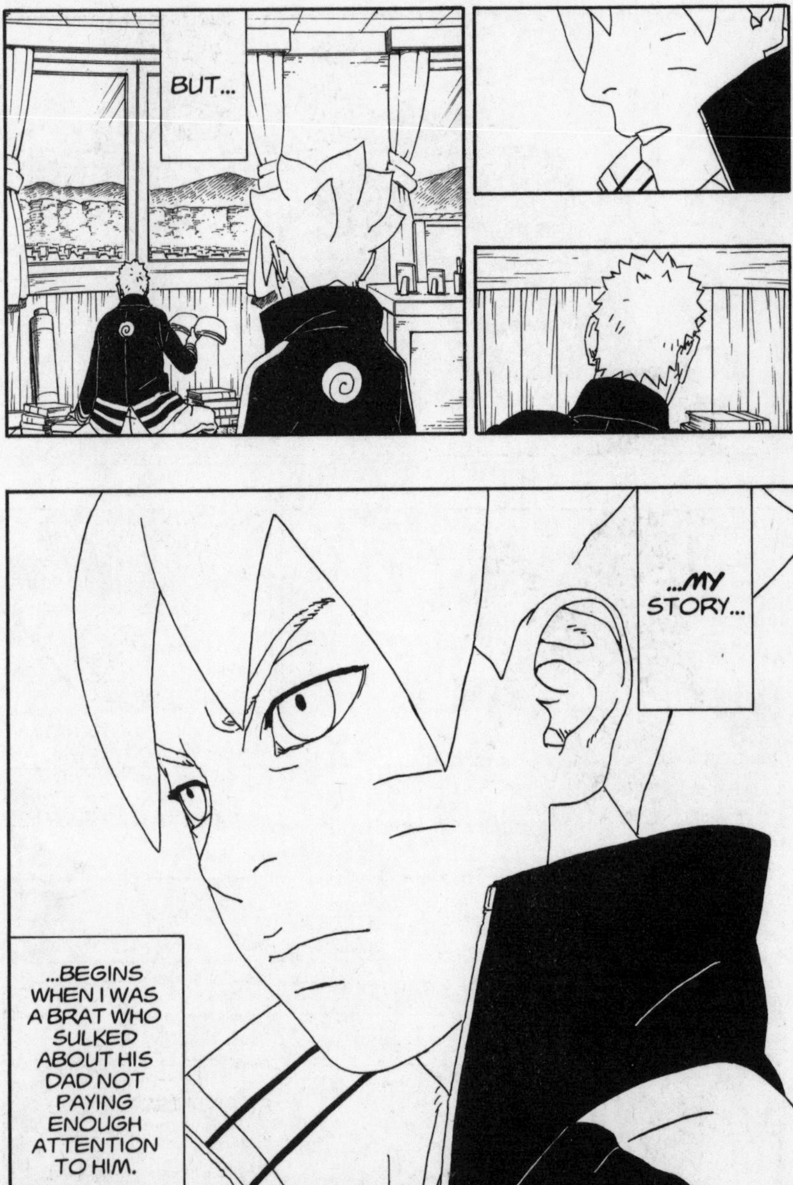
BUT...
...MY STORY...
...BEGINS WHEN I WAS A BRAT WHO SULKED ABOUT HIS DAD NOT PAYING ENOUGH ATTENTION TO HIM.

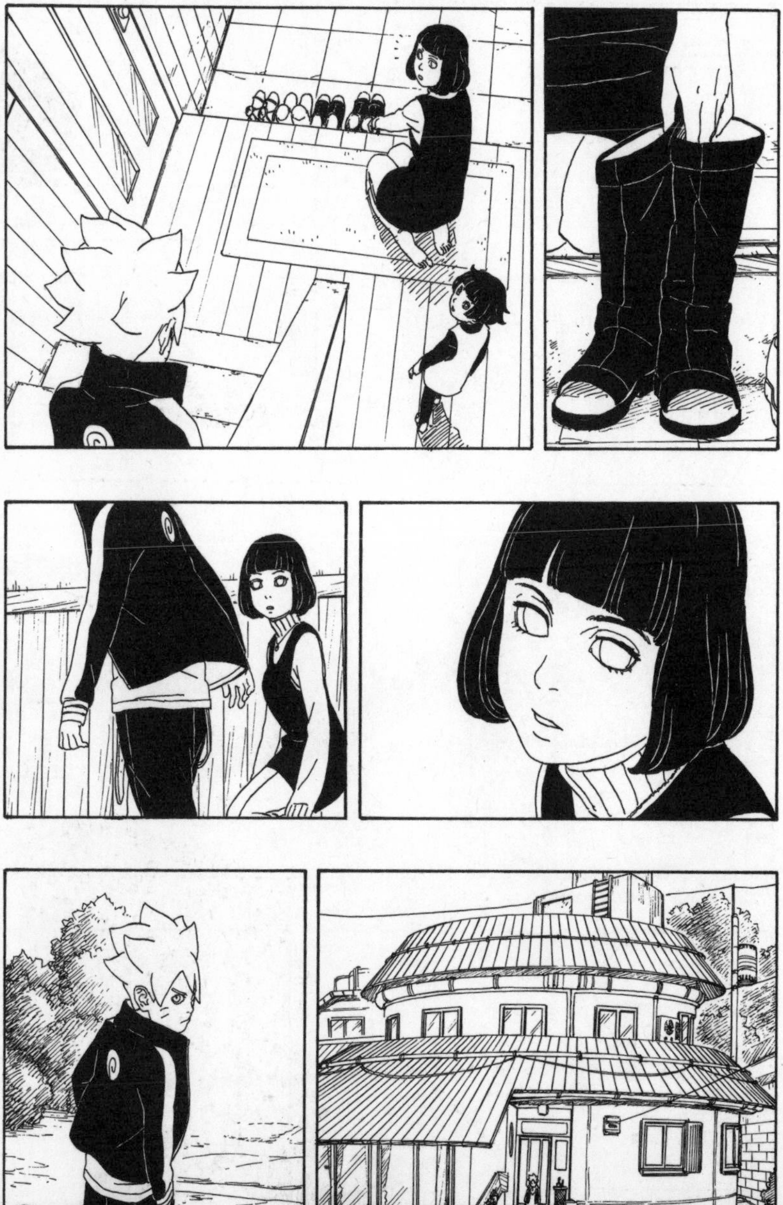

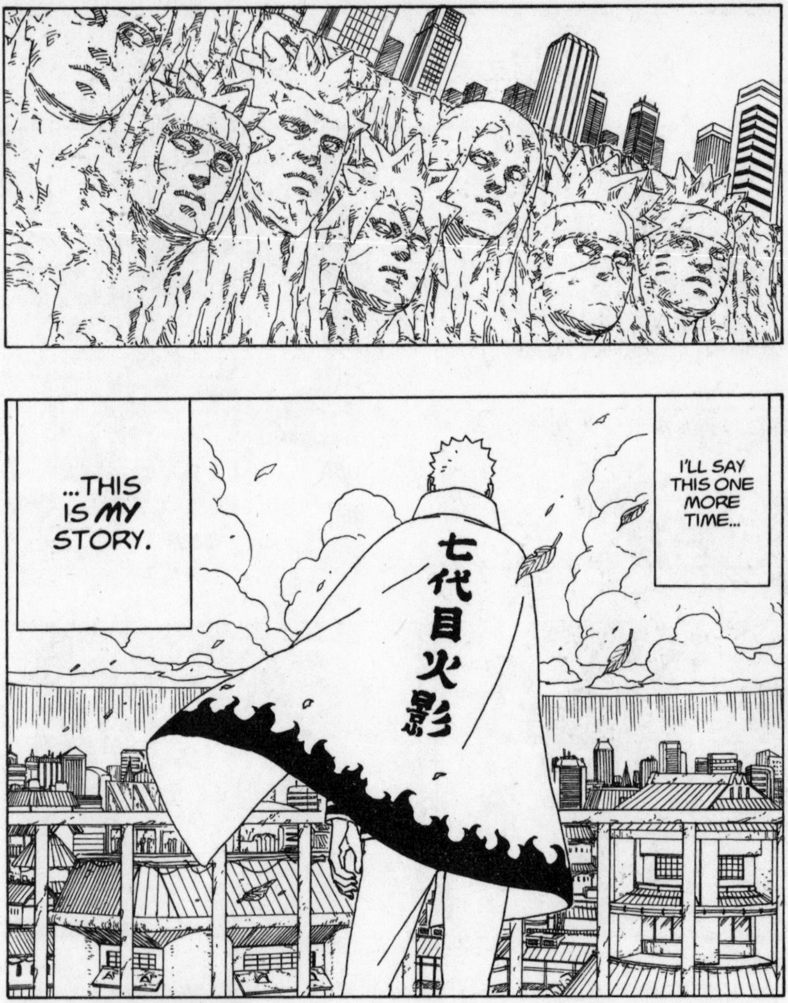
七代目火影
I'LL SAY THIS ONE MORE TIME...
...THIS IS MY STORY.

*COAT: SEVENTH HOKAGE

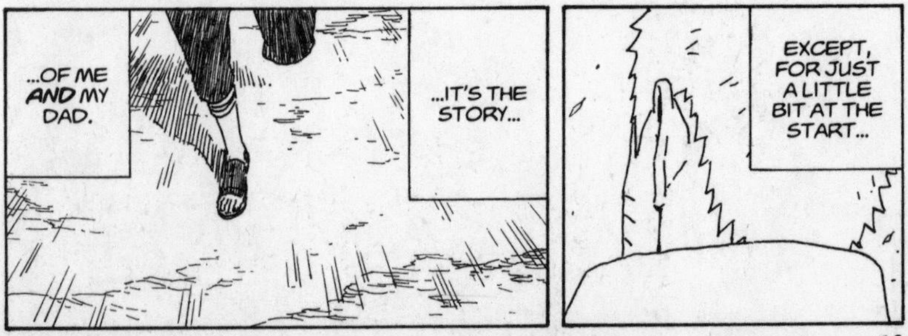
EXCEPT, FOR JUST A LITTLE BIT AT THE START...
...IT'S THE STORY...
...OF ME AND MY DAD.

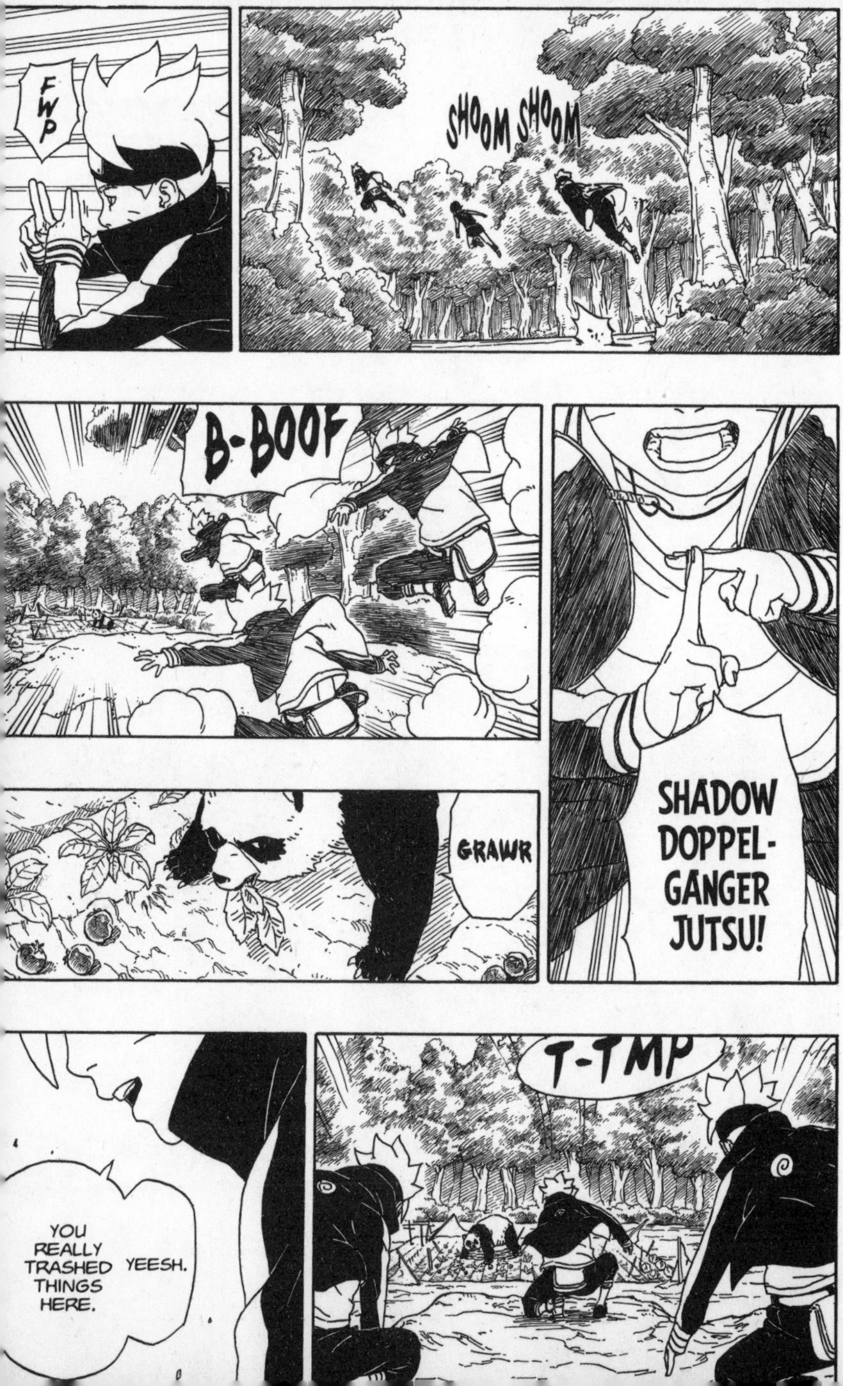
SHOOM SHOOM
FWP
SHADOW DOPPEL-GANGER JUTSU!
B-BOOF
GRAWR
T-TMP
YEESH.
YOU REALLY TRASHED THINGS HERE.

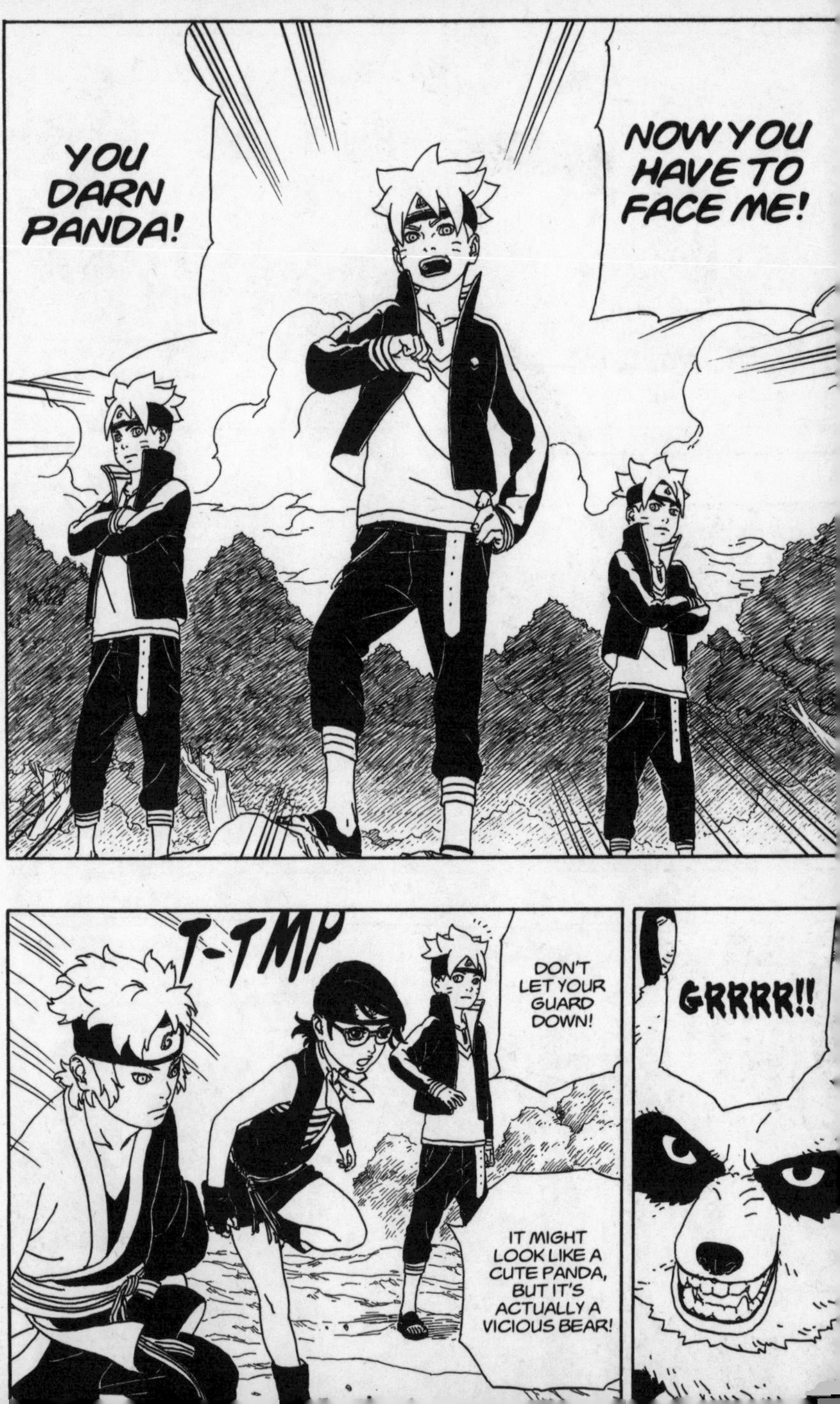
NOW YOU HAVE TO FACE ME!
YOU DARN PANDA!
GRRRR!!
T-TMP
DON'T LET YOUR GUARD DOWN!
IT MIGHT LOOK LIKE A CUTE PANDA, BUT IT'S ACTUALLY A VICIOUS BEAR!

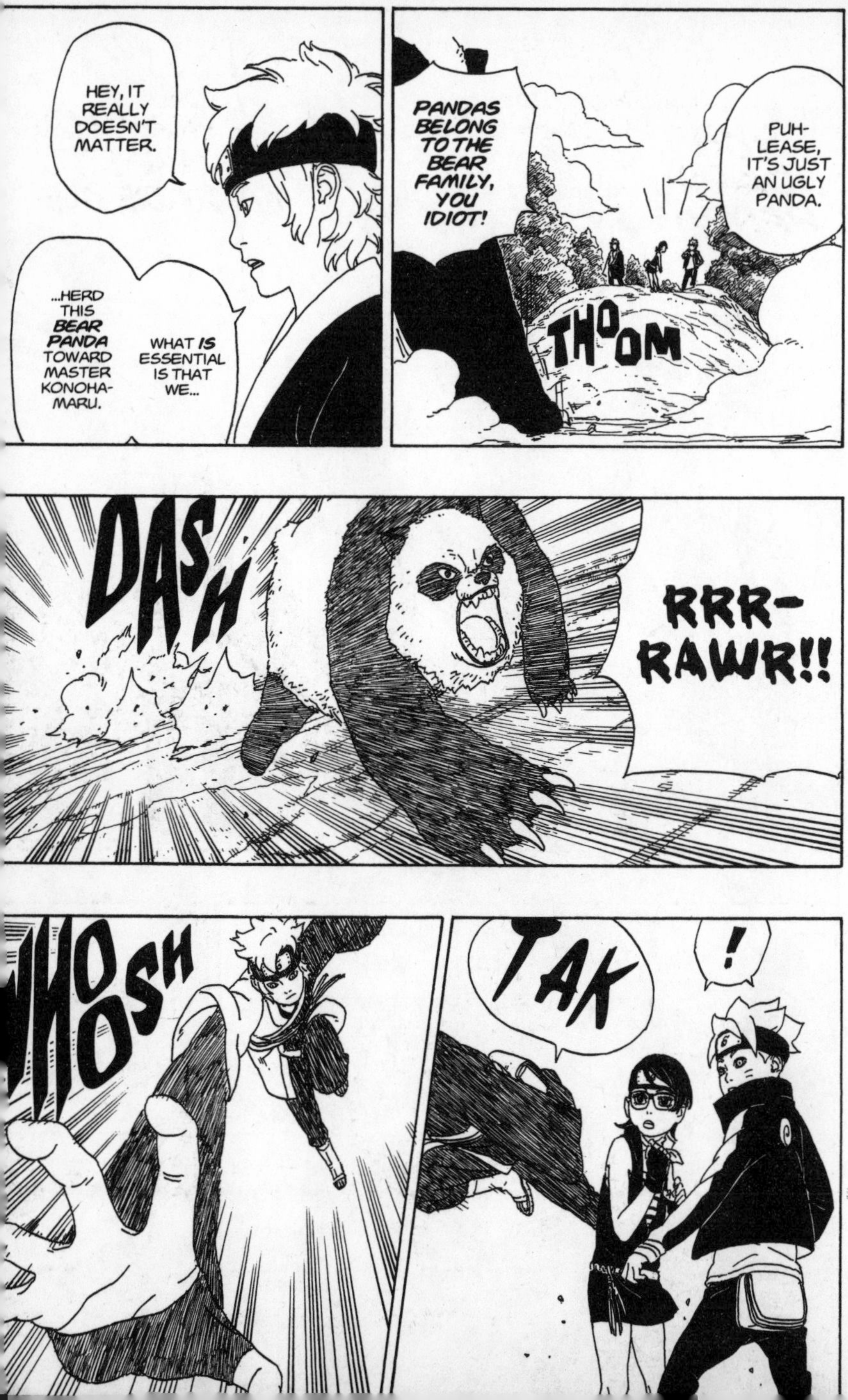
PUH-LEASE, IT'S JUST AN UGLY PANDA.
PANDAS BELONG TO THE BEAR FAMILY, YOU IDIOT!
THOOM
HEY, IT REALLY DOESN'T MATTER.
WHAT IS ESSENTIAL IS THAT WE...
...HERD THIS BEAR PANDA TOWARD MASTER KONOHA-MARU.
RRR-RAWR!!
DASH
!
TAK
WHOOSH

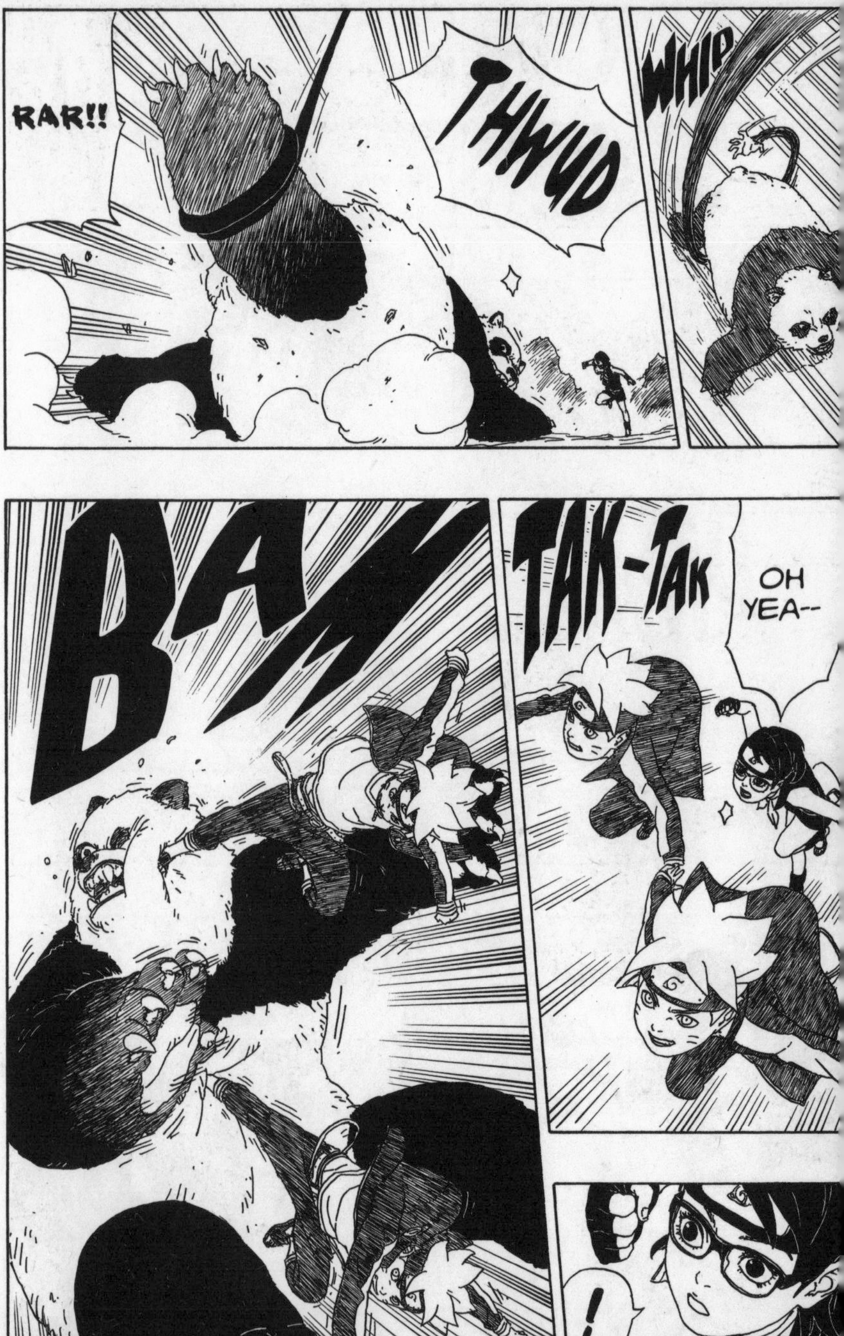
WHIP
THWUD
RAR!!
OH YEA--
TAK-TAK
!
BAM

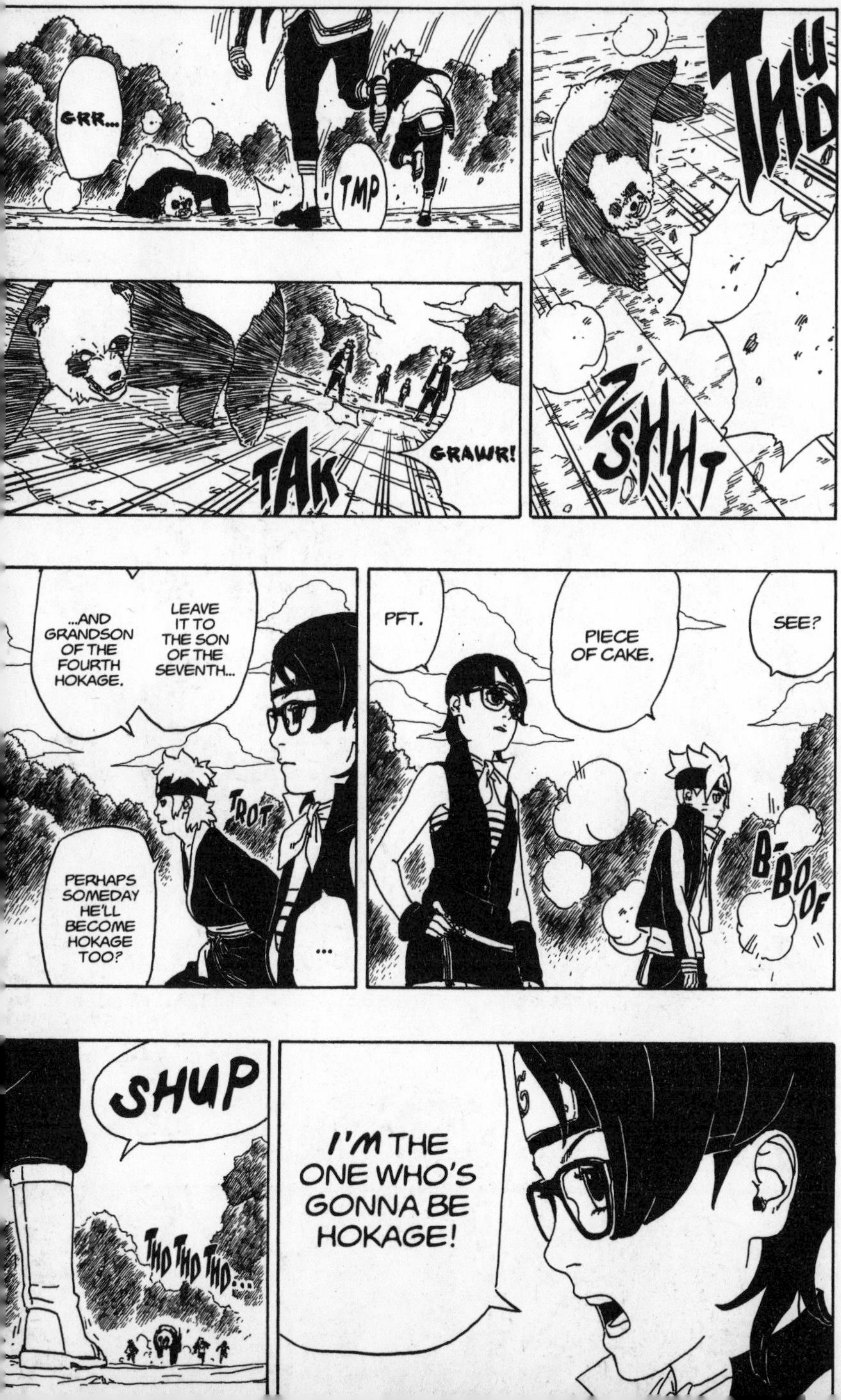
THUD
ZSHHT
GRR...
TMP
GRAWR!
TAK
SEE?
PIECE OF CAKE.
B-BOOF
PFT.
LEAVE IT TO THE SON OF THE SEVENTH...
...AND GRANDSON OF THE FOURTH HOKAGE.
TROT
PERHAPS SOMEDAY HE'LL BECOME HOKAGE TOO?
...
I'M THE ONE WHO'S GONNA BE HOKAGE!
SHUP
THD THD THD...

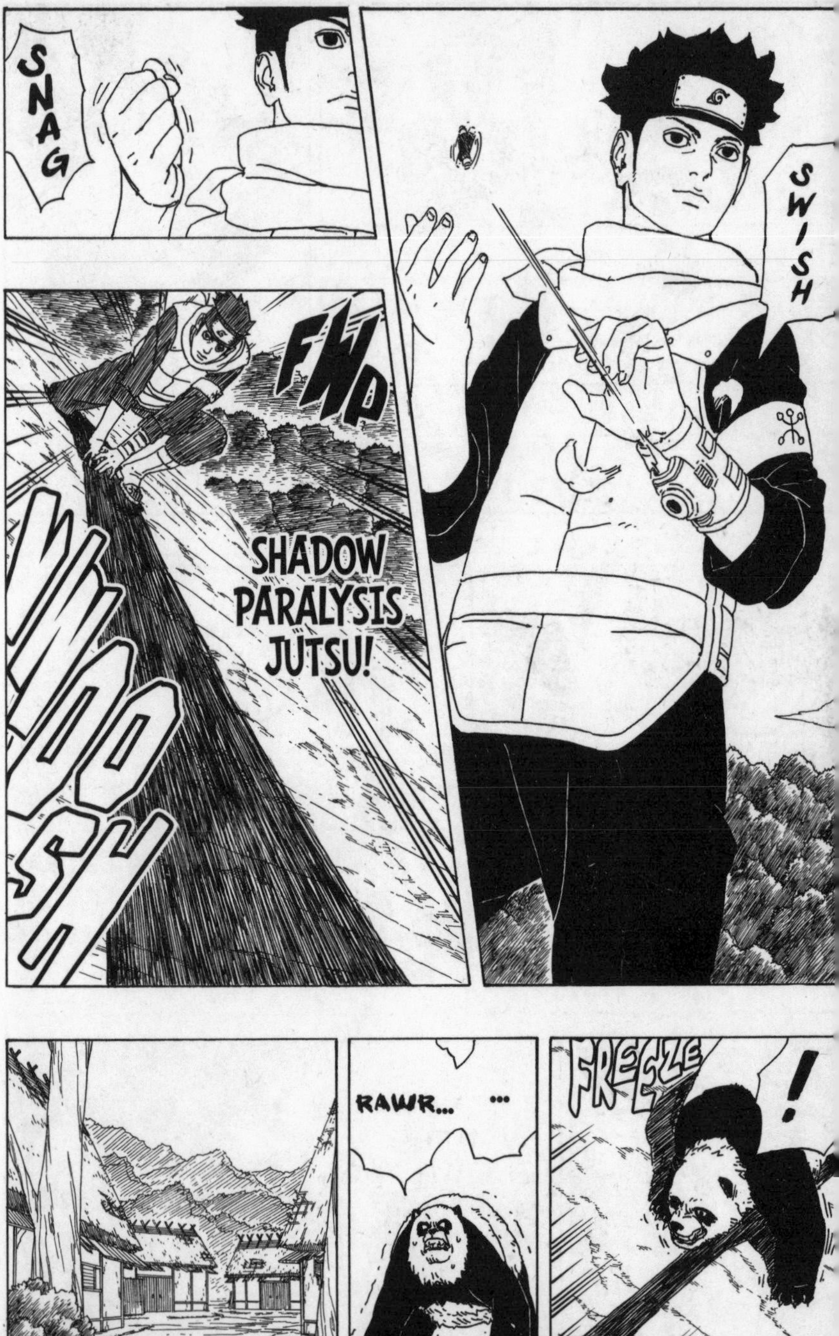
SWISH
SNAG
FWP
SHADOW PARALYSIS JUTSU!
WHOOSH
FREEZE
!
RAWR...
...

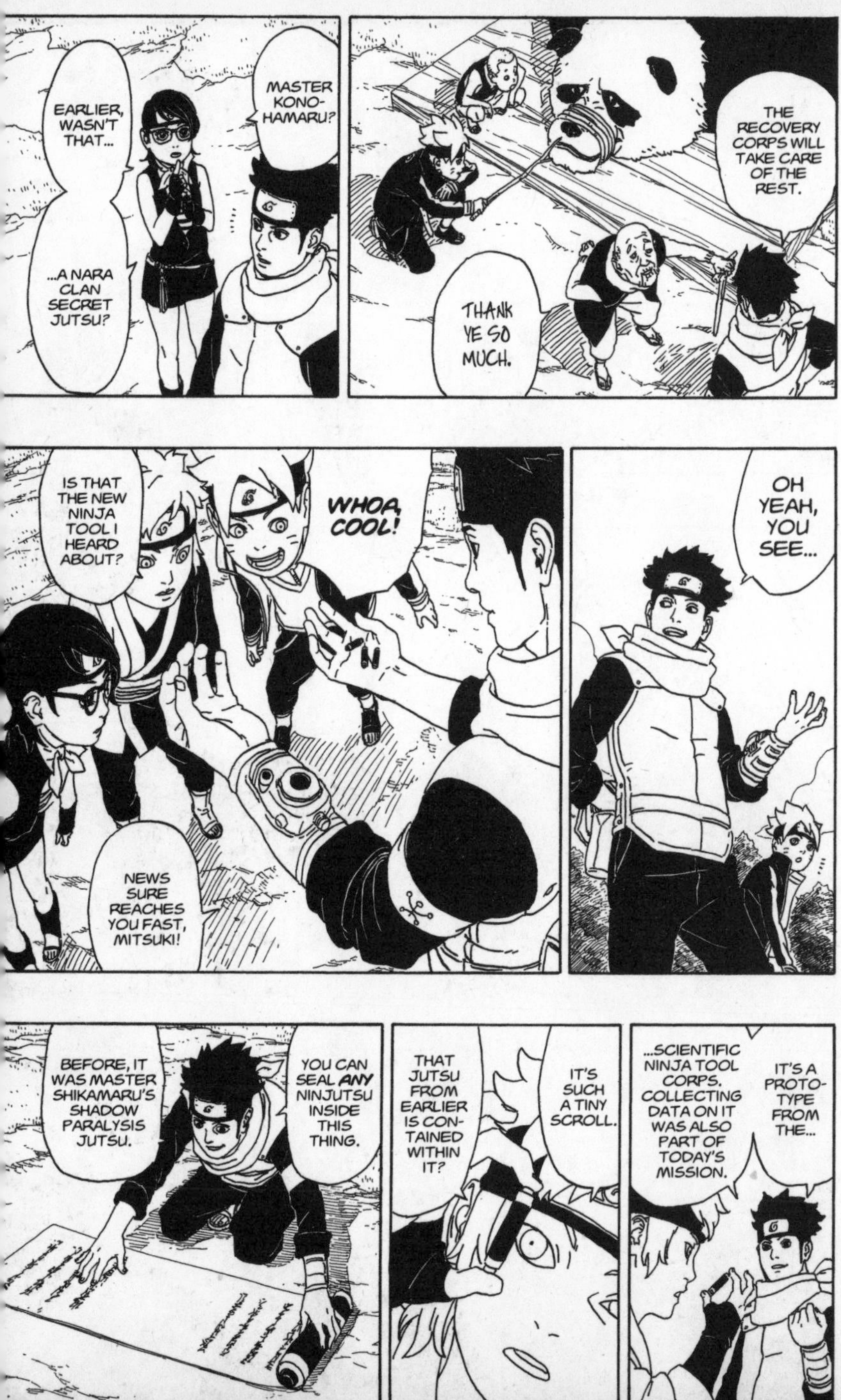
THE RECOVERY CORPS WILL TAKE CARE OF THE REST.
THANK YE SO MUCH.
MASTER KONO-HAMARU?
EARLIER, WASN'T THAT...
...A NARA CLAN SECRET JUTSU?
OH YEAH, YOU SEE...
WHOA, COOL!
IS THAT THE NEW NINJA TOOL I HEARD ABOUT?
NEWS SURE REACHES YOU FAST, MITSUKI!
IT'S A PROTO-TYPE FROM THE...
...SCIENTIFIC NINJA TOOL CORPS. COLLECTING DATA ON IT WAS ALSO PART OF TODAY'S MISSION.
IT'S SUCH A TINY SCROLL.
THAT JUTSU FROM EARLIER IS CON-TAINED WITHIN IT?
YOU CAN SEAL ANY NINJUTSU INSIDE THIS THING.
BEFORE, IT WAS MASTER SHIKAMARU'S SHADOW PARALYSIS JUTSU.

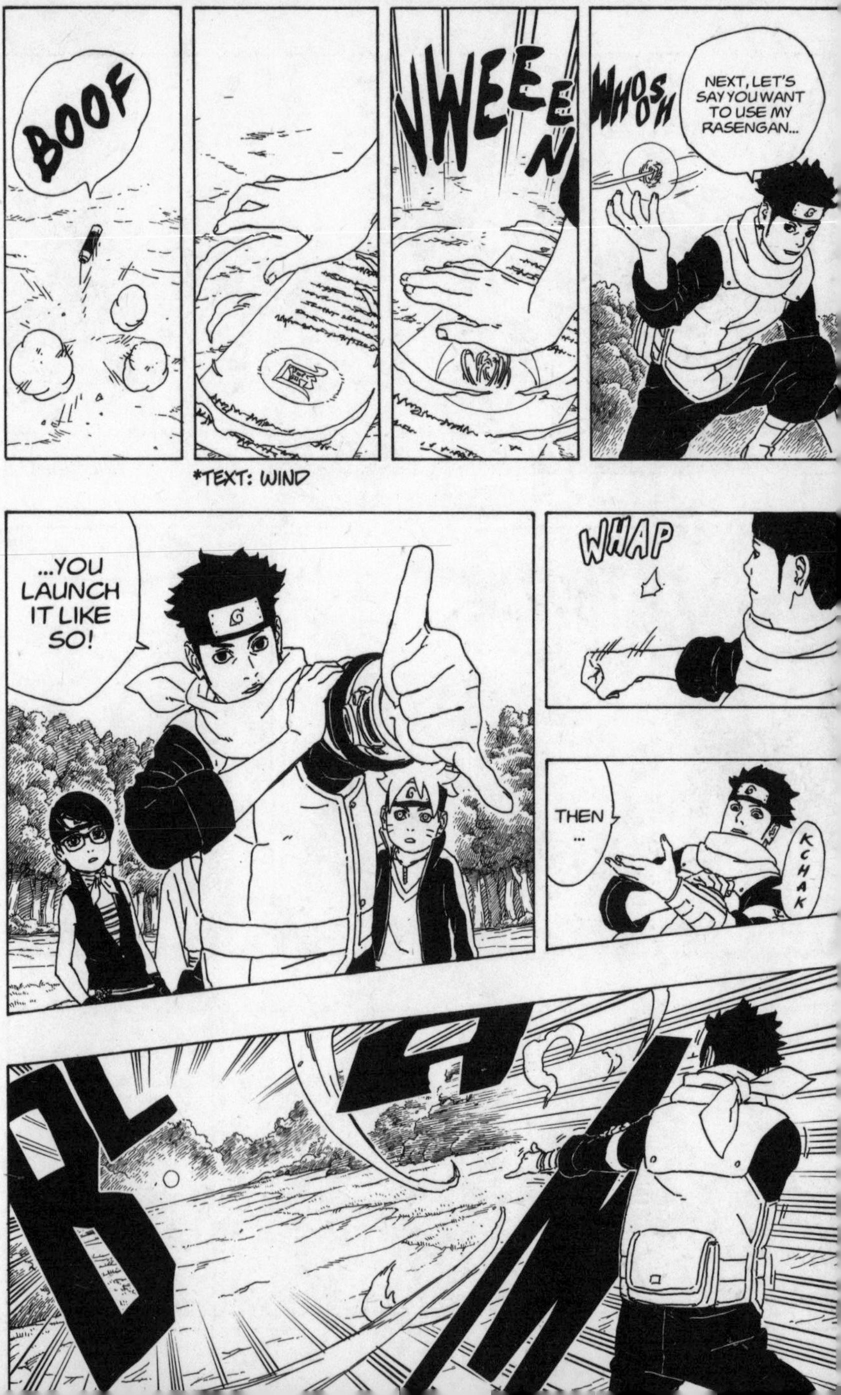
NEXT, LET'S SAY YOU WANT TO USE MY RASENGAN...
WHOOSH
VWEEEEN
BOOF
*TEXT: WIND
WHAP
THEN...
KCHAK
...YOU LAUNCH IT LIKE SO!

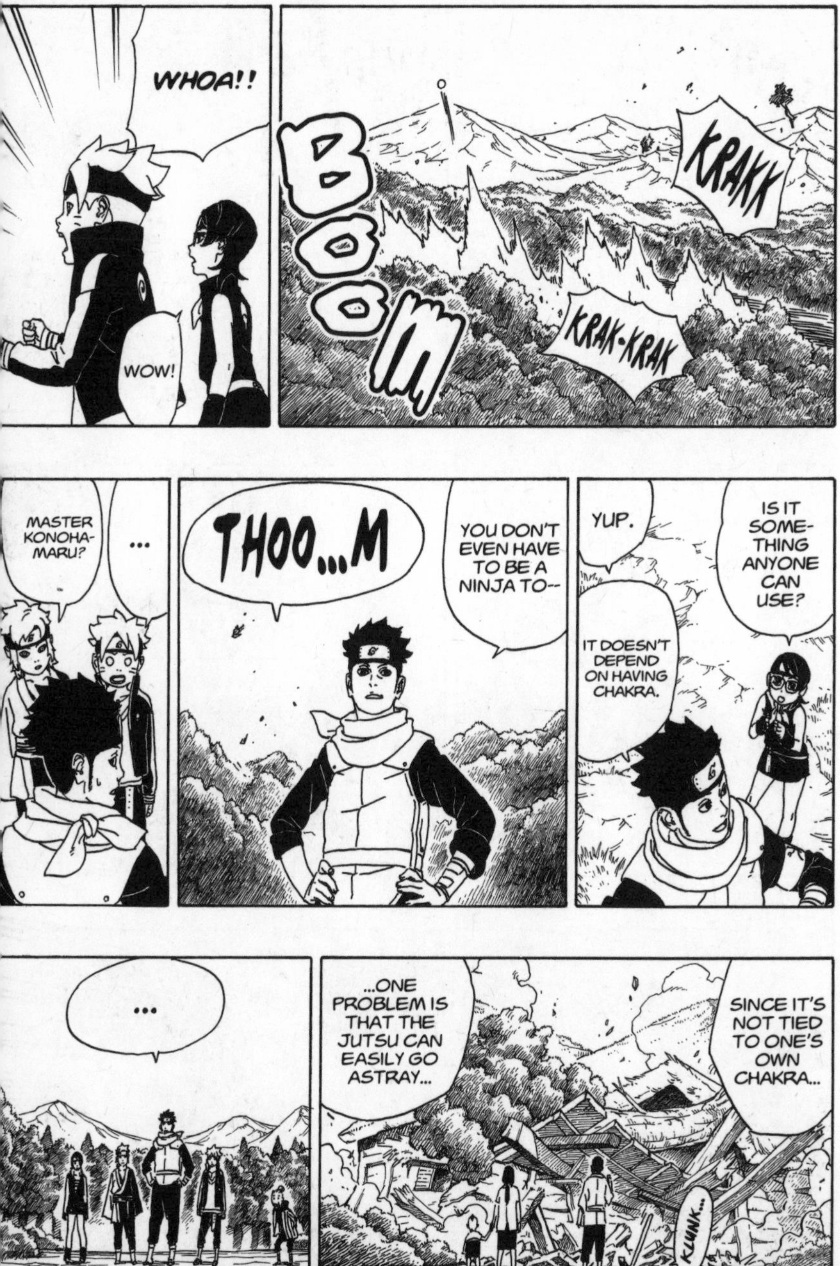
BOOM
KRAKK
KRAK-KRAK
WHOA!!
WOW!
IS IT SOMETHING ANYONE CAN USE?
YUP.
IT DOESN'T DEPEND ON HAVING CHAKRA.
YOU DON'T EVEN HAVE TO BE A NINJA TO--
THOO...M
...
MASTER KONOHAMARU?
SINCE IT'S NOT TIED TO ONE'S OWN CHAKRA...
...ONE PROBLEM IS THAT THE JUTSU CAN EASILY GO ASTRAY...
KLUNK...
...

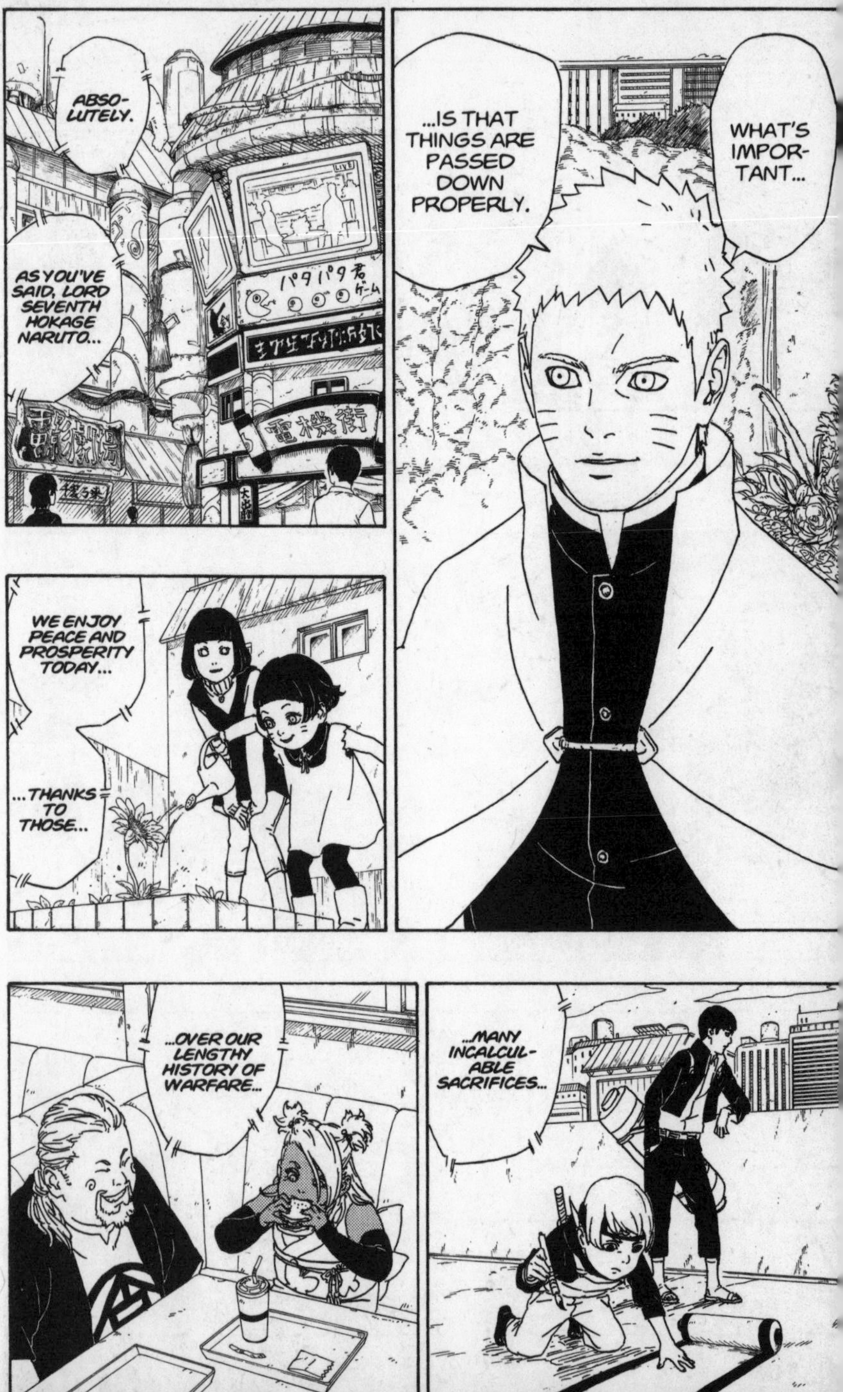

WHAT'S IMPORTANT...
...IS THAT THINGS ARE PASSED DOWN PROPERLY.
ABSOLUTELY.
AS YOU'VE SAID, LORD SEVENTH HOKAGE NARUTO...
LIVE
パタパタ君
ゲーム
電機街
WE ENJOY PEACE AND PROSPERITY TODAY...
...THANKS TO THOSE...
...MANY INCALCULABLE SACRIFICES...
...OVER OUR LENGTHY HISTORY OF WARFARE...

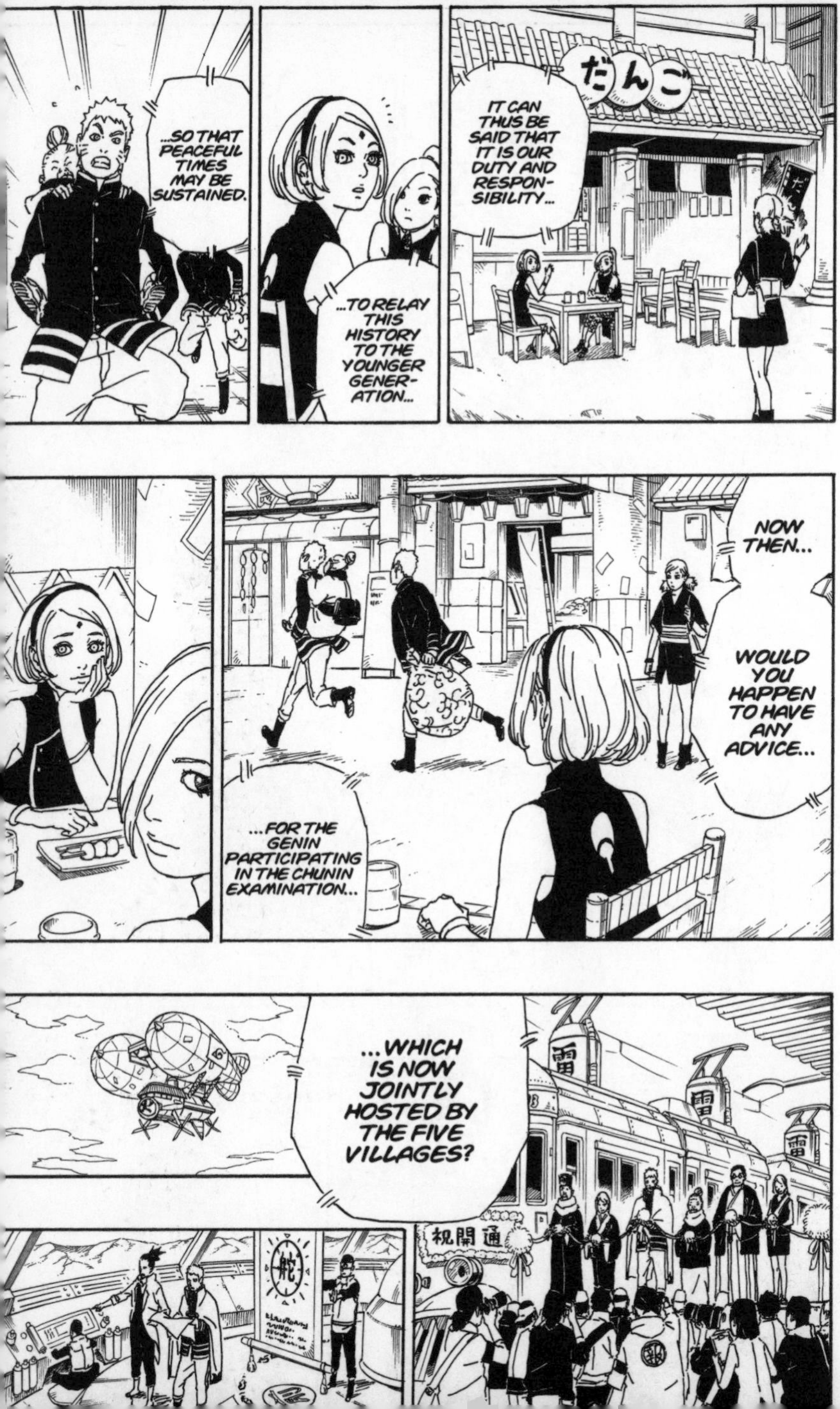
だんご
IT CAN THUS BE SAID THAT IT IS OUR DUTY AND RESPONSIBILITY...
...TO RELAY THIS HISTORY TO THE YOUNGER GENERATION...
...SO THAT PEACEFUL TIMES MAY BE SUSTAINED.
NOW THEN...
WOULD YOU HAPPEN TO HAVE ANY ADVICE...
...FOR THE GENIN PARTICIPATING IN THE CHUNIN EXAMINATION...
...WHICH IS NOW JOINTLY HOSTED BY THE FIVE VILLAGES?
雷
祝開通

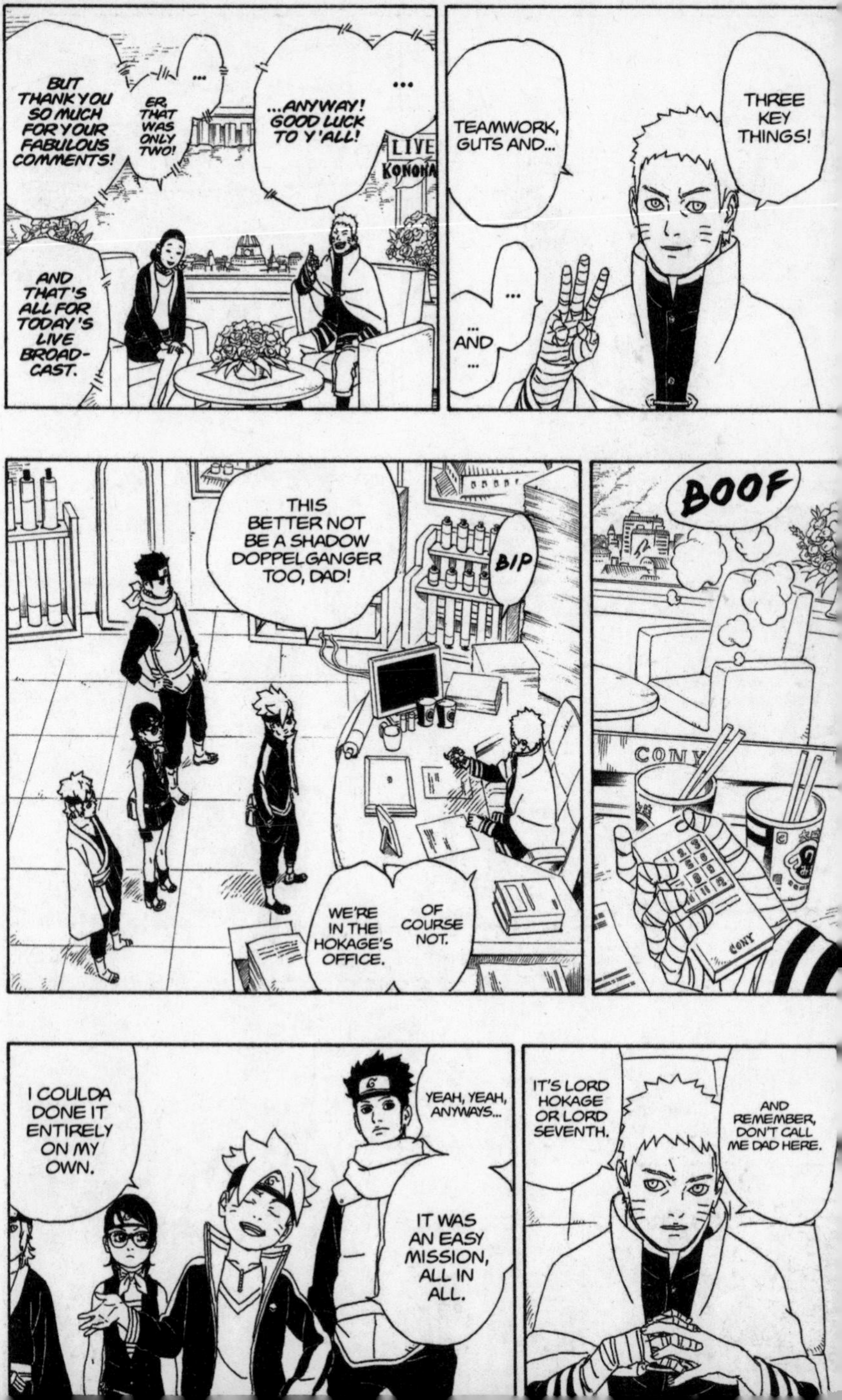
THREE KEY THINGS!
TEAMWORK, GUTS AND...
...
... AND ...
...
...ANYWAY! GOOD LUCK TO Y'ALL!
LIVE KONOHA
...
ER, THAT WAS ONLY TWO!
BUT THANK YOU SO MUCH FOR YOUR FABULOUS COMMENTS!
AND THAT'S ALL FOR TODAY'S LIVE BROADCAST.
BOOF
CONY
BIP
THIS BETTER NOT BE A SHADOW DOPPELGANGER TOO, DAD!
OF COURSE NOT.
WE'RE IN THE HOKAGE'S OFFICE.
AND REMEMBER, DON'T CALL ME DAD HERE.
IT'S LORD HOKAGE OR LORD SEVENTH.
YEAH, YEAH, ANYWAYS...
IT WAS AN EASY MISSION, ALL IN ALL.
I COULDA DONE IT ENTIRELY ON MY OWN.

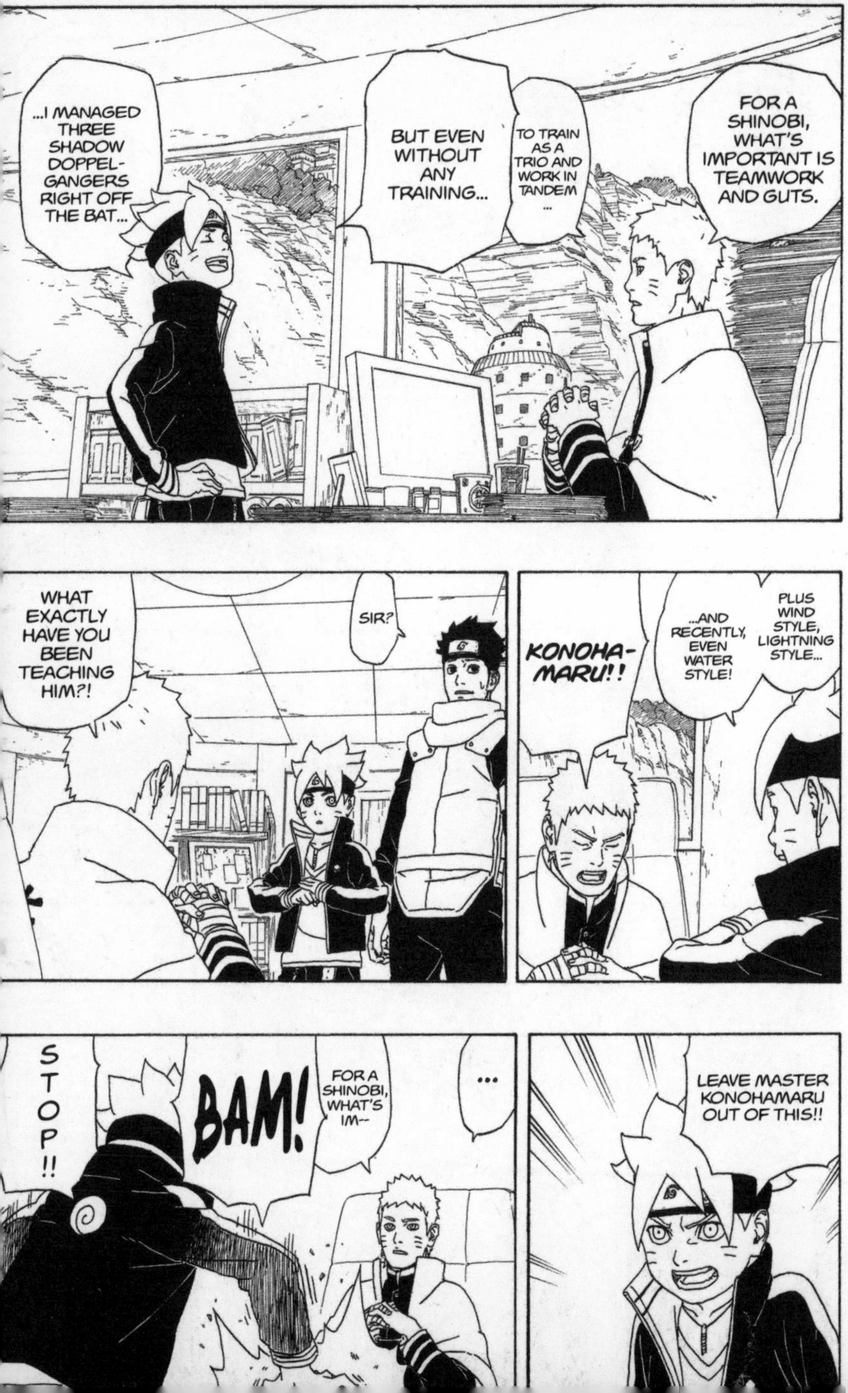
FOR A SHINOBI, WHAT'S IMPORTANT IS TEAMWORK AND GUTS.
TO TRAIN AS A TRIO AND WORK IN TANDEM ...
BUT EVEN WITHOUT ANY TRAINING...
...I MANAGED THREE SHADOW DOPPEL-GANGERS RIGHT OFF THE BAT...
PLUS WIND STYLE, LIGHTNING STYLE...
...AND RECENTLY, EVEN WATER STYLE!
KONOHA-MARU!!
SIR?
WHAT EXACTLY HAVE YOU BEEN TEACHING HIM?!
LEAVE MASTER KONOHAMARU OUT OF THIS!!
...
FOR A SHINOBI, WHAT'S IM--
BAM!
STOP!!

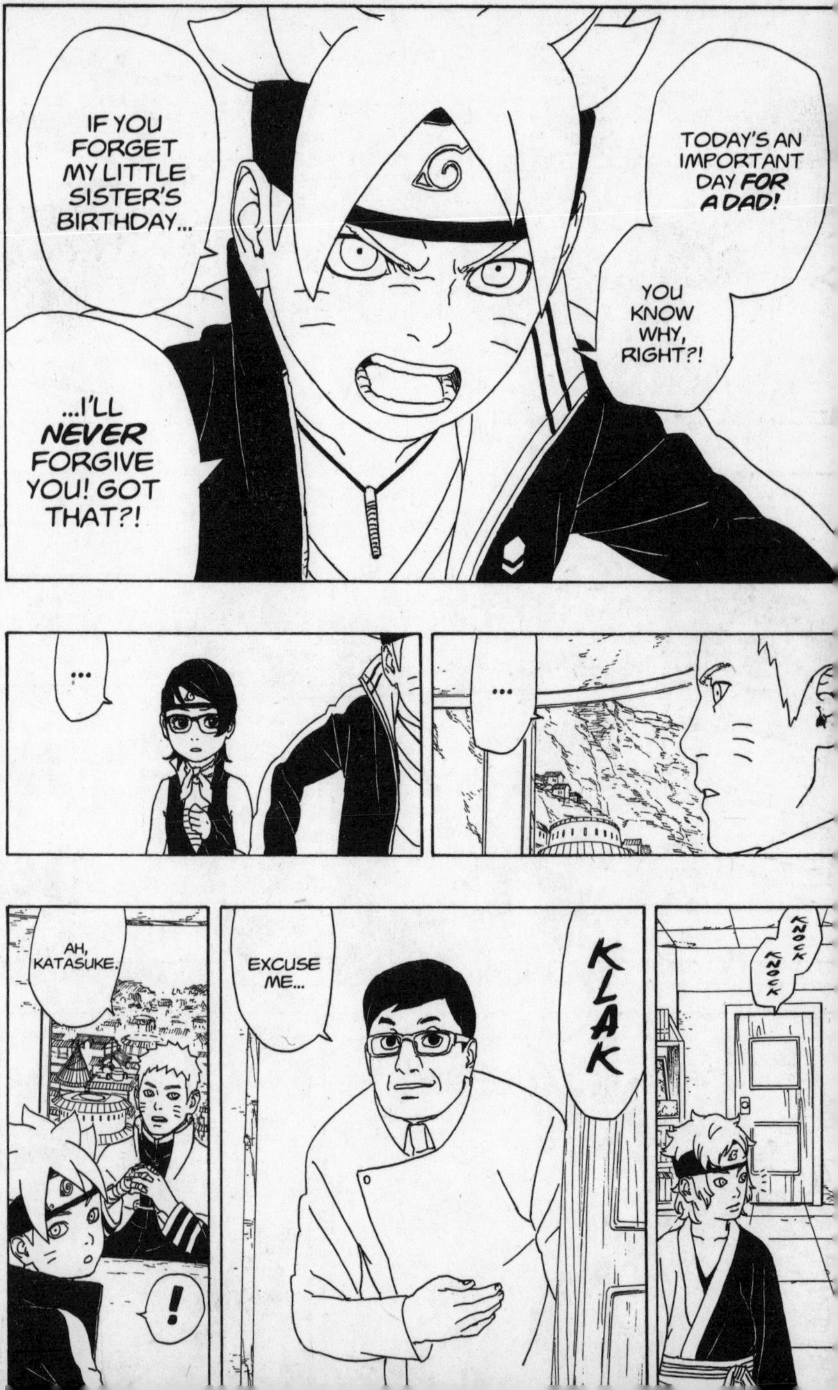
TODAY'S AN IMPORTANT DAY FOR A DAD!
YOU KNOW WHY, RIGHT?!
IF YOU FORGET MY LITTLE SISTER'S BIRTHDAY...
...I'LL NEVER FORGIVE YOU! GOT THAT?!
...
...
KNOCK KNOCK
KLAK
EXCUSE ME...
AH, KATASUKE.
!

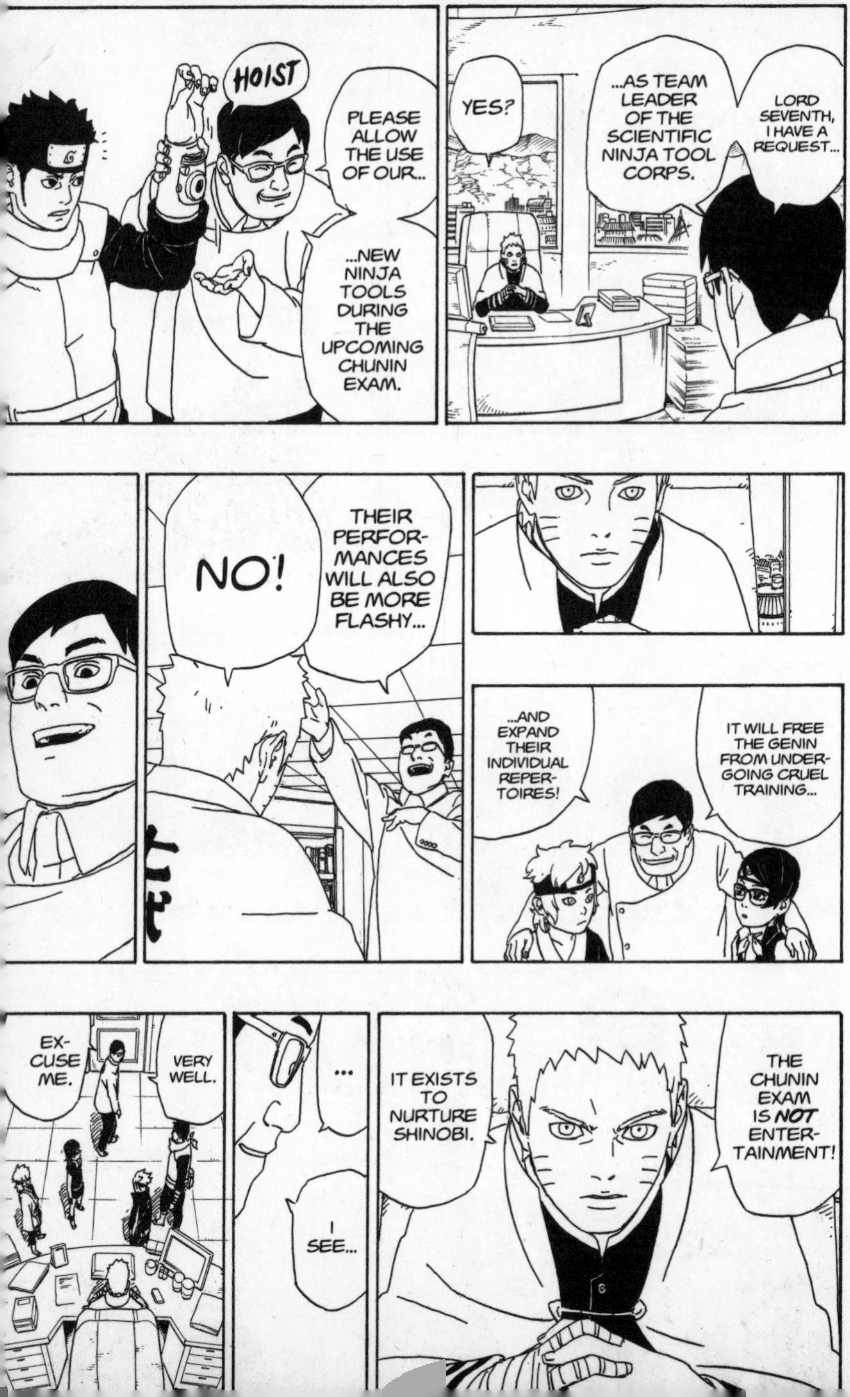
LORD SEVENTH, I HAVE A REQUEST...
...AS TEAM LEADER OF THE SCIENTIFIC NINJA TOOL CORPS.
YES?
PLEASE ALLOW THE USE OF OUR...
HOIST
...NEW NINJA TOOLS DURING THE UPCOMING CHUNIN EXAM.
IT WILL FREE THE GENIN FROM UNDER-GOING CRUEL TRAINING...
...AND EXPAND THEIR INDIVIDUAL REPER-TOIRES!
THEIR PERFOR-MANCES WILL ALSO BE MORE FLASHY...
NO!
THE CHUNIN EXAM IS **NOT** ENTER-TAINMENT!
IT EXISTS TO NURTURE SHINOBI.
...
I SEE...
VERY WELL.
EX-CUSE ME.

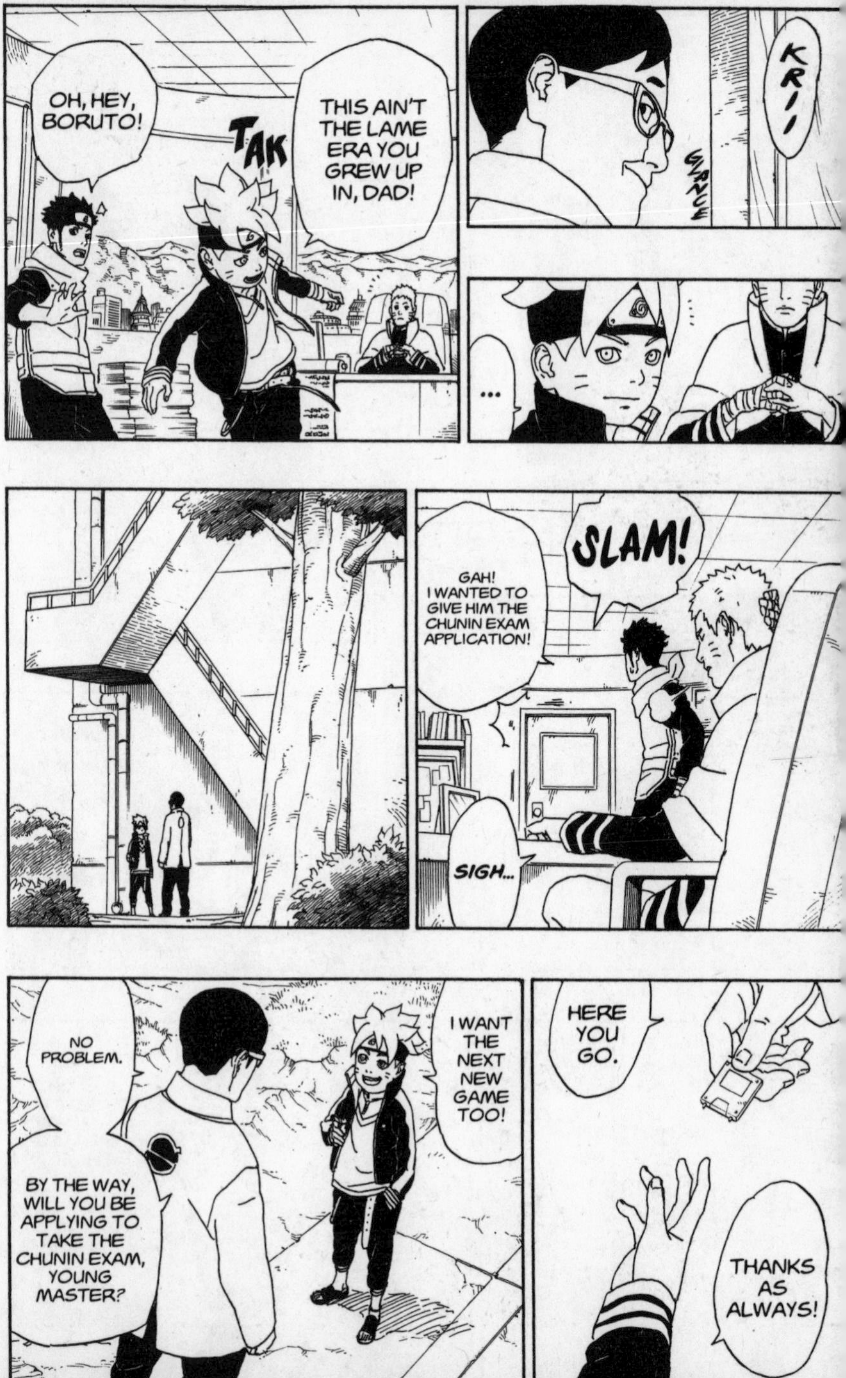
KRII
GLANCE
...
THIS AIN'T THE LAME ERA YOU GREW UP IN, DAD!
TAK
OH, HEY, BORUTO!
SLAM!
GAH! I WANTED TO GIVE HIM THE CHUNIN EXAM APPLICATION!
SIGH...
HERE YOU GO.
THANKS AS ALWAYS!
I WANT THE NEXT NEW GAME TOO!
NO PROBLEM.
BY THE WAY, WILL YOU BE APPLYING TO TAKE THE CHUNIN EXAM, YOUNG MASTER?

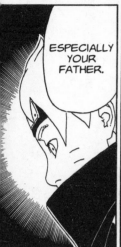

HUH?
NO WAY.
OH?
WELL, THAT'S A SHAME.
I'M SURE EVERYONE'S LOOKING FORWARD TO SEEING YOUR CAPABILITIES.
ESPECIALLY YOUR FATHER.
...

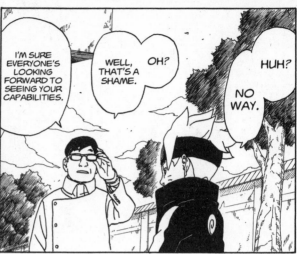

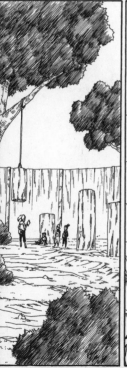

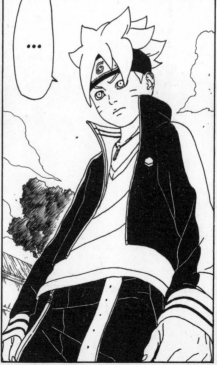

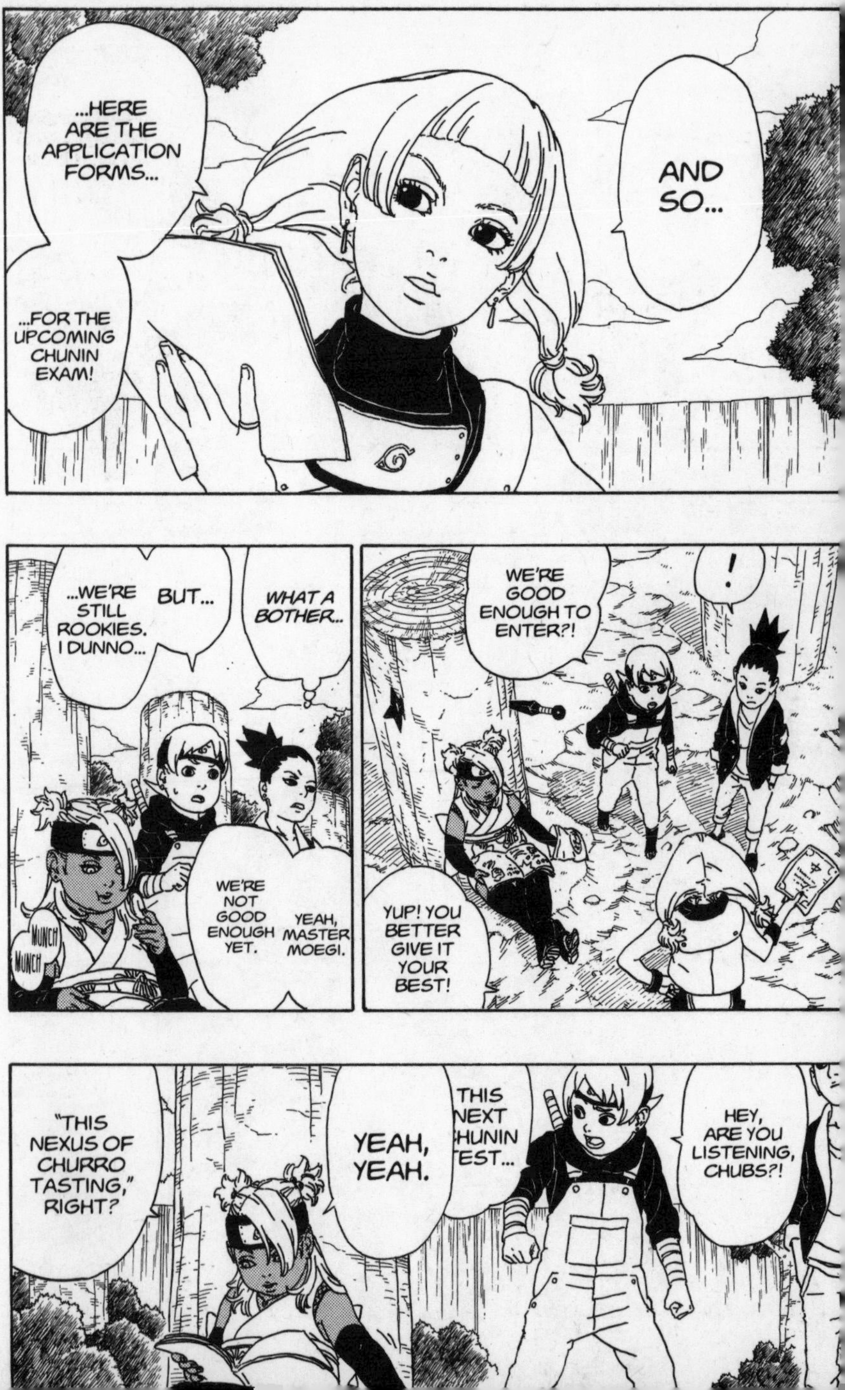
AND SO...
...HERE ARE THE APPLICATION FORMS...
...FOR THE UPCOMING CHUNIN EXAM!
!
WE'RE GOOD ENOUGH TO ENTER?!
YUP! YOU BETTER GIVE IT YOUR BEST!
WHAT A BOTHER..
BUT...
...WE'RE STILL ROOKIES. I DUNNO...
YEAH, MASTER MOEGI.
WE'RE NOT GOOD ENOUGH YET.
MUNCH
MUNCH
HEY, ARE YOU LISTENING, CHUBS?!
THIS NEXT CHUNIN TEST...
YEAH, YEAH.
"THIS NEXUS OF CHURRO TASTING," RIGHT?

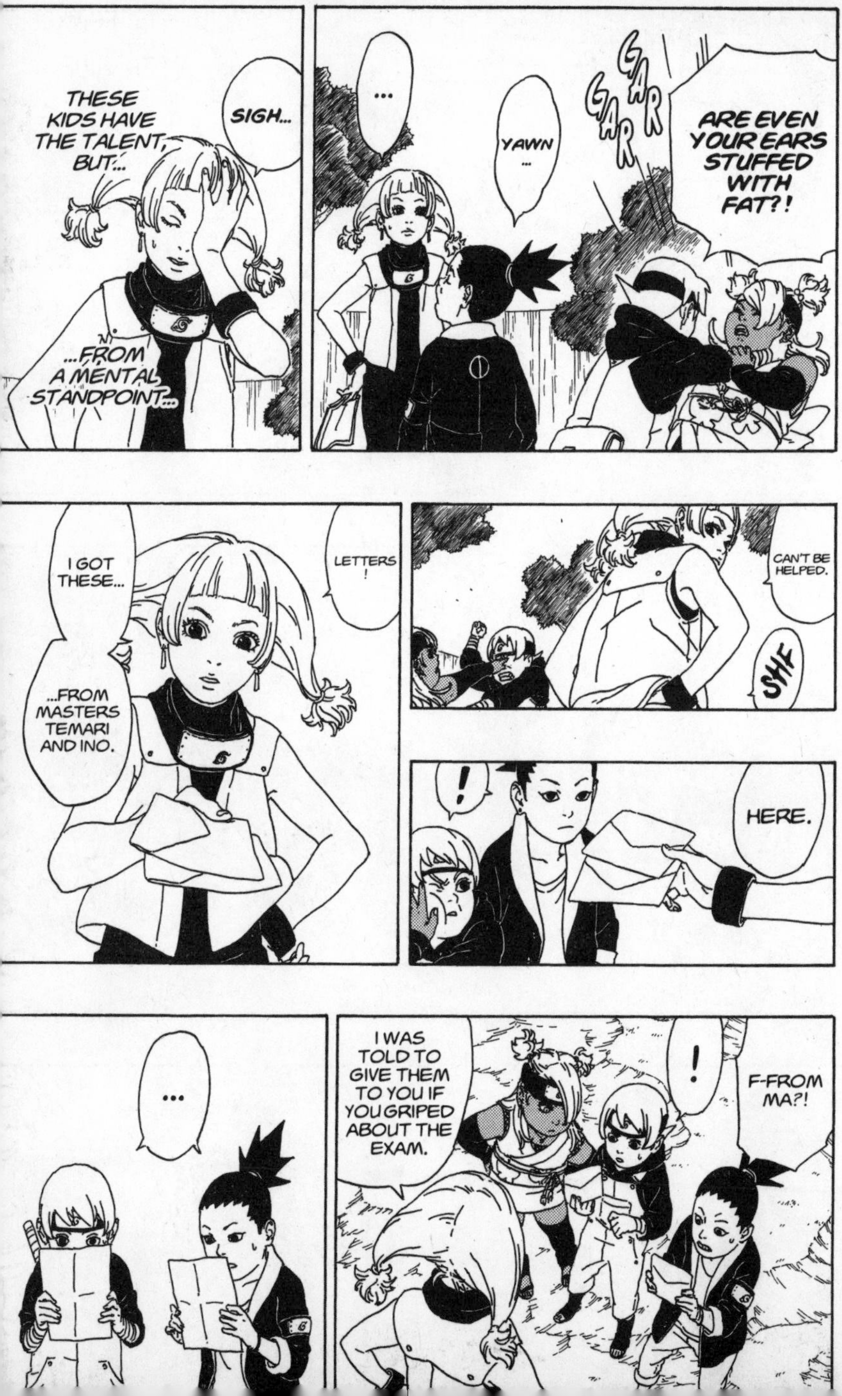
GAR
GAR
ARE EVEN YOUR EARS STUFFED WITH FAT?!
YAWN...
...
SIGH...
THESE KIDS HAVE THE TALENT, BUT...
...FROM A MENTAL STANDPOINT...
CAN'T BE HELPED.
SHF
HERE.
!
LETTERS!
I GOT THESE...
...FROM MASTERS TEMARI AND INO.
F-FROM MA?!
!
I WAS TOLD TO GIVE THEM TO YOU IF YOU GRIPED ABOUT THE EXAM.
...

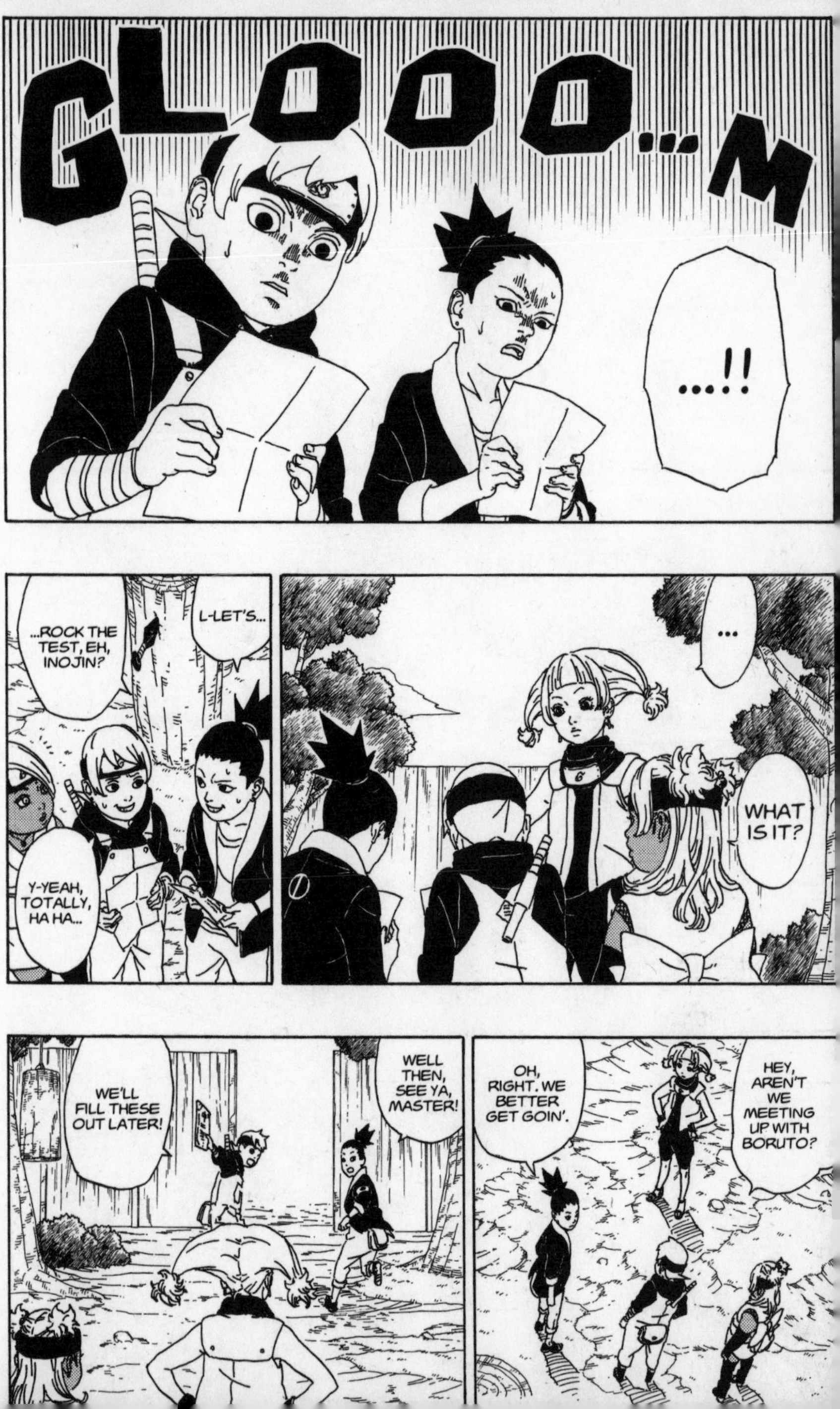
GLOOOO...M
...!!
...
WHAT IS IT?
L-LET'S...
...ROCK THE TEST, EH, INOJIN?
Y-YEAH, TOTALLY, HA HA...
HEY, AREN'T WE MEETING UP WITH BORUTO?
OH, RIGHT. WE BETTER GET GOIN'.
WELL THEN, SEE YA, MASTER!
WE'LL FILL THESE OUT LATER!

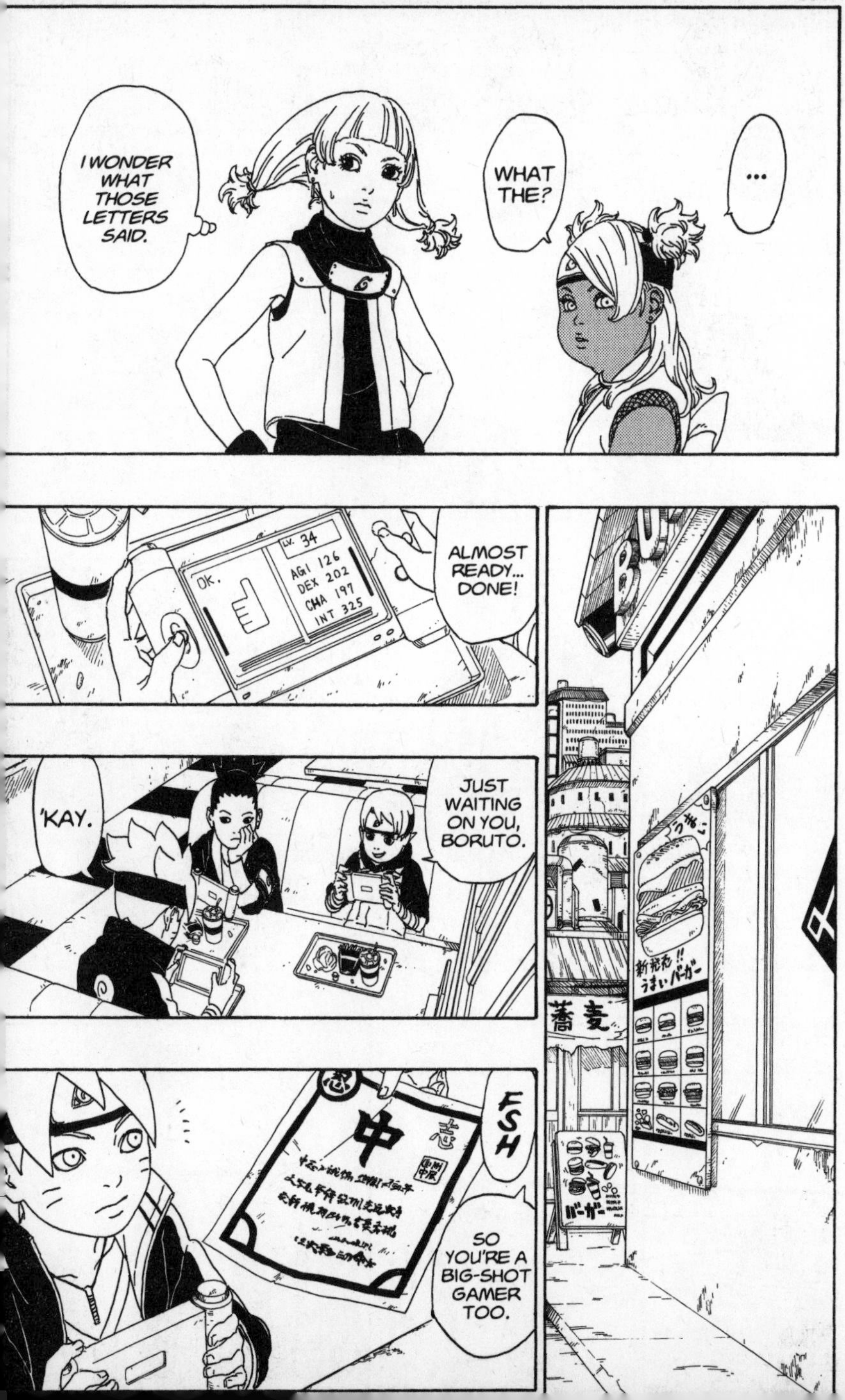
...
WHAT THE?
I WONDER WHAT THOSE LETTERS SAID.
新発売!!
うまいバーガー
蕎麦
バーガー
ALMOST READY... DONE!
LV. 34
AGI 126
DEX 202
CHA 197
INT 325
OK.
JUST WAITING ON YOU, BORUTO.
'KAY.
FSH
SO YOU'RE A BIG-SHOT GAMER TOO.

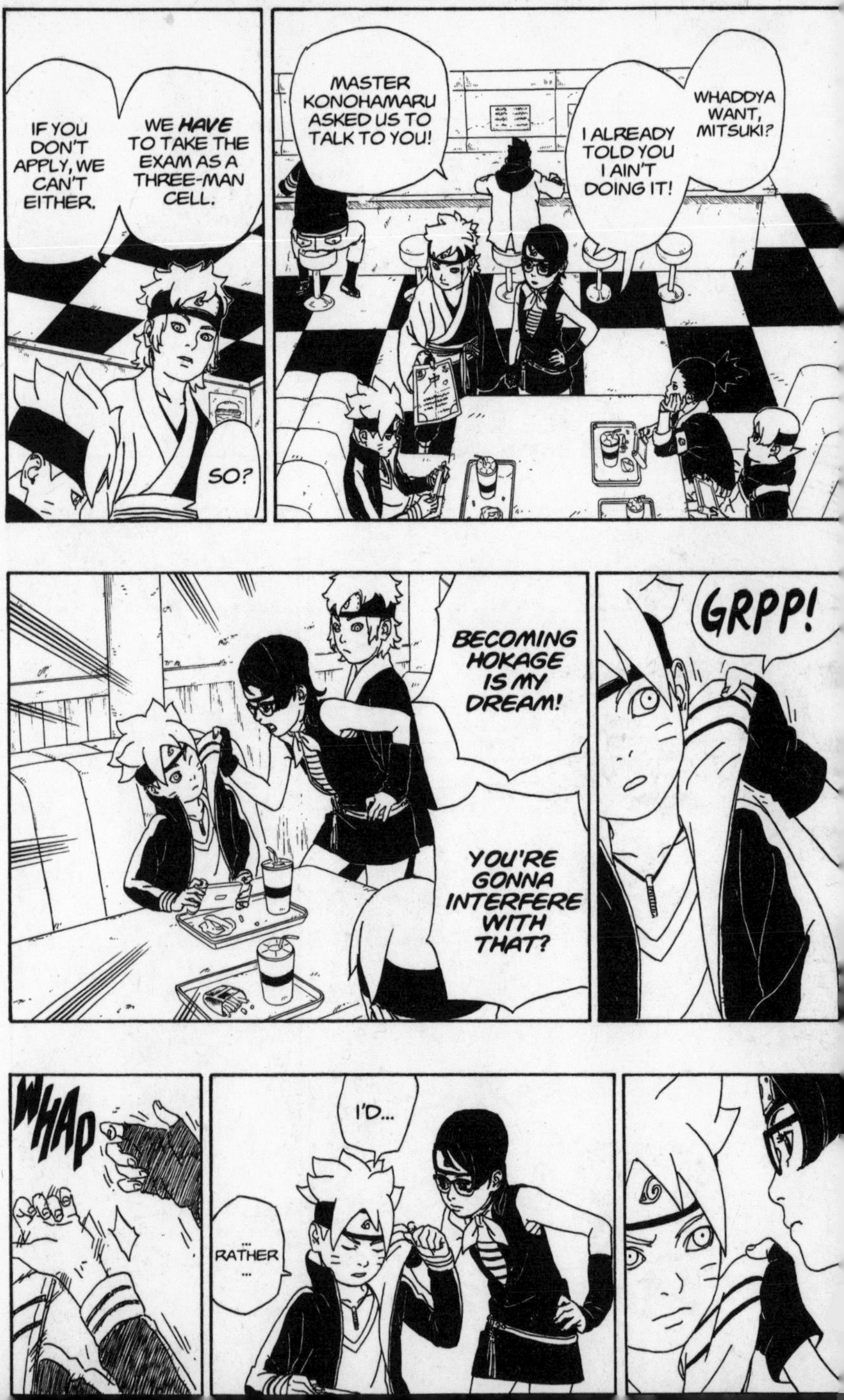
WHADDYA WANT, MITSUKI?
I ALREADY TOLD YOU I AIN'T DOING IT!
MASTER KONOHAMARU ASKED US TO TALK TO YOU!
WE HAVE TO TAKE THE EXAM AS A THREE-MAN CELL.
IF YOU DON'T APPLY, WE CAN'T EITHER.
SO?
GRPP!
BECOMING HOKAGE IS MY DREAM!
YOU'RE GONNA INTERFERE WITH THAT?
I'D...
...RATHER...
WHAP

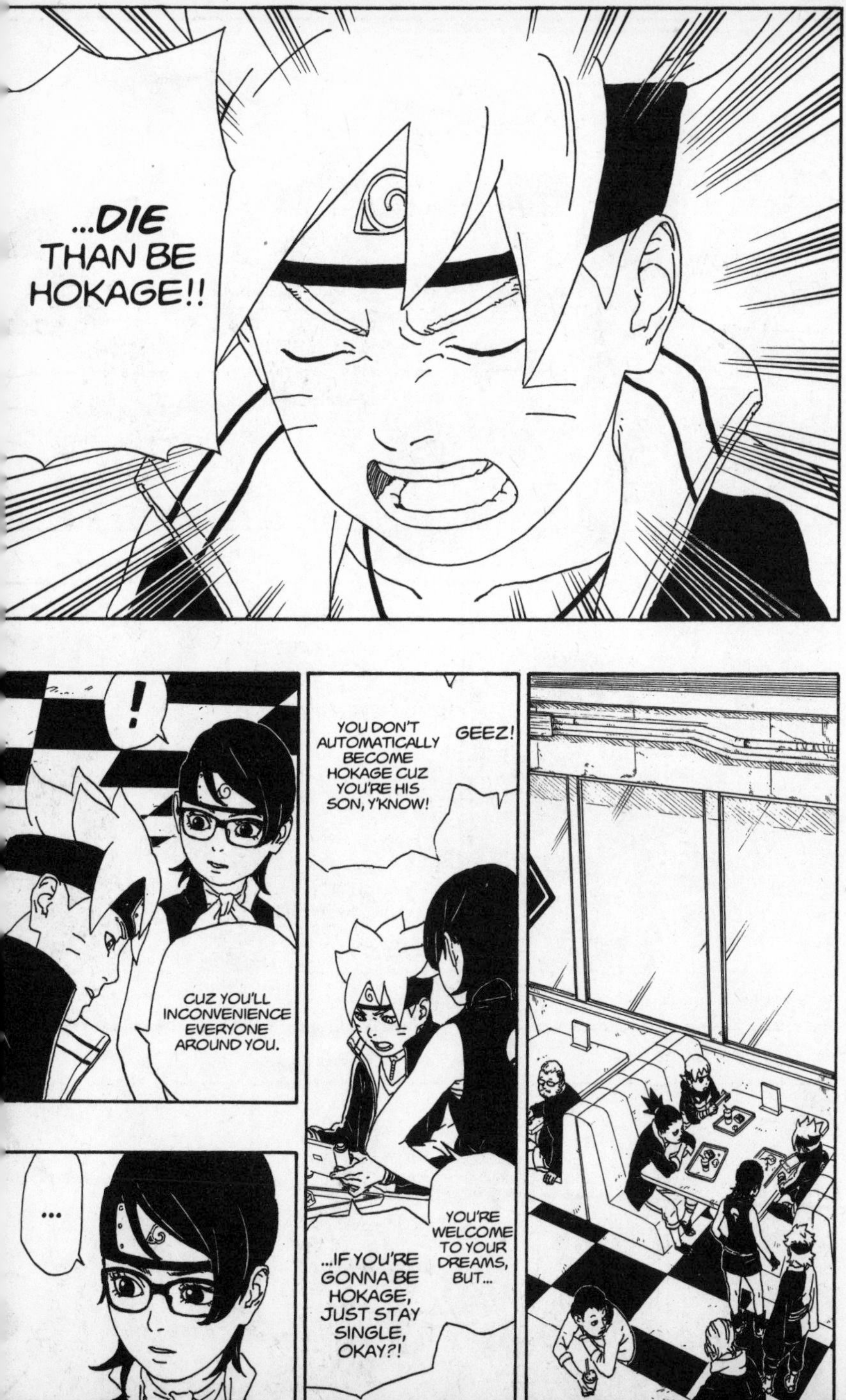
...DIE THAN BE HOKAGE!!
GEEZ!
YOU DON'T AUTOMATICALLY BECOME HOKAGE CUZ YOU'RE HIS SON, Y'KNOW!
YOU'RE WELCOME TO YOUR DREAMS, BUT...
...IF YOU'RE GONNA BE HOKAGE, JUST STAY SINGLE, OKAY?!
!
CUZ YOU'LL INCONVENIENCE EVERYONE AROUND YOU.
...

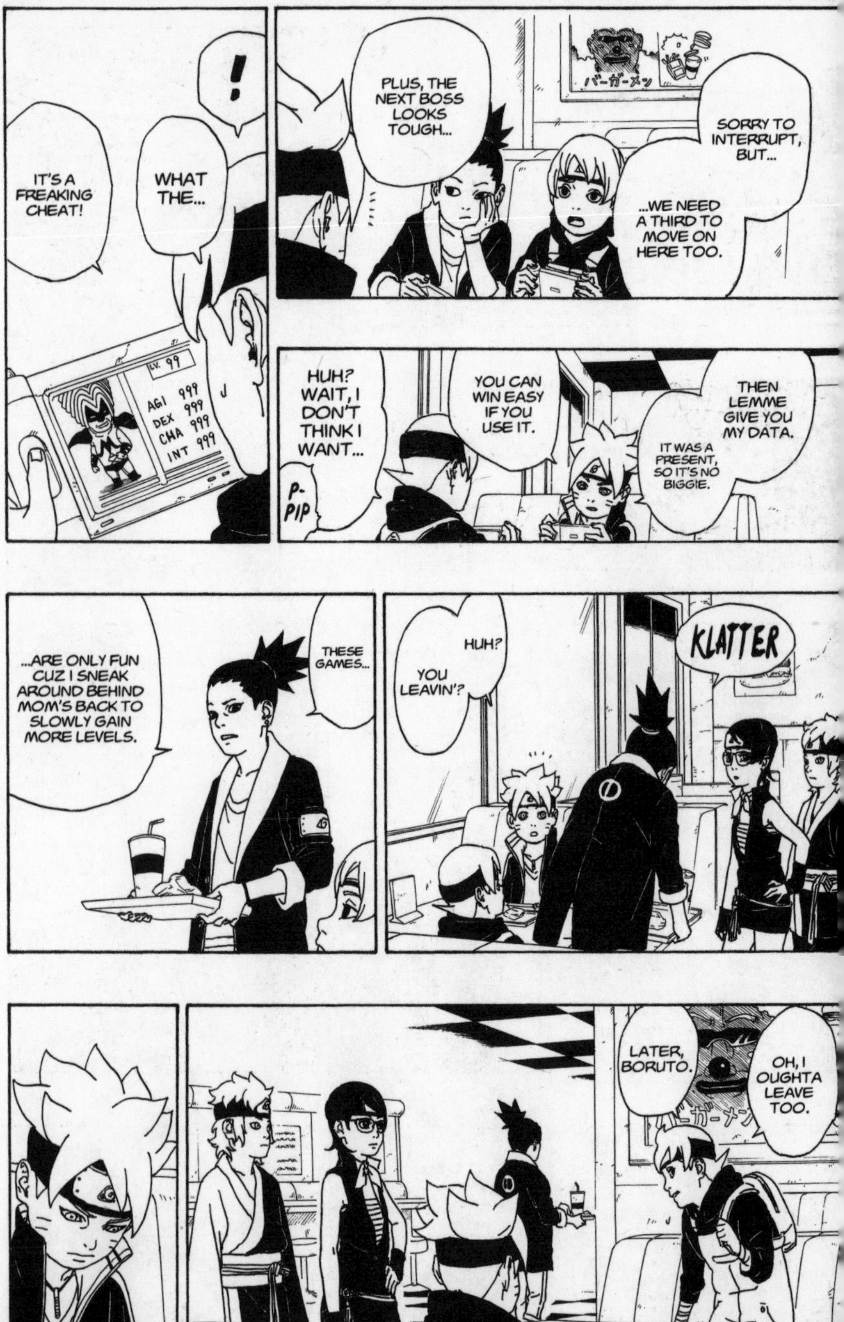

バーガーメン
PLUS, THE NEXT BOSS LOOKS TOUGH...
SORRY TO INTERRUPT, BUT...
...WE NEED A THIRD TO MOVE ON HERE TOO.
THEN LEMME GIVE YOU MY DATA.
IT WAS A PRESENT, SO IT'S NO BIGGIE.
YOU CAN WIN EASY IF YOU USE IT.
HUH? WAIT, I DON'T THINK I WANT...
P-PIP
!
WHAT THE...
IT'S A FREAKING CHEAT!
LV. 99
AGI 999
DEX 999
CHA 999
INT 999
KLATTER
HUH?
YOU LEAVIN'?
THESE GAMES...
...ARE ONLY FUN CUZ I SNEAK AROUND BEHIND MOM'S BACK TO SLOWLY GAIN MORE LEVELS.
OH, I OUGHTA LEAVE TOO.
LATER, BORUTO.

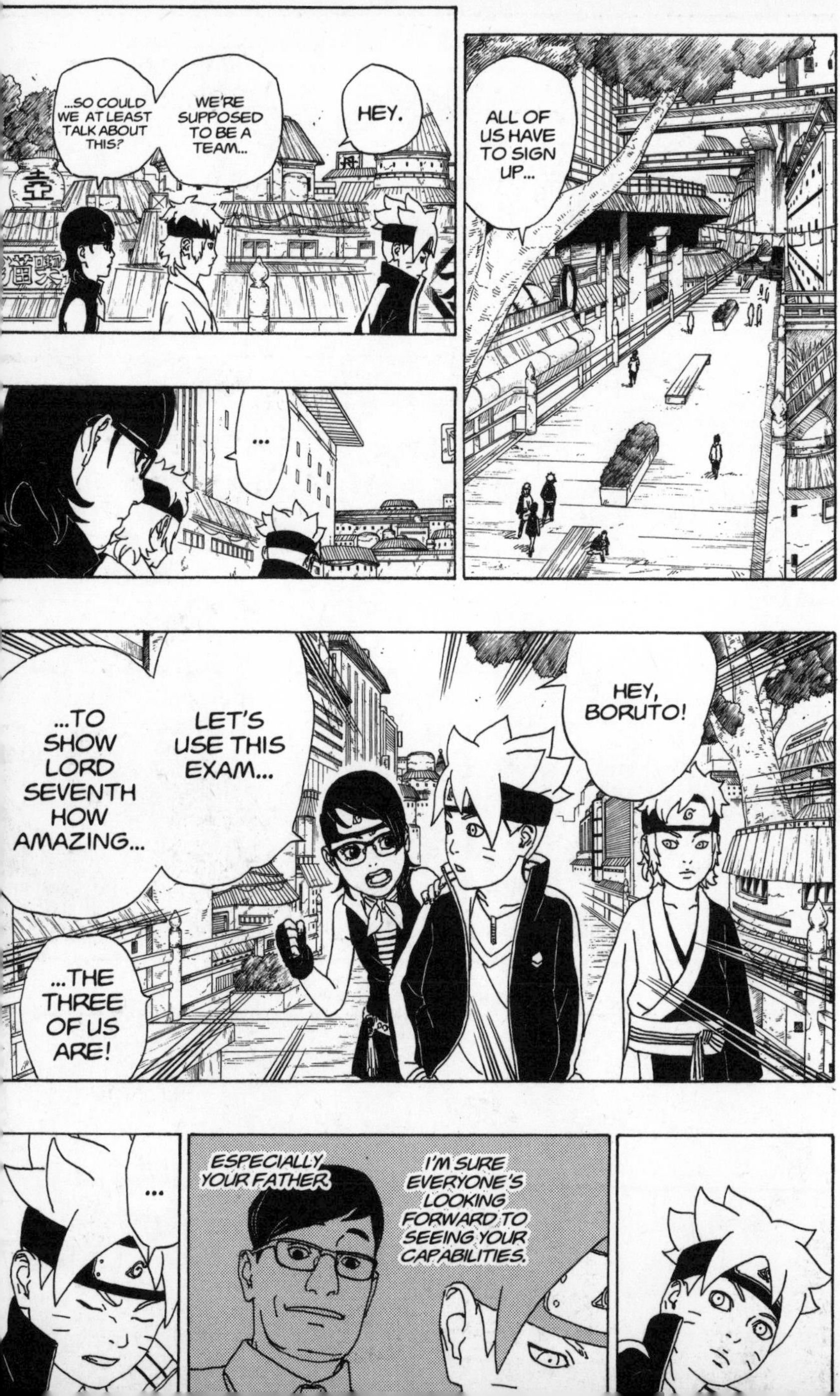
ALL OF US HAVE TO SIGN UP...
HEY.
WE'RE SUPPOSED TO BE A TEAM...
...SO COULD WE AT LEAST TALK ABOUT THIS?
...
HEY, BORUTO!
LET'S USE THIS EXAM...
...TO SHOW LORD SEVENTH HOW AMAZING...
...THE THREE OF US ARE!
I'M SURE EVERYONE'S LOOKING FORWARD TO SEEING YOUR CAPABILITIES.
ESPECIALLY YOUR FATHER.
...

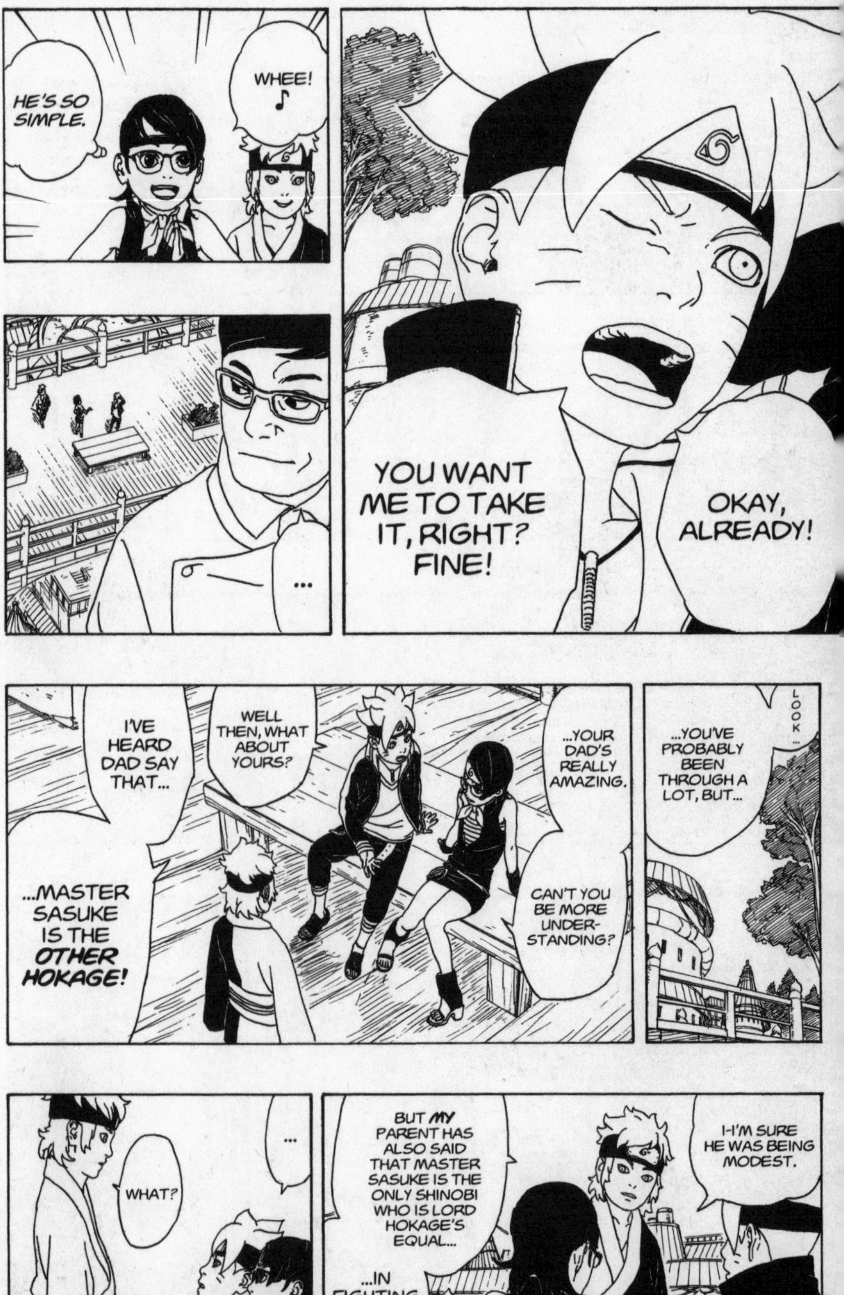
OKAY, ALREADY!
YOU WANT ME TO TAKE IT, RIGHT? FINE!
WHEE! ♪
HE'S SO SIMPLE.
...
LOOK...
...YOU'VE PROBABLY BEEN THROUGH A LOT, BUT...
...YOUR DAD'S REALLY AMAZING.
CAN'T YOU BE MORE UNDER-STANDING?
WELL THEN, WHAT ABOUT YOURS?
I'VE HEARD DAD SAY THAT...
...MASTER SASUKE IS THE *OTHER HOKAGE!*
I-I'M SURE HE WAS BEING MODEST.
BUT *MY* PARENT HAS ALSO SAID THAT MASTER SASUKE IS THE ONLY SHINOBI WHO IS LORD HOKAGE'S EQUAL...
...IN FIGHTING ABILITY.
...
WHAT?

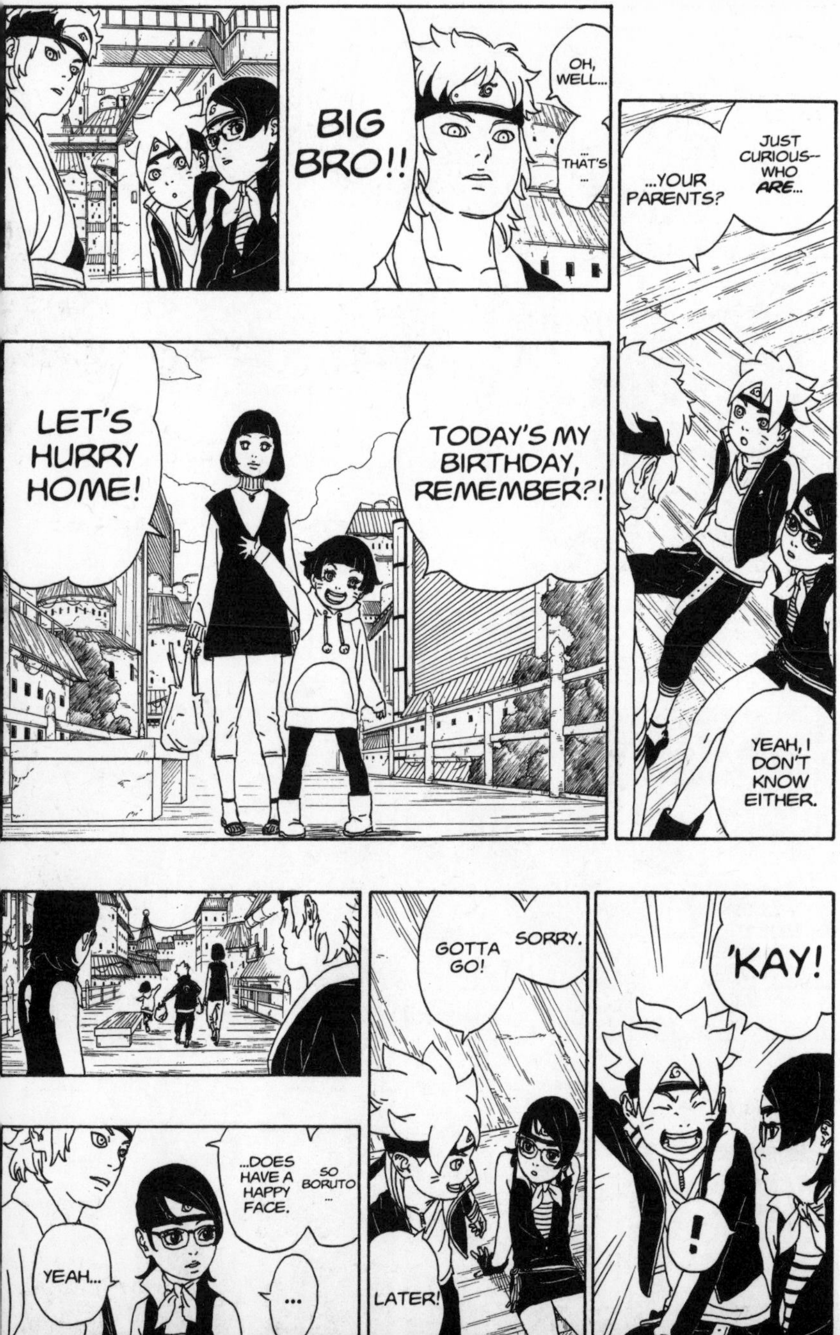
JUST CURIOUS-- WHO ARE...
...YOUR PARENTS?
YEAH, I DON'T KNOW EITHER.
OH, WELL...
... THAT'S ...
BIG BRO!!
TODAY'S MY BIRTHDAY, REMEMBER?!
LET'S HURRY HOME!
'KAY!
!
SORRY.
GOTTA GO!
LATER!
SO BORUTO ...
...DOES HAVE A HAPPY FACE.
YEAH...
...

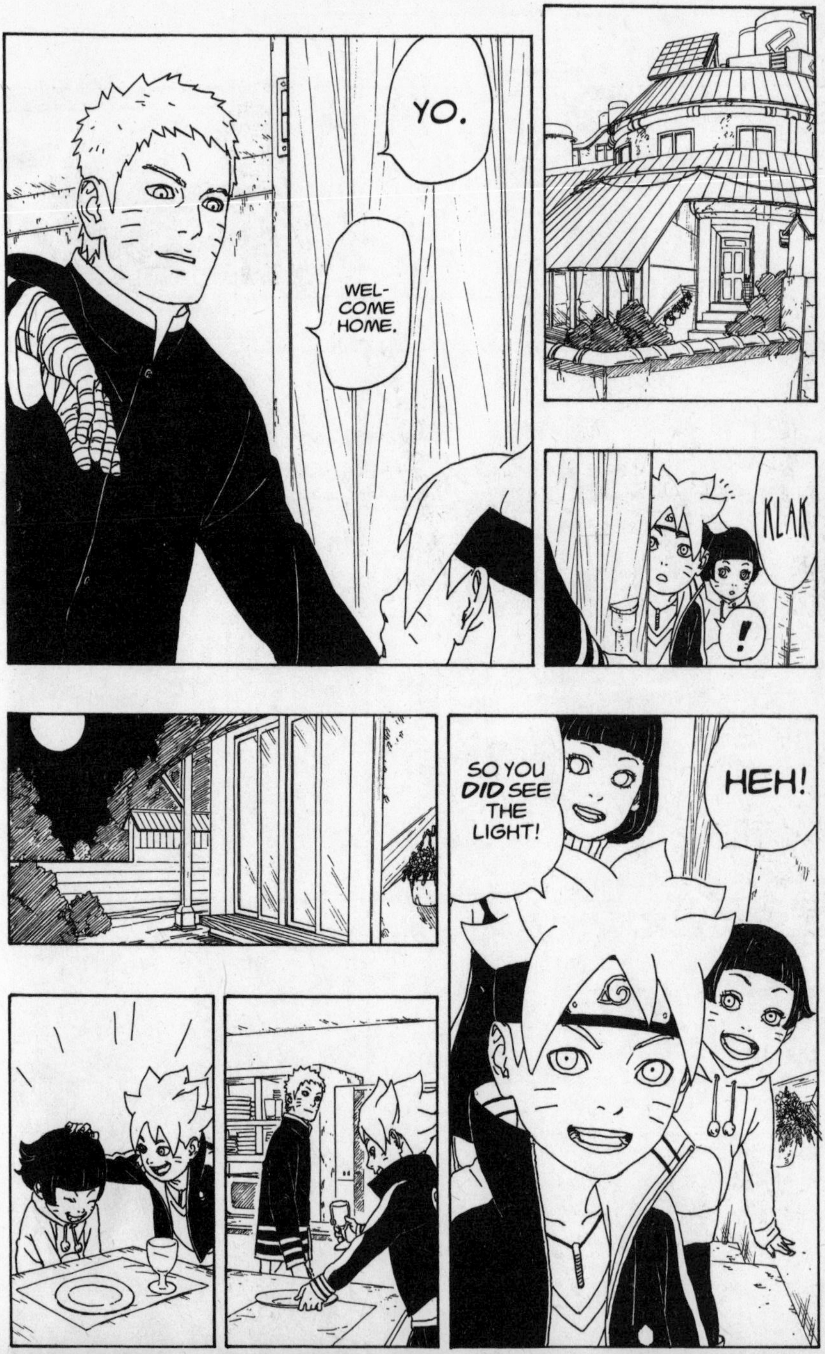
KLAK
!
YO.
WEL-COME HOME.
HEH!
SO YOU **DID** SEE THE LIGHT!

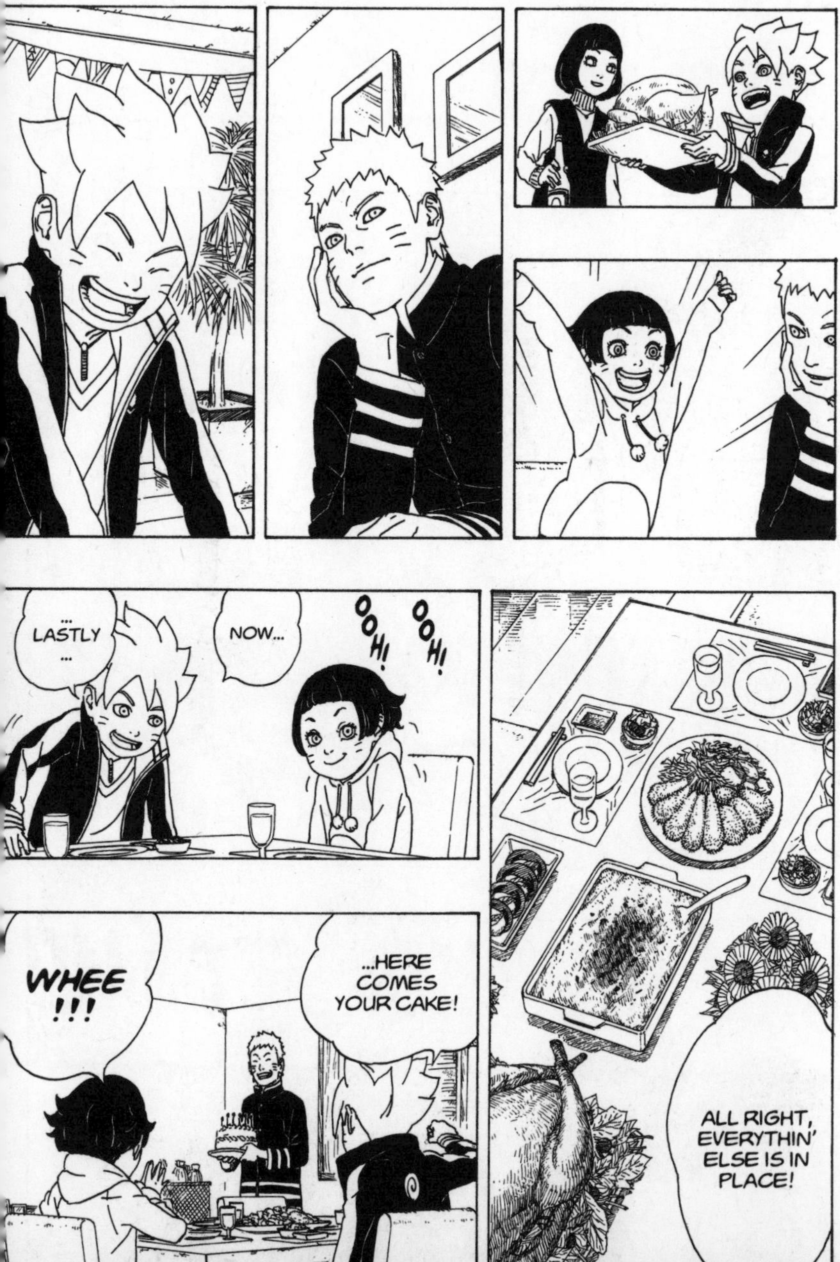
ALL RIGHT, EVERYTHIN' ELSE IS IN PLACE!
OOH! OOH!
NOW...
...LASTLY...
...HERE COMES YOUR CAKE!
WHEE!!!

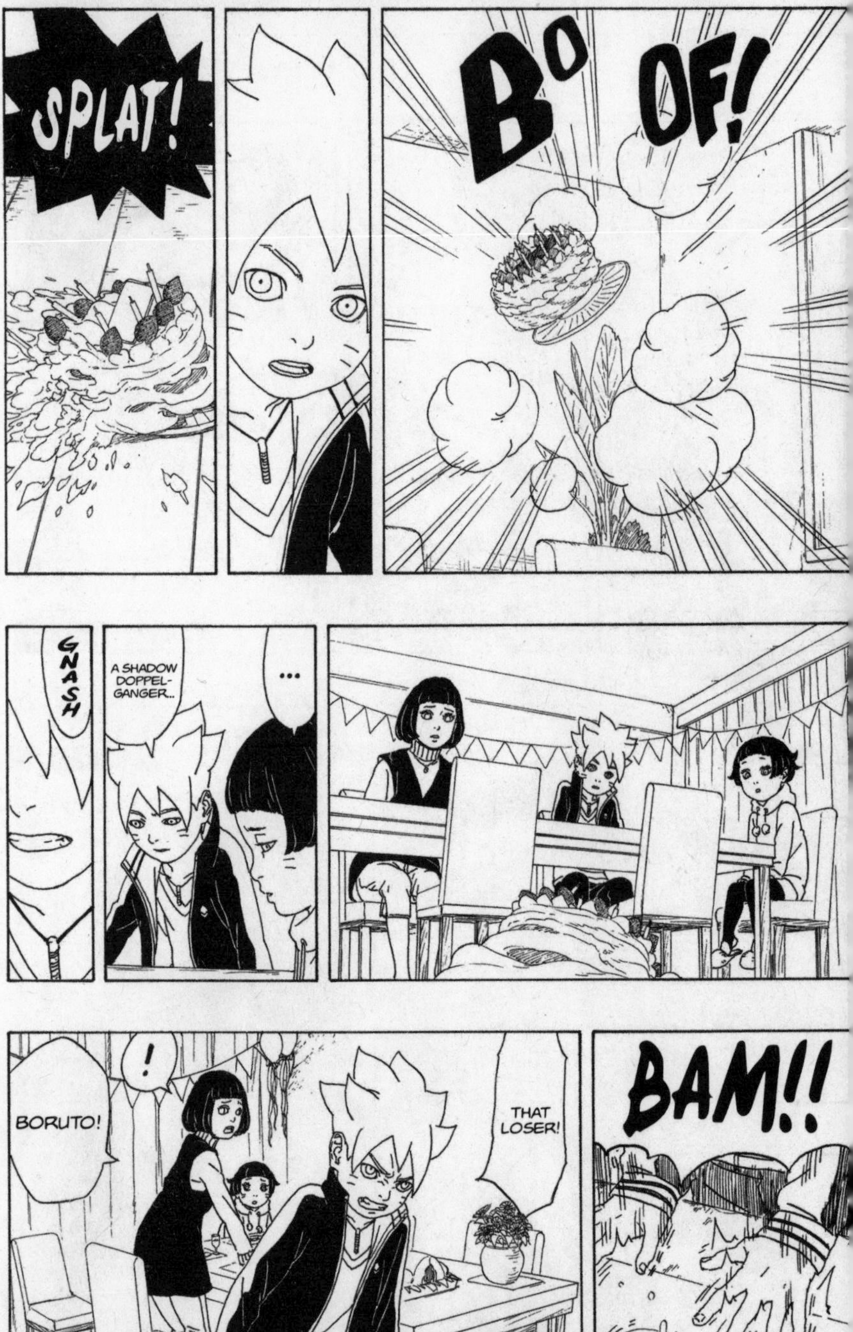
BOOF!
SPLAT!
...
A SHADOW DOPPEL-GANGER...
GNASH
BAM!!
THAT LOSER!
!
BORUTO!

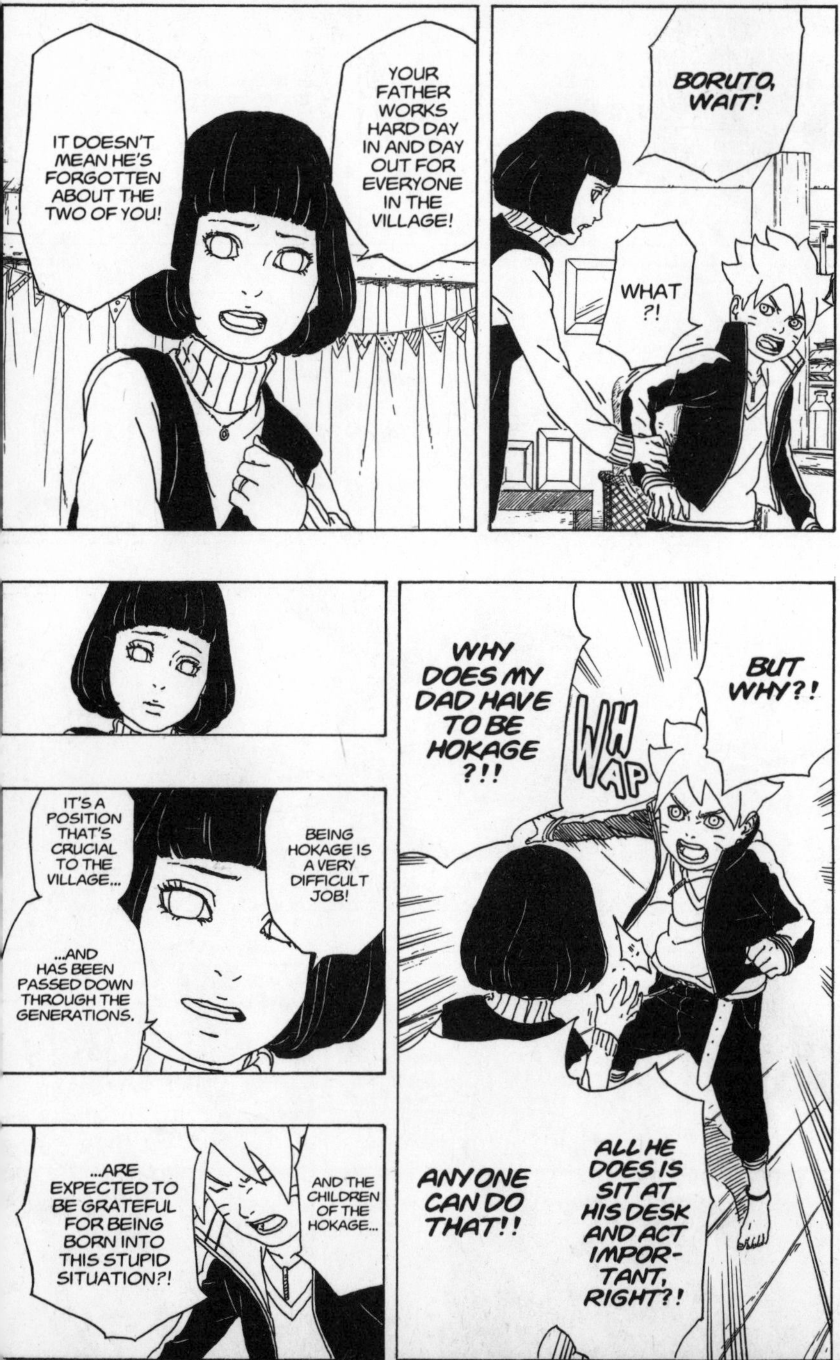
BORUTO, WAIT!
WHAT?!
YOUR FATHER WORKS HARD DAY IN AND DAY OUT FOR EVERYONE IN THE VILLAGE!
IT DOESN'T MEAN HE'S FORGOTTEN ABOUT THE TWO OF YOU!
BUT WHY?!
WHY DOES MY DAD HAVE TO BE HOKAGE?!!
WHWAP
ALL HE DOES IS SIT AT HIS DESK AND ACT IMPOR-TANT, RIGHT?!
ANYONE CAN DO THAT!!
BEING HOKAGE IS A VERY DIFFICULT JOB!
IT'S A POSITION THAT'S CRUCIAL TO THE VILLAGE...
...AND HAS BEEN PASSED DOWN THROUGH THE GENERATIONS.
AND THE CHILDREN OF THE HOKAGE...
...ARE EXPECTED TO BE GRATEFUL FOR BEING BORN INTO THIS STUPID SITUATION?!

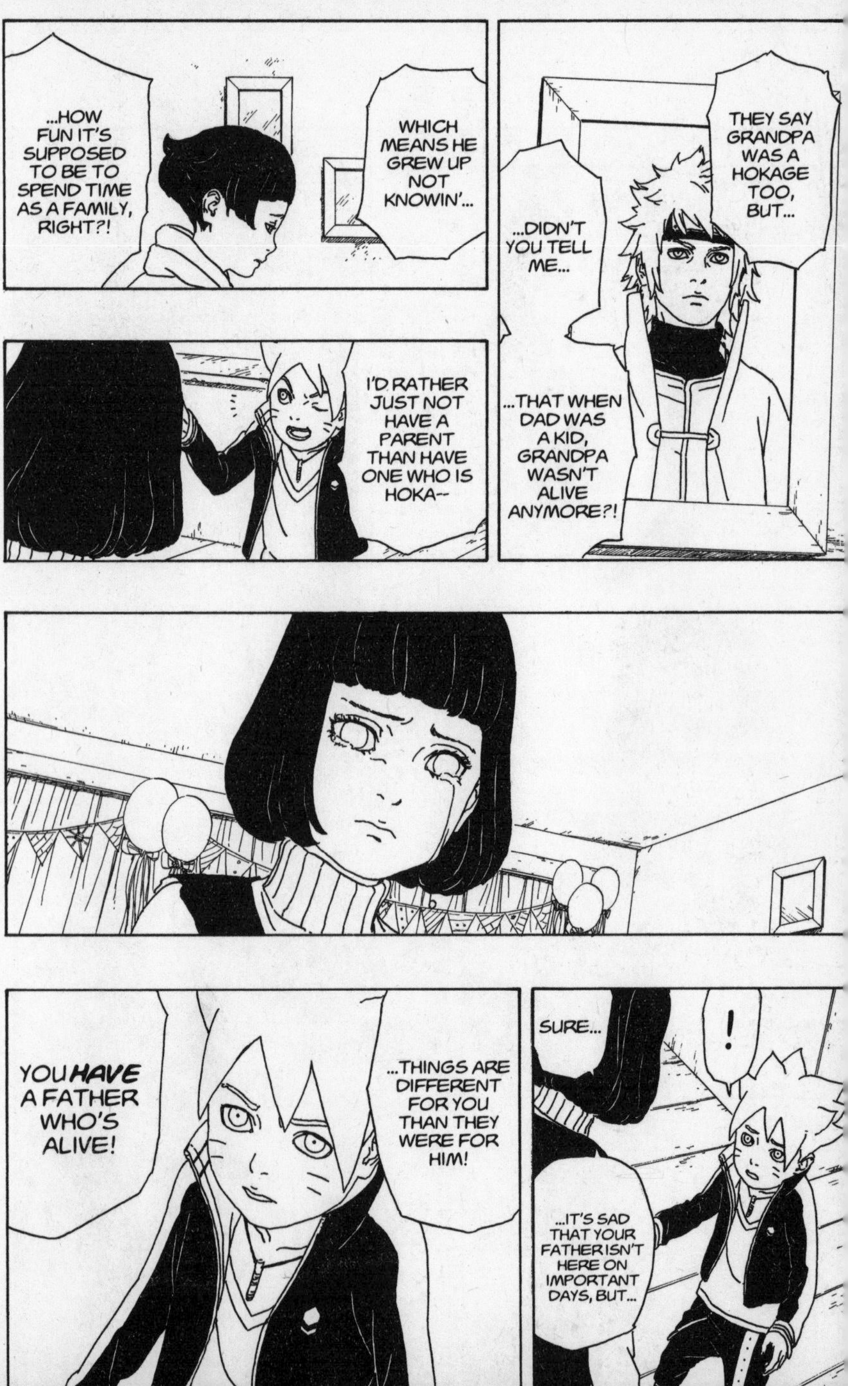
THEY SAY GRANDPA WAS A HOKAGE TOO, BUT...
...DIDN'T YOU TELL ME...
...THAT WHEN DAD WAS A KID, GRANDPA WASN'T ALIVE ANYMORE?!
WHICH MEANS HE GREW UP NOT KNOWIN'...
...HOW FUN IT'S SUPPOSED TO BE TO SPEND TIME AS A FAMILY, RIGHT?!
I'D RATHER JUST NOT HAVE A PARENT THAN HAVE ONE WHO IS HOKA--
!
SURE...
...IT'S SAD THAT YOUR FATHER ISN'T HERE ON IMPORTANT DAYS, BUT...
...THINGS ARE DIFFERENT FOR YOU THAN THEY WERE FOR HIM!
YOU **HAVE** A FATHER WHO'S ALIVE!

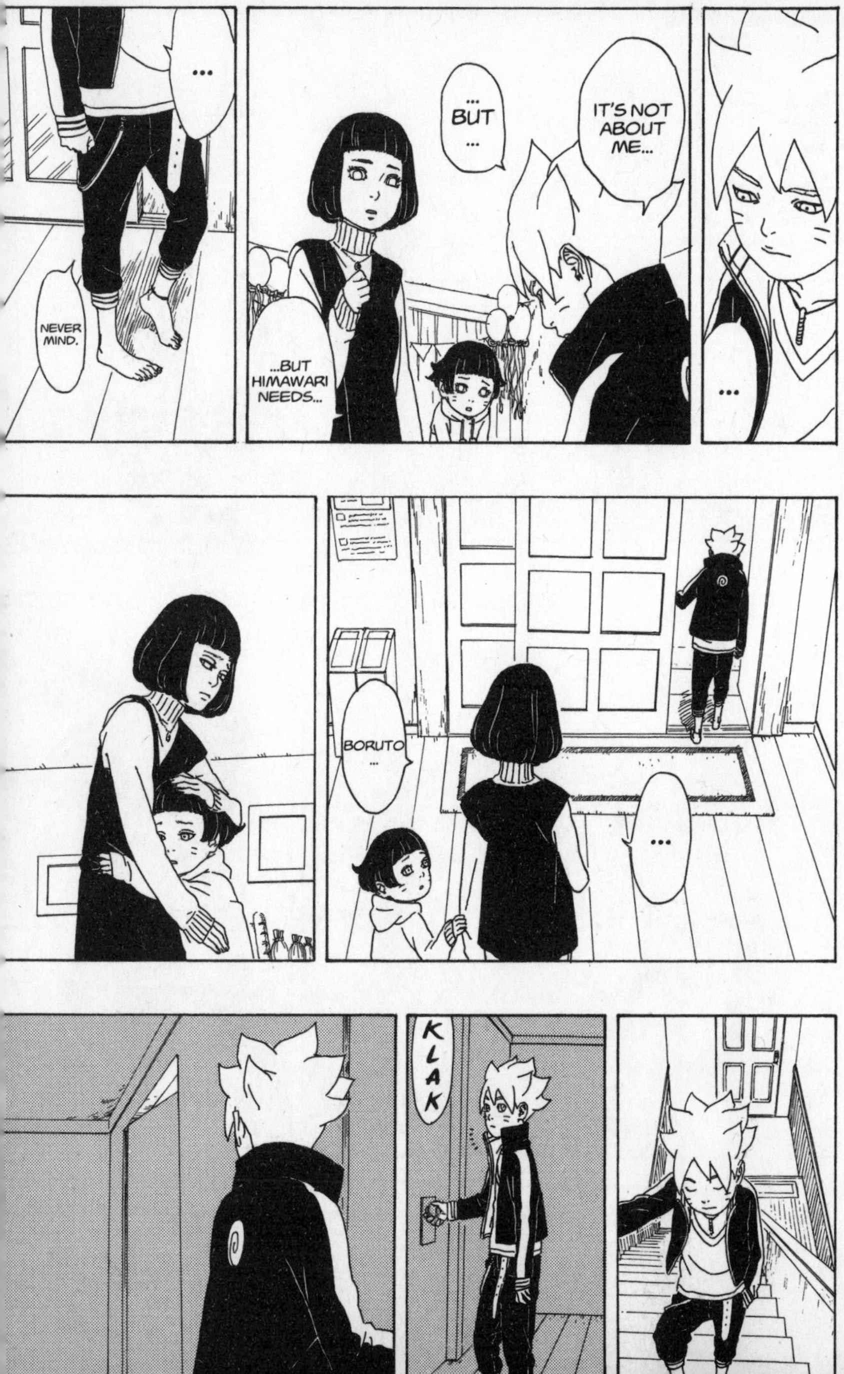
...
IT'S NOT ABOUT ME...
... BUT ...
...BUT HIMAWARI NEEDS...
...
NEVER MIND.
BORUTO ...
...
KLAK

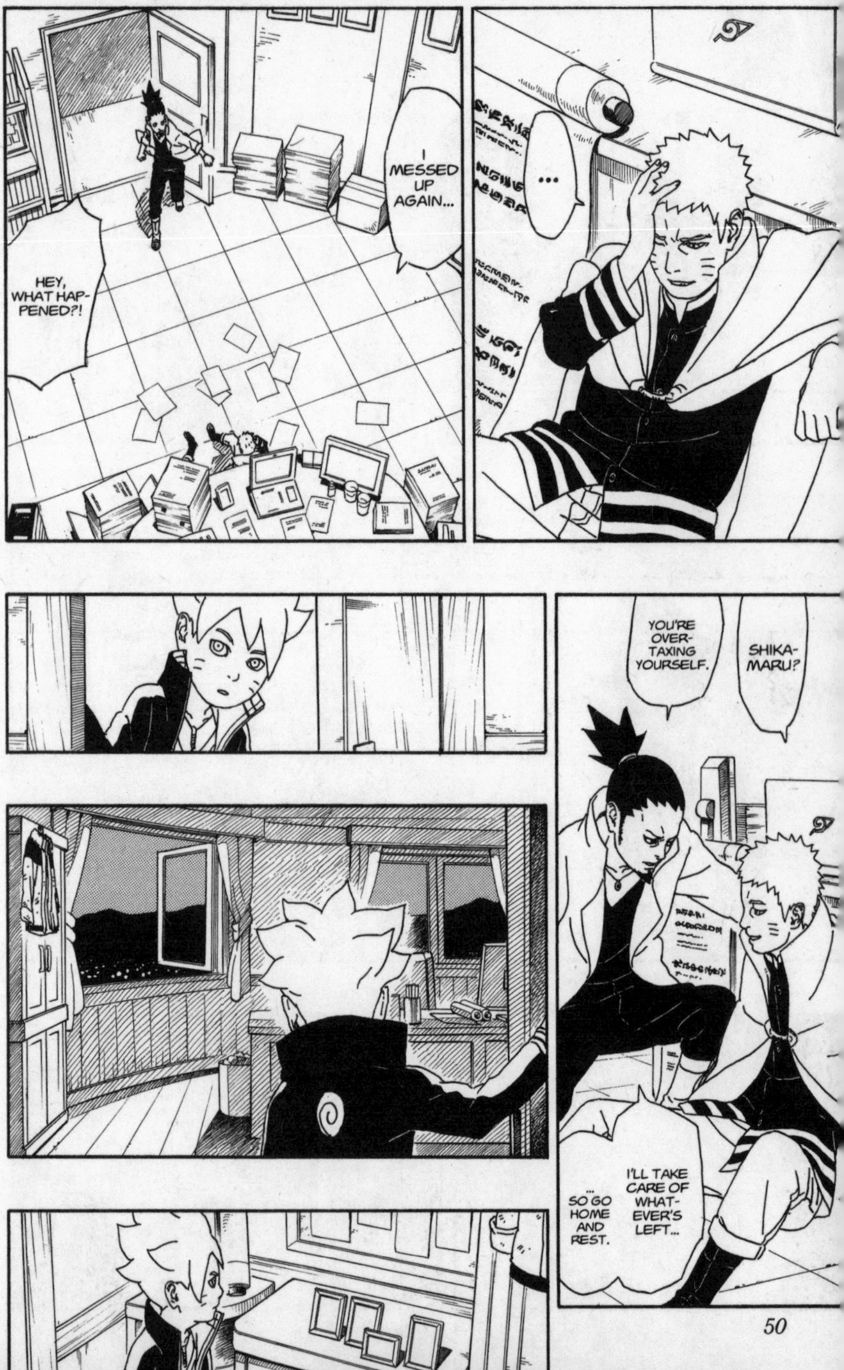
...
I MESSED UP AGAIN...
HEY, WHAT HAPPENED?!
SHIKA-MARU?
YOU'RE OVER-TAXING YOURSELF.
I'LL TAKE CARE OF WHAT-EVER'S LEFT...
... SO GO HOME AND REST.

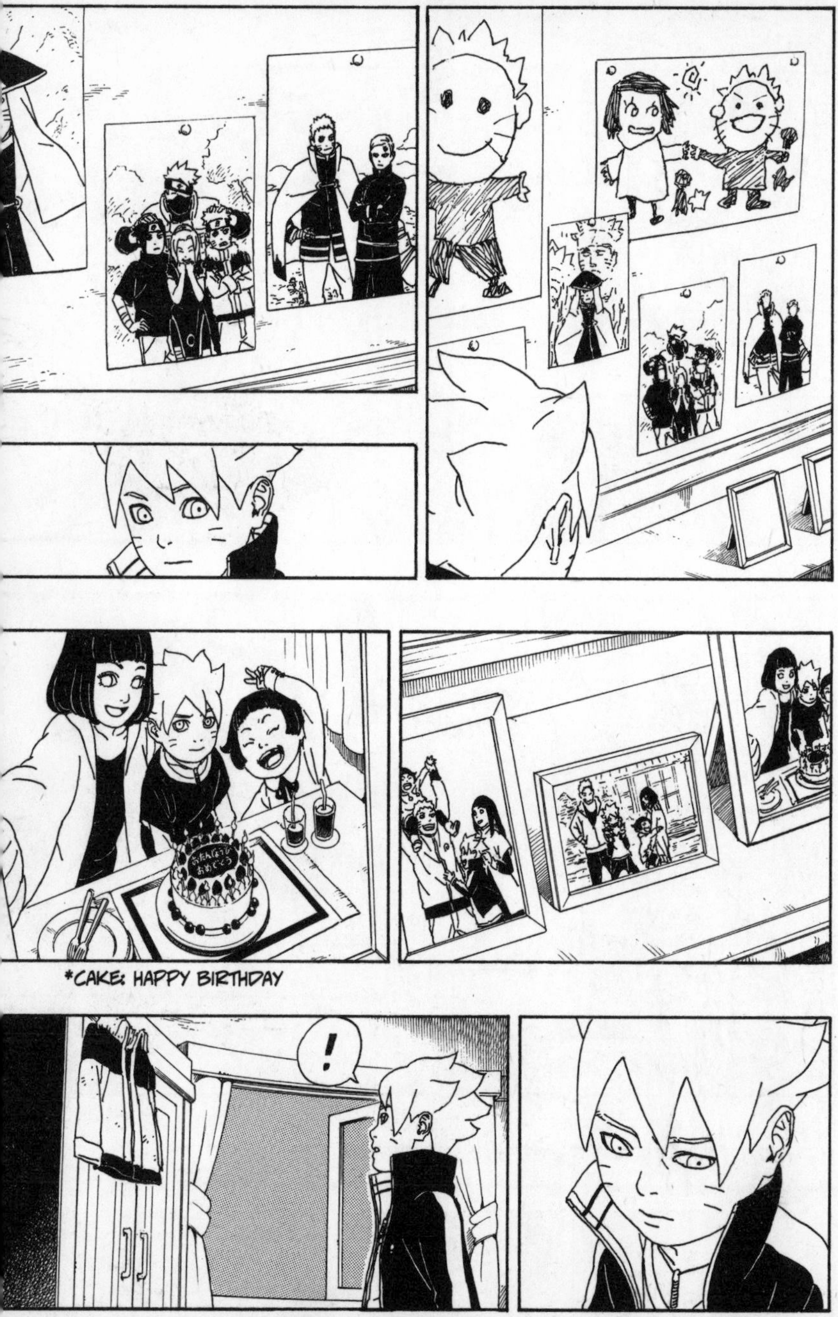
*CAKE: HAPPY BIRTHDAY
!

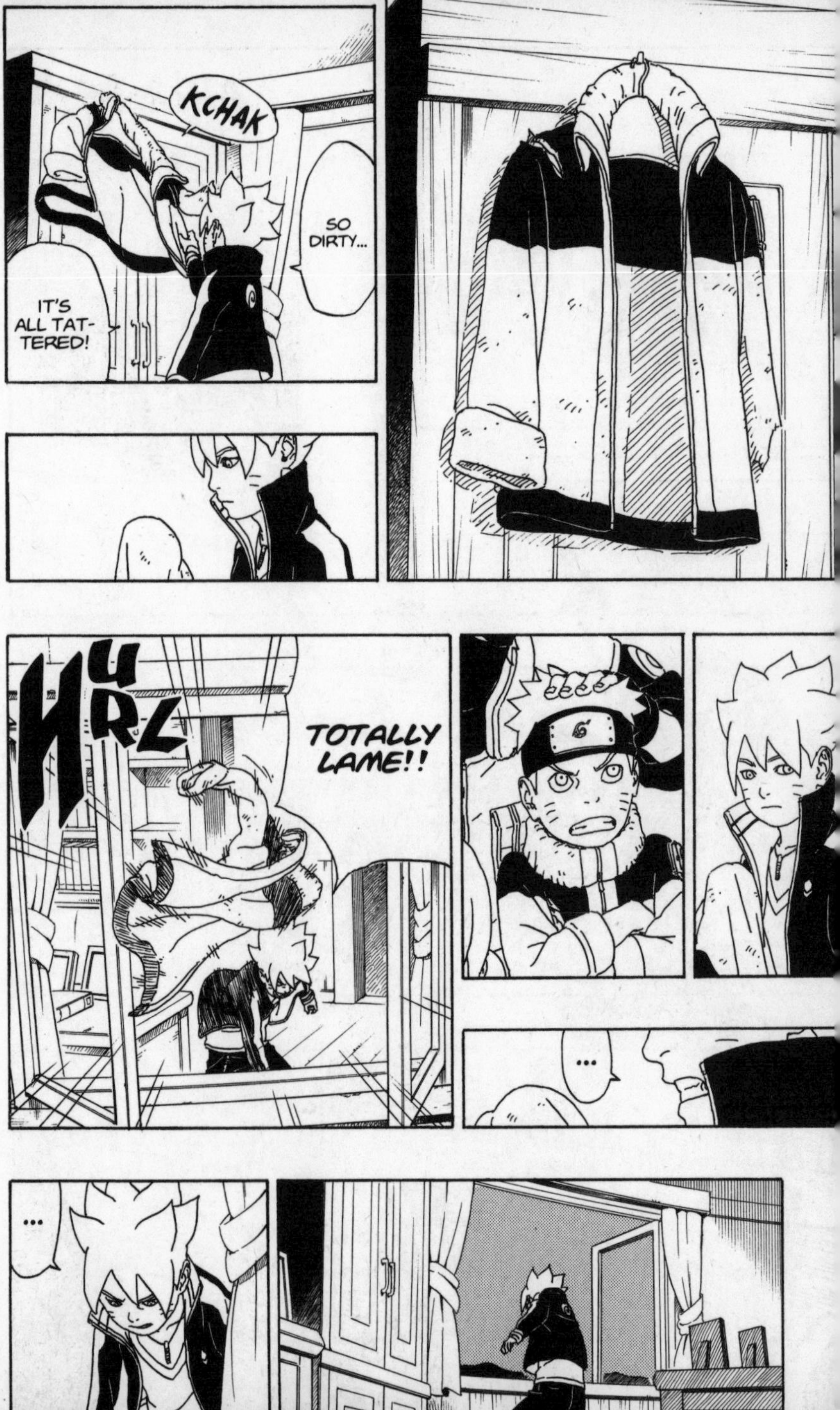
KCHAK
SO DIRTY...
IT'S ALL TATTERED!
...
TOTALLY LAME!!
HURL
...

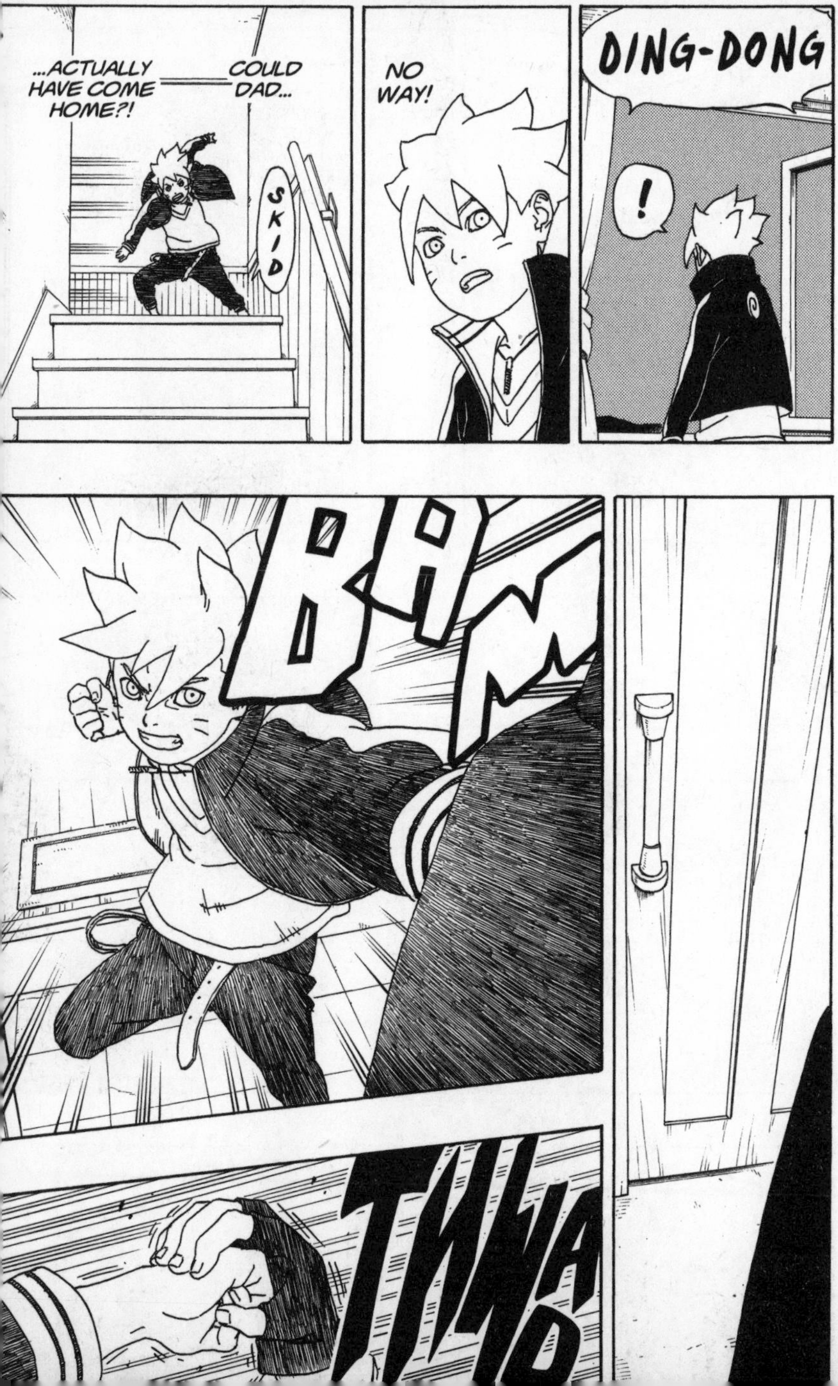
DING-DONG
!
NO WAY!
COULD DAD...
...ACTUALLY HAVE COME HOME?!
SKID
BAM
THWAP

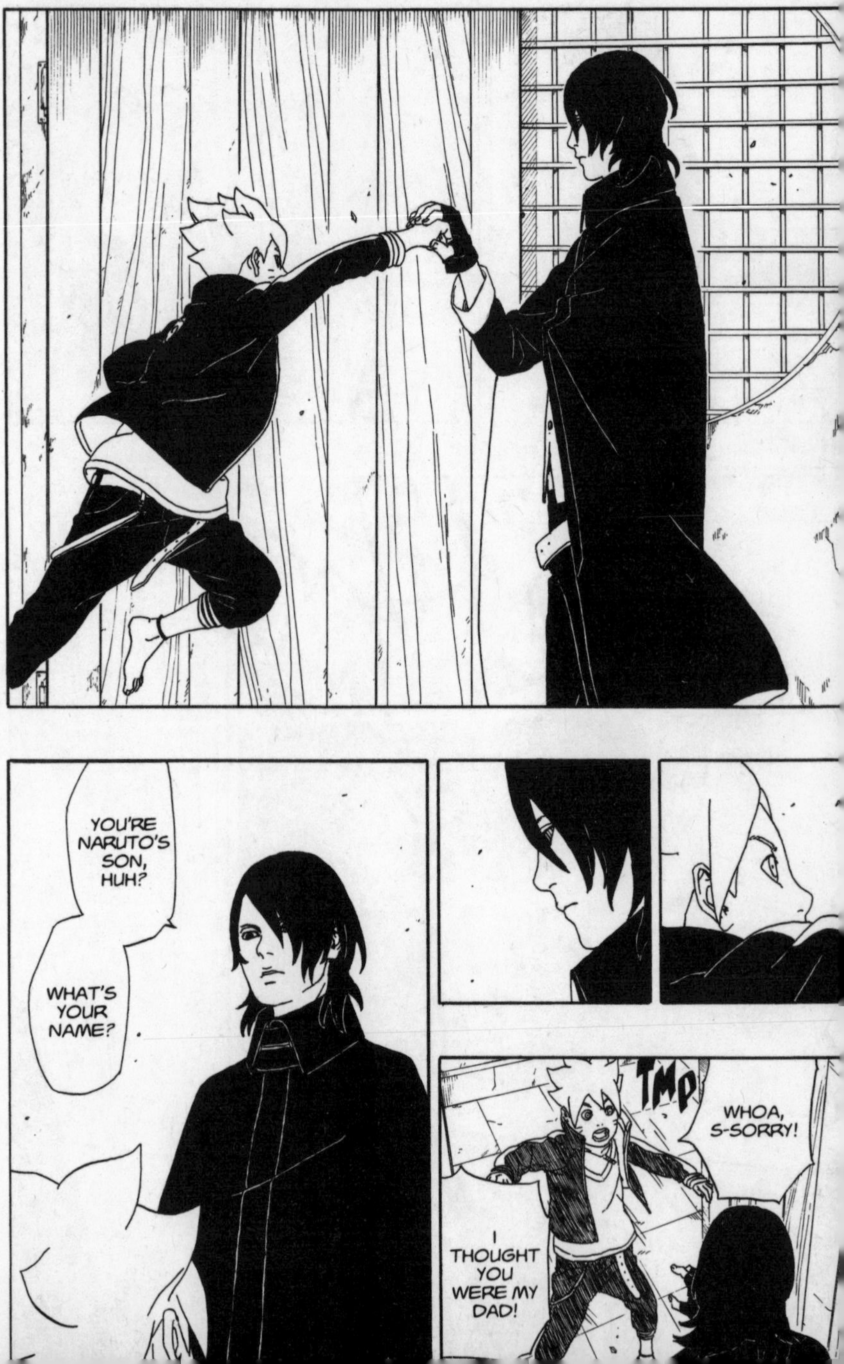
TMP
WHOA, S-SORRY!
I THOUGHT YOU WERE MY DAD!
YOU'RE NARUTO'S SON, HUH?
WHAT'S YOUR NAME?

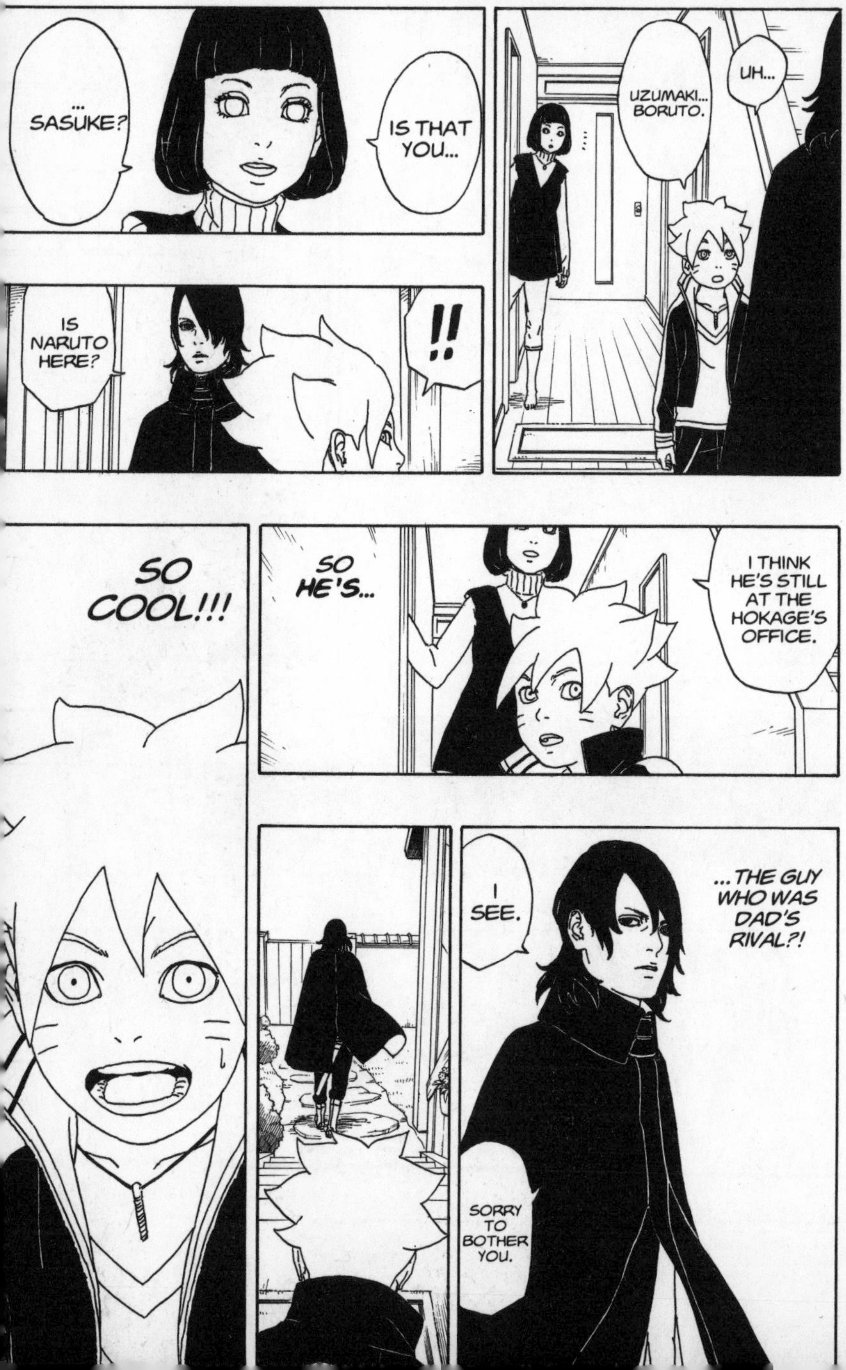
UH...
UZUMAKI... BORUTO.
IS THAT YOU...
... SASUKE?
!!
IS NARUTO HERE?
I THINK HE'S STILL AT THE HOKAGE'S OFFICE.
SO HE'S...
...THE GUY WHO WAS DAD'S RIVAL?!
I SEE.
SORRY TO BOTHER YOU.
SO COOL!!!

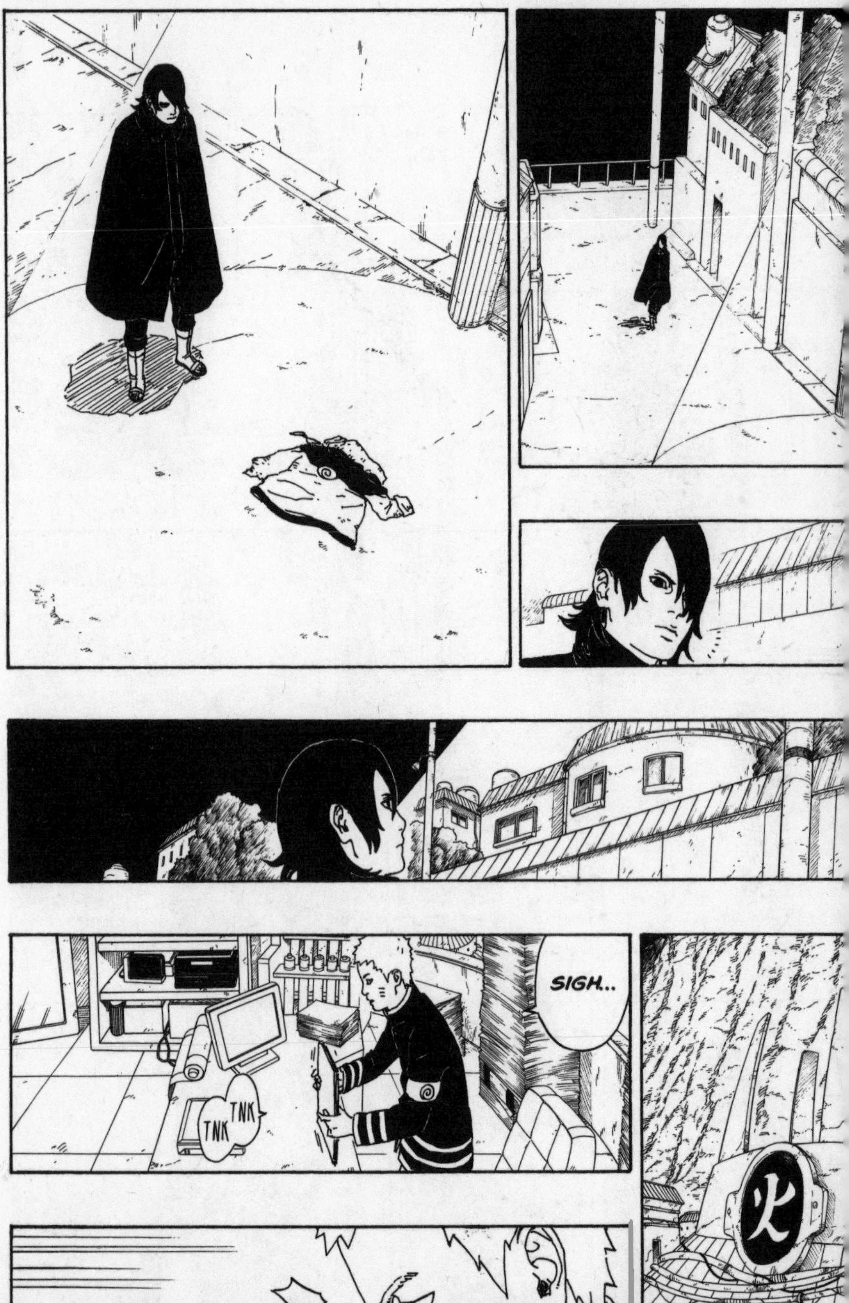
SIGH...
TNK
TNK

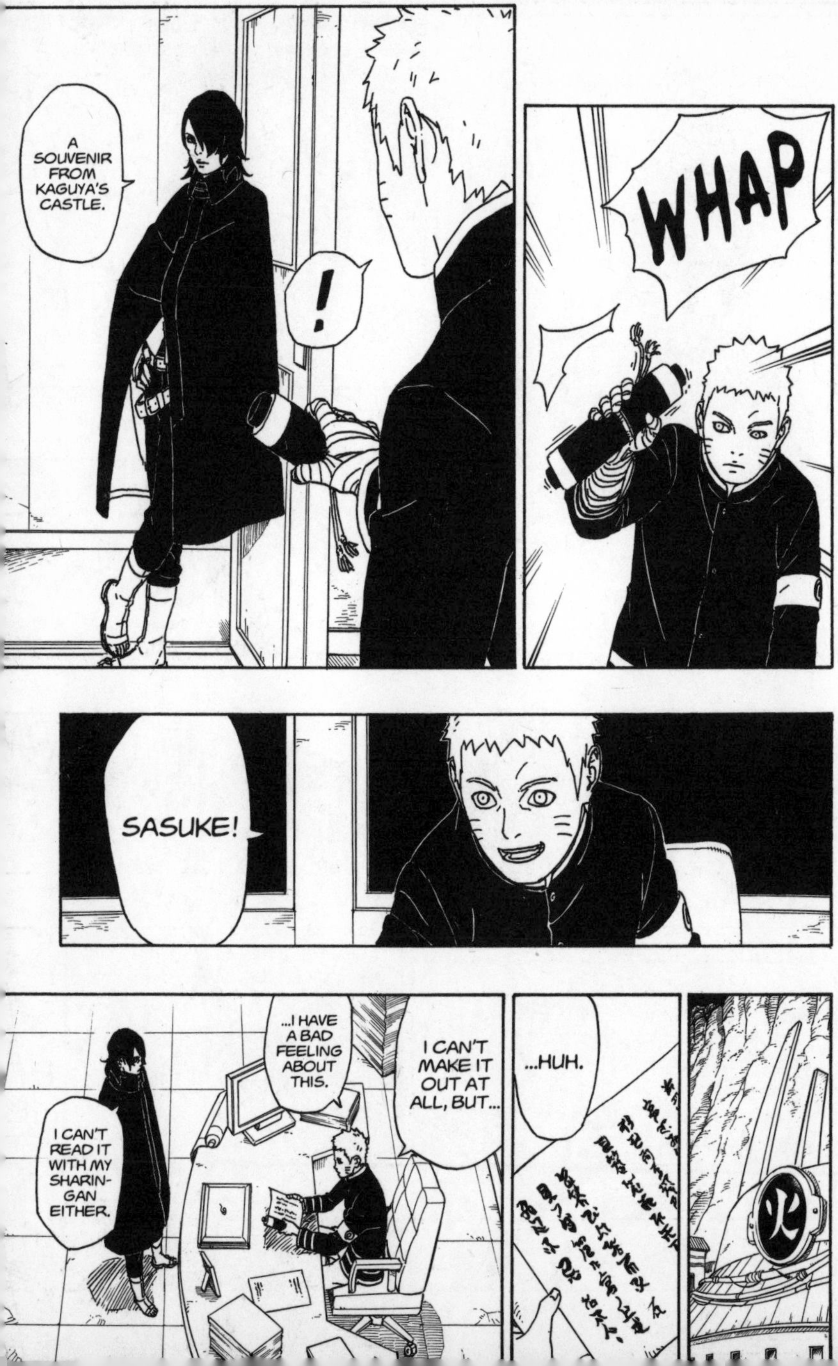
WHAP
A SOUVENIR FROM KAGUYA'S CASTLE.
!
SASUKE!
...HUH.
I CAN'T MAKE IT OUT AT ALL, BUT...
...I HAVE A BAD FEELING ABOUT THIS.
I CAN'T READ IT WITH MY SHARINGAN EITHER.

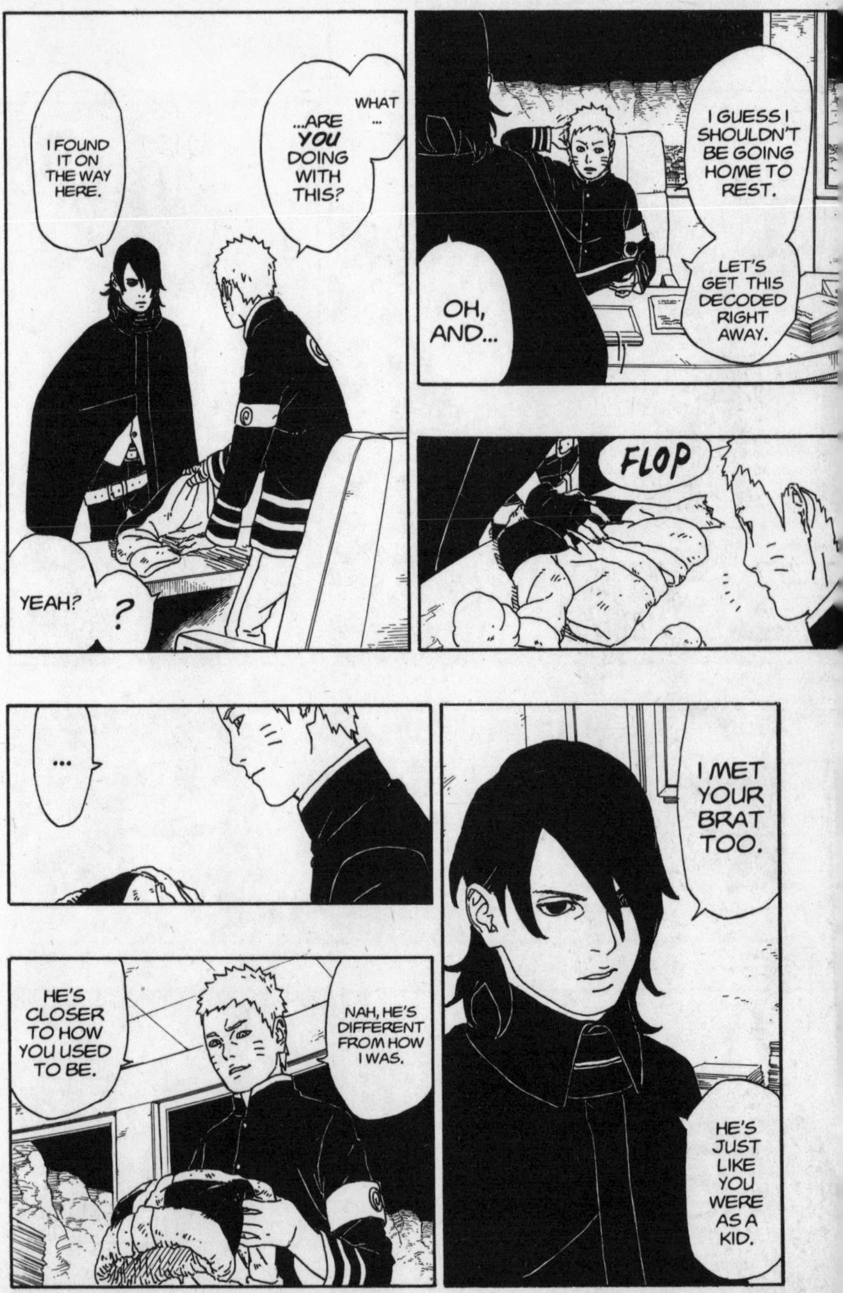
I GUESS I SHOULDN'T BE GOING HOME TO REST.
LET'S GET THIS DECODED RIGHT AWAY.
OH, AND...
FLOP
WHAT ...
...ARE YOU DOING WITH THIS?
I FOUND IT ON THE WAY HERE.
YEAH?
?
I MET YOUR BRAT TOO.
HE'S JUST LIKE YOU WERE AS A KID.
...
NAH, HE'S DIFFERENT FROM HOW I WAS.
HE'S CLOSER TO HOW YOU USED TO BE.

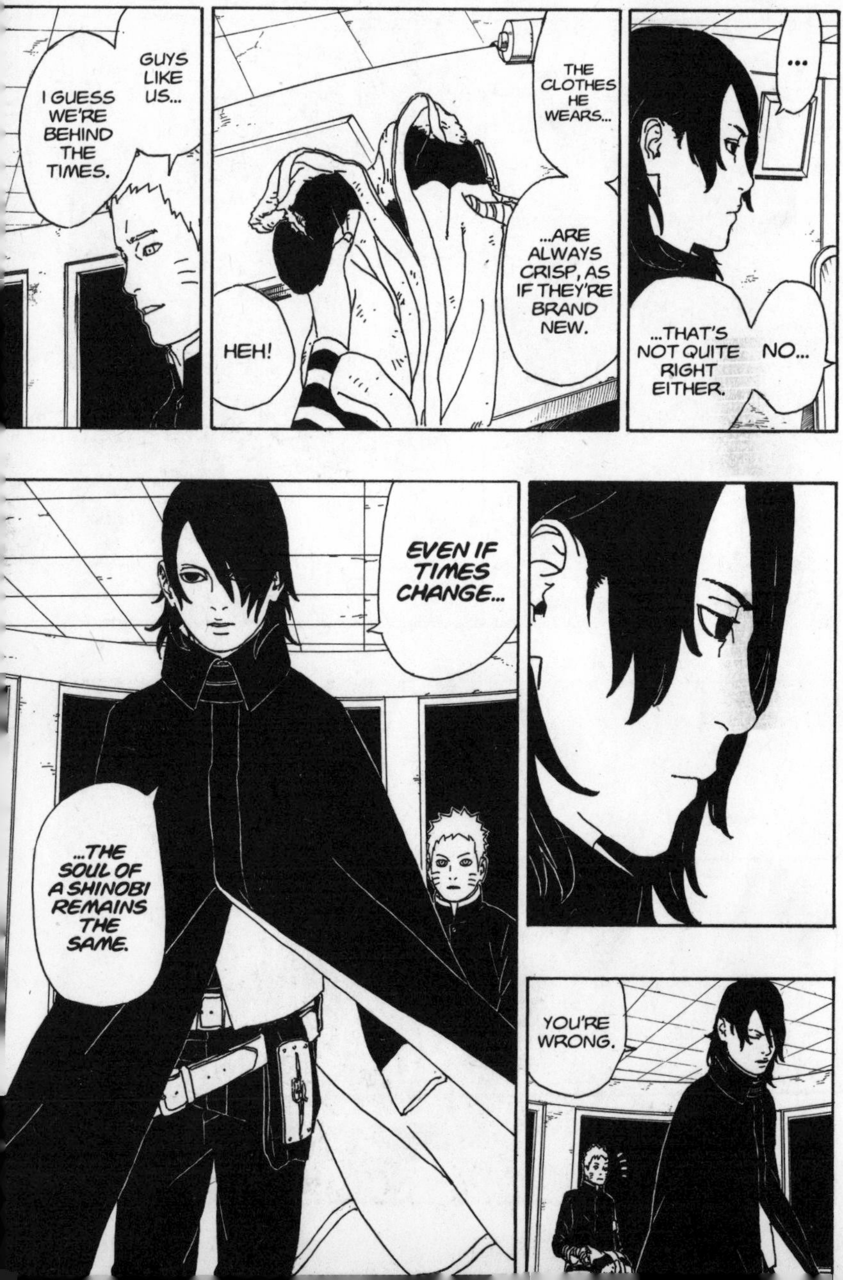
...
NO...
...THAT'S NOT QUITE RIGHT EITHER.
THE CLOTHES HE WEARS...
...ARE ALWAYS CRISP, AS IF THEY'RE BRAND NEW.
HEH!
GUYS LIKE US...
I GUESS WE'RE BEHIND THE TIMES.
YOU'RE WRONG.
EVEN IF TIMES CHANGE...
...THE SOUL OF A SHINOBI REMAINS THE SAME.

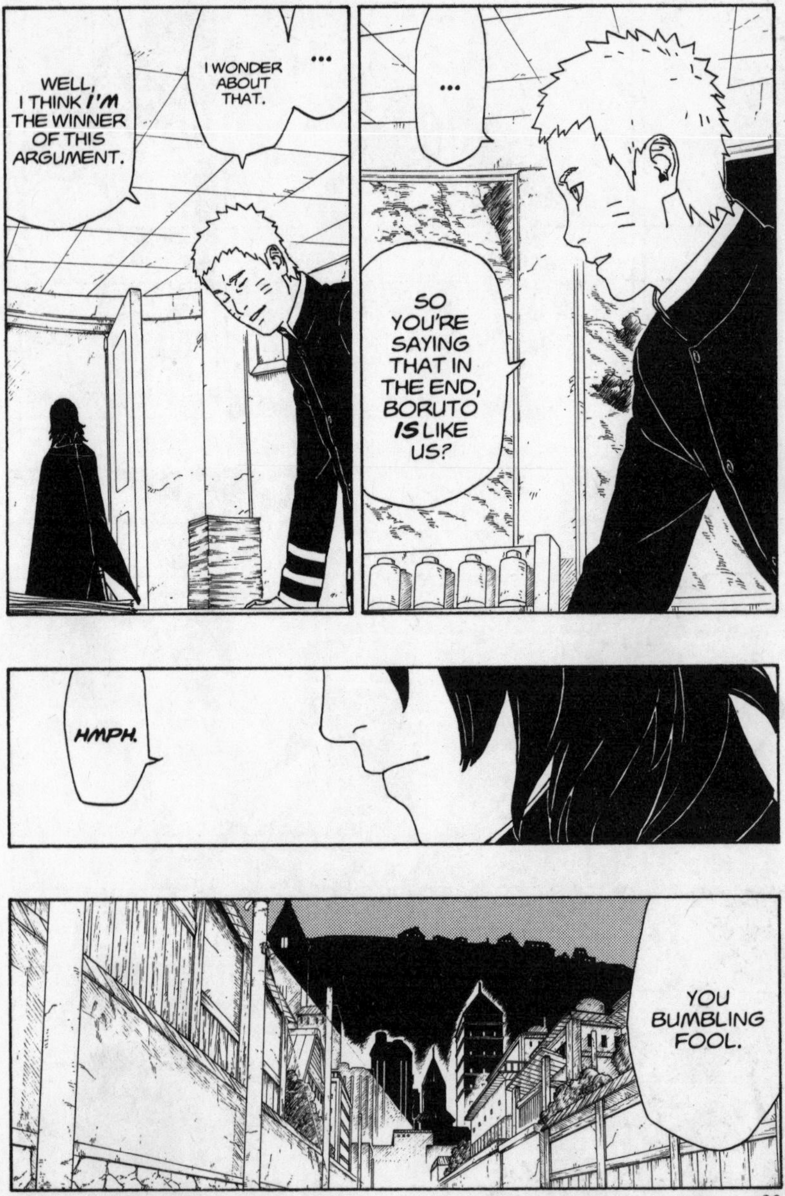
...
SO YOU'RE SAYING THAT IN THE END, BORUTO IS LIKE US?
...
I WONDER ABOUT THAT.
WELL, I THINK I'M THE WINNER OF THIS ARGUMENT.
HMPH.
YOU BUMBLING FOOL.

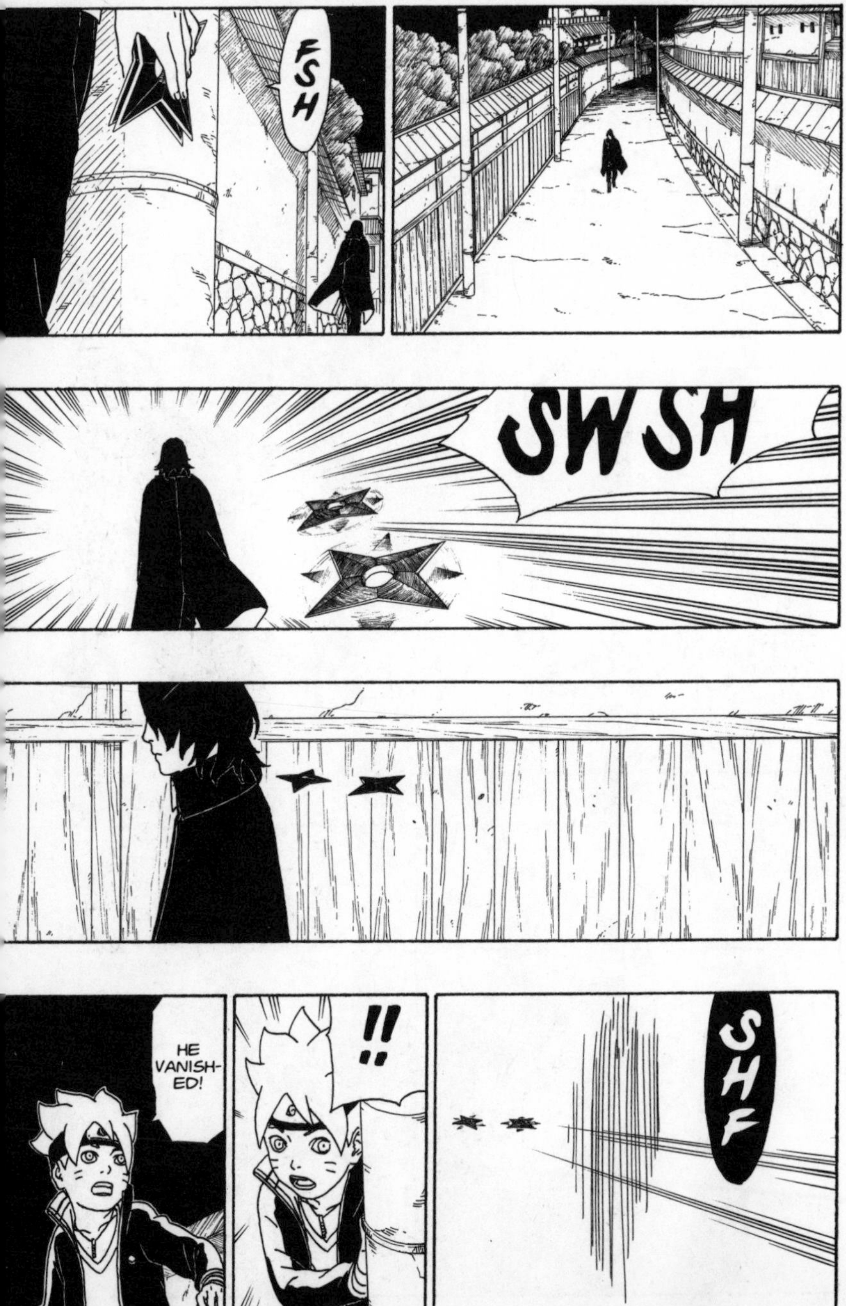
FSH
SWSH
SHF
!!
HE VANISH-ED!

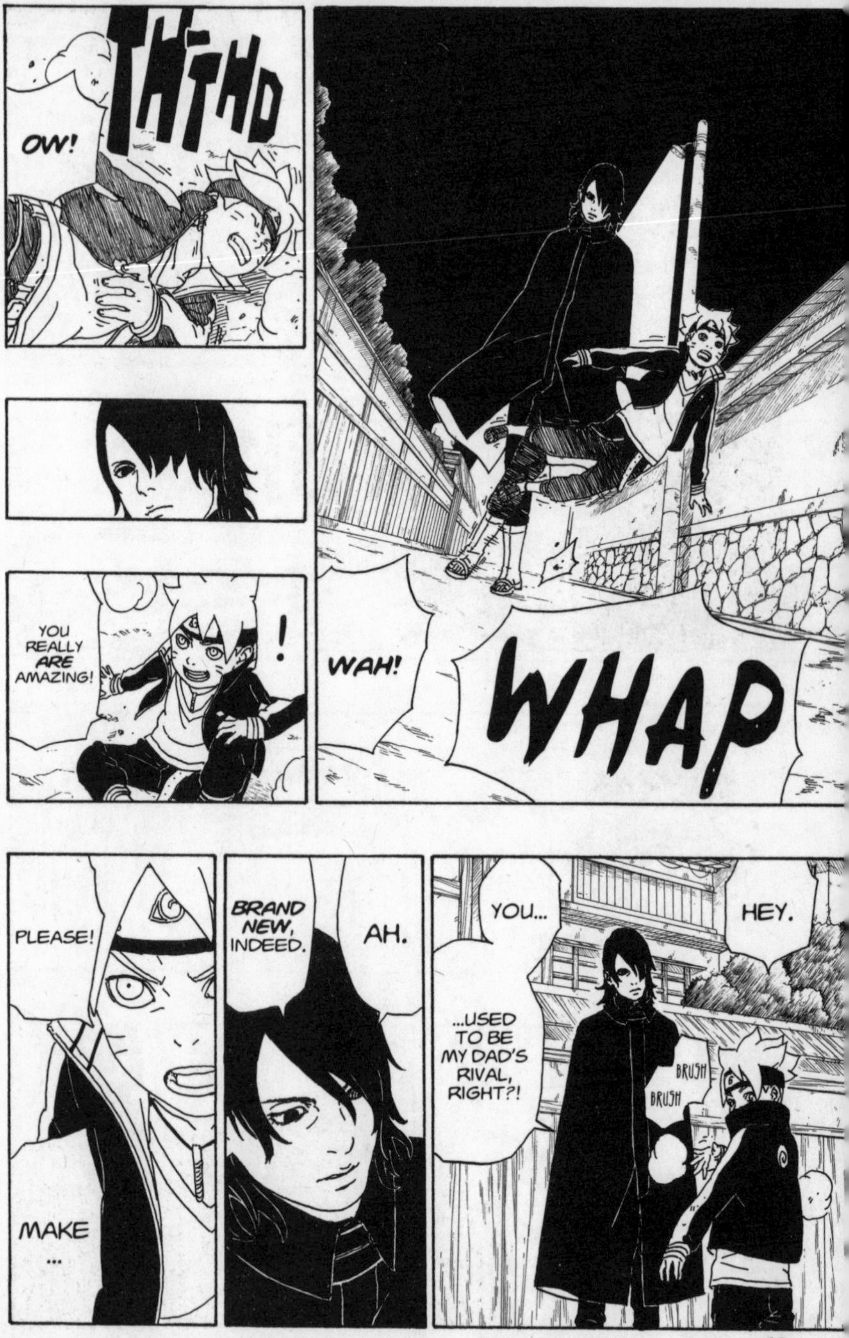
WHAP
WAH!
THTHD
OW!
!
YOU REALLY ARE AMAZING!
HEY.
YOU...
...USED TO BE MY DAD'S RIVAL, RIGHT?!
BRUSH
BRUSH
AH.
BRAND NEW, INDEED.
PLEASE!
MAKE ...

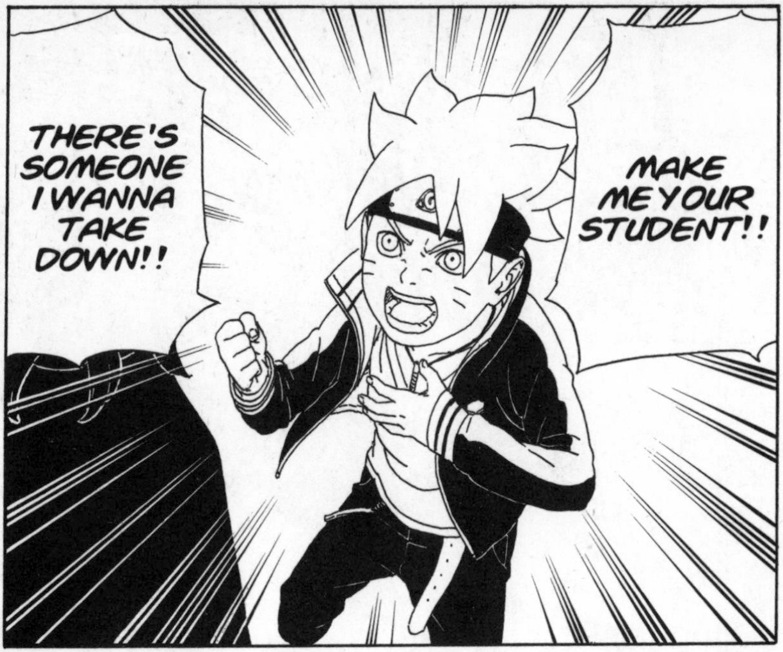
THERE'S SOMEONE I WANNA TAKE DOWN!!
MAKE ME YOUR STUDENT!!
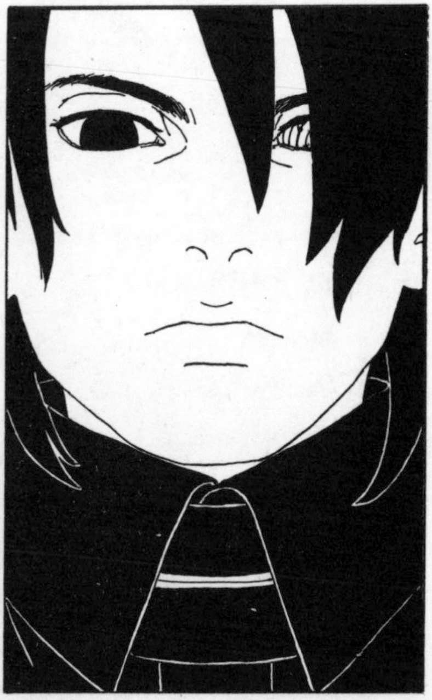
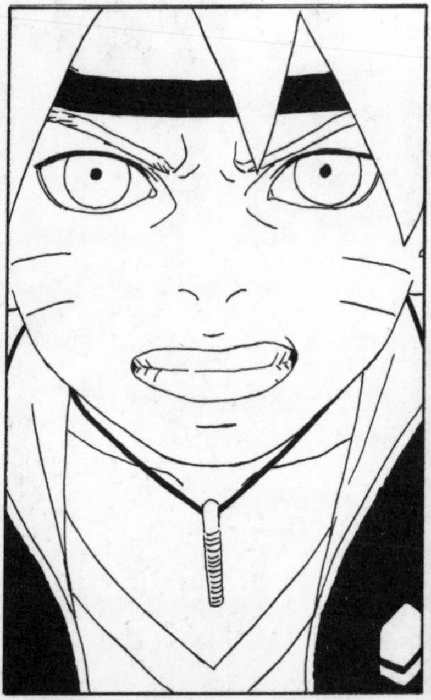

NINJA ENCYCLOPEDIA • ENTRY 1

UZUMAKI BORUTO

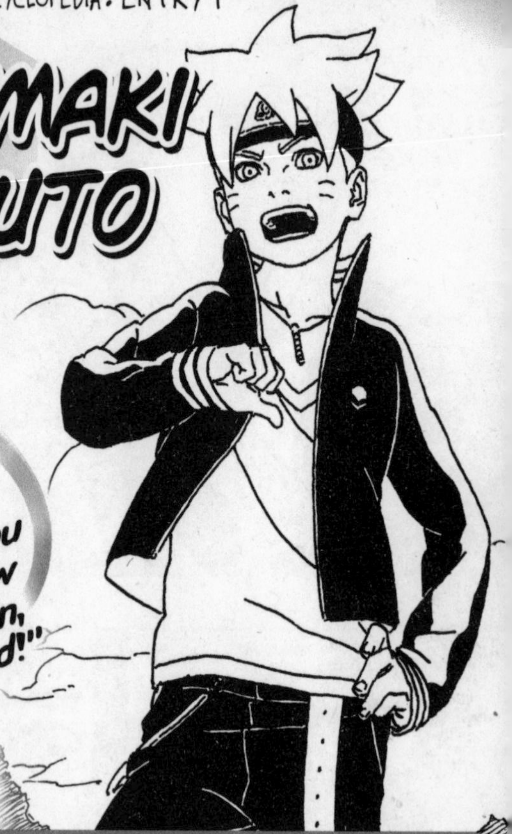

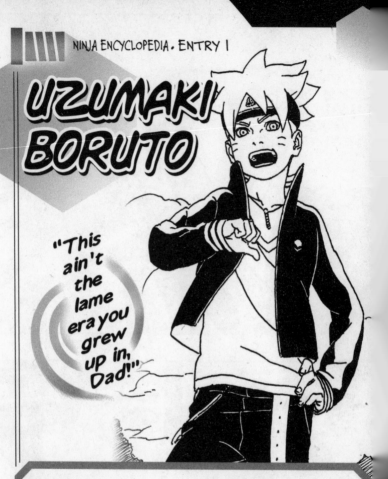

"This ain't the lame era you grew up in, Dad!"

Attributes

Strength	120	Dexterity	160
Intelligence	90	Chakra	140
Perception	130	Negotiation	90

Skills

Evasion ☆☆☆☆ Unarmed combat ☆☆☆ Ninjutsu ☆☆☆☆ etc

Ninja Arts

Suiton: Spatter Bullet, Fuuton: Gale Palm, Raiton: Purple Lightning, Shadow Doppelganger Jutsu, etc.

*Average attribute value is 60 for ordinary people and 90 for genin.
Skill values range from 1 to 5☆ with 5☆ signifying super-topnotch.

2: The Training Begins!!

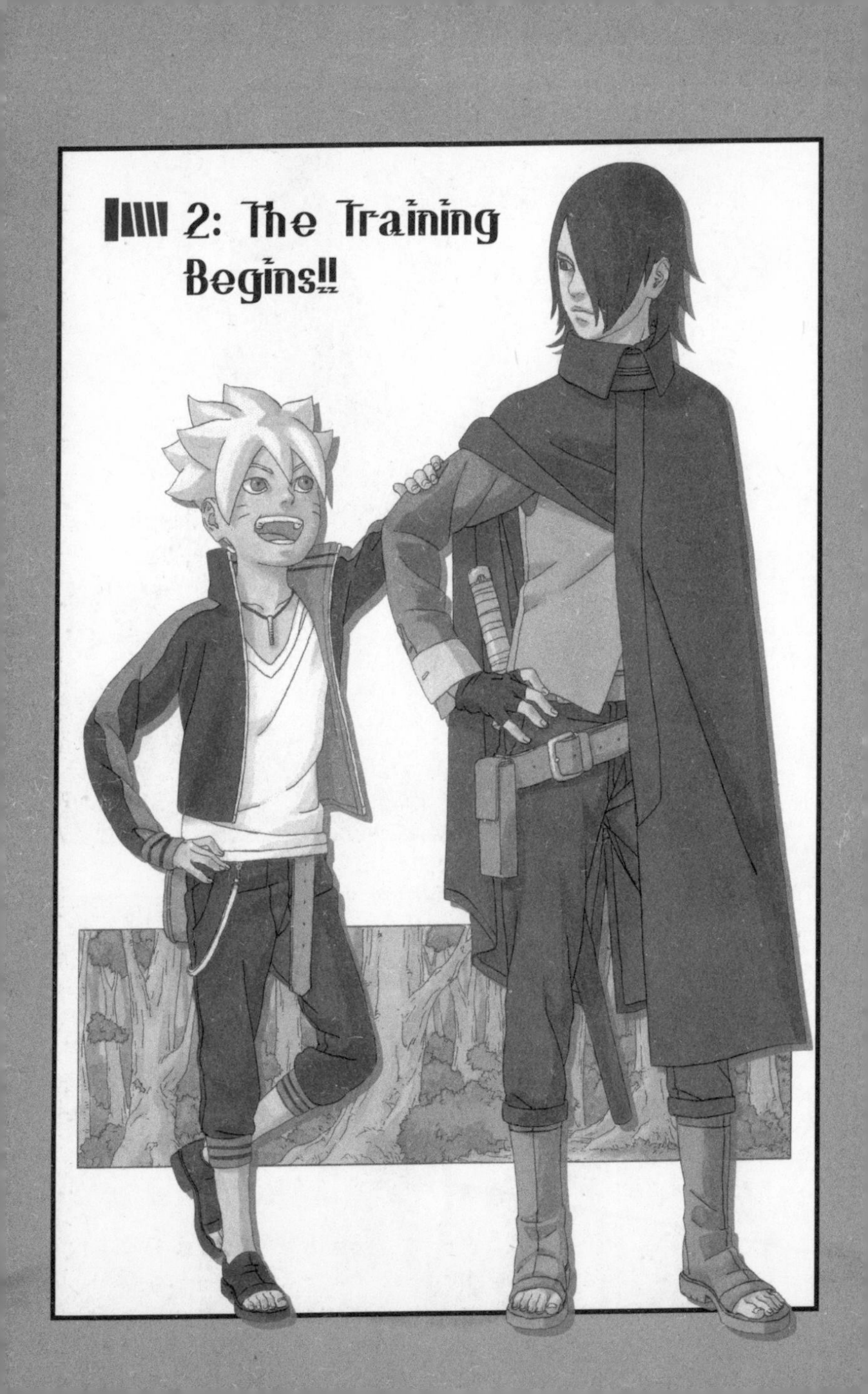

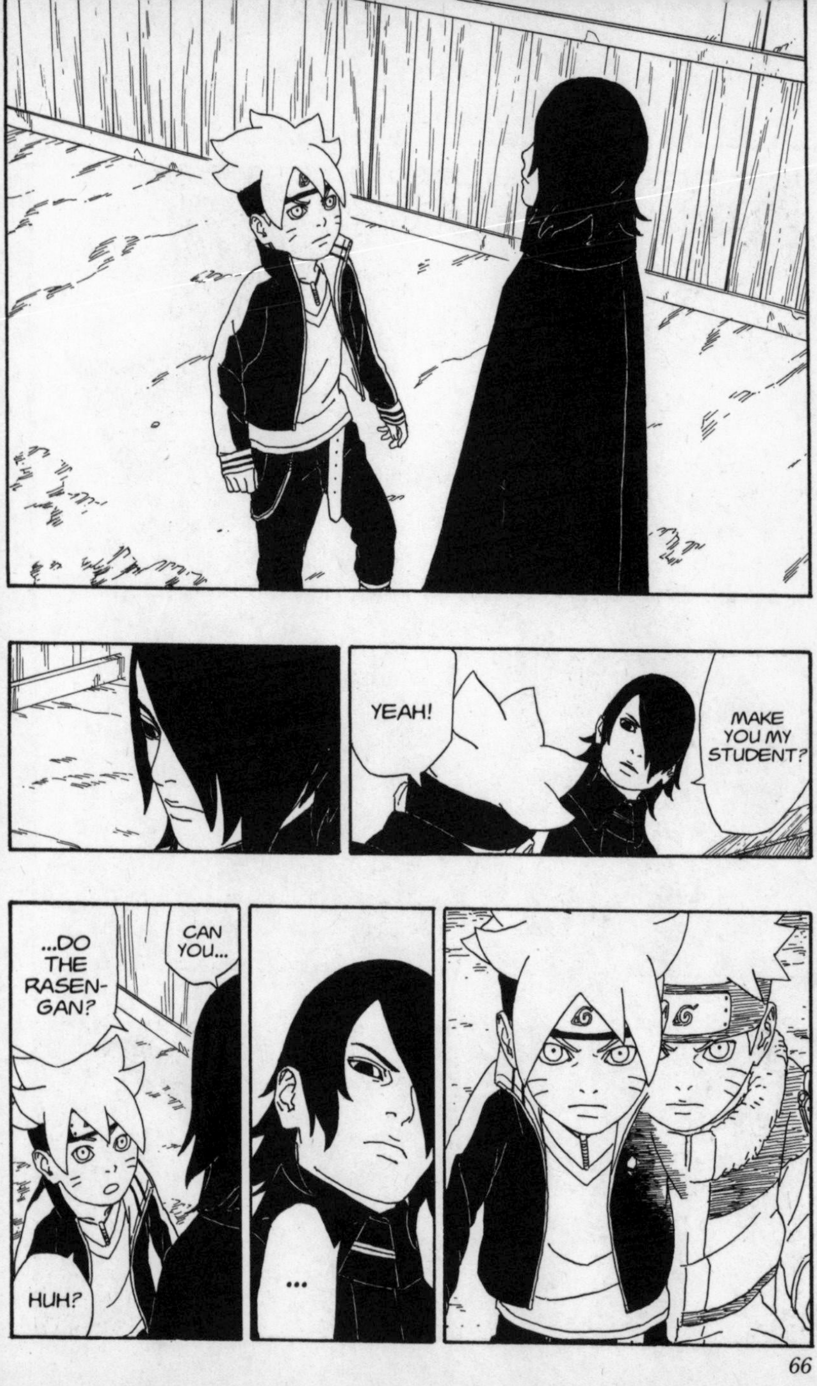
MAKE YOU MY STUDENT?
YEAH!
...
CAN YOU...
...DO THE RASEN-GAN?
HUH?

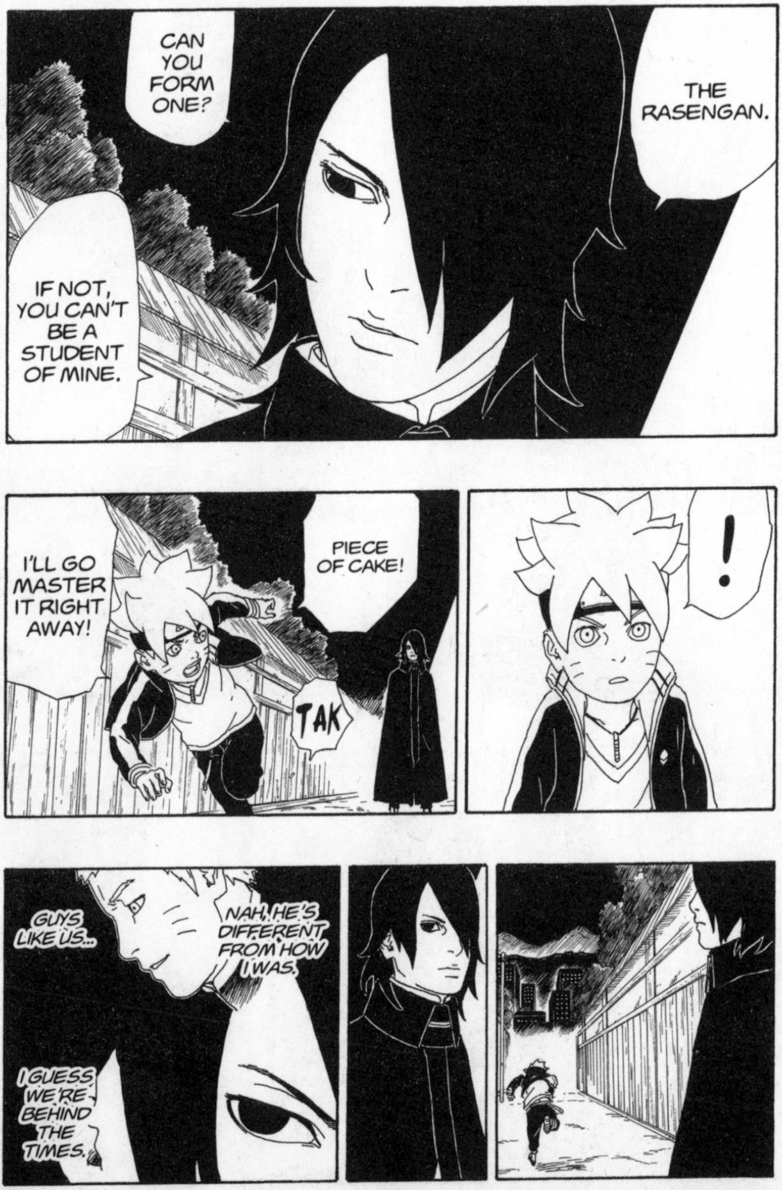

THE RASENGAN.
CAN YOU FORM ONE?
IF NOT, YOU CAN'T BE A STUDENT OF MINE.
!
PIECE OF CAKE!
I'LL GO MASTER IT RIGHT AWAY!
TAK
NAH, HE'S DIFFERENT FROM HOW I WAS.
GUYS LIKE US...
I GUESS WE'RE BEHIND THE TIMES.

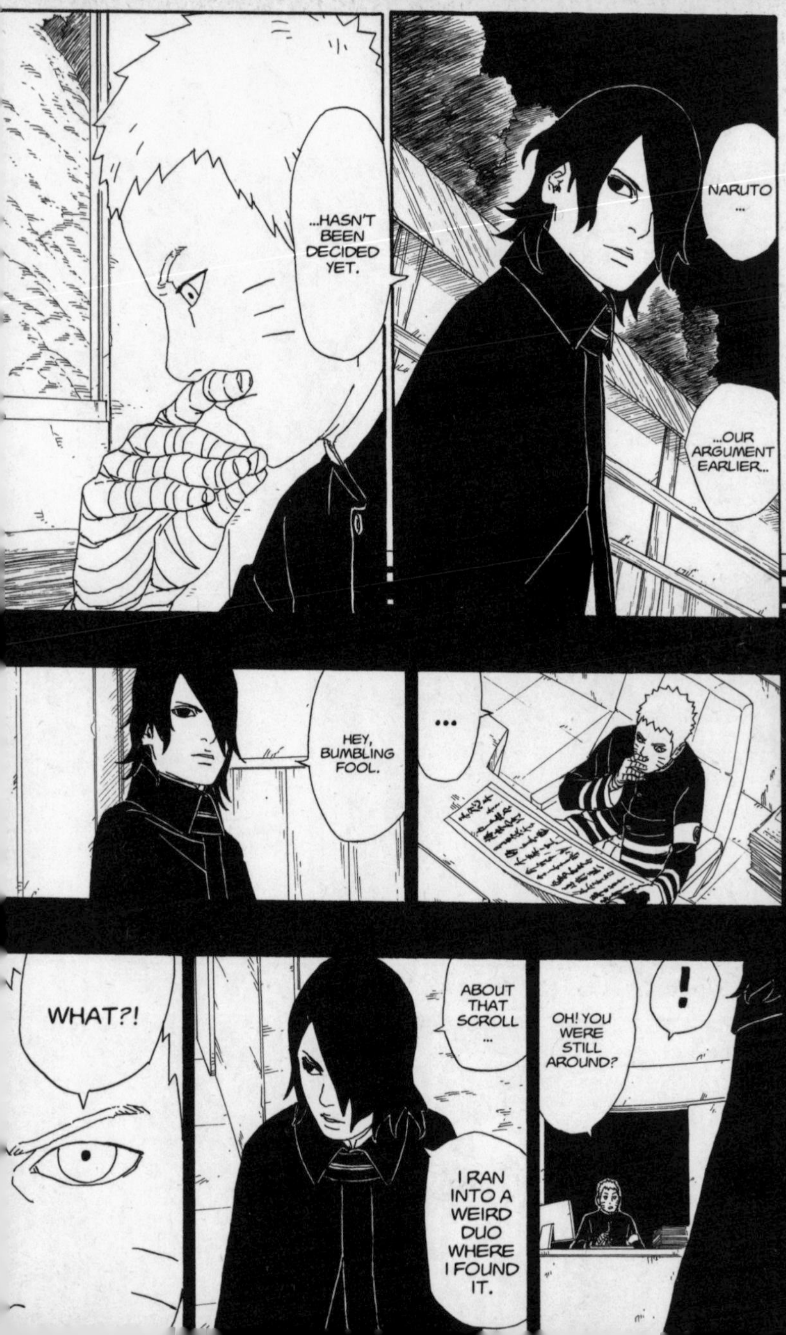
NARUTO ...
...OUR ARGUMENT EARLIER..
...HASN'T BEEN DECIDED YET.
...
HEY, BUMBLING FOOL.
!
OH! YOU WERE STILL AROUND?
ABOUT THAT SCROLL ...
I RAN INTO A WEIRD DUO WHERE I FOUND IT.
WHAT?!

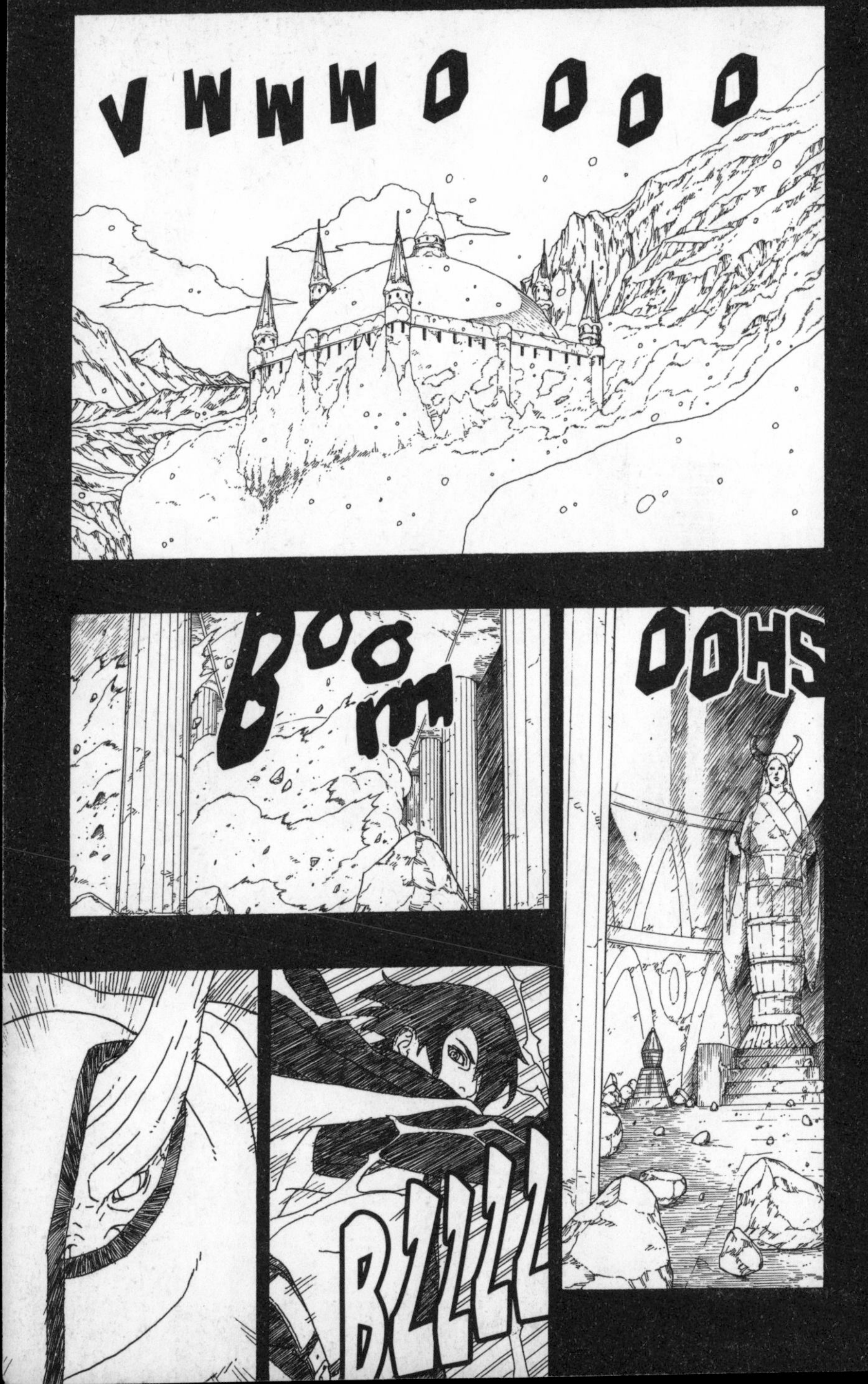
VWWWOOOO
OOHS
BOOM
BZZZZ

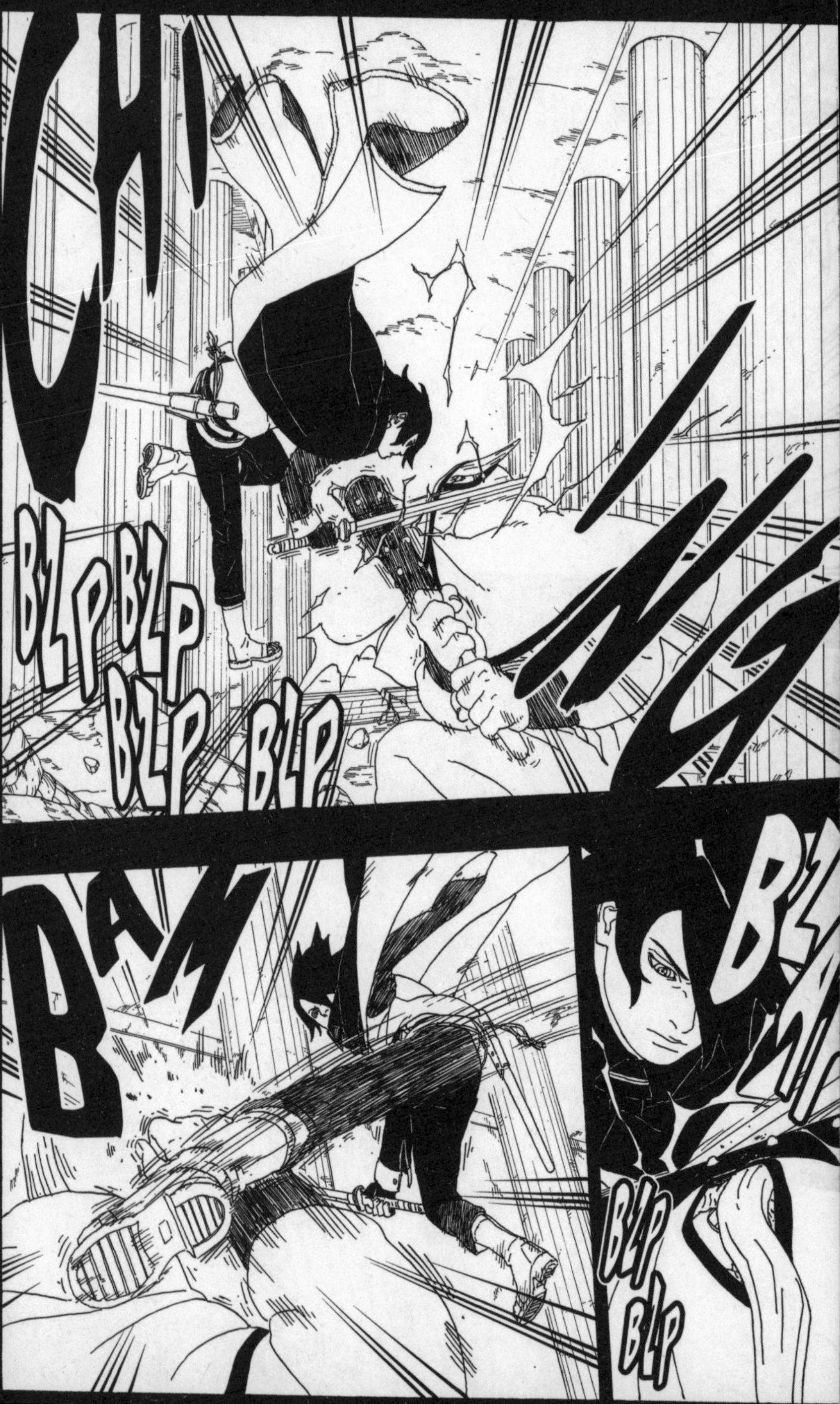

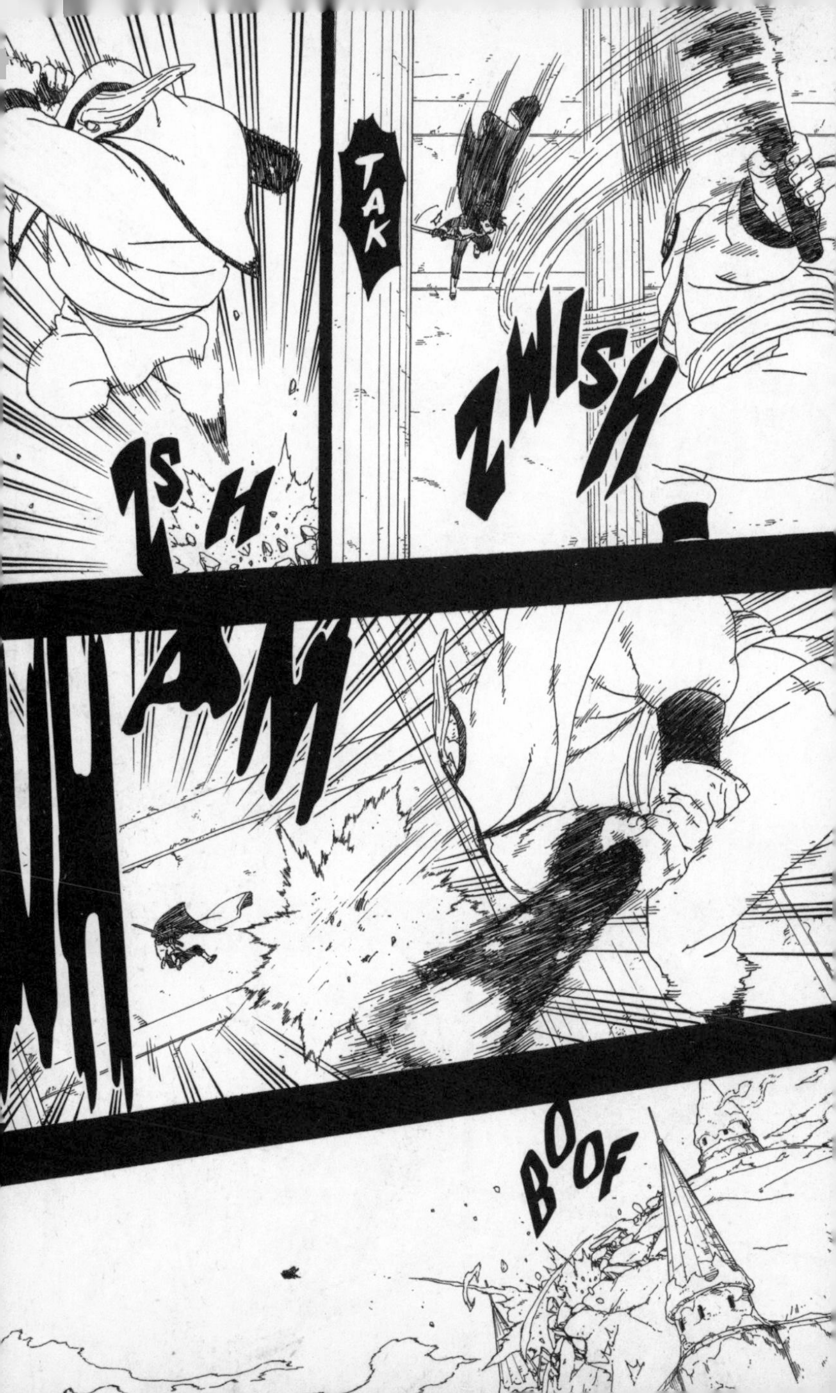
TAK
ZWISH
TSH
WHAM
BOOF

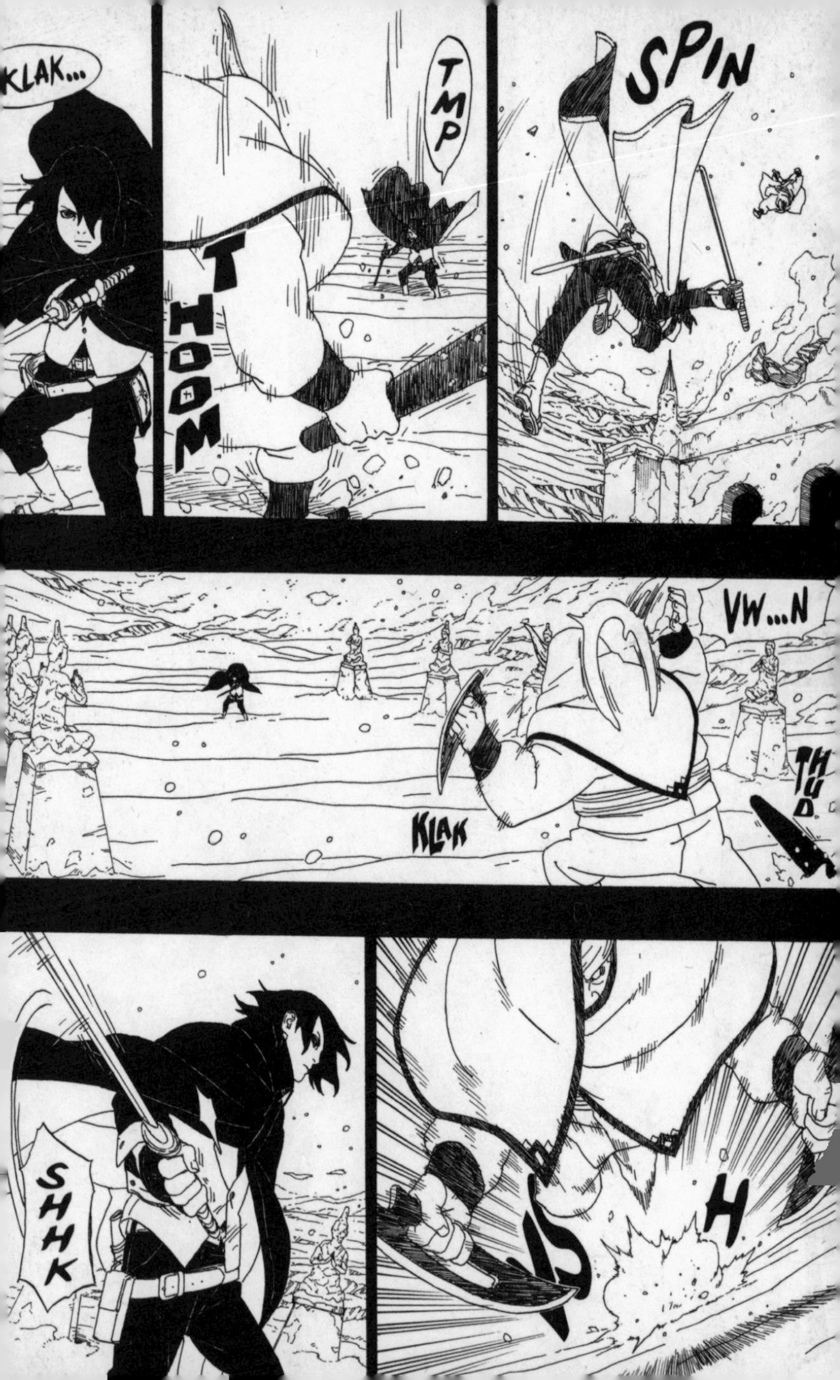
SPIN
TMP
THOOM
KLAK...
VW...N
THUD
KLAK
H.
SHHK

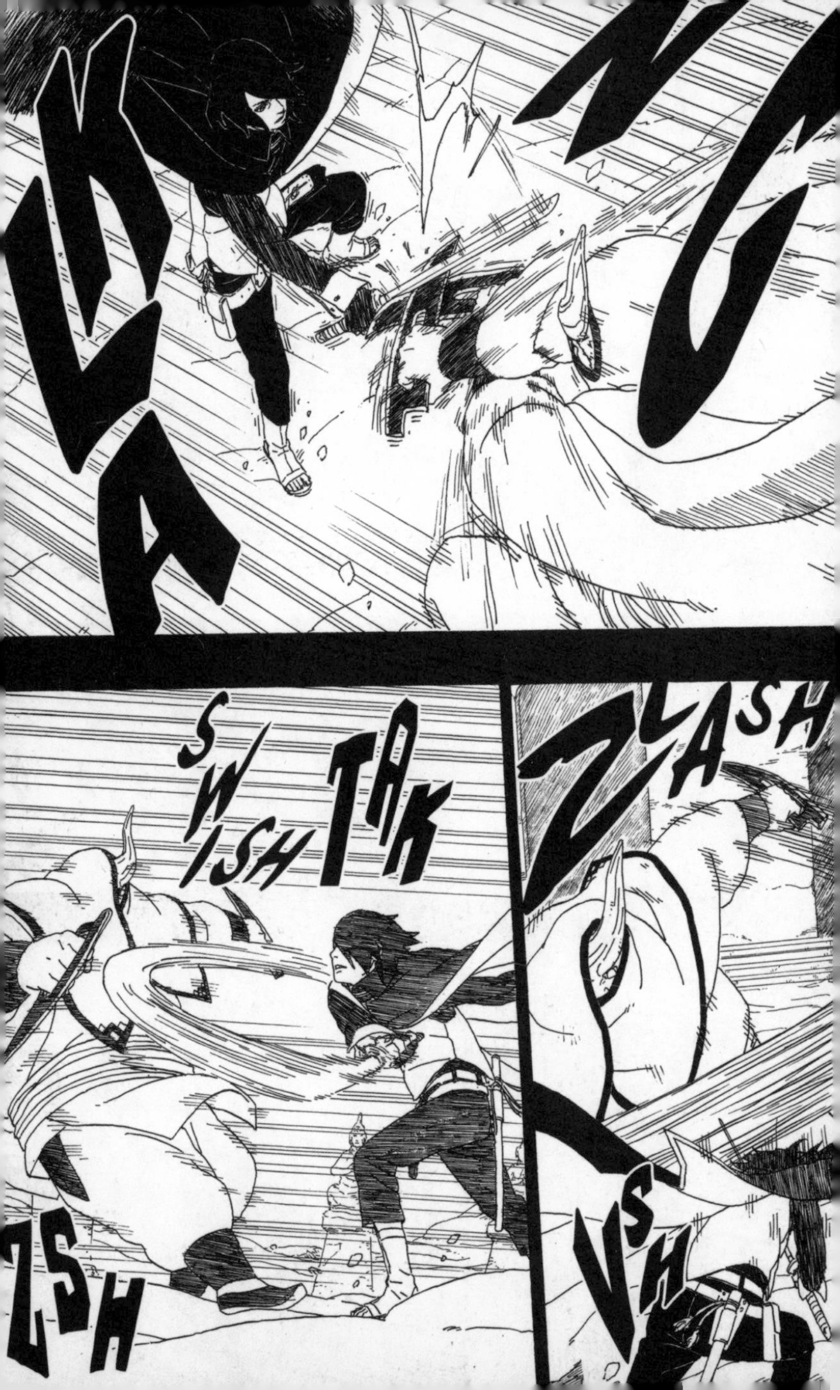
ZLASH
VSH
SWISH
TAK
ZSH

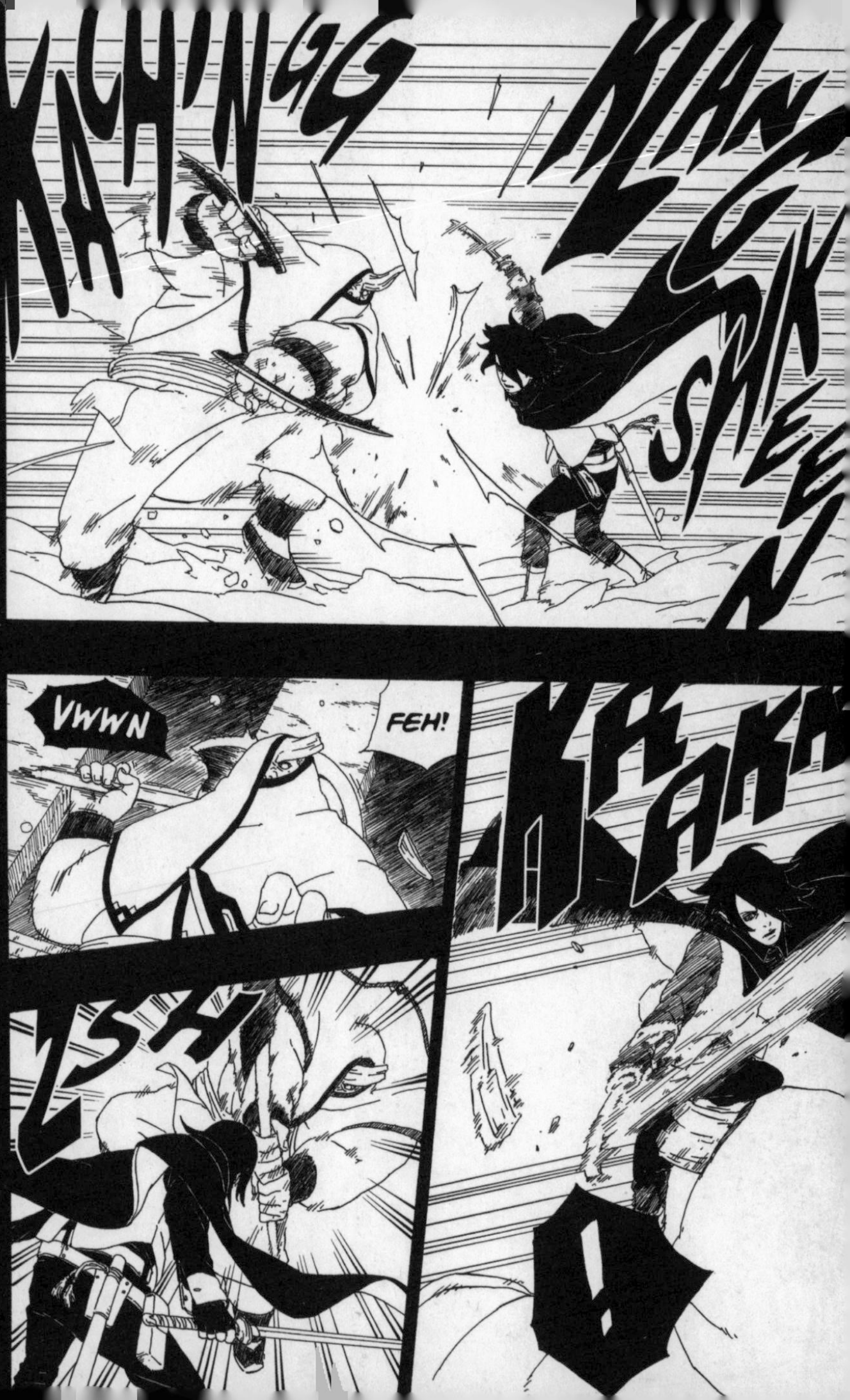
KACHINGG
VWWN
FEH!
ZSH

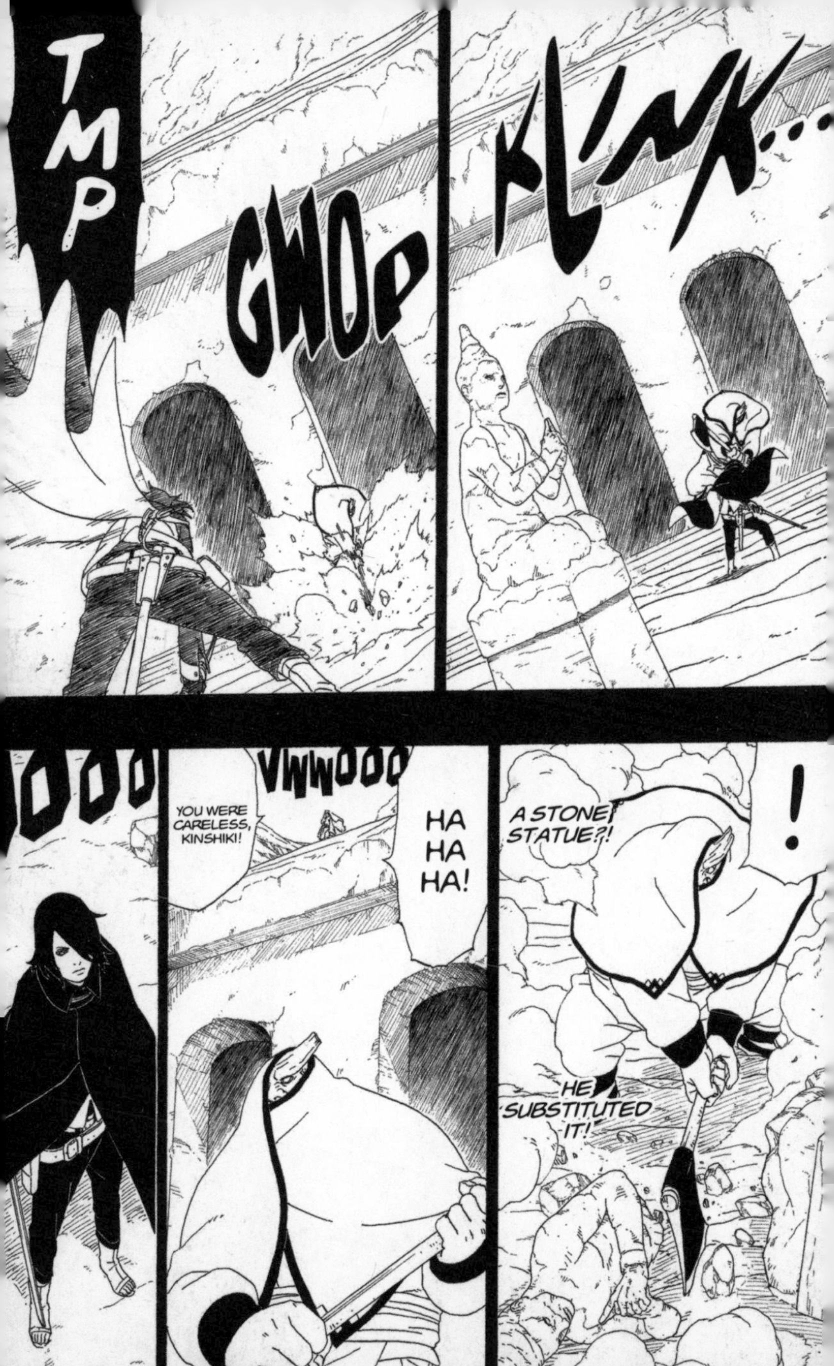
KLINK...
GWOP
TMP
!
A STONE STATUE?!
HE SUBSTITUTED IT!
VWWOOO
HA HA HA!
YOU WERE CARELESS, KINSHIKI!
OOO

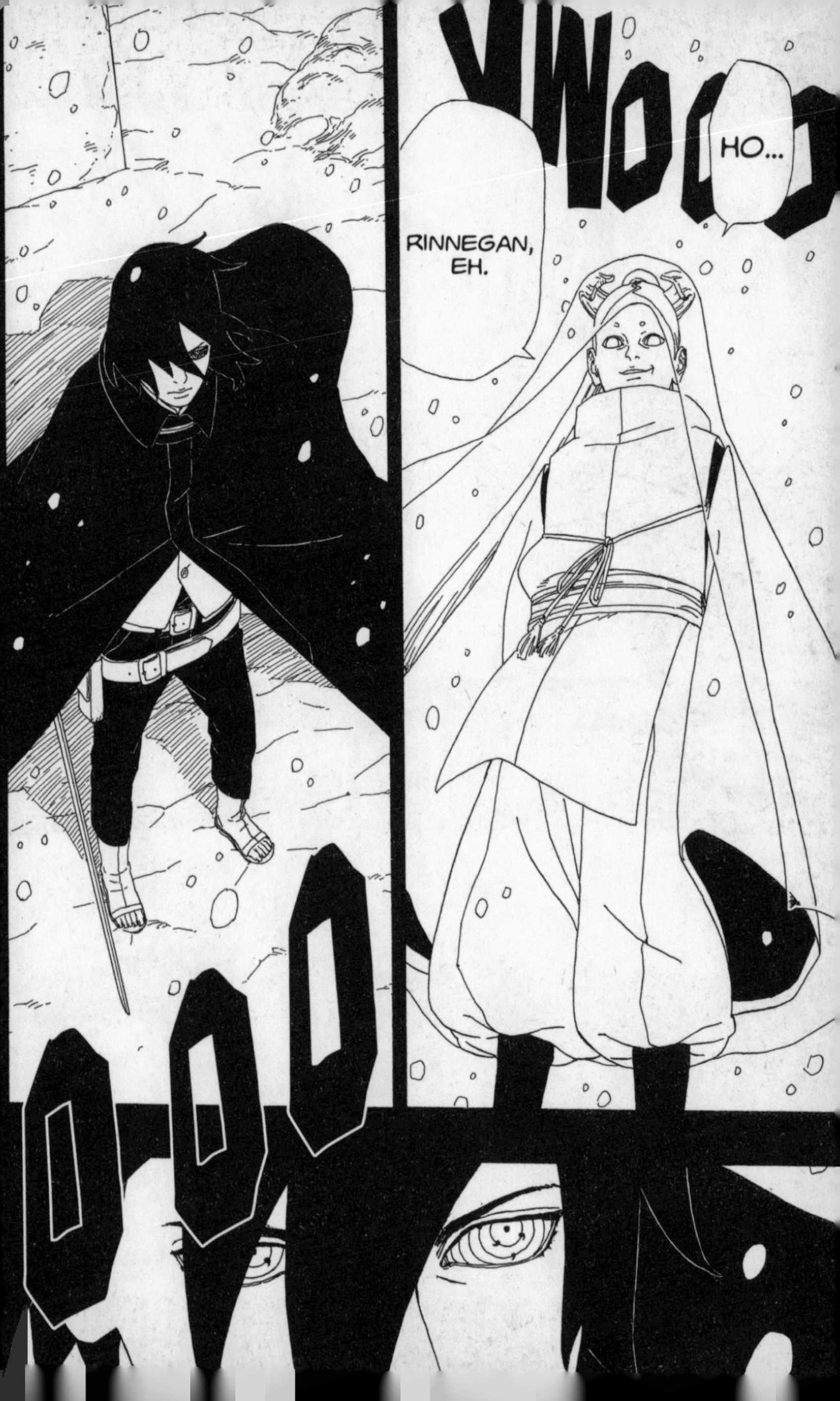
VWOO
HO...
RINNEGAN, EH.
OOOO

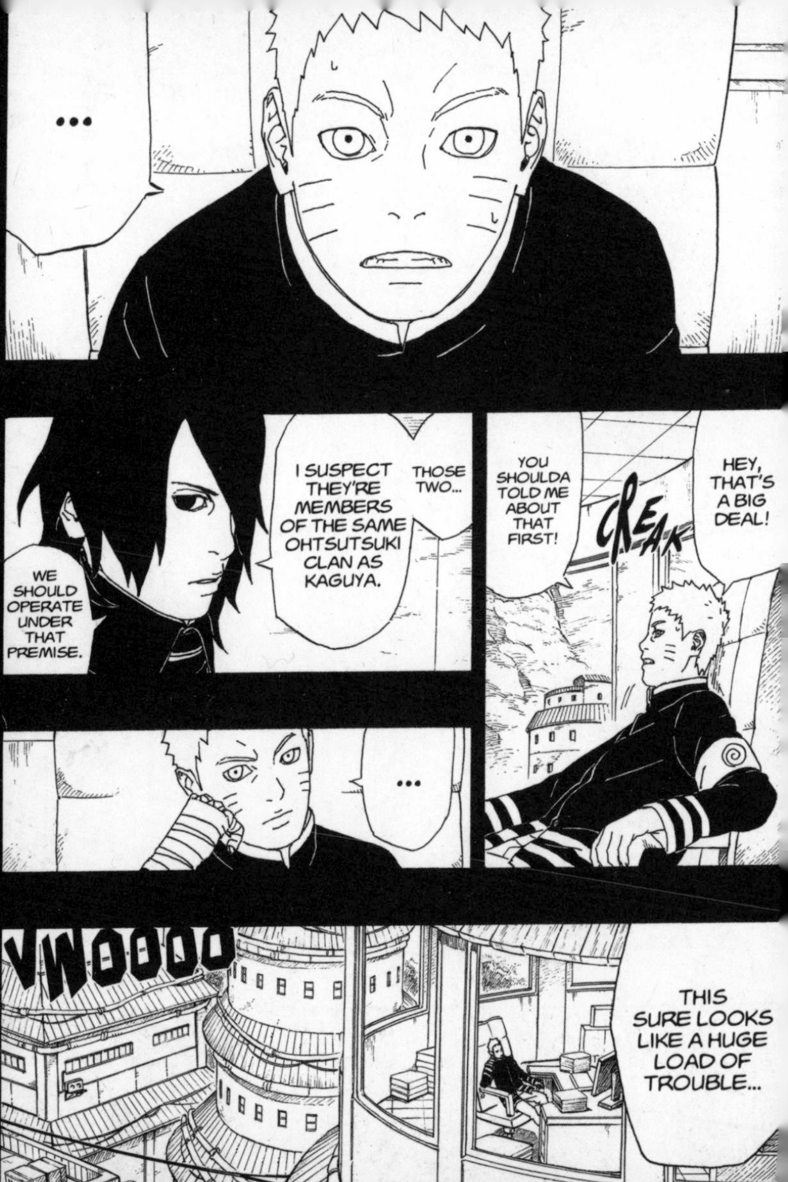
...
HEY, THAT'S A BIG DEAL!
YOU SHOULDA TOLD ME ABOUT THAT FIRST!
CREAK
THOSE TWO...
I SUSPECT THEY'RE MEMBERS OF THE SAME OHTSUTSUKI CLAN AS KAGUYA.
WE SHOULD OPERATE UNDER THAT PREMISE.
...
THIS SURE LOOKS LIKE A HUGE LOAD OF TROUBLE...
VWOOOO

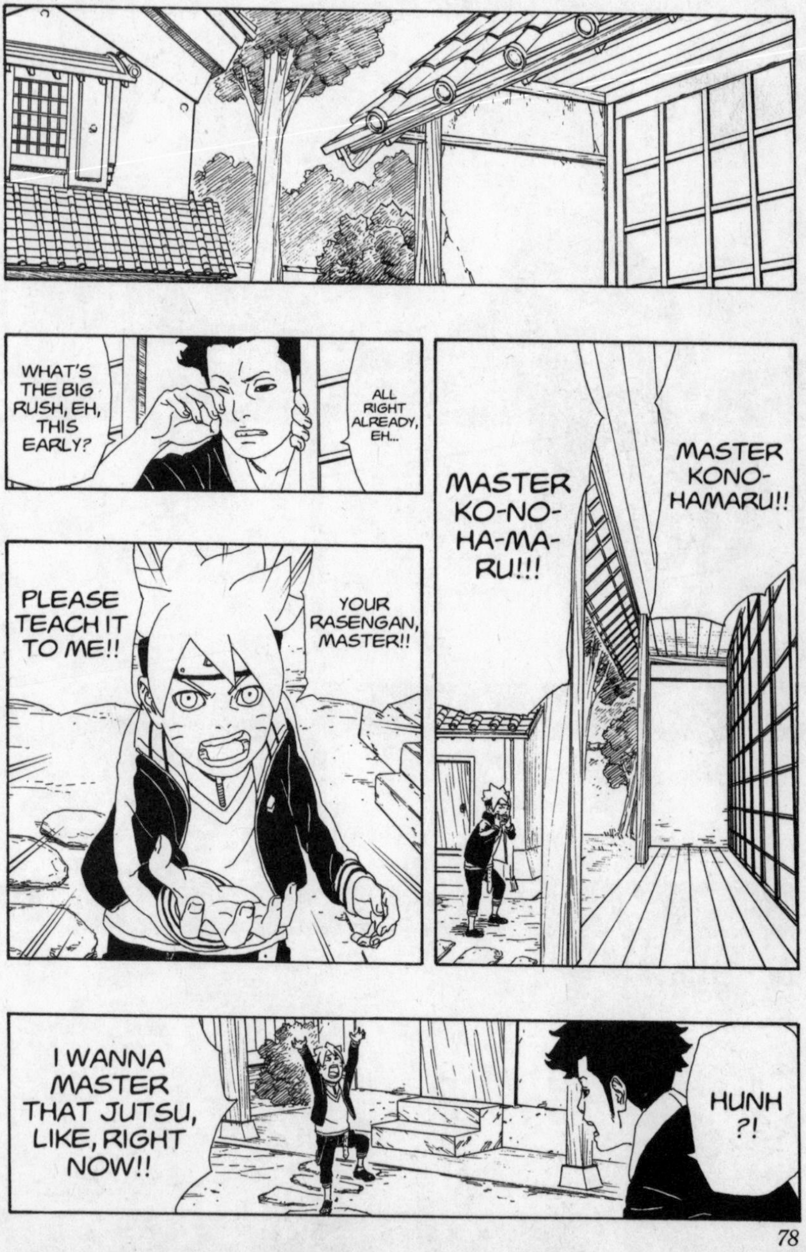
MASTER KONO-HAMARU!!
MASTER KO-NO-HA-MA-RU!!!
ALL RIGHT ALREADY, EH...
WHAT'S THE BIG RUSH, EH, THIS EARLY?
YOUR RASENGAN, MASTER!!
PLEASE TEACH IT TO ME!!
HUNH ?!
I WANNA MASTER THAT JUTSU, LIKE, RIGHT NOW!!

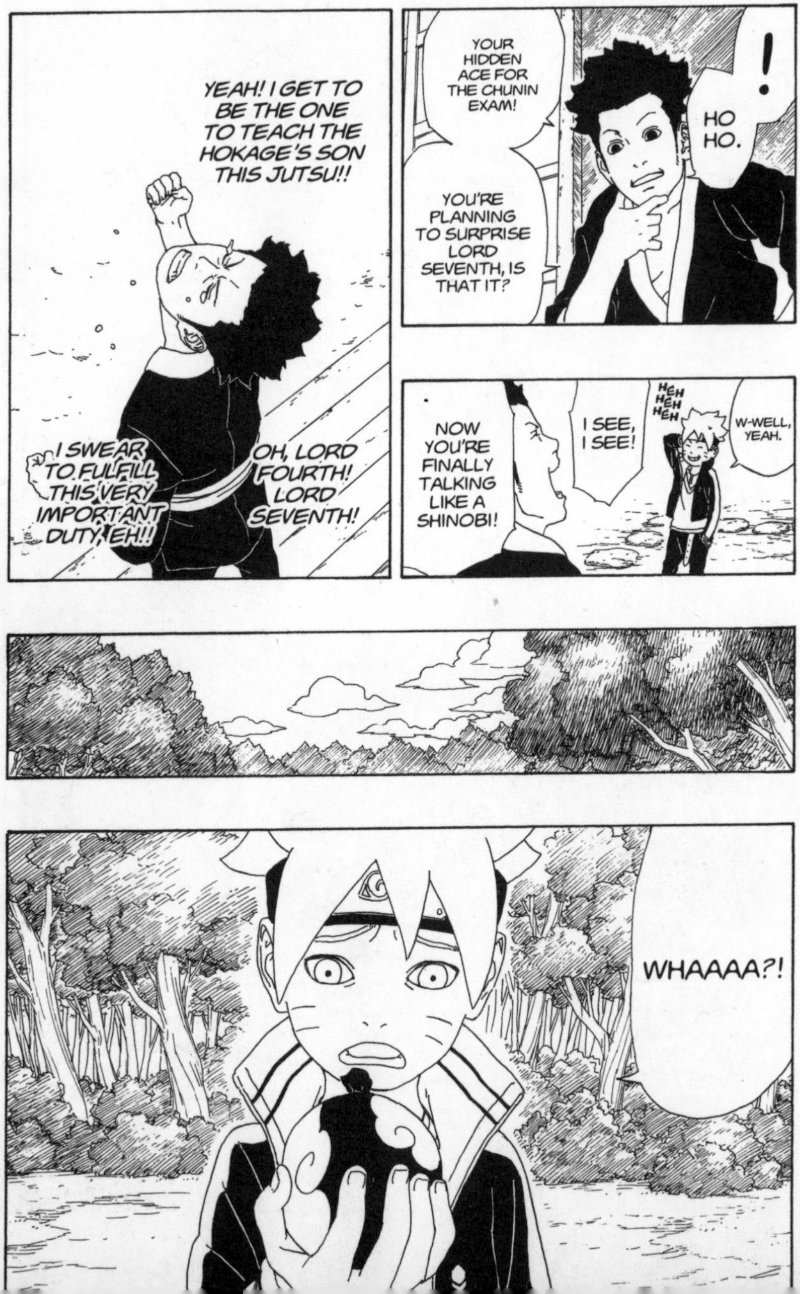
!
HO HO.
YOUR HIDDEN ACE FOR THE CHUNIN EXAM!
YOU'RE PLANNING TO SURPRISE LORD SEVENTH, IS THAT IT?
W-WELL, YEAH.
HEH HEH HEH HEH
I SEE, I SEE!
NOW YOU'RE FINALLY TALKING LIKE A SHINOBI!
YEAH! I GET TO BE THE ONE TO TEACH THE HOKAGE'S SON THIS JUTSU!!
OH, LORD FOURTH! LORD SEVENTH!
I SWEAR TO FULFILL THIS VERY IMPORTANT DUTY, EH!!
WHAAAA?!

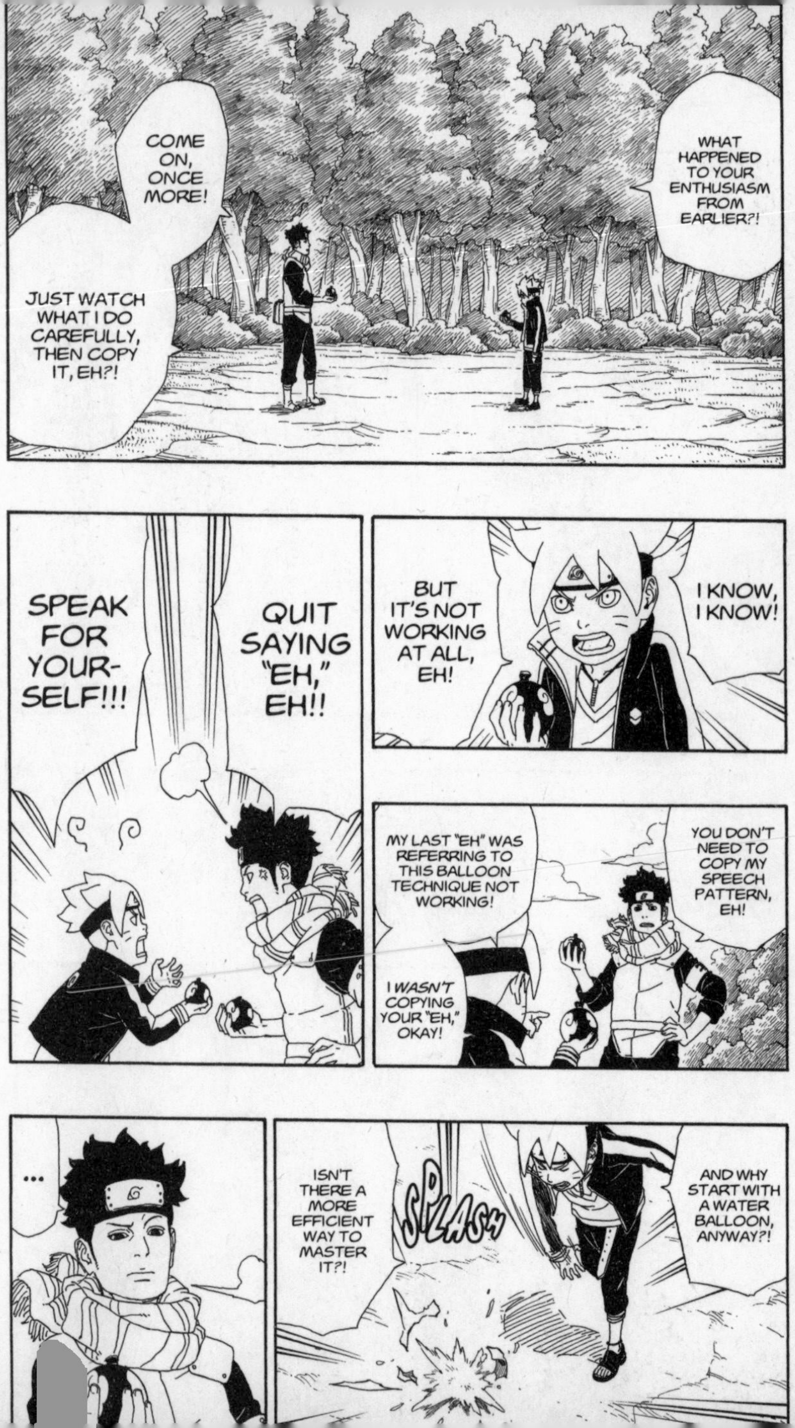
WHAT HAPPENED TO YOUR ENTHUSIASM FROM EARLIER?!
COME ON, ONCE MORE!
JUST WATCH WHAT I DO CAREFULLY, THEN COPY IT, EH?!
I KNOW, I KNOW!
BUT IT'S NOT WORKING AT ALL, EH!
YOU DON'T NEED TO COPY MY SPEECH PATTERN, EH!
MY LAST "EH" WAS REFERRING TO THIS BALLOON TECHNIQUE NOT WORKING!
I WASN'T COPYING YOUR "EH," OKAY!
QUIT SAYING "EH," EH!!
SPEAK FOR YOURSELF!!!
AND WHY START WITH A WATER BALLOON, ANYWAY?!
SPLASH
ISN'T THERE A MORE EFFICIENT WAY TO MASTER IT?!
...

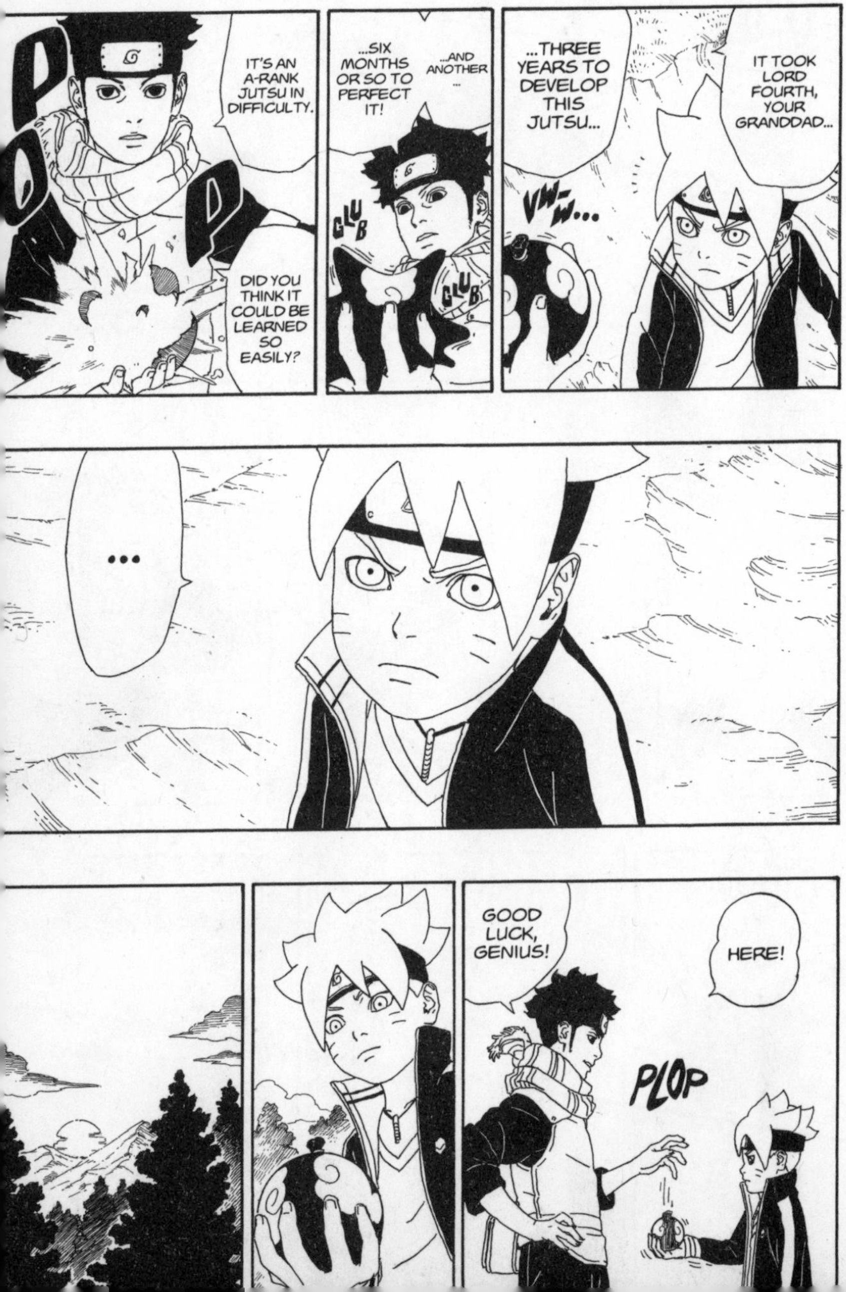
IT TOOK LORD FOURTH, YOUR GRANDDAD...
...THREE YEARS TO DEVELOP THIS JUTSU...
VW-W...
...AND ANOTHER ...
...SIX MONTHS OR SO TO PERFECT IT!
GLUB
GLUB
IT'S AN A-RANK JUTSU IN DIFFICULTY.
DID YOU THINK IT COULD BE LEARNED SO EASILY?
POP
POP
...
HERE!
PLOP
GOOD LUCK, GENIUS!

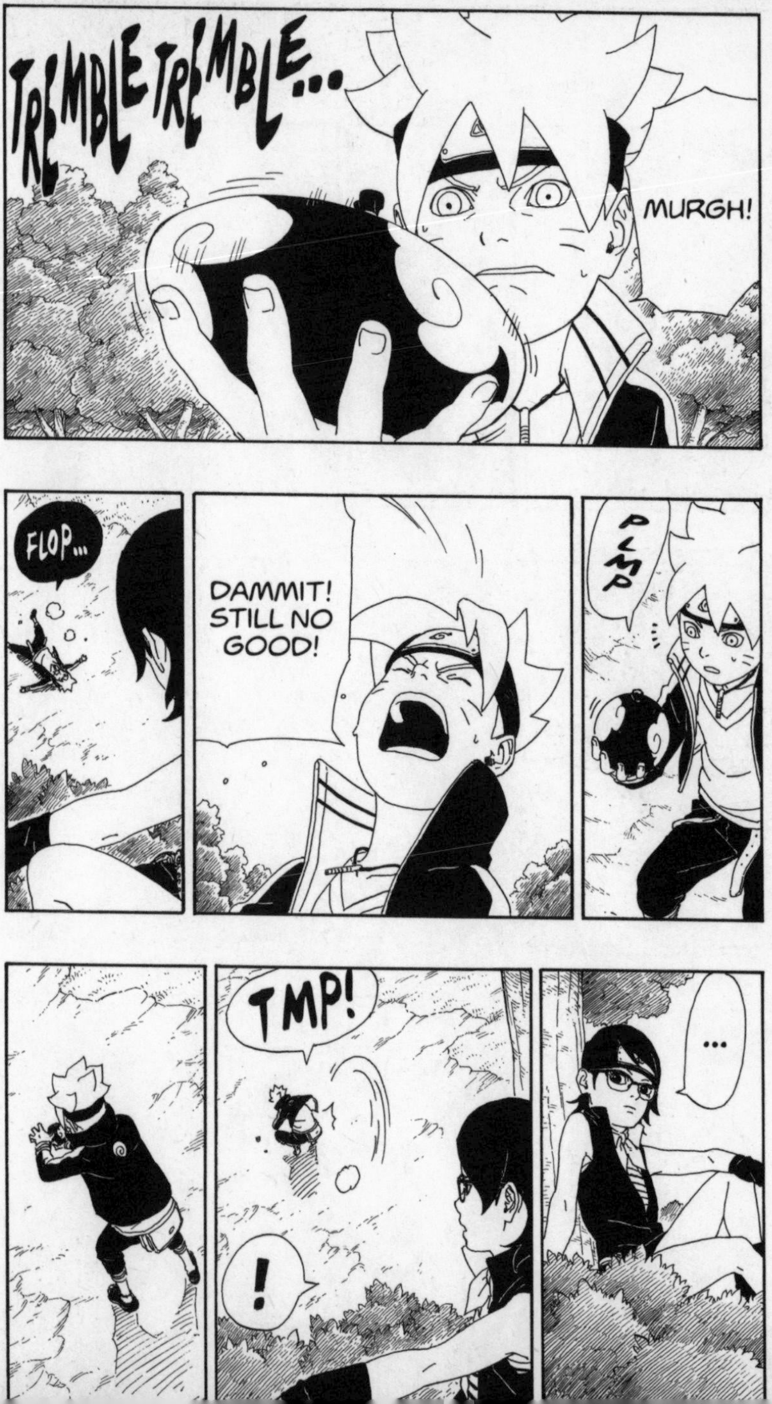
TREMBLE TREMBLE...
MURGH!
PLMP
DAMMIT! STILL NO GOOD!
FLOP...
...
TMP!
!

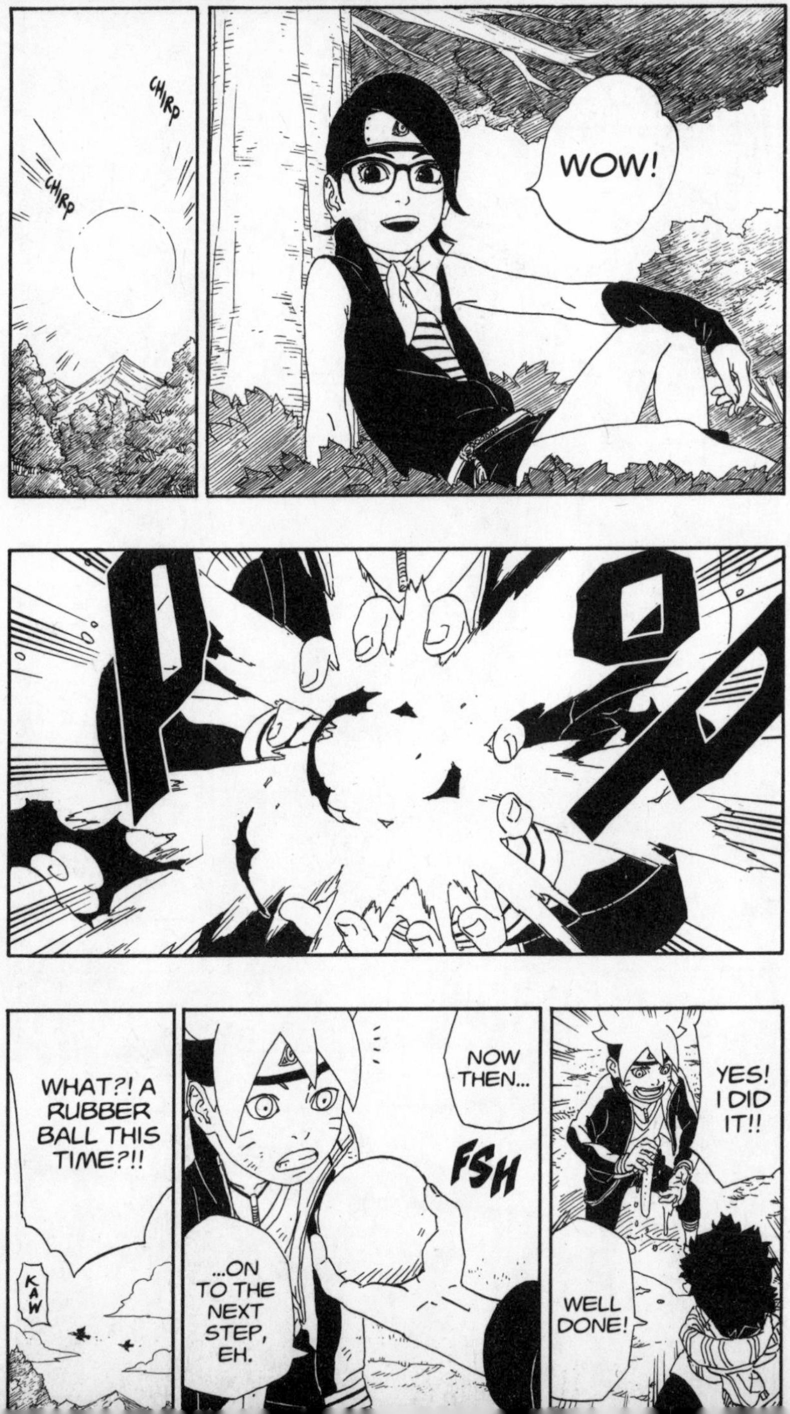
WOW!
CHIRP
CHIRP
YES! I DID IT!!
WELL DONE!
NOW THEN...
FSH
...ON TO THE NEXT STEP, EH.
WHAT?! A RUBBER BALL THIS TIME?!!
KAW

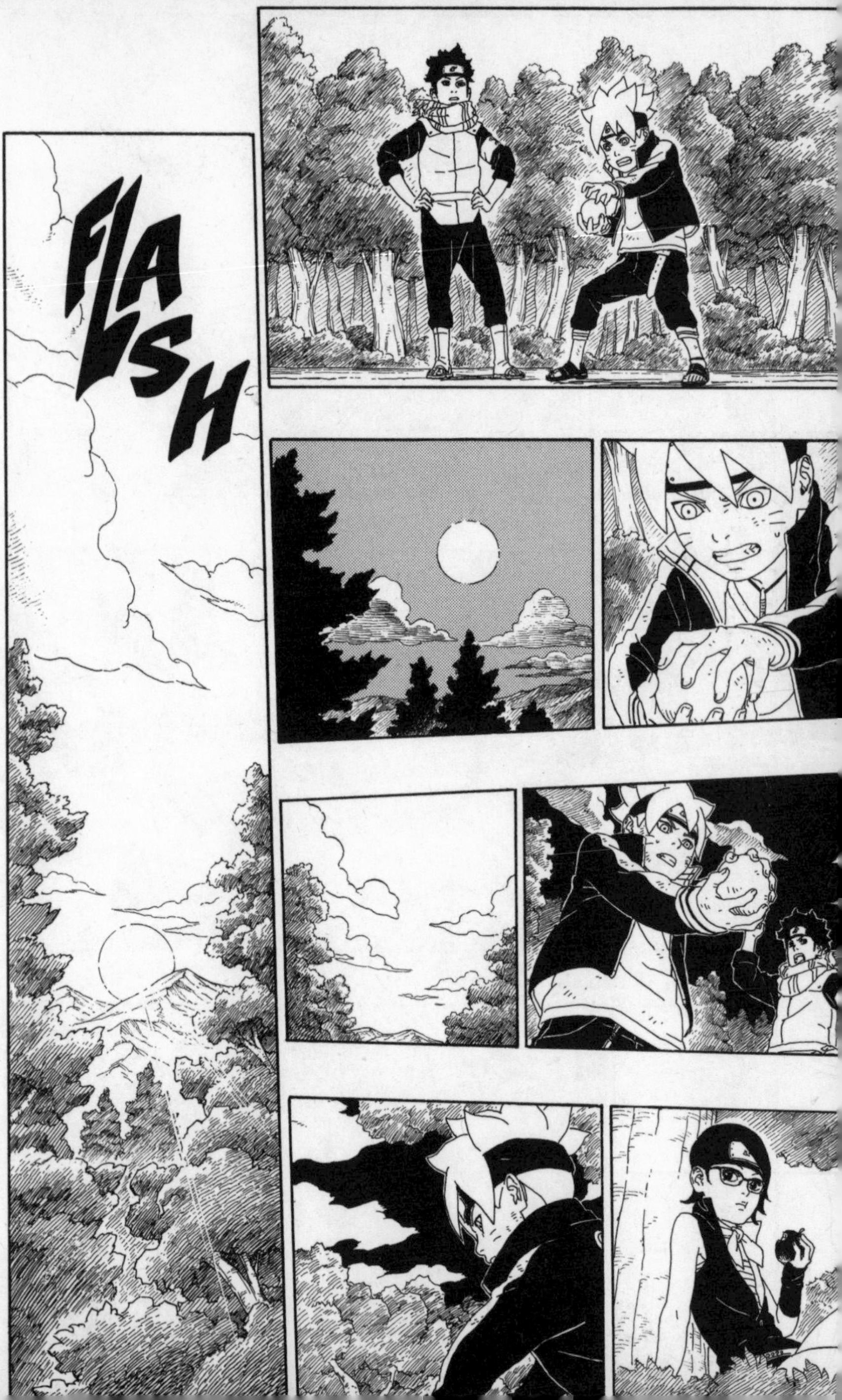
FLASH

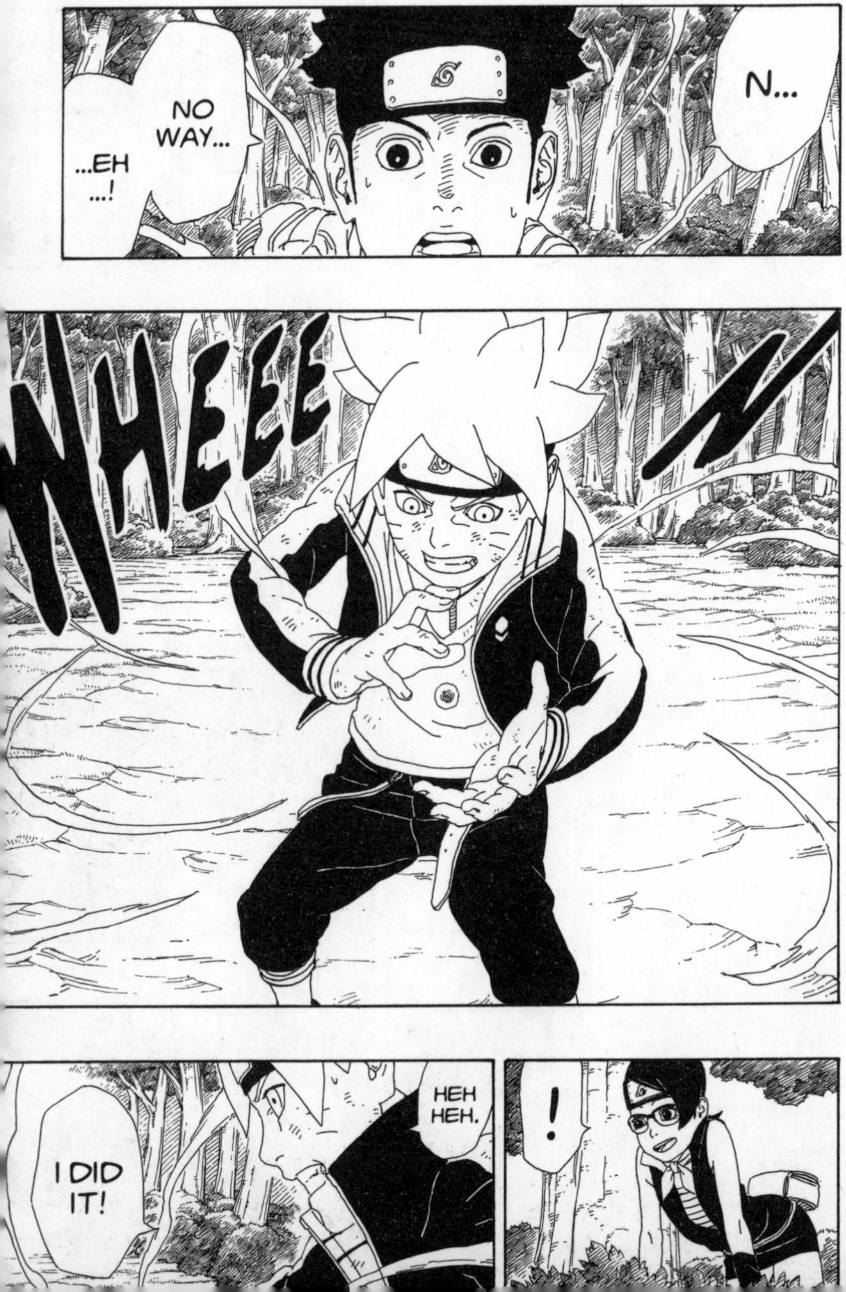
N...
NO WAY...
...EH ...!
WHEEEN
!
HEH HEH.
I DID IT!

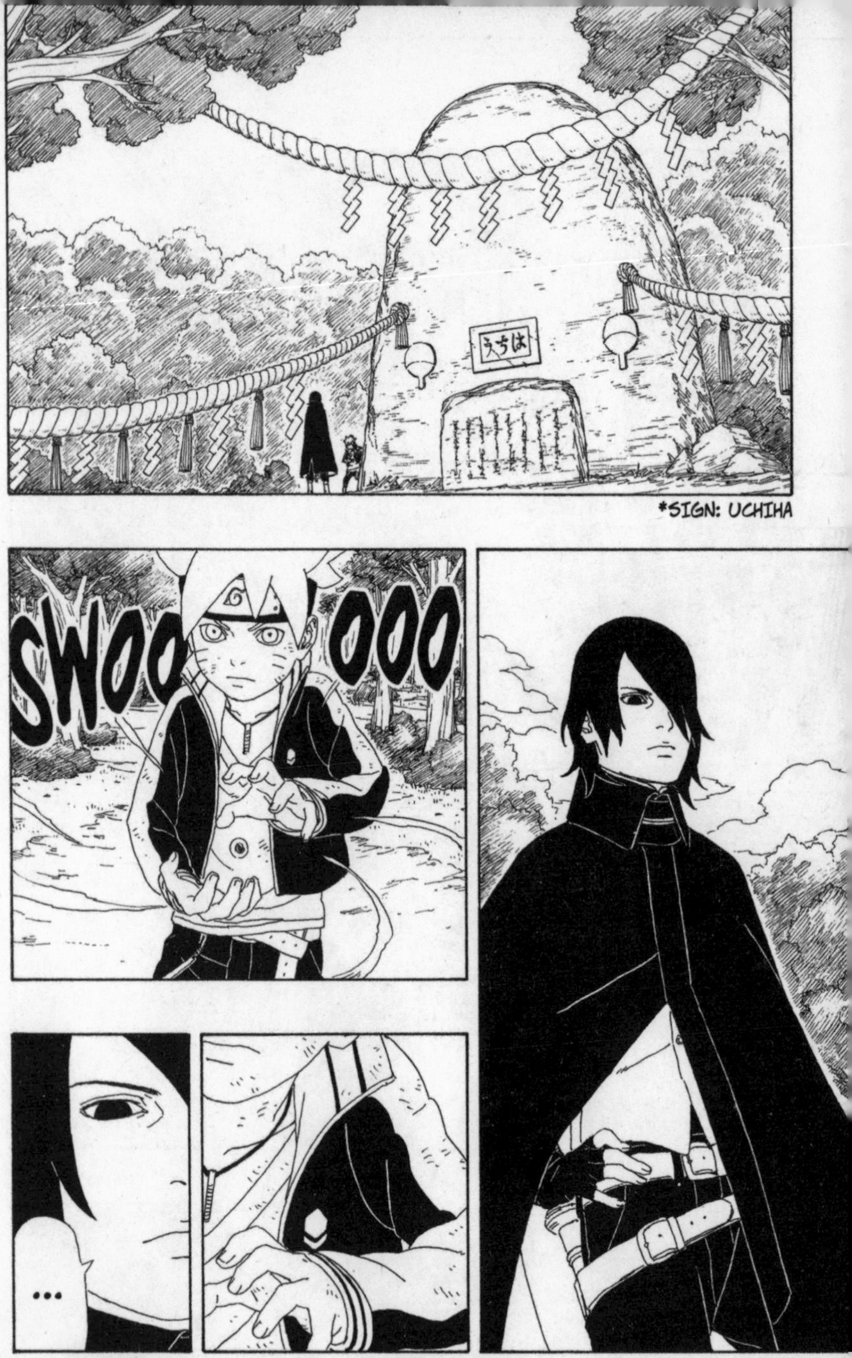
うちは
*SIGN: UCHIHA
SWOO
OOO
...

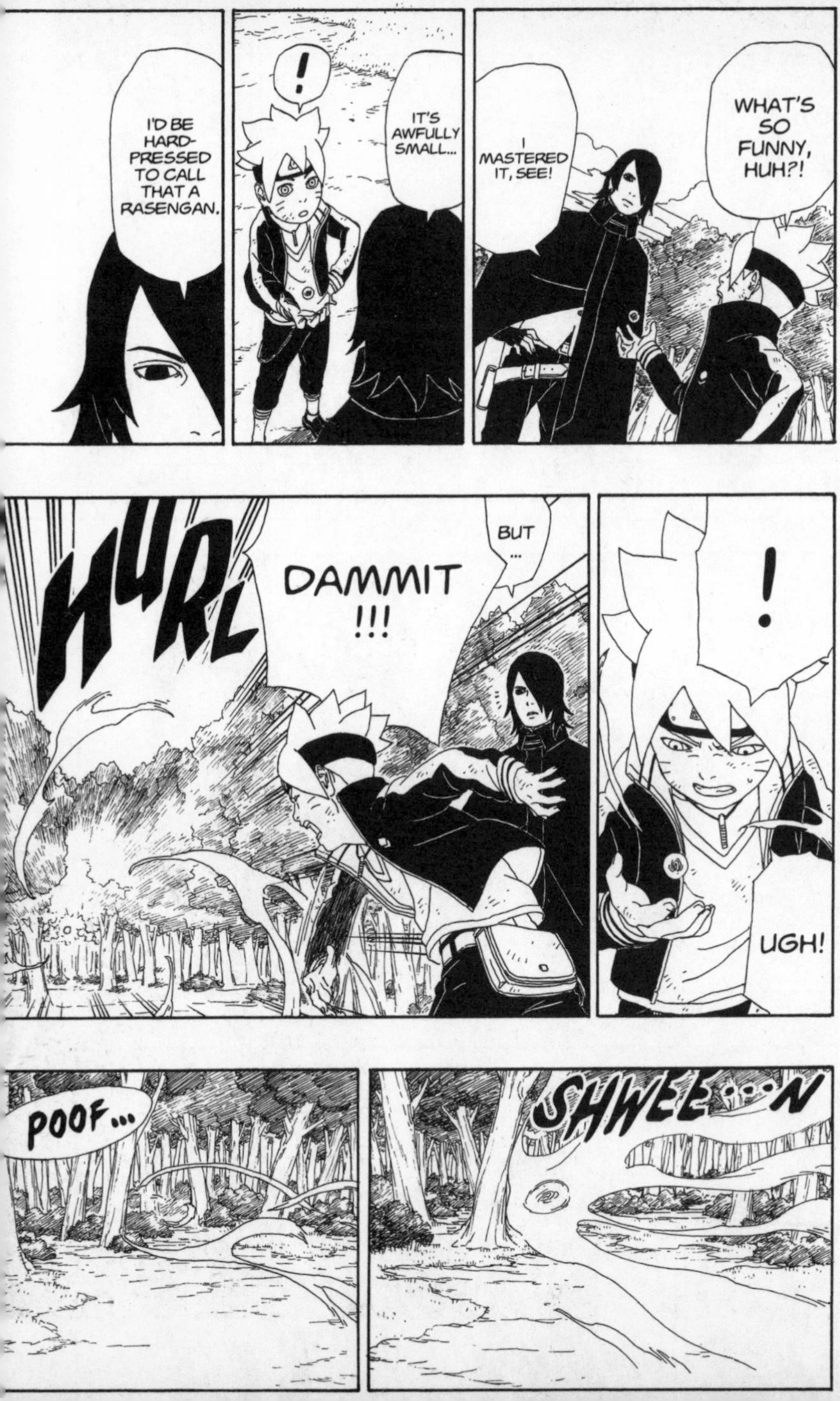
WHAT'S SO FUNNY, HUH?!
I MASTERED IT, SEE!
IT'S AWFULLY SMALL...
!
I'D BE HARD-PRESSED TO CALL THAT A RASENGAN.
!
UGH!
BUT ...
DAMMIT !!!
HURL
SHWEE...N
POOF...

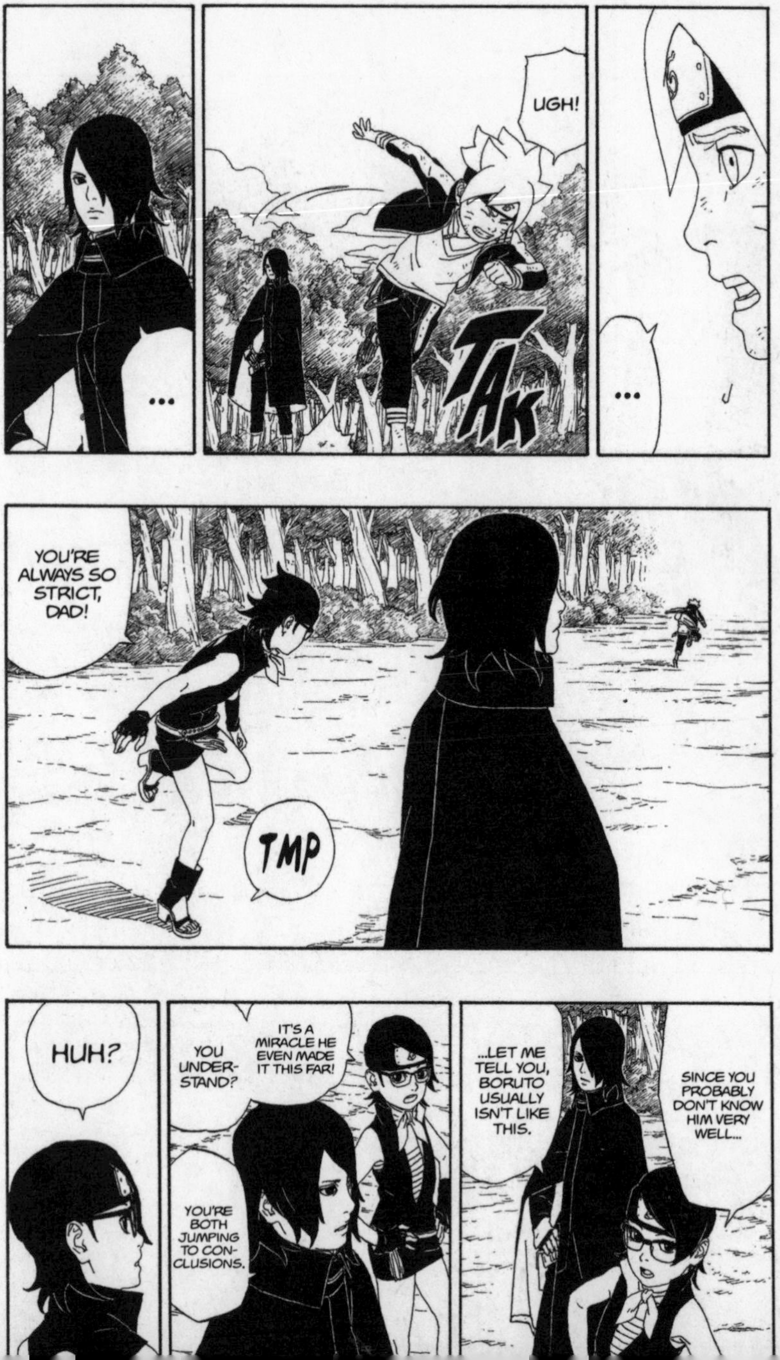
...
UGH!
TAK
...
YOU'RE ALWAYS SO STRICT, DAD!
TMP
SINCE YOU PROBABLY DON'T KNOW HIM VERY WELL...
...LET ME TELL YOU, BORUTO USUALLY ISN'T LIKE THIS.
IT'S A MIRACLE HE EVEN MADE IT THIS FAR!
YOU UNDER-STAND?
YOU'RE BOTH JUMPING TO CON-CLUSIONS.
HUH?

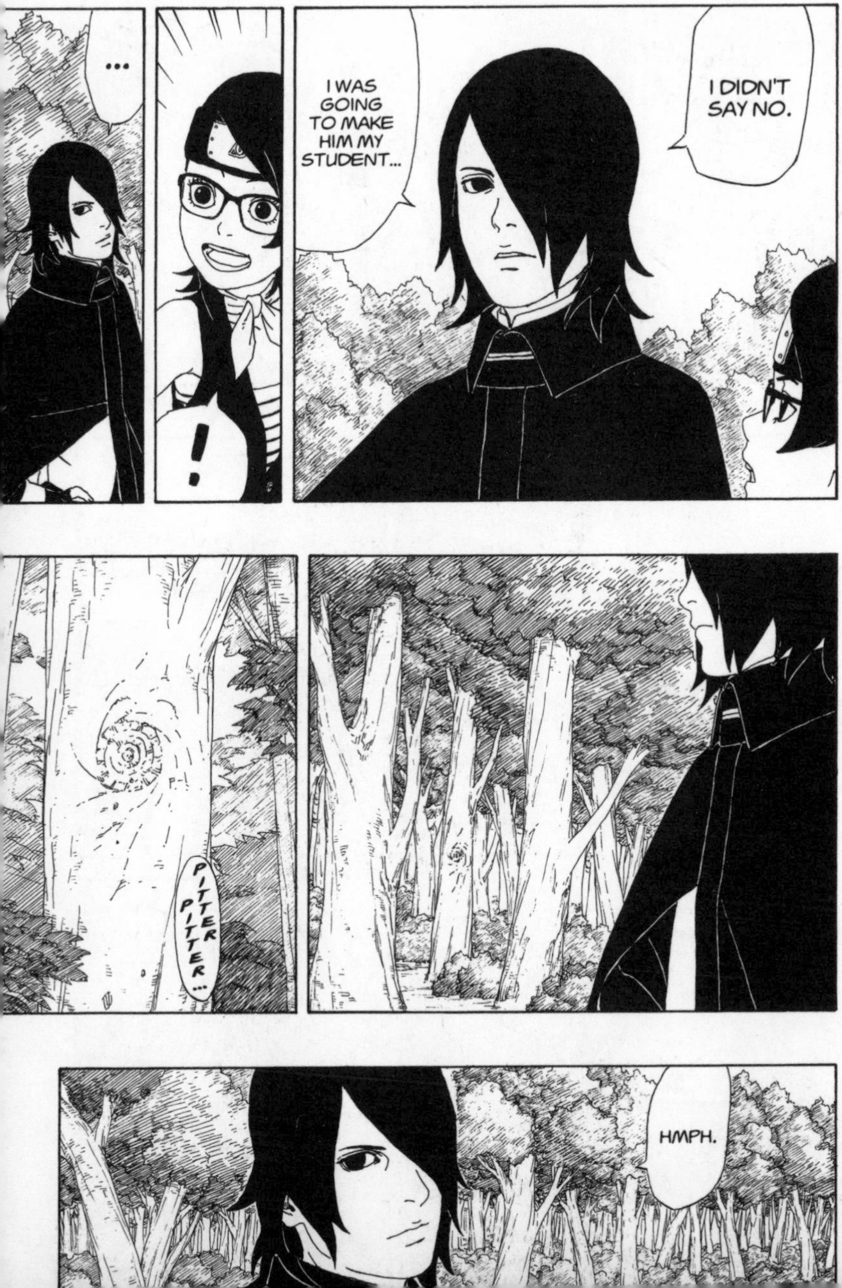
I DIDN'T SAY NO.
I WAS GOING TO MAKE HIM MY STUDENT...
!
...
PITTER PITTER...
HMPH.

*SIGN: THE CHUNIN EXAM IS HERE!

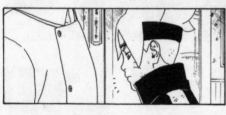

DAMMIT.

BAH...

OH, YOUNG MASTER.

WHAT'S WRONG?

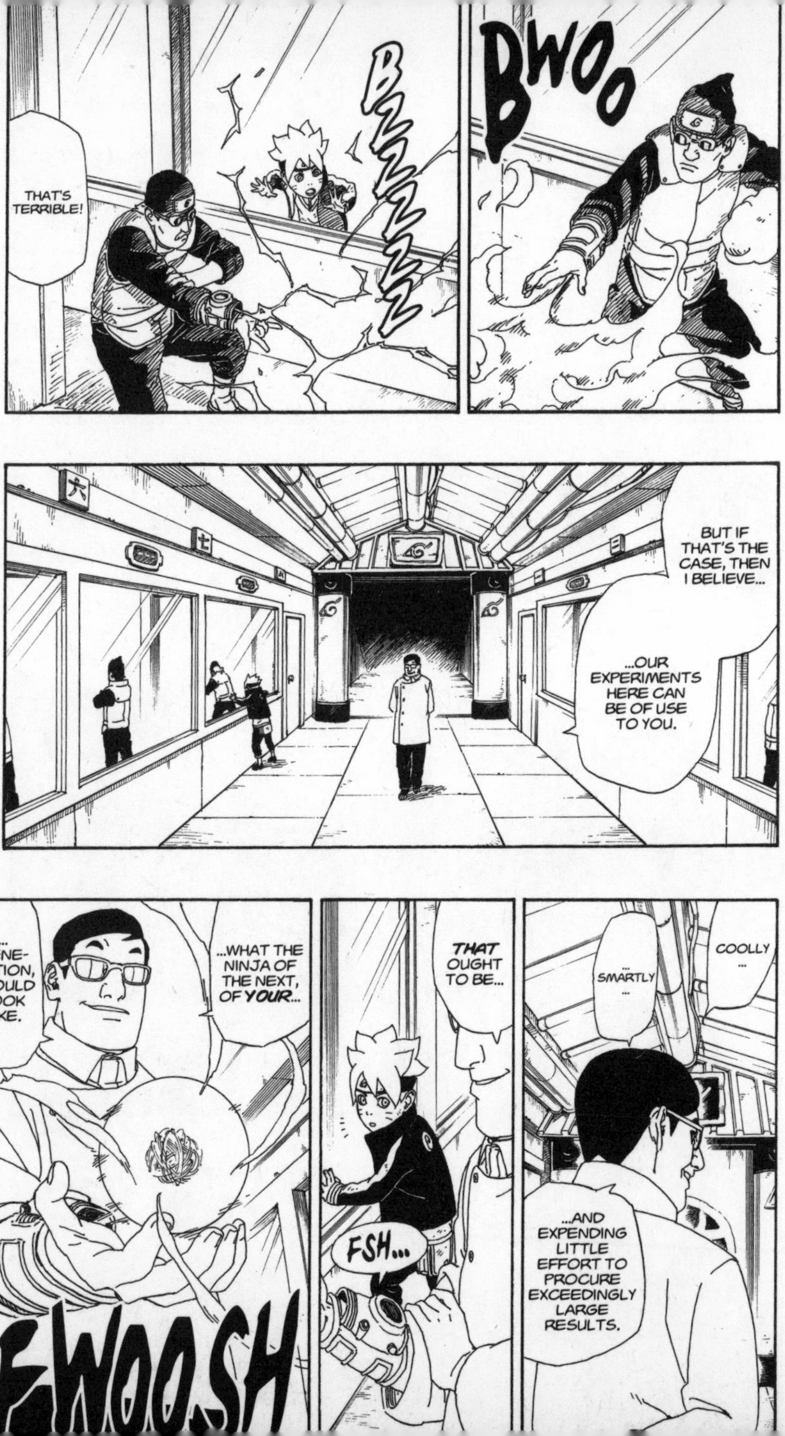
BWOO
BZZZZZ
THAT'S TERRIBLE!
BUT IF THAT'S THE CASE, THEN I BELIEVE...
...OUR EXPERIMENTS HERE CAN BE OF USE TO YOU.
COOLLY...
...SMARTLY...
...AND EXPENDING LITTLE EFFORT TO PROCURE EXCEEDINGLY LARGE RESULTS.
THAT OUGHT TO BE...
FSH...
...WHAT THE NINJA OF THE NEXT, OF ***YOUR***...
...GENERATION, SHOULD LOOK LIKE.
FWOOSH

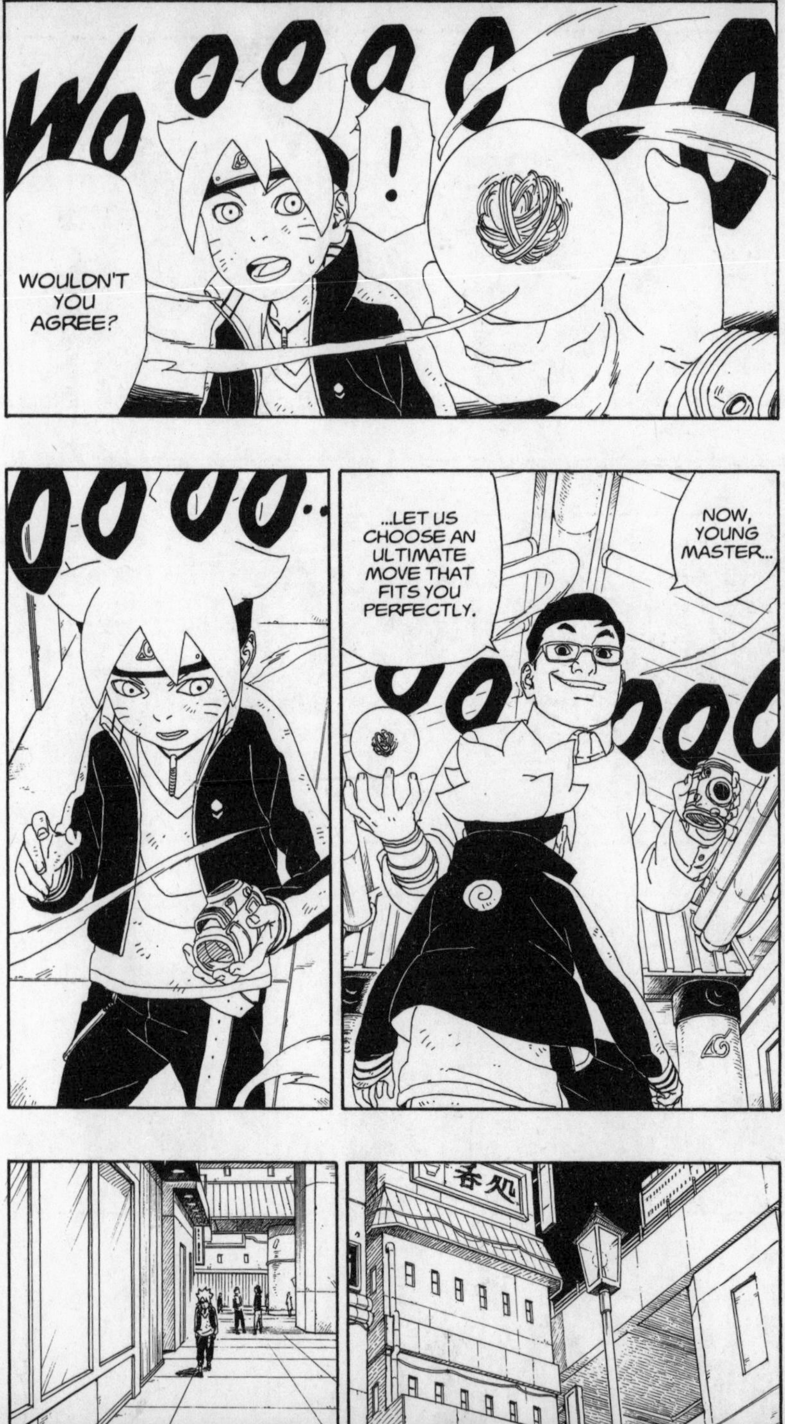
WOOOOOOO
!
WOULDN'T YOU AGREE?
NOW, YOUNG MASTER...
...LET US CHOOSE AN ULTIMATE MOVE THAT FITS YOU PERFECTLY.
OOOO..

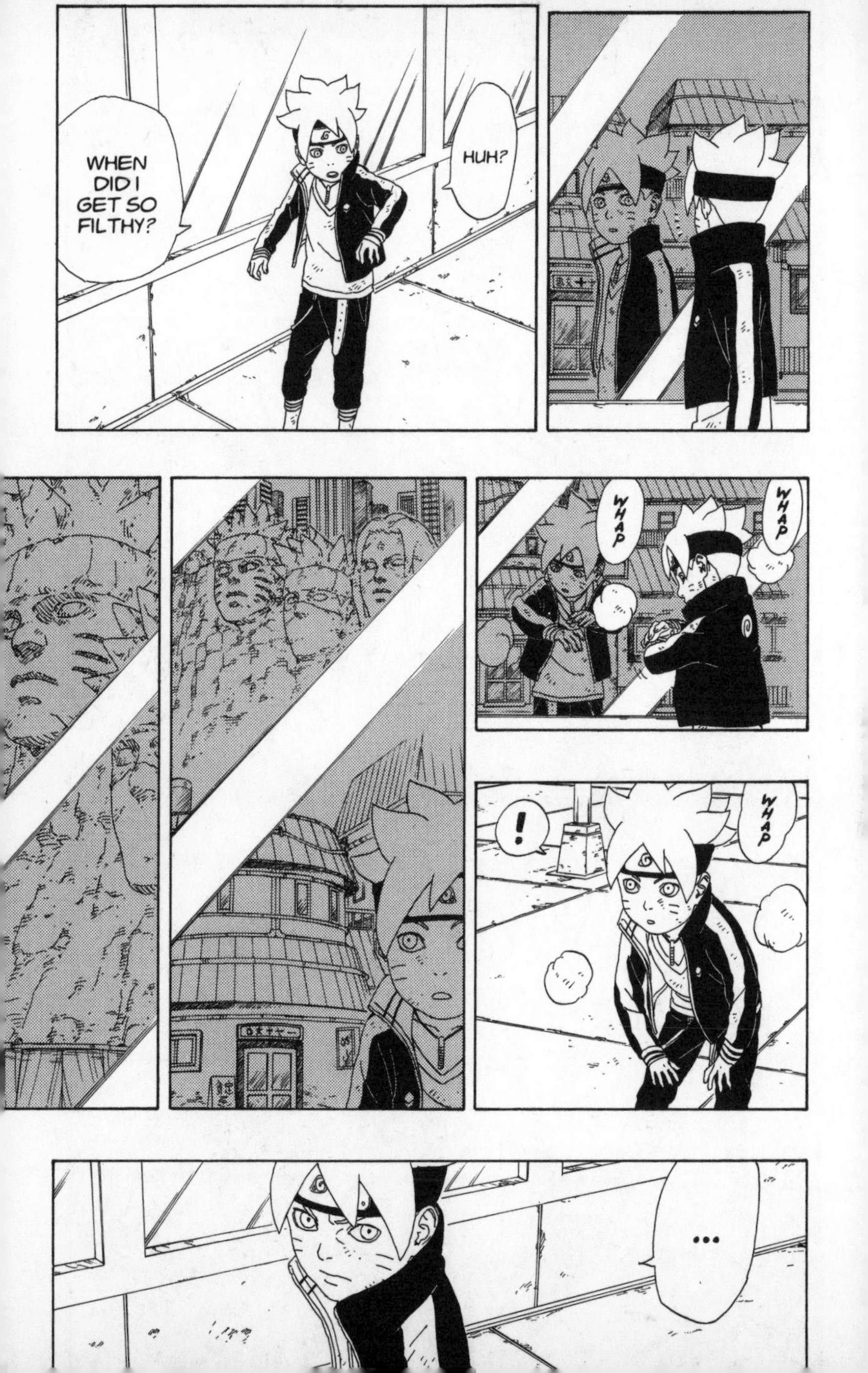
HUH?
WHEN DID I GET SO FILTHY?
WHAP
WHAP
WHAP
!
...

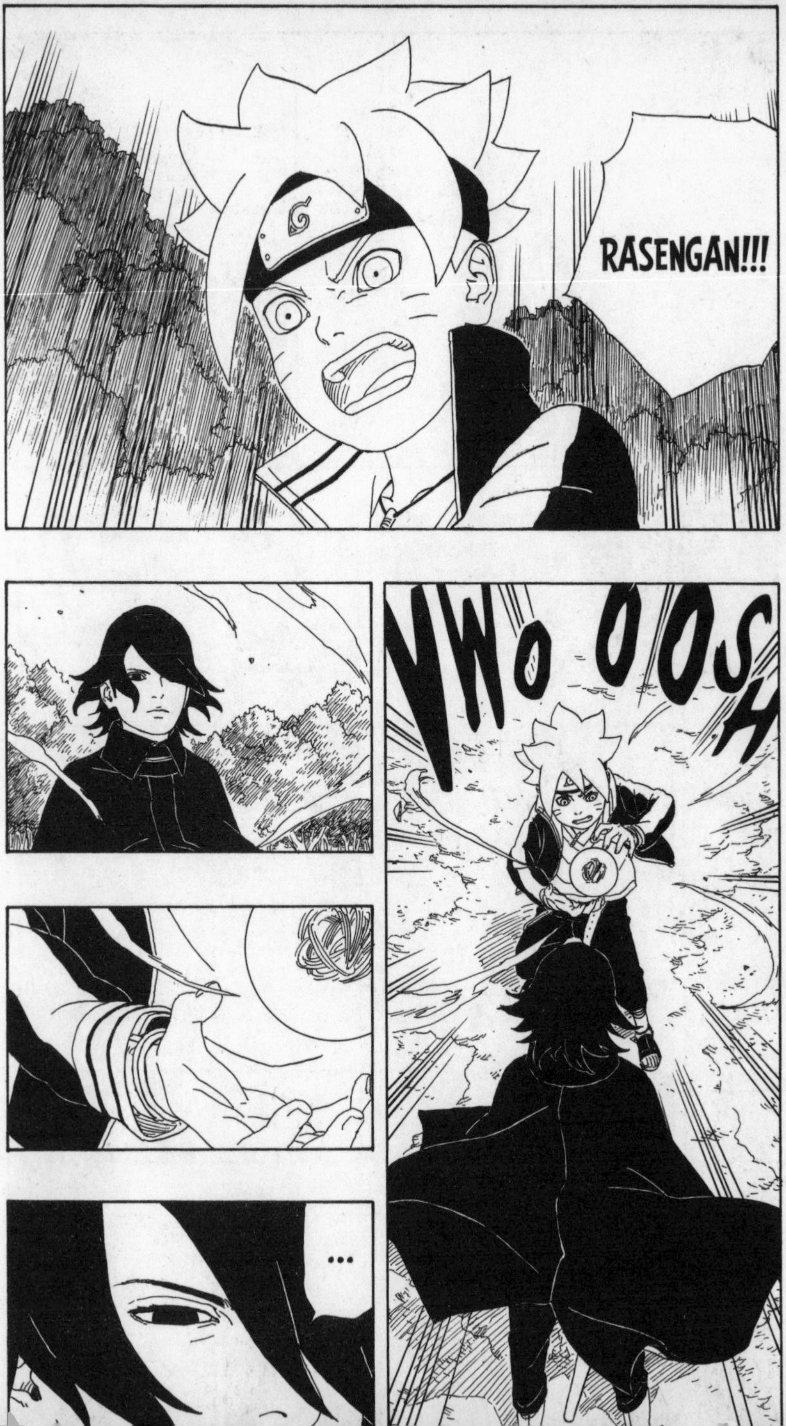
RASENGAN!!!
WHOOOSH
...

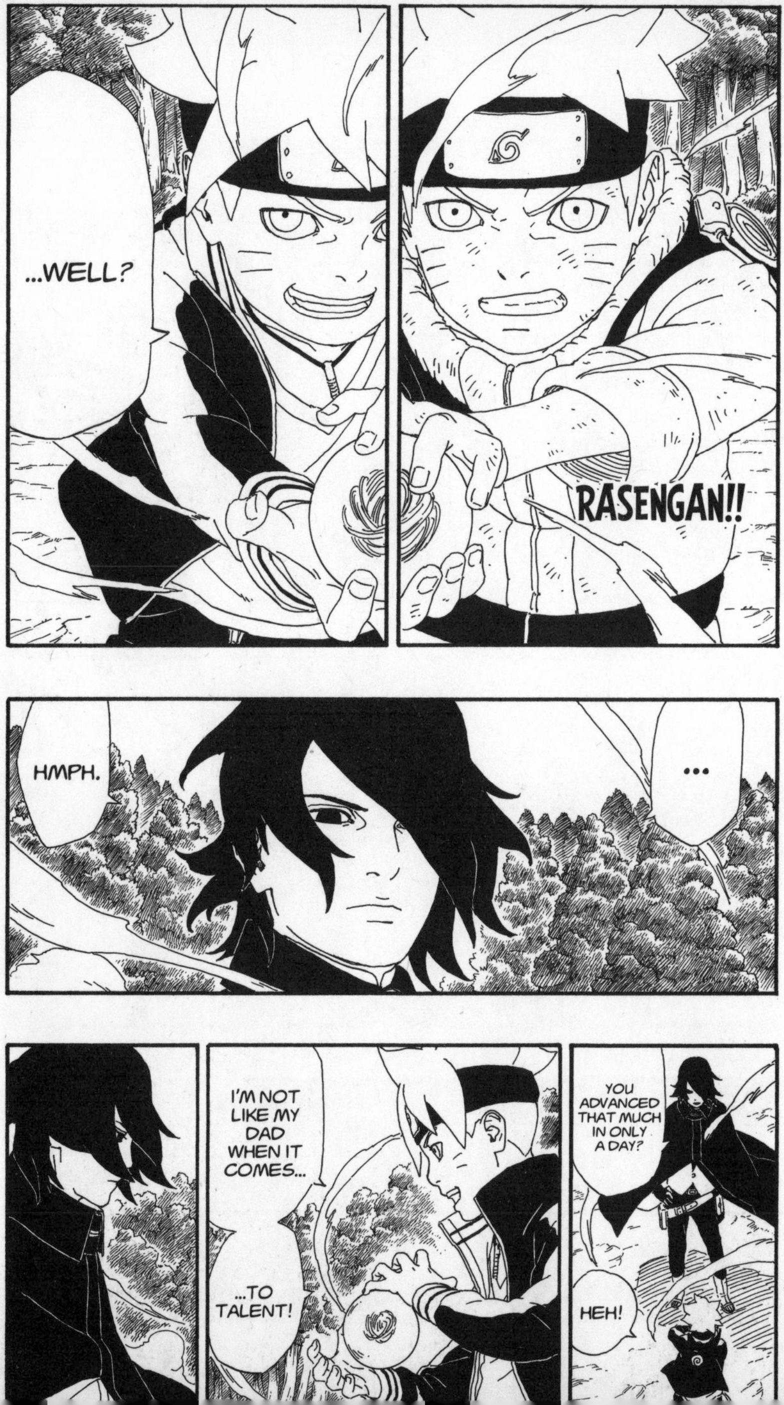
RASENGAN!!
...WELL?
...
HMPH.
YOU ADVANCED THAT MUCH IN ONLY A DAY?
HEH!
I'M NOT LIKE MY DAD WHEN IT COMES...
...TO TALENT!

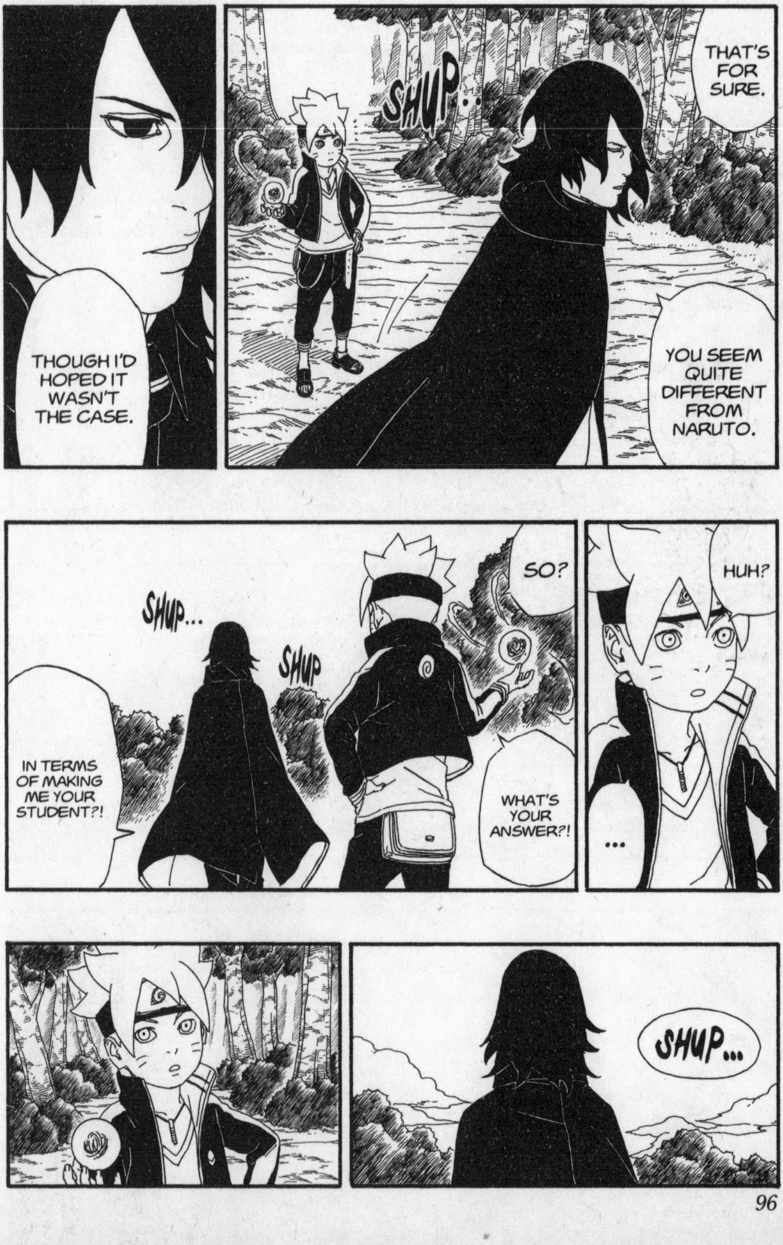
THAT'S FOR SURE.
SHUP...
YOU SEEM QUITE DIFFERENT FROM NARUTO.
THOUGH I'D HOPED IT WASN'T THE CASE.
HUH?
...
SO?
WHAT'S YOUR ANSWER?!
SHUP
SHUP...
IN TERMS OF MAKING ME YOUR STUDENT?!
SHUP...

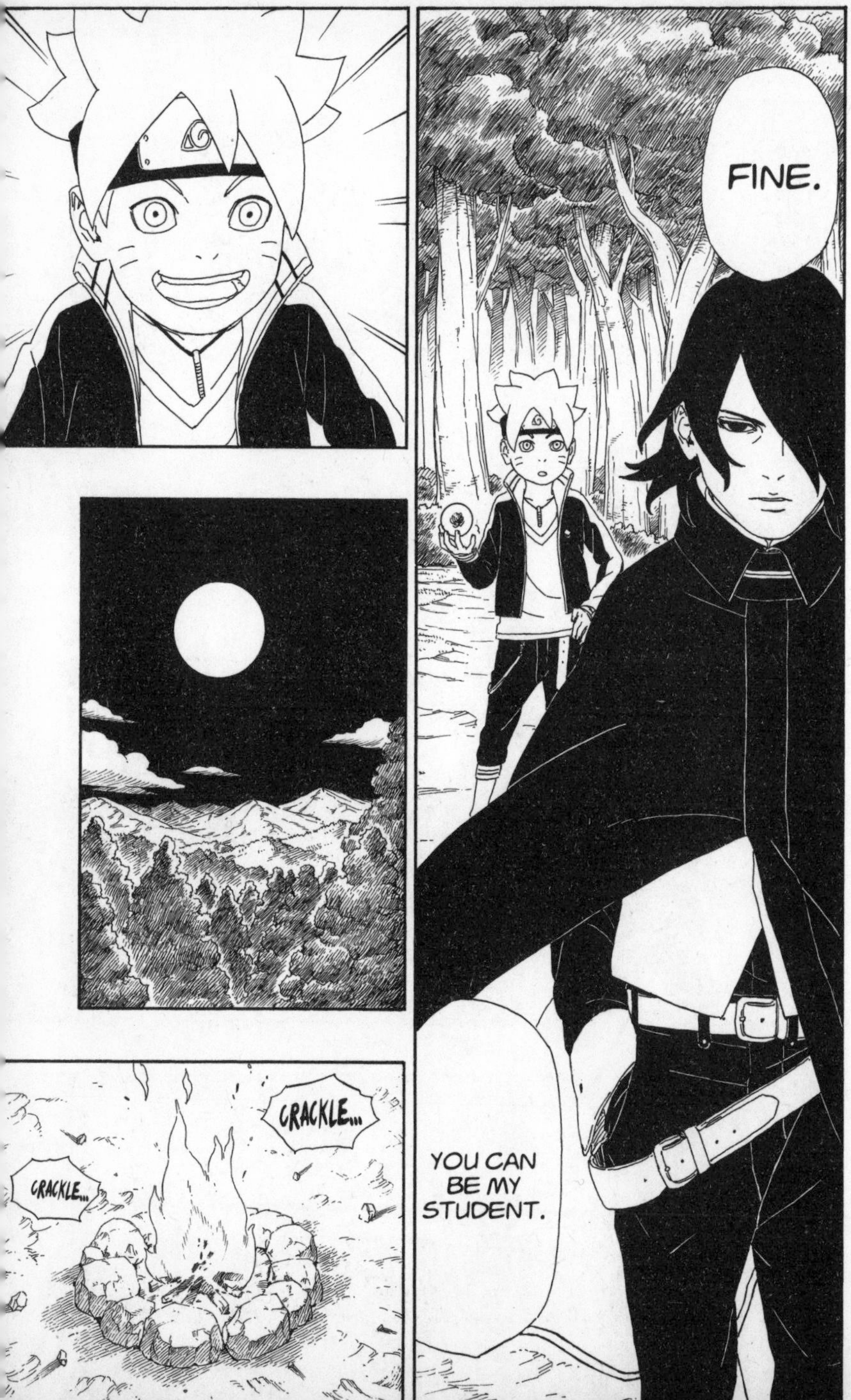
FINE.
YOU CAN BE MY STUDENT.
CRACKLE...
CRACKLE...

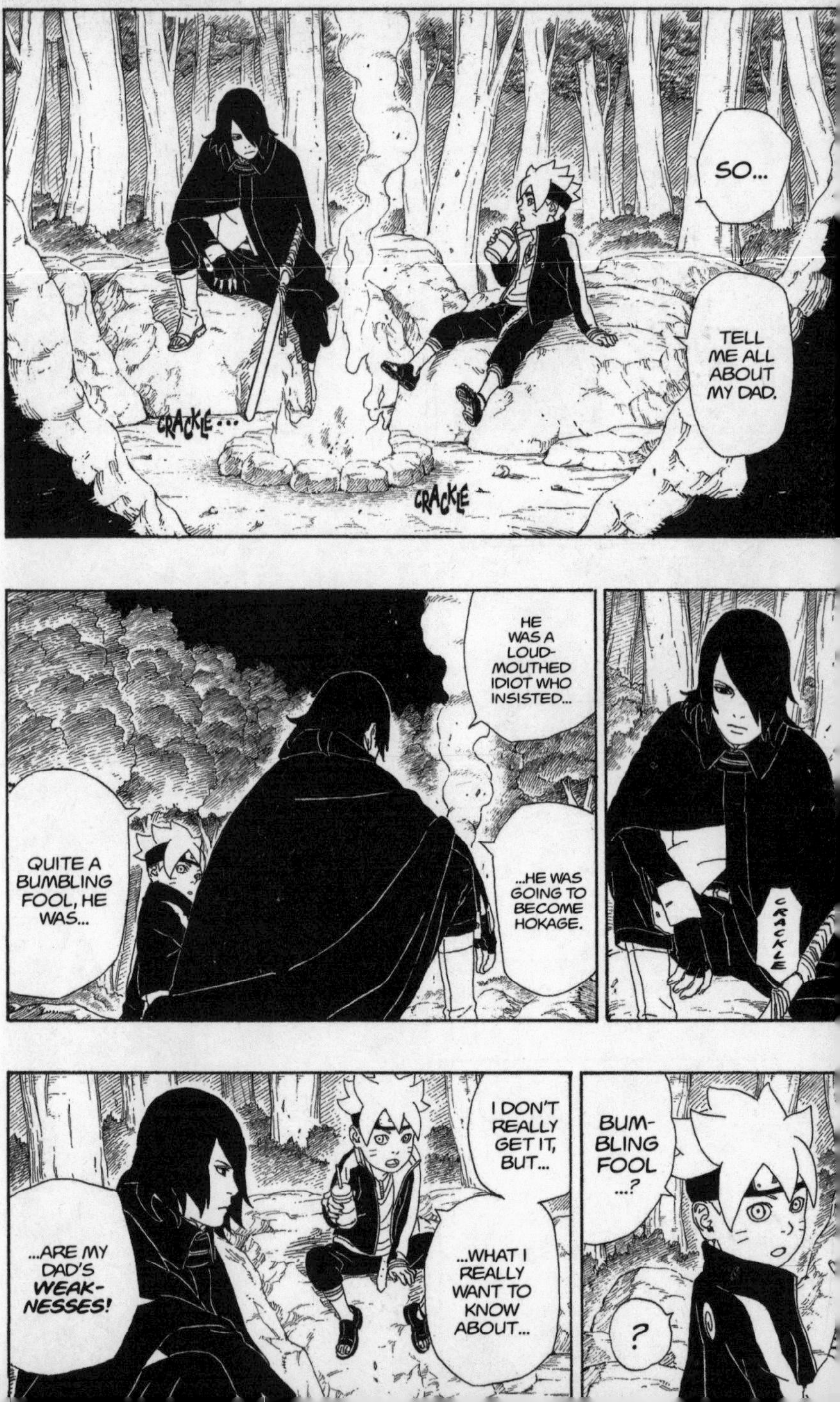
SO...
TELL ME ALL ABOUT MY DAD.
CRACKLE...
CRACKLE
CRACKLE
HE WAS A LOUD-MOUTHED IDIOT WHO INSISTED...
...HE WAS GOING TO BECOME HOKAGE.
QUITE A BUMBLING FOOL, HE WAS...
BUM-BLING FOOL ...?
?
I DON'T REALLY GET IT, BUT...
...WHAT I REALLY WANT TO KNOW ABOUT...
...ARE MY DAD'S WEAK-NESSES!

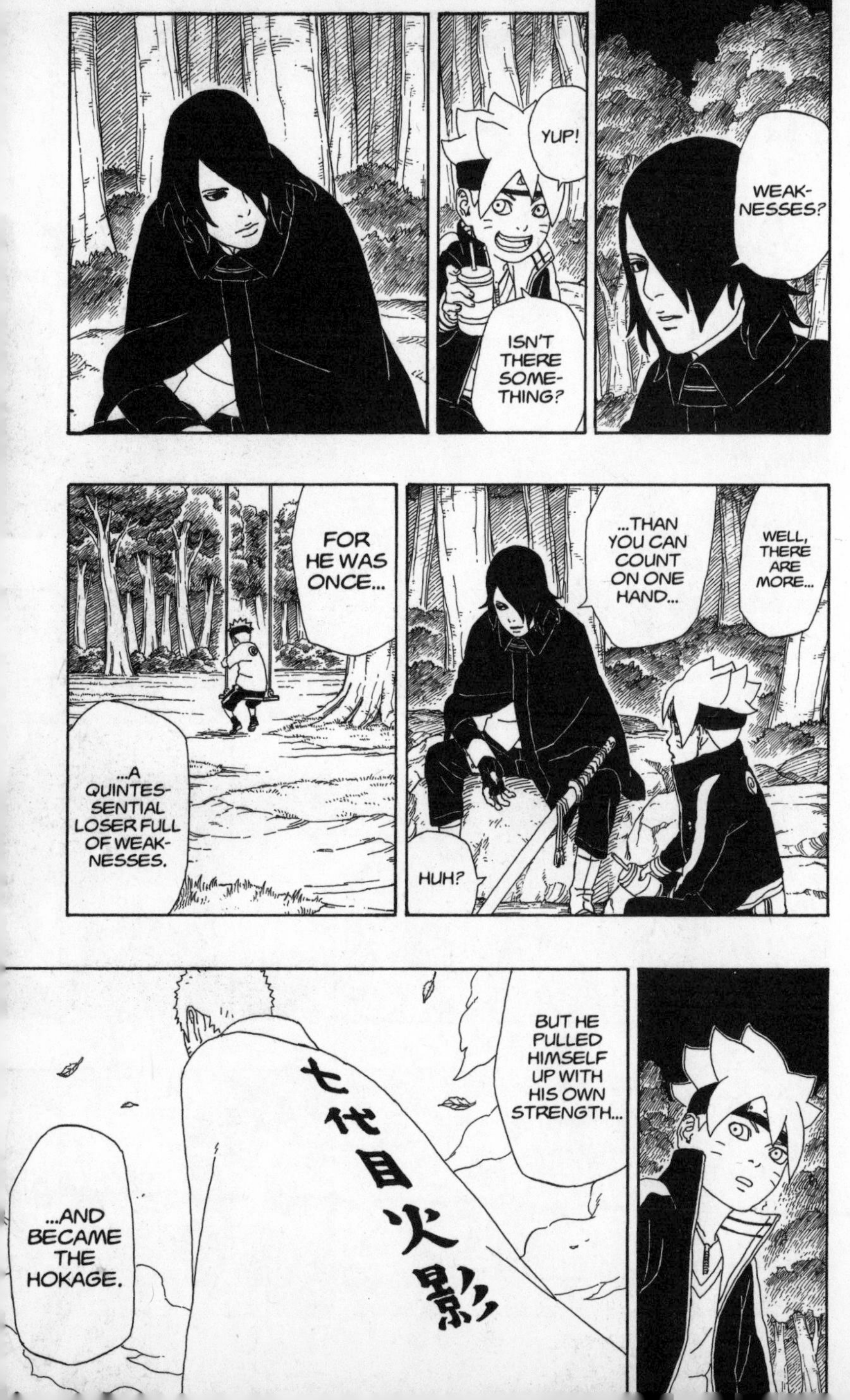
WEAK-NESSES?
YUP!
ISN'T THERE SOME-THING?
WELL, THERE ARE MORE...
...THAN YOU CAN COUNT ON ONE HAND...
HUH?
FOR HE WAS ONCE...
...A QUINTES-SENTIAL LOSER FULL OF WEAK-NESSES.
BUT HE PULLED HIMSELF UP WITH HIS OWN STRENGTH...
七代目火影
...AND BECAME THE HOKAGE.

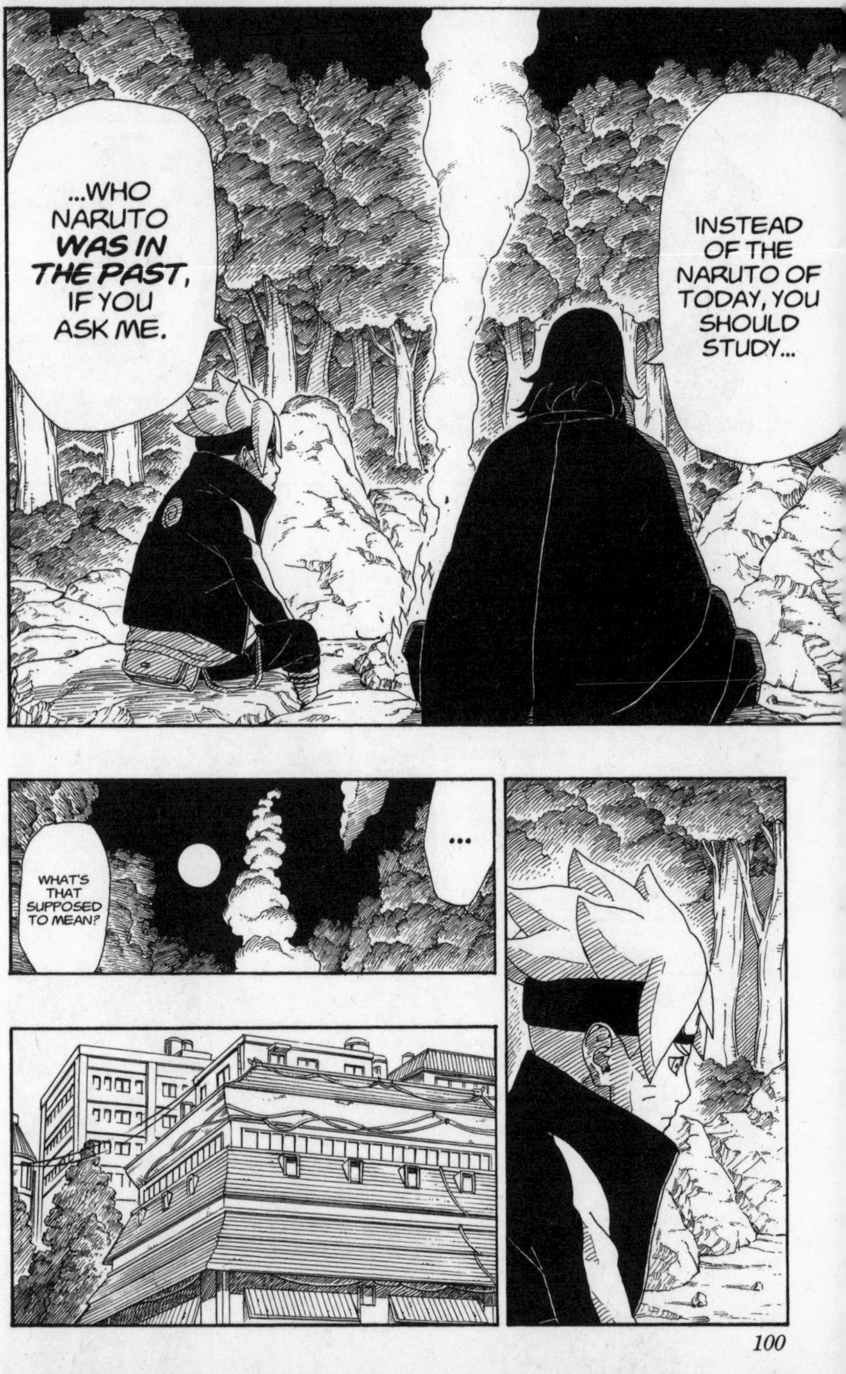
INSTEAD OF THE NARUTO OF TODAY, YOU SHOULD STUDY...
...WHO NARUTO **WAS IN THE PAST**, IF YOU ASK ME.
...
WHAT'S THAT SUPPOSED TO MEAN?

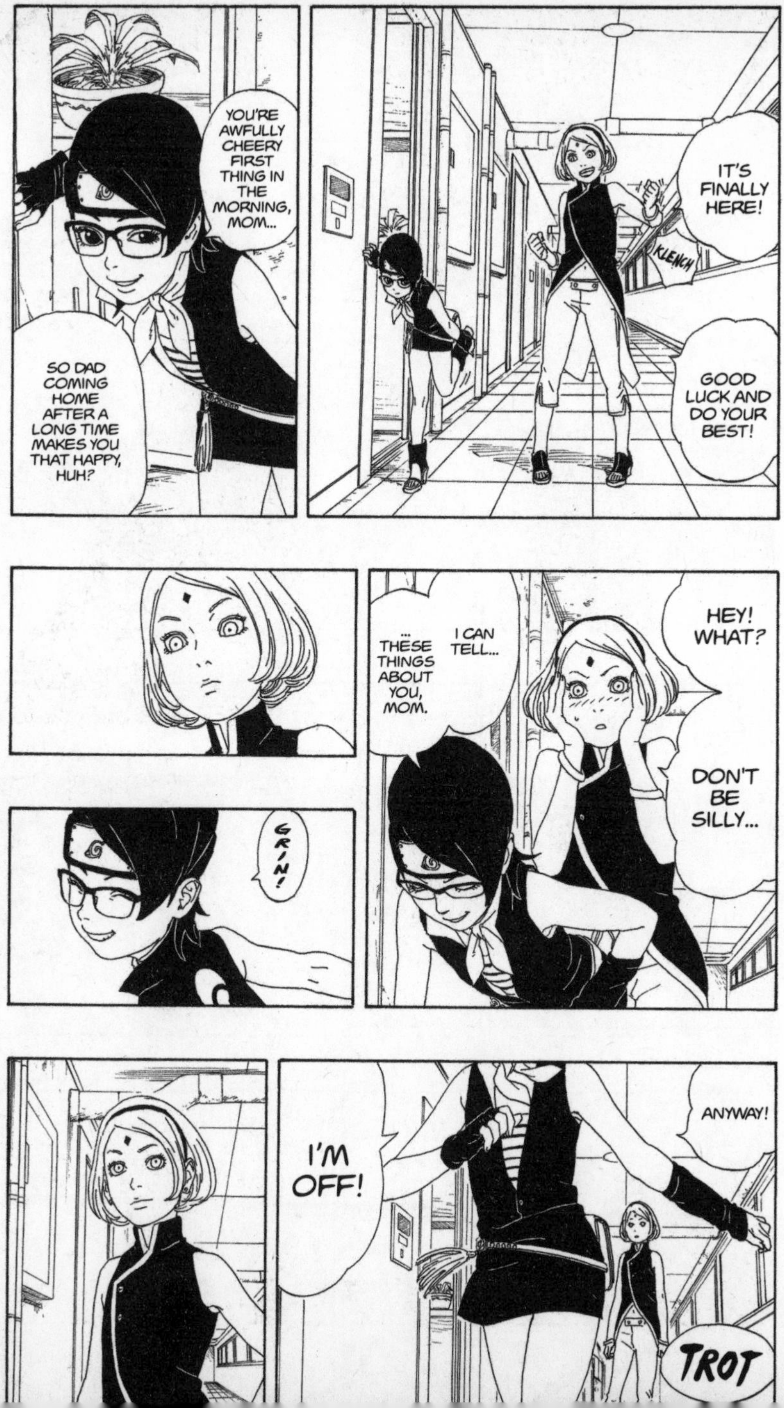
IT'S FINALLY HERE!
KLENCH
GOOD LUCK AND DO YOUR BEST!
YOU'RE AWFULLY CHEERY FIRST THING IN THE MORNING, MOM...
SO DAD COMING HOME AFTER A LONG TIME MAKES YOU THAT HAPPY, HUH?
HEY! WHAT?
DON'T BE SILLY...
I CAN TELL...
...THESE THINGS ABOUT YOU, MOM.
GRIN!
ANYWAY!
I'M OFF!
TROT

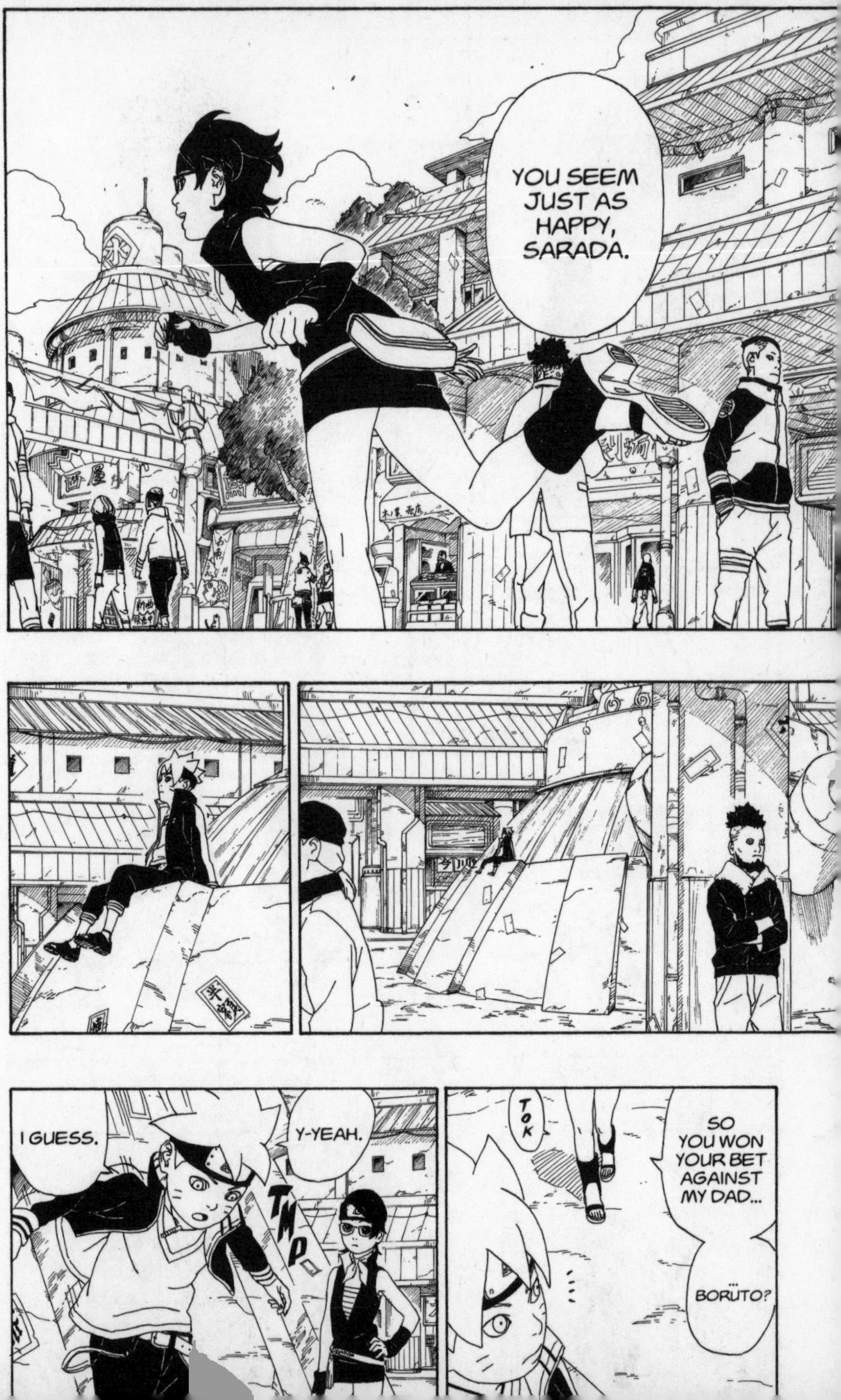
YOU SEEM JUST AS HAPPY, SARADA.
TOK
SO YOU WON YOUR BET AGAINST MY DAD...
... BORUTO?
...
Y-YEAH.
TMP
I GUESS.

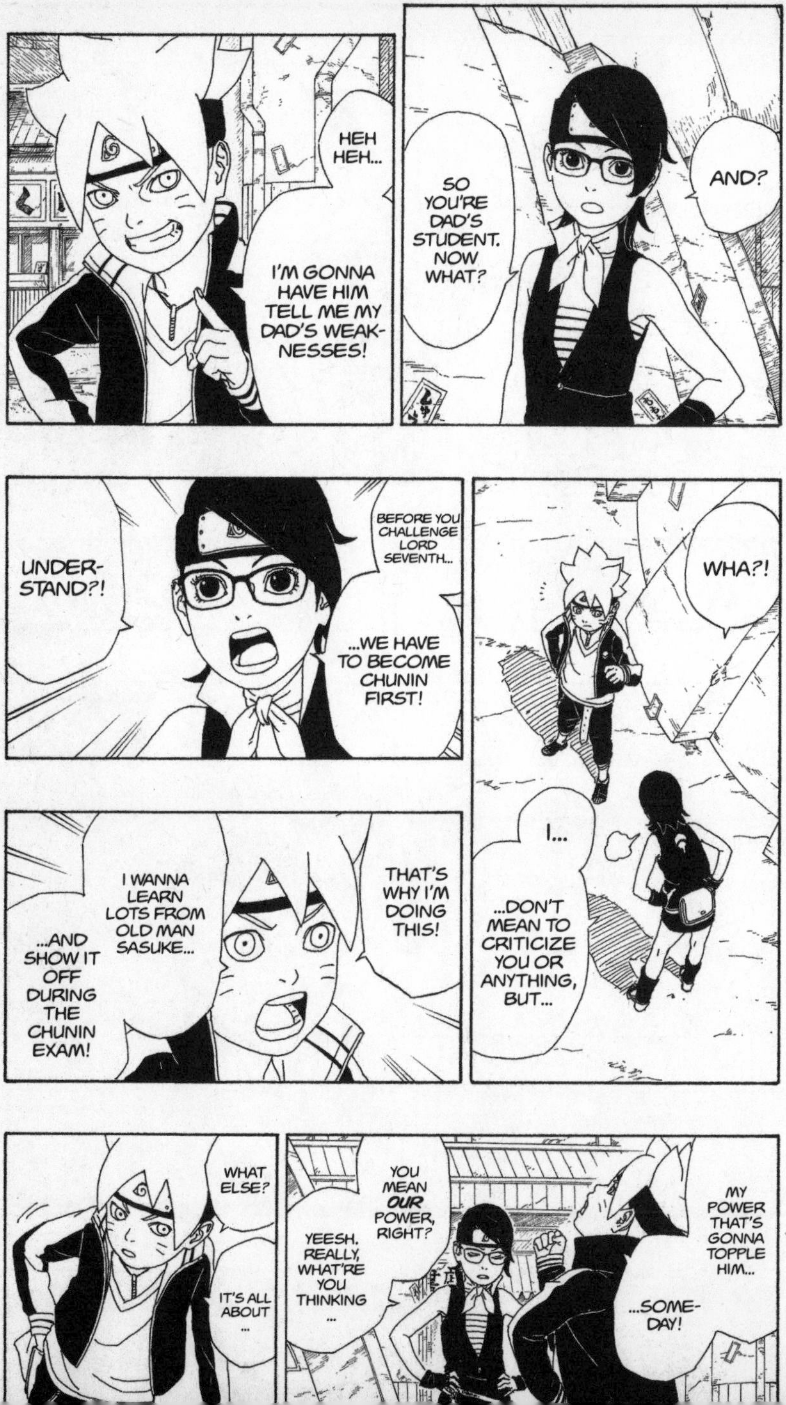
AND?
SO YOU'RE DAD'S STUDENT. NOW WHAT?
HEH HEH...
I'M GONNA HAVE HIM TELL ME MY DAD'S WEAK-NESSES!
WHA?!
I...
...DON'T MEAN TO CRITICIZE YOU OR ANYTHING, BUT...
BEFORE YOU CHALLENGE LORD SEVENTH...
...WE HAVE TO BECOME CHUNIN FIRST!
UNDER-STAND?!
THAT'S WHY I'M DOING THIS!
I WANNA LEARN LOTS FROM OLD MAN SASUKE...
...AND SHOW IT OFF DURING THE CHUNIN EXAM!
MY POWER THAT'S GONNA TOPPLE HIM...
...SOME-DAY!
YOU MEAN **OUR** POWER, RIGHT?
YEESH. REALLY, WHAT'RE YOU THINKING...
WHAT ELSE?
IT'S ALL ABOUT...

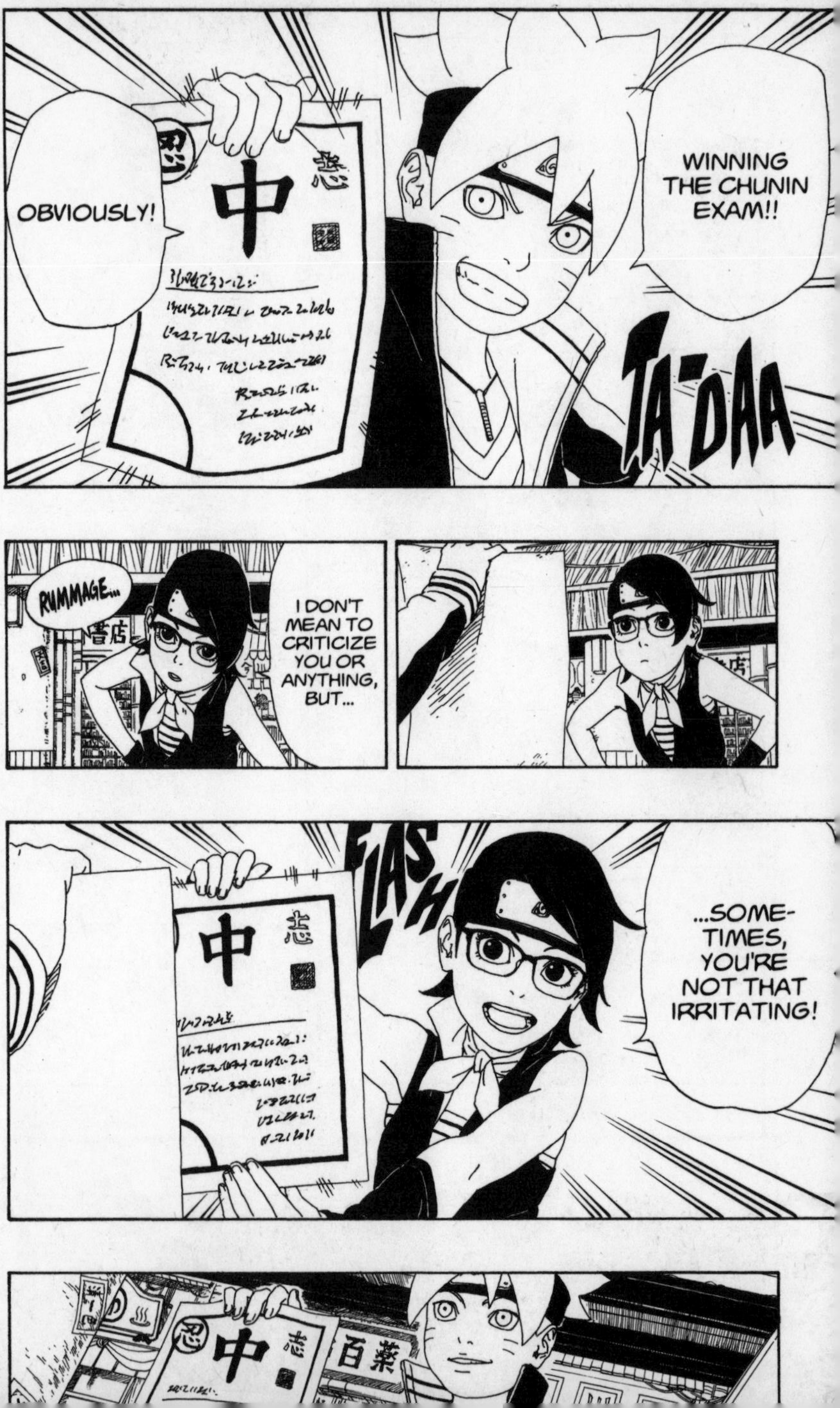
WINNING THE CHUNIN EXAM!!
TA-DAA
OBVIOUSLY!
I DON'T MEAN TO CRITICIZE YOU OR ANYTHING, BUT...
RUMMAGE...
...SOME-TIMES, YOU'RE NOT THAT IRRITATING!
FLASH

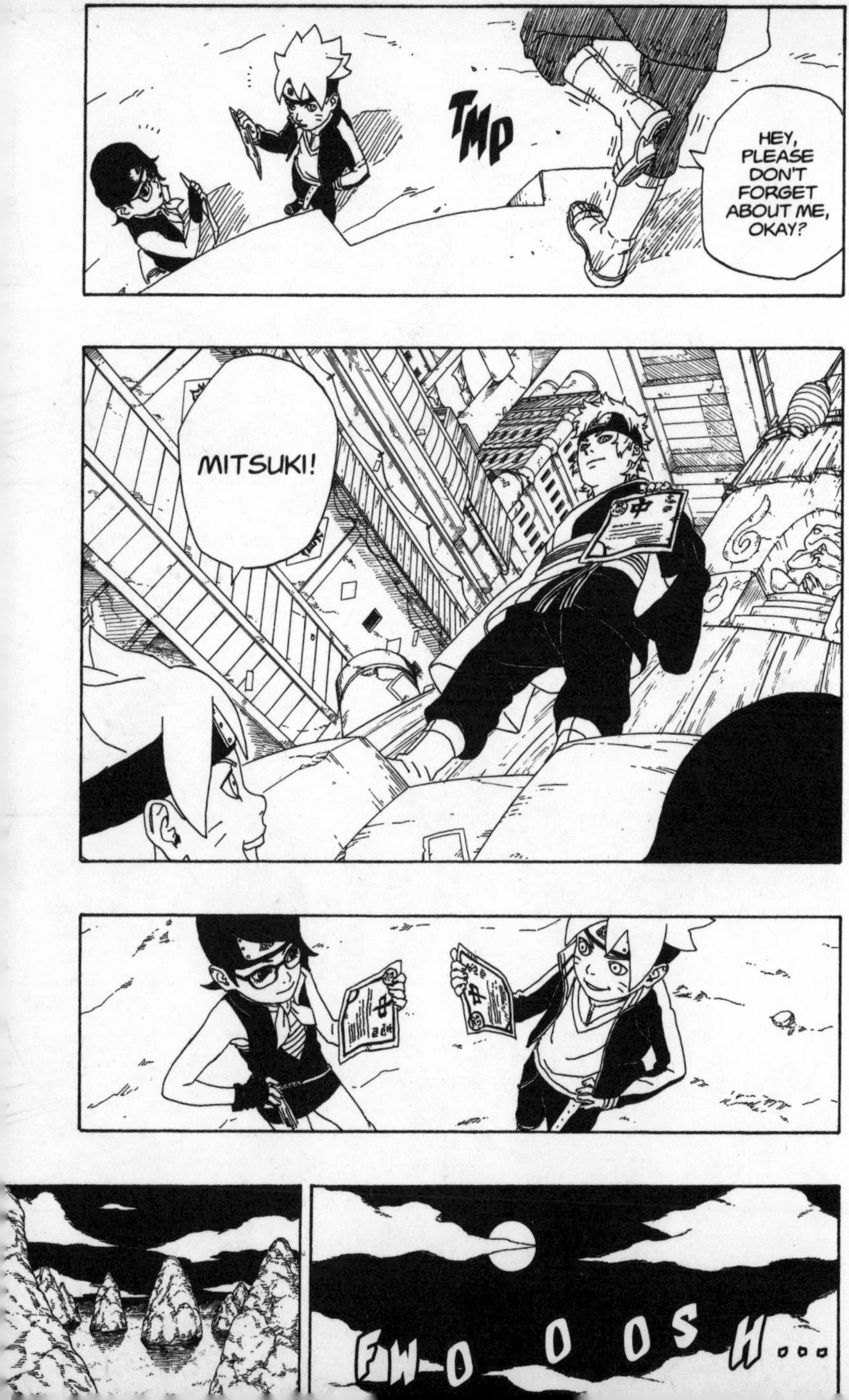
HEY, PLEASE DON'T FORGET ABOUT ME, OKAY?
TMP
MITSUKI!
FWOOOSH...

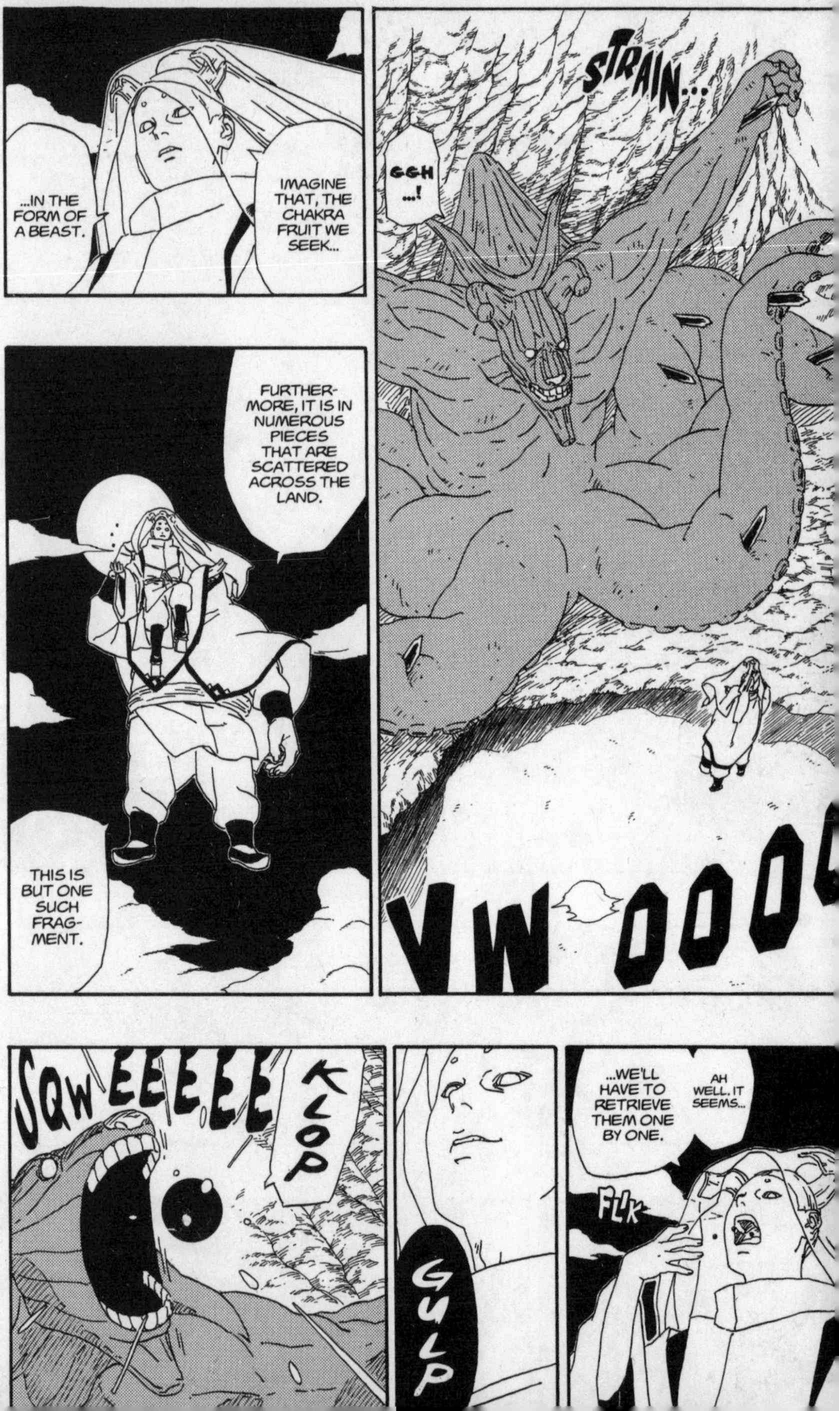
STRAIN...
GGH ...!
VWOOO
IMAGINE THAT, THE CHAKRA FRUIT WE SEEK...
...IN THE FORM OF A BEAST.
FURTHER-MORE, IT IS IN NUMEROUS PIECES THAT ARE SCATTERED ACROSS THE LAND.
THIS IS BUT ONE SUCH FRAG-MENT.
AH WELL. IT SEEMS...
...WE'LL HAVE TO RETRIEVE THEM ONE BY ONE.
FLIK
GULP
KLOP
SQWEEEEE

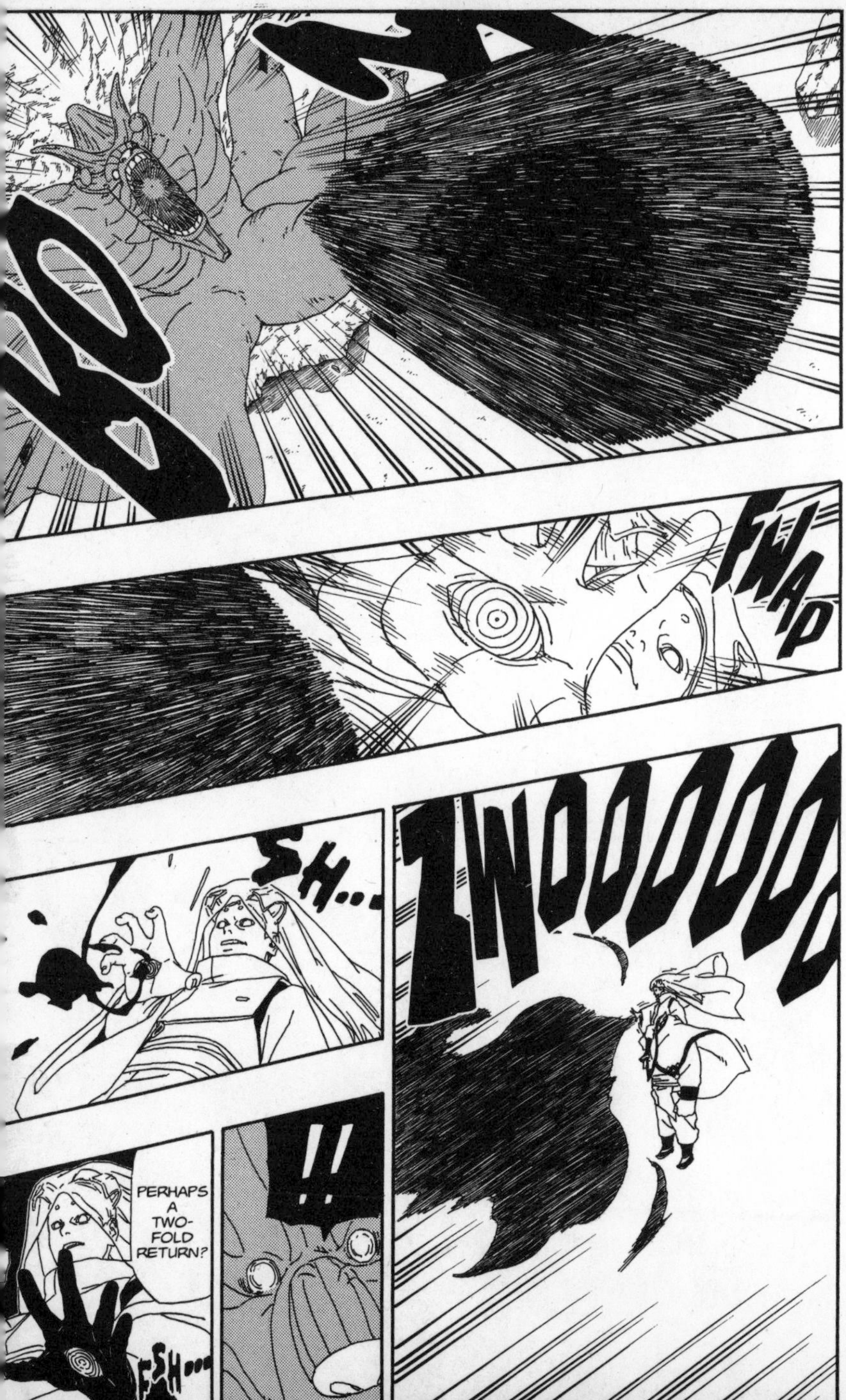

FWAP
SH...
!!
PERHAPS A TWO-FOLD RETURN?
FSH...

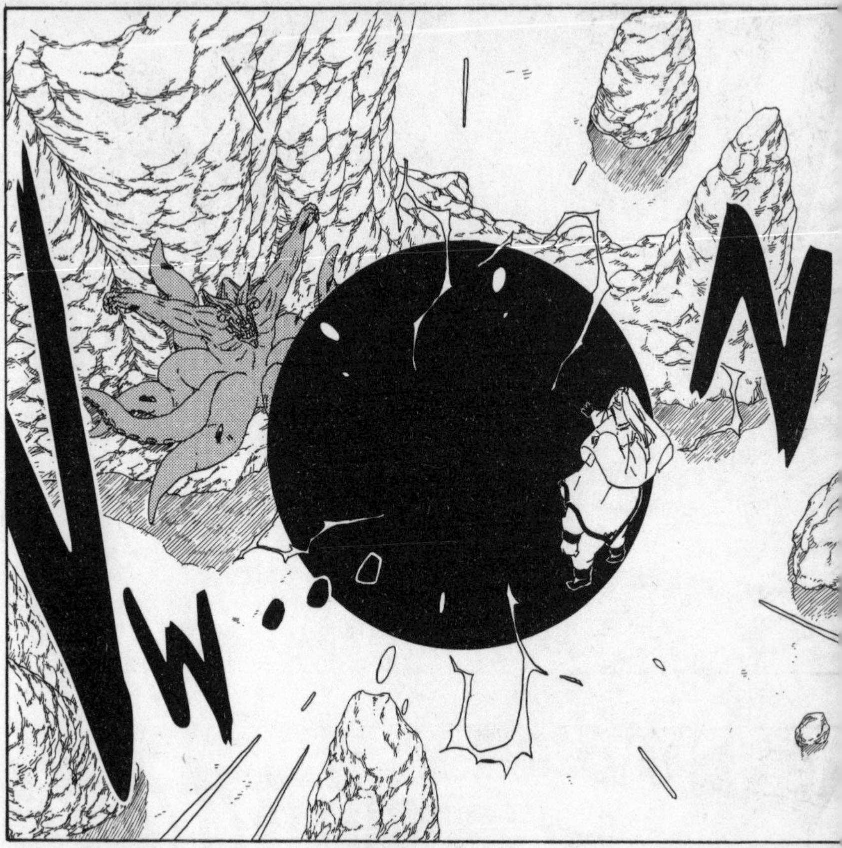
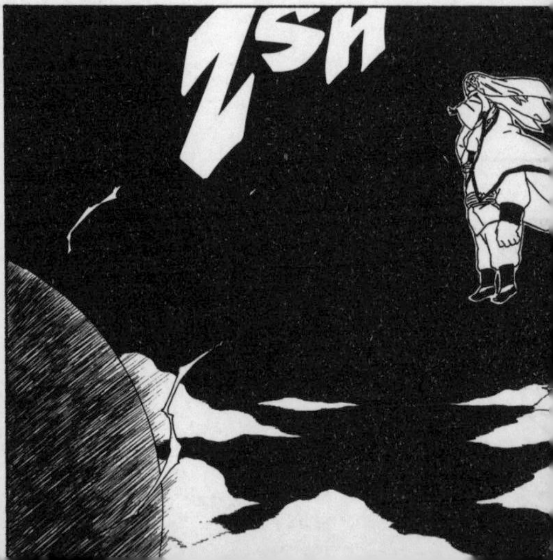
ZSH
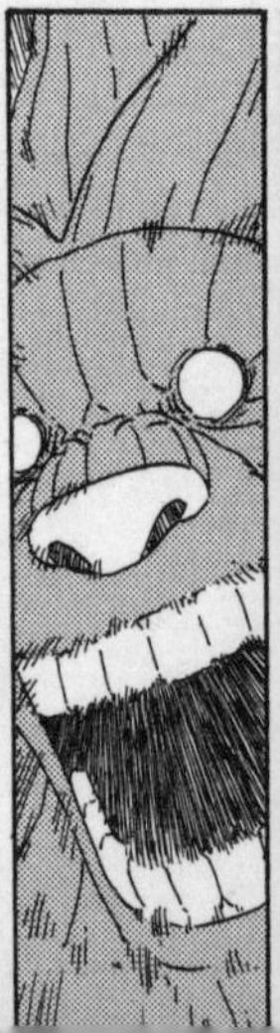
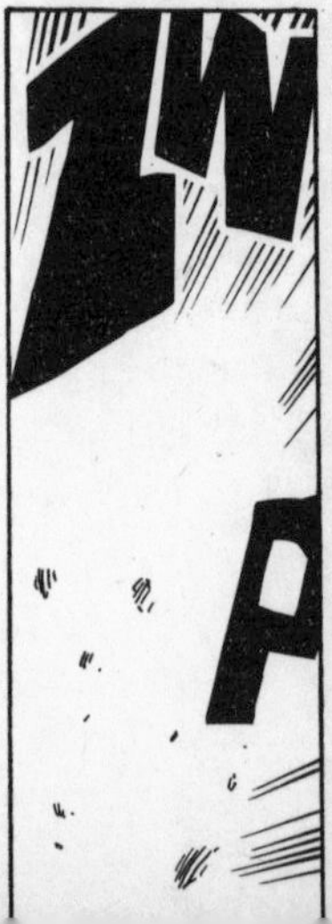

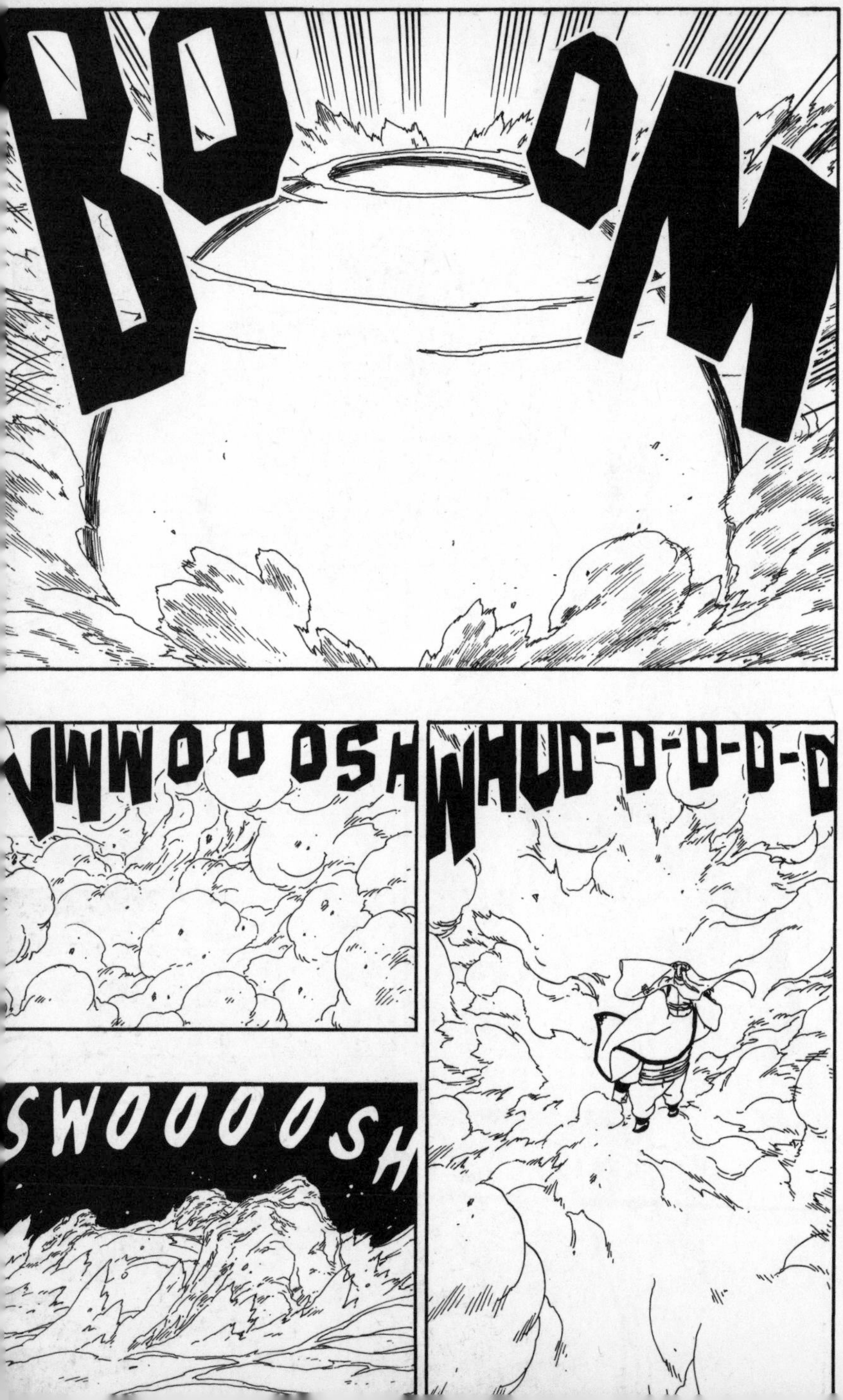
BOOM
WHUD-D-D-D-D
WWWOOOSH
SWOOOOSH

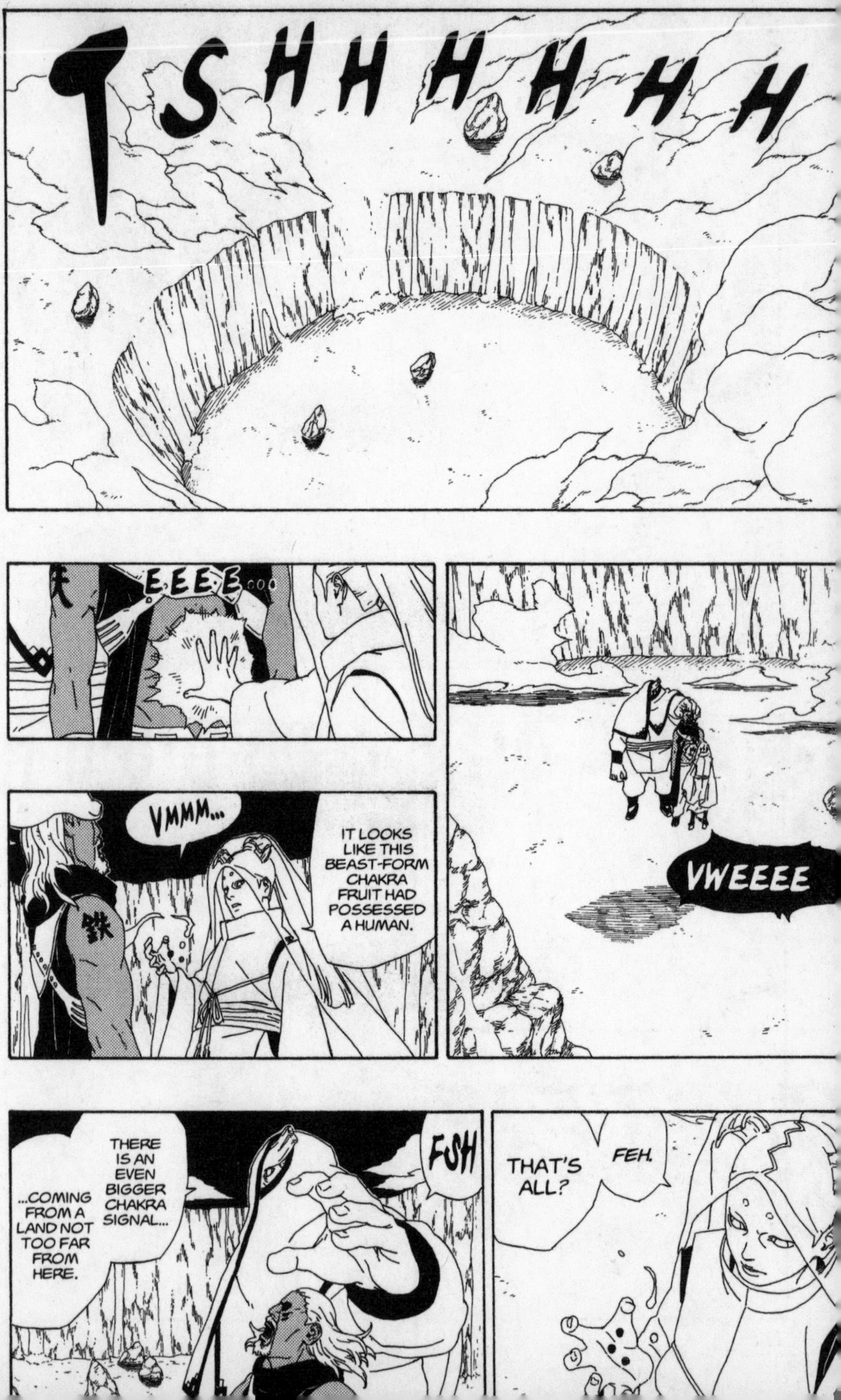
TSHHHHHH
VWEEEE
EEEE...
VMMM...
IT LOOKS LIKE THIS BEAST-FORM CHAKRA FRUIT HAD POSSESSED A HUMAN.
FEH.
THAT'S ALL?
FSH
THERE IS AN EVEN BIGGER CHAKRA SIGNAL...
...COMING FROM A LAND NOT TOO FAR FROM HERE.

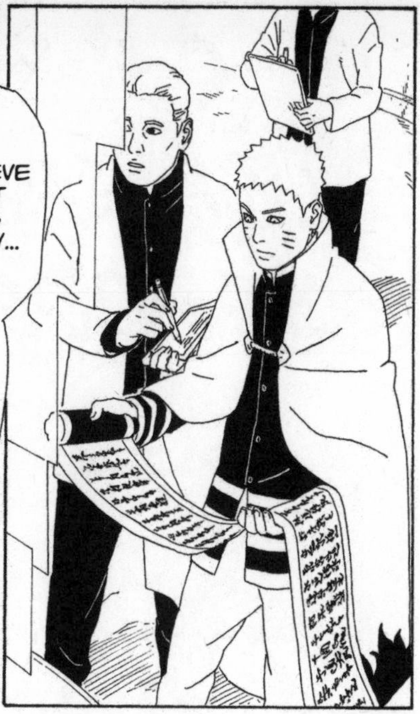

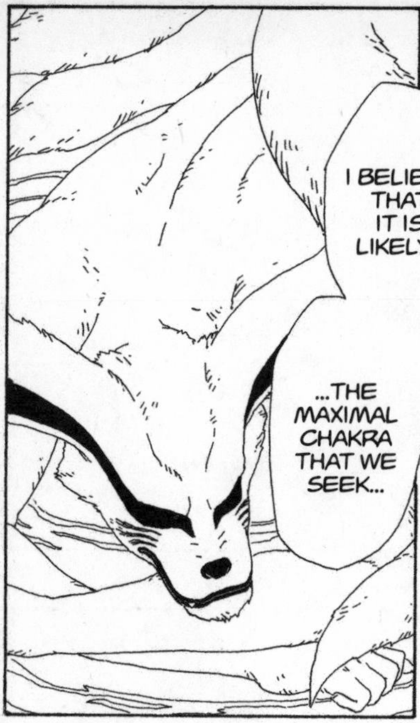
I BELIEVE THAT IT IS LIKELY...
...THE MAXIMAL CHAKRA THAT WE SEEK...

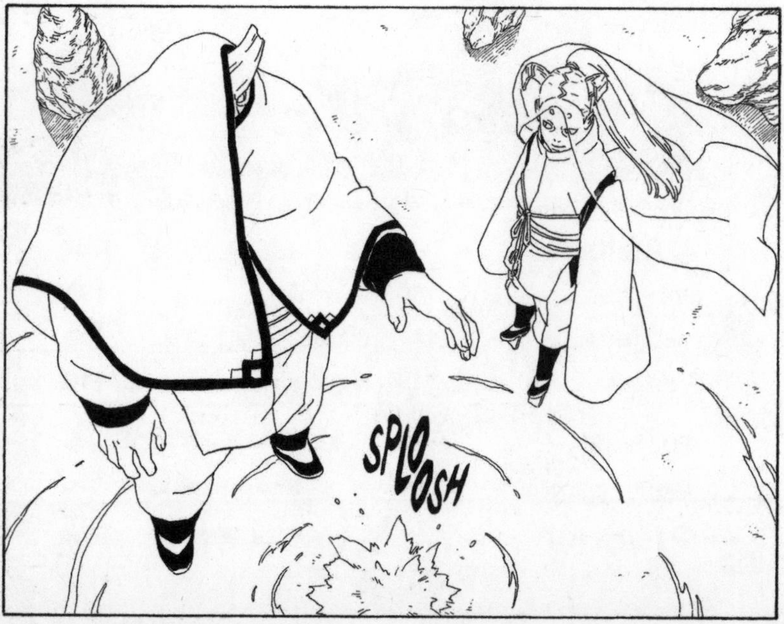
SPLOOSH

NINJA ENCYCLOPEDIA • ENTRY 2

UCHIHA SARADA

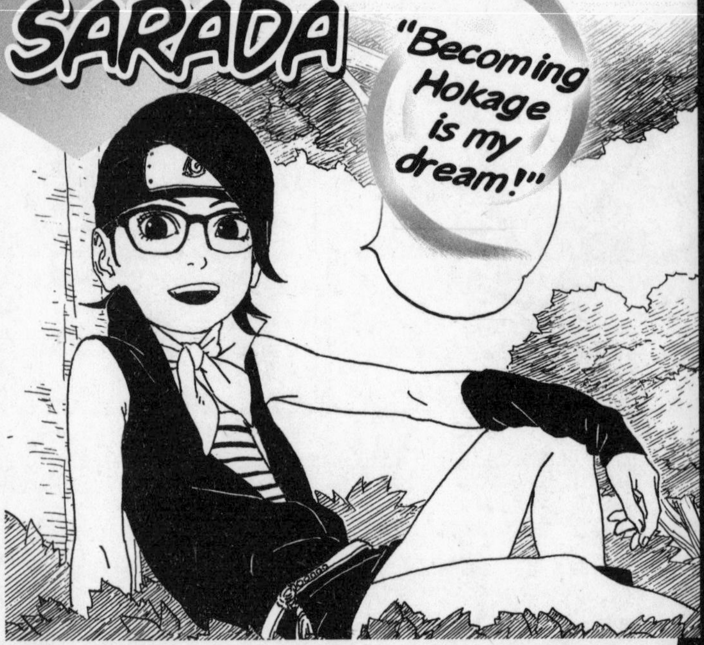
"Becoming Hokage is my dream!"

Attributes

Strength	160	Dexterity	130
Intelligence	145	Chakra	150
Perception	140	Negotiation	146

Skills

Marksmanship ☆☆☆☆ Genjutsu ☆☆☆☆ Ninjutsu knowledge ☆☆☆☆

etc

Ninja Arts

Sharingan, Demon Wind Shuriken: Windmill of Shadows, Lightning Flash, etc.

*Average attribute value is 60 for ordinary people and 90 for genin.
Skill values range from 1 to 5☆ with 5☆ signifying super-topnotch.

Number 3: The Chunin Exam Begins!!

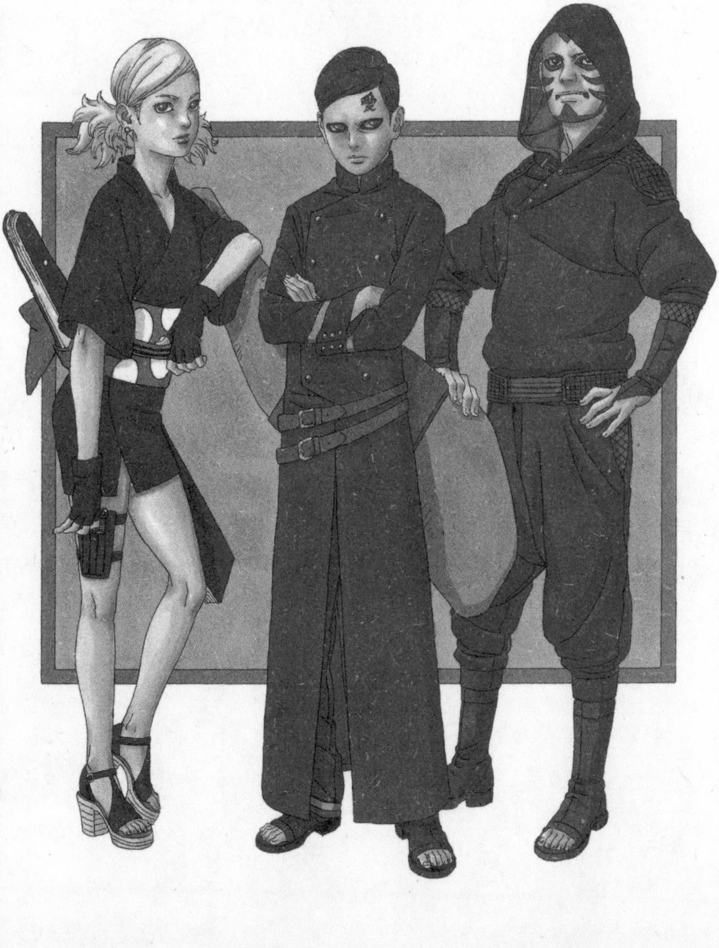

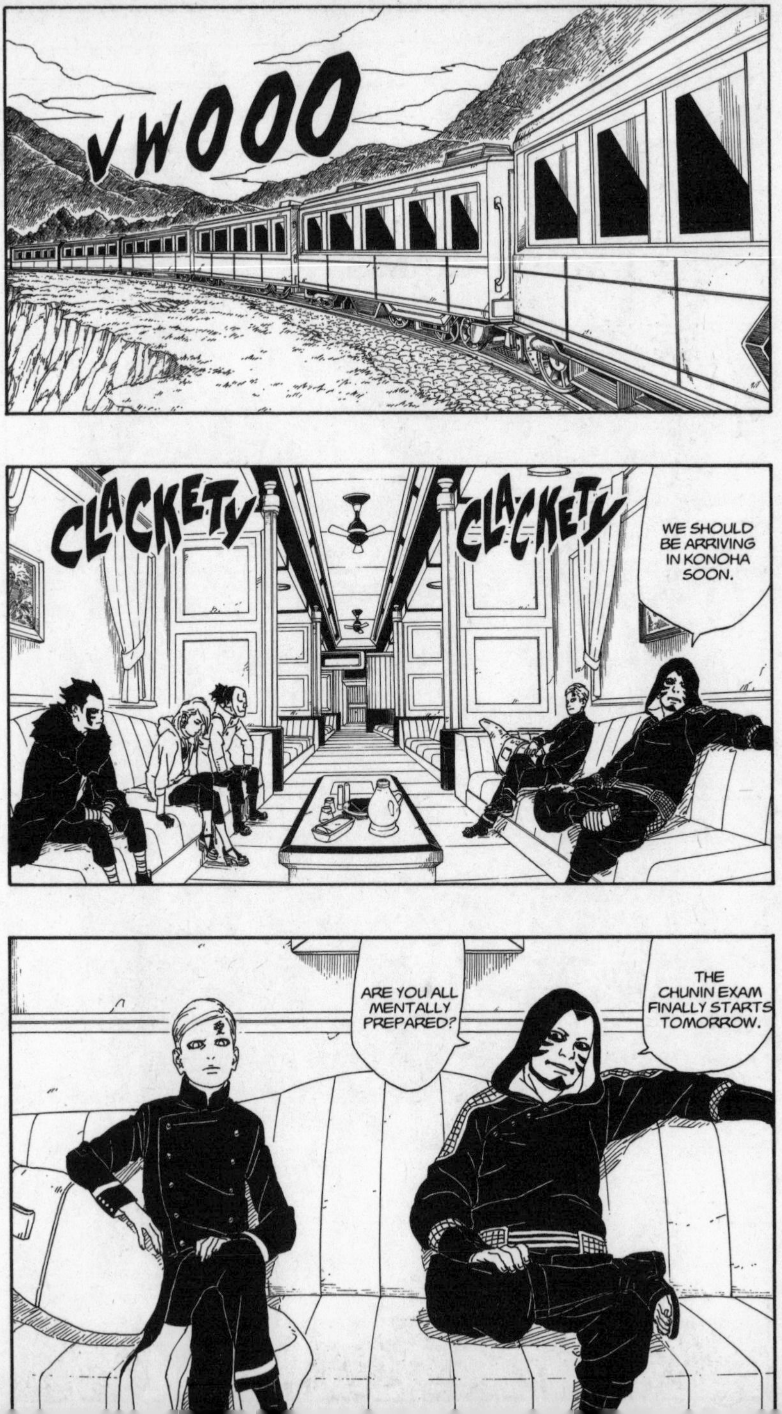
VWOOO
CLACKETY
CLACKETY
WE SHOULD BE ARRIVING IN KONOHA SOON.
THE CHUNIN EXAM FINALLY STARTS TOMORROW.
ARE YOU ALL MENTALLY PREPARED?

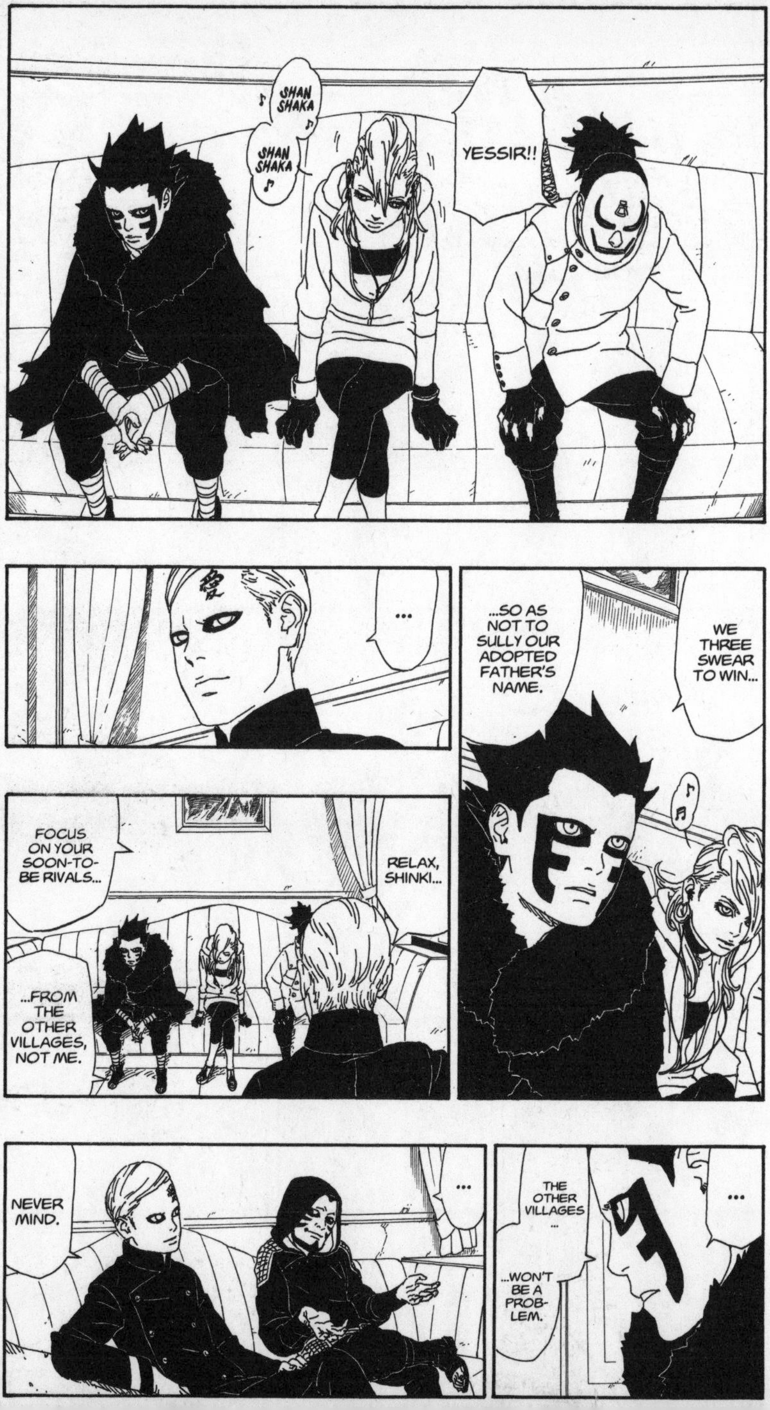
YESSIR!!
♪ SHAN SHAKA ♪
SHAN SHAKA ♪
WE THREE SWEAR TO WIN...
...SO AS NOT TO SULLY OUR ADOPTED FATHER'S NAME.
♪ ♪
...
RELAX, SHINKI...
FOCUS ON YOUR SOON-TO-BE RIVALS...
...FROM THE OTHER VILLAGES, NOT ME.
...
THE OTHER VILLAGES ...
...WON'T BE A PROB-LEM.
...
NEVER MIND.

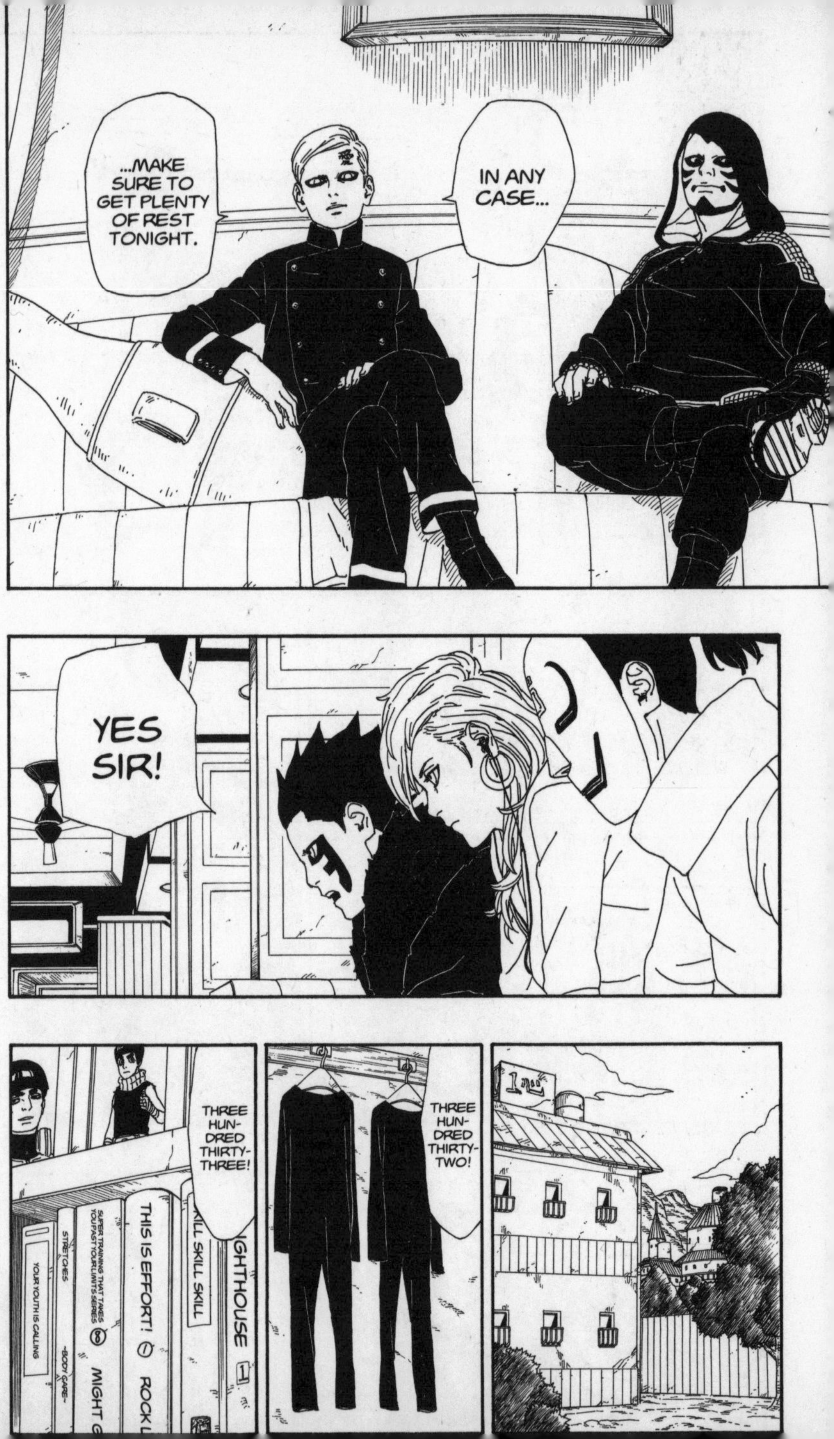
IN ANY CASE...
...MAKE SURE TO GET PLENTY OF REST TONIGHT.
YES SIR!
THREE HUNDRED THIRTY-TWO!
THREE HUNDRED THIRTY-THREE!
THIS IS EFFORT!
SUPER TRAINING THAT TAKES YOU PAST YOUR LIMITS SERIES
STRETCHES ~BODY CARE~
YOUR YOUTH IS CALLING

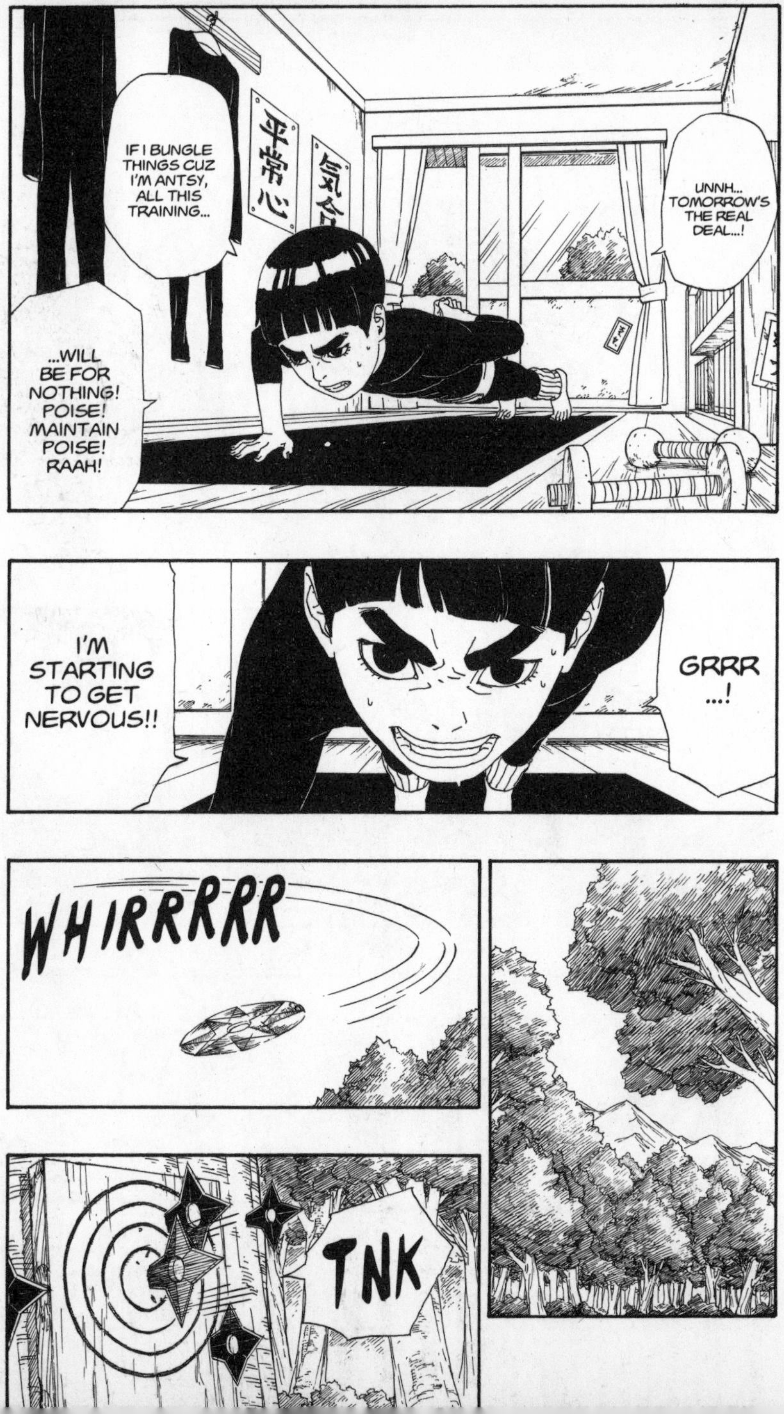
UNNH... TOMORROW'S THE REAL DEAL...!
IF I BUNGLE THINGS CUZ I'M ANTSY, ALL THIS TRAINING...
...WILL BE FOR NOTHING! POISE! MAINTAIN POISE! RAAH!
平常心
GRRR ...!
I'M STARTING TO GET NERVOUS!!
WHIRRRRR
TNK

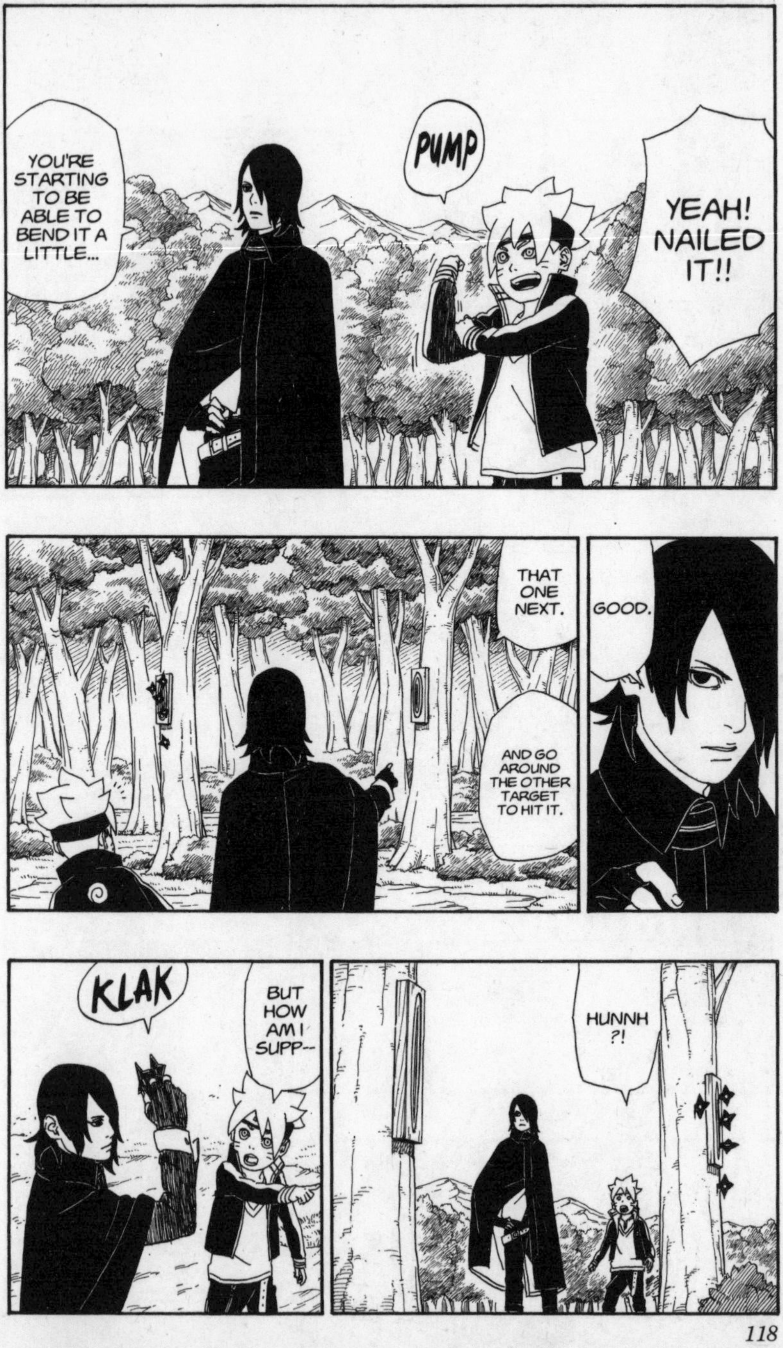
YEAH! NAILED IT!!
PUMP
YOU'RE STARTING TO BE ABLE TO BEND IT A LITTLE...
GOOD.
THAT ONE NEXT.
AND GO AROUND THE OTHER TARGET TO HIT IT.
HUNNH ?!
BUT HOW AM I SUPP--
KLAK

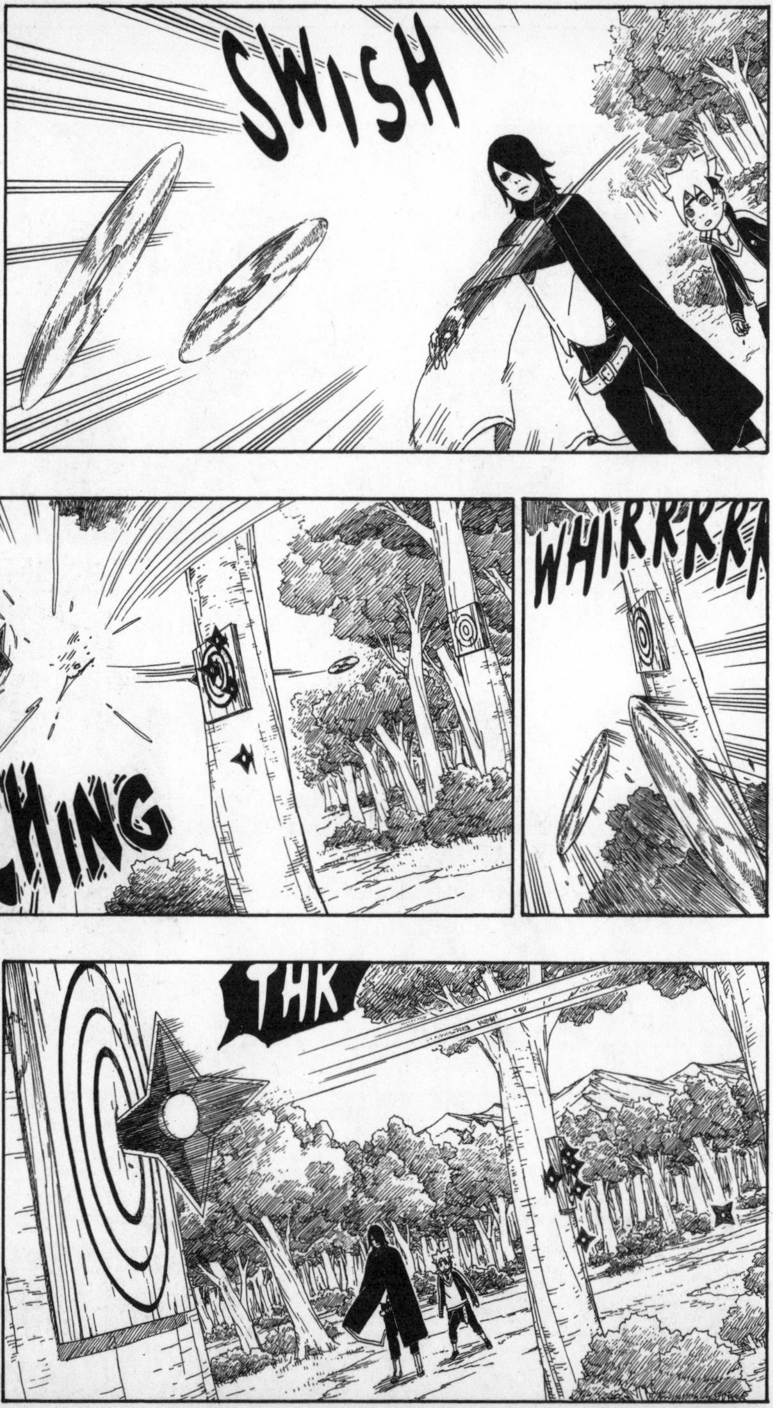
SWISH
WHIRRRR
CHING
THK

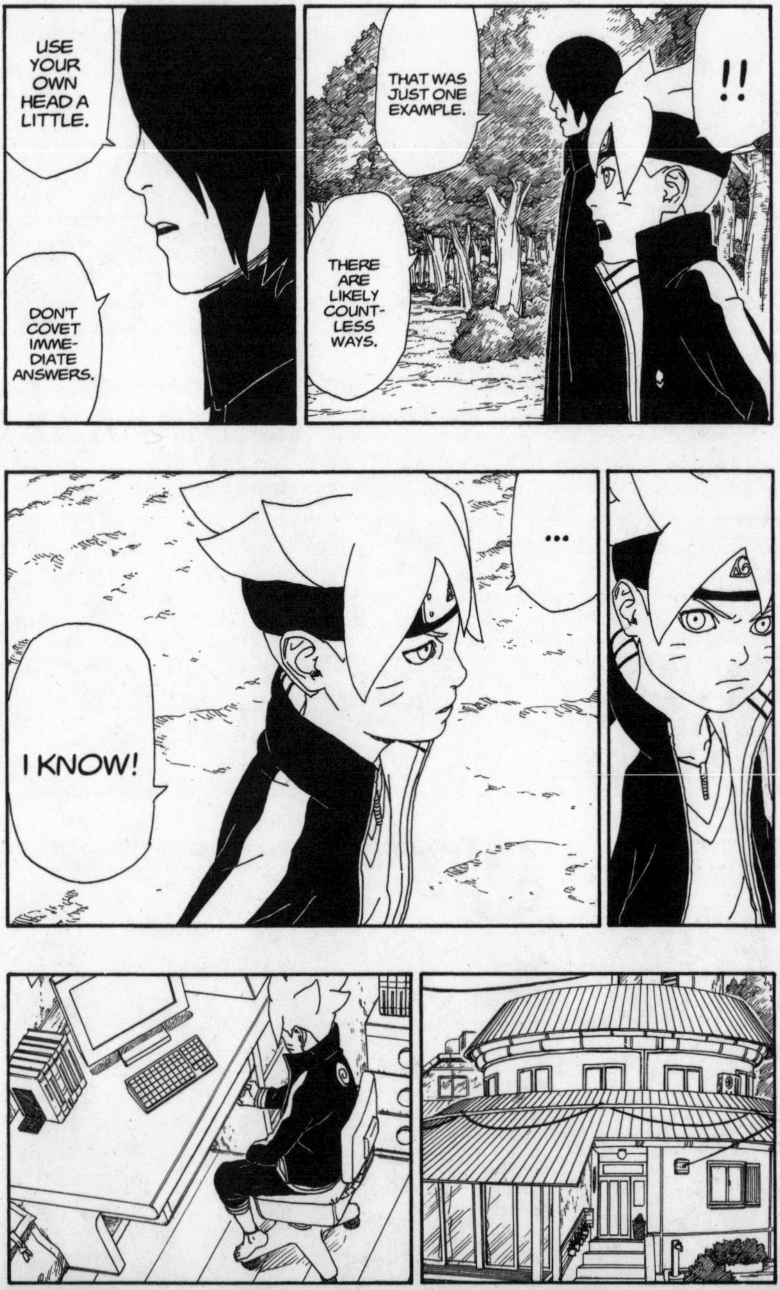
!!
THAT WAS JUST ONE EXAMPLE.
THERE ARE LIKELY COUNTLESS WAYS.
USE YOUR OWN HEAD A LITTLE.
DON'T COVET IMMEDIATE ANSWERS.
...
I KNOW!

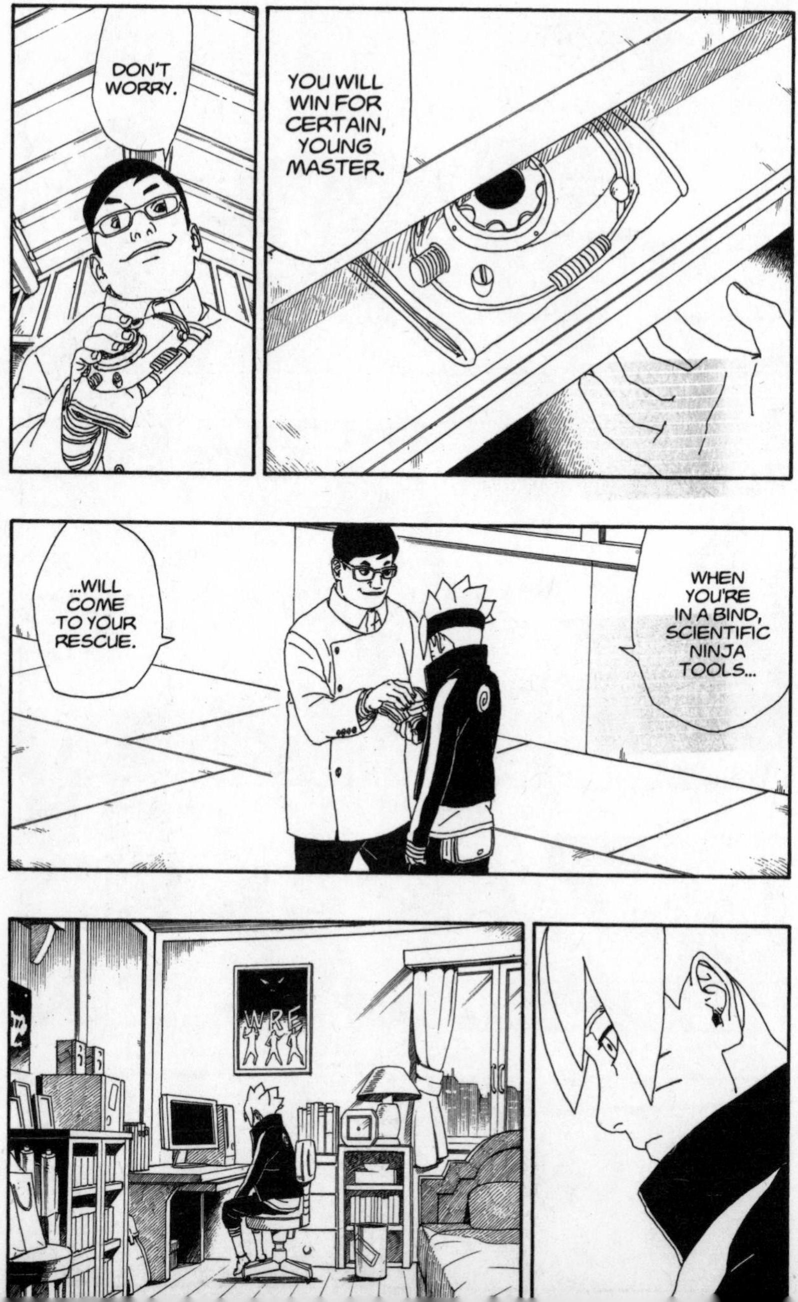
YOU WILL WIN FOR CERTAIN, YOUNG MASTER.
DON'T WORRY.
WHEN YOU'RE IN A BIND, SCIENTIFIC NINJA TOOLS...
...WILL COME TO YOUR RESCUE.

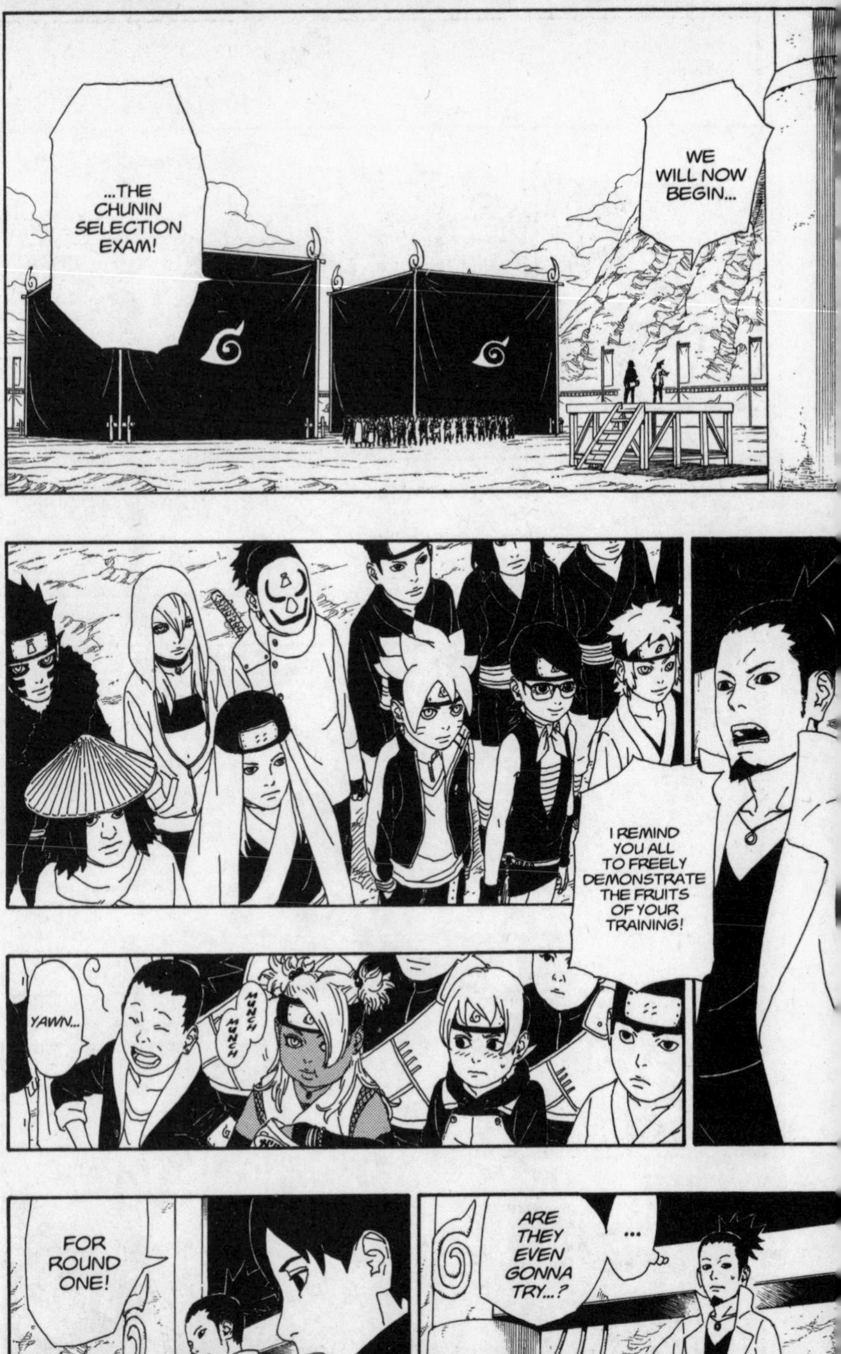
WE WILL NOW BEGIN...
...THE CHUNIN SELECTION EXAM!
I REMIND YOU ALL TO FREELY DEMONSTRATE THE FRUITS OF YOUR TRAINING!
MUNCH MUNCH
YAWN...
...
ARE THEY EVEN GONNA TRY...?
FOR ROUND ONE!

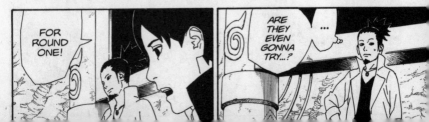

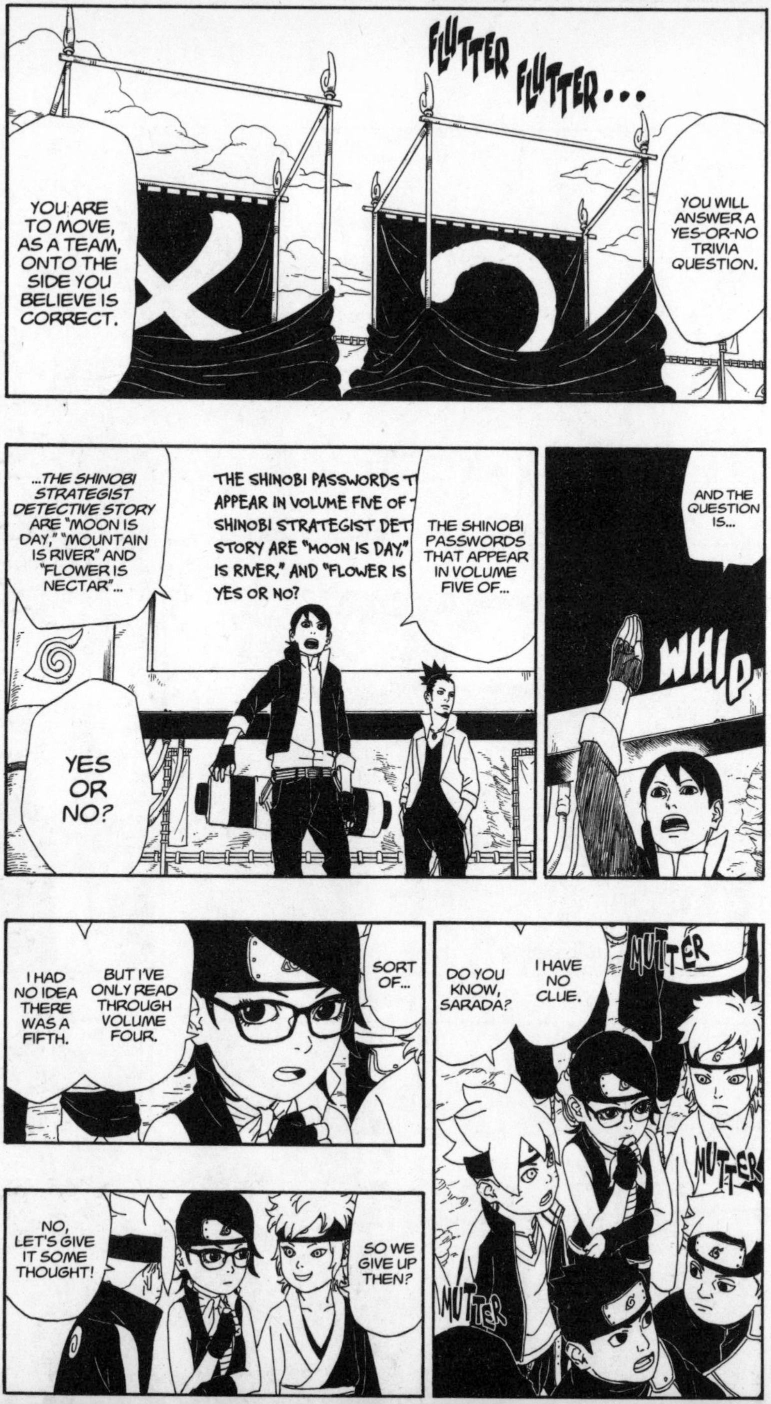
FLUTTER FLUTTER...
YOU WILL ANSWER A YES-OR-NO TRIVIA QUESTION.
YOU ARE TO MOVE, AS A TEAM, ONTO THE SIDE YOU BELIEVE IS CORRECT.
AND THE QUESTION IS...
WHIP
THE SHINOBI PASSWORDS THAT APPEAR IN VOLUME FIVE OF...
THE SHINOBI PASSWORDS T
APPEAR IN VOLUME FIVE OF
SHINOBI STRATEGIST DET
STORY ARE "MOON IS DAY,"
IS RIVER," AND "FLOWER IS
YES OR NO?
...THE SHINOBI STRATEGIST DETECTIVE STORY ARE "MOON IS DAY," "MOUNTAIN IS RIVER" AND "FLOWER IS NECTAR"...
YES OR NO?
MUTTER
I HAVE NO CLUE.
DO YOU KNOW, SARADA?
MUTTER
MUTTER
SORT OF...
BUT I'VE ONLY READ THROUGH VOLUME FOUR.
I HAD NO IDEA THERE WAS A FIFTH.
SO WE GIVE UP THEN?
NO, LET'S GIVE IT SOME THOUGHT!

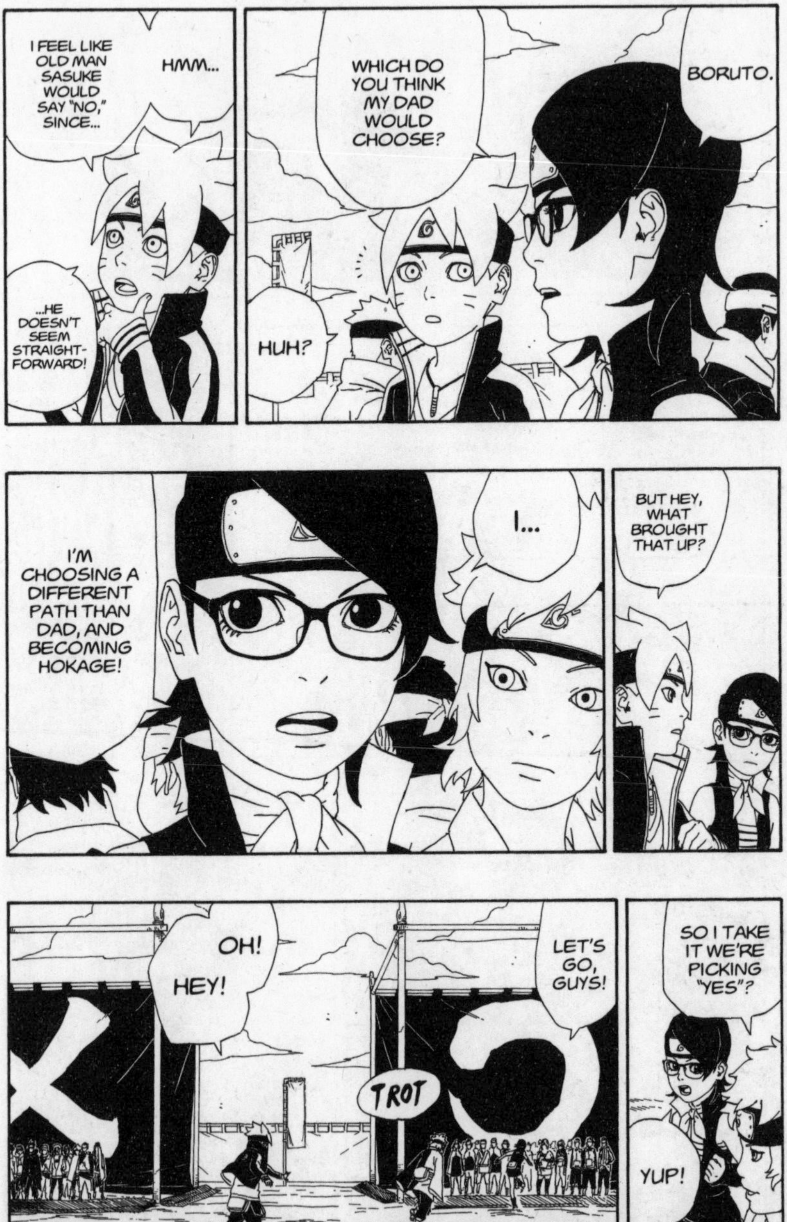
BORUTO.
WHICH DO YOU THINK MY DAD WOULD CHOOSE?
HUH?
HMM...
I FEEL LIKE OLD MAN SASUKE WOULD SAY "NO," SINCE...
...HE DOESN'T SEEM STRAIGHT-FORWARD!
BUT HEY, WHAT BROUGHT THAT UP?
I...
I'M CHOOSING A DIFFERENT PATH THAN DAD, AND BECOMING HOKAGE!
SO I TAKE IT WE'RE PICKING "YES"?
YUP!
LET'S GO, GUYS!
TROT
OH!
HEY!

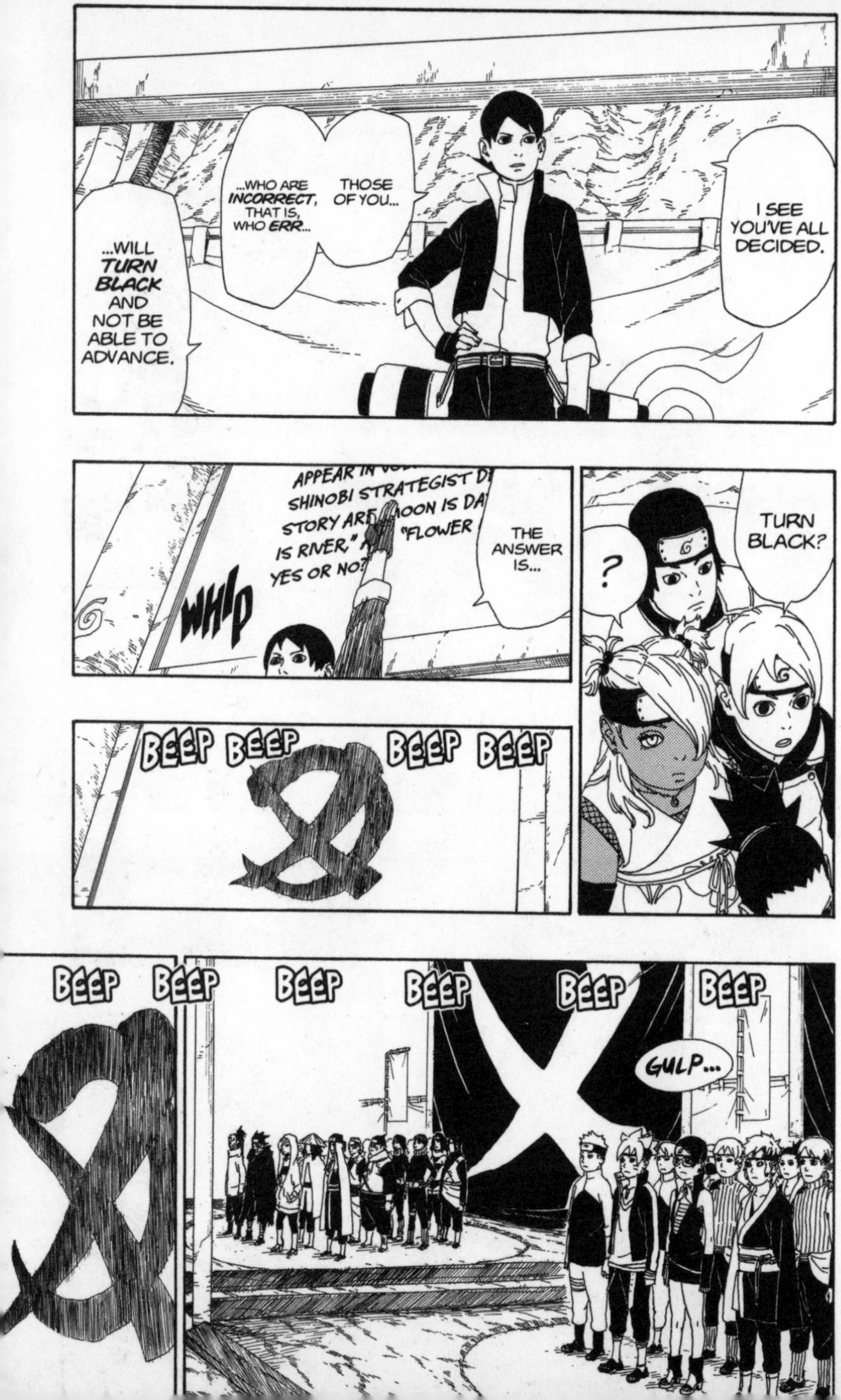
I SEE YOU'VE ALL DECIDED.
THOSE OF YOU...
...WHO ARE **INCORRECT**, THAT IS, WHO **ERR**...
...WILL **TURN BLACK** AND NOT BE ABLE TO ADVANCE.
TURN BLACK?
?
THE ANSWER IS...
YES OR NO?
WHIP
BEEP BEEP
BEEP BEEP
BEEP
BEEP
BEEP
BEEP
BEEP
BEEP
GULP...

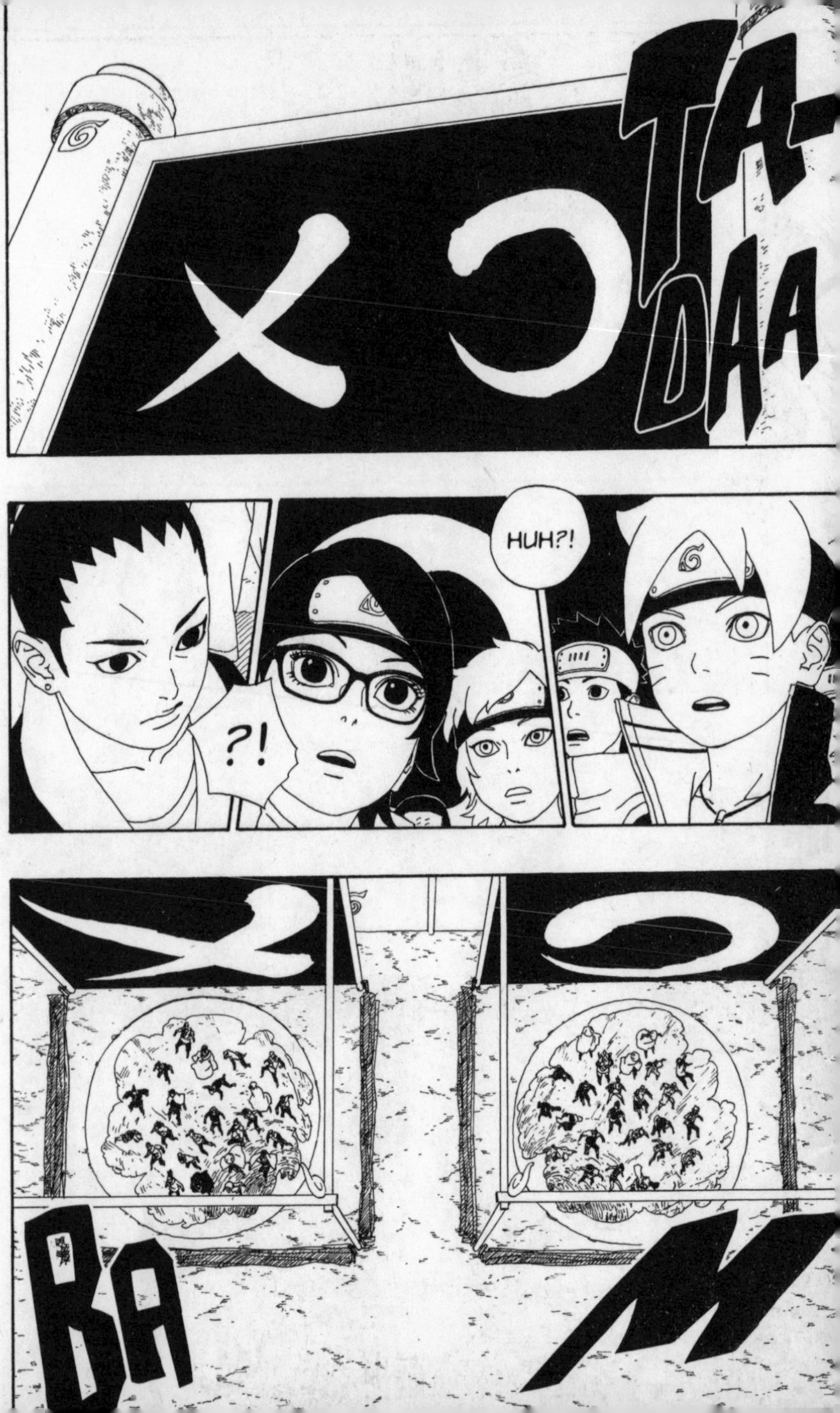
TA-DAA
HUH?!
?!
BAM

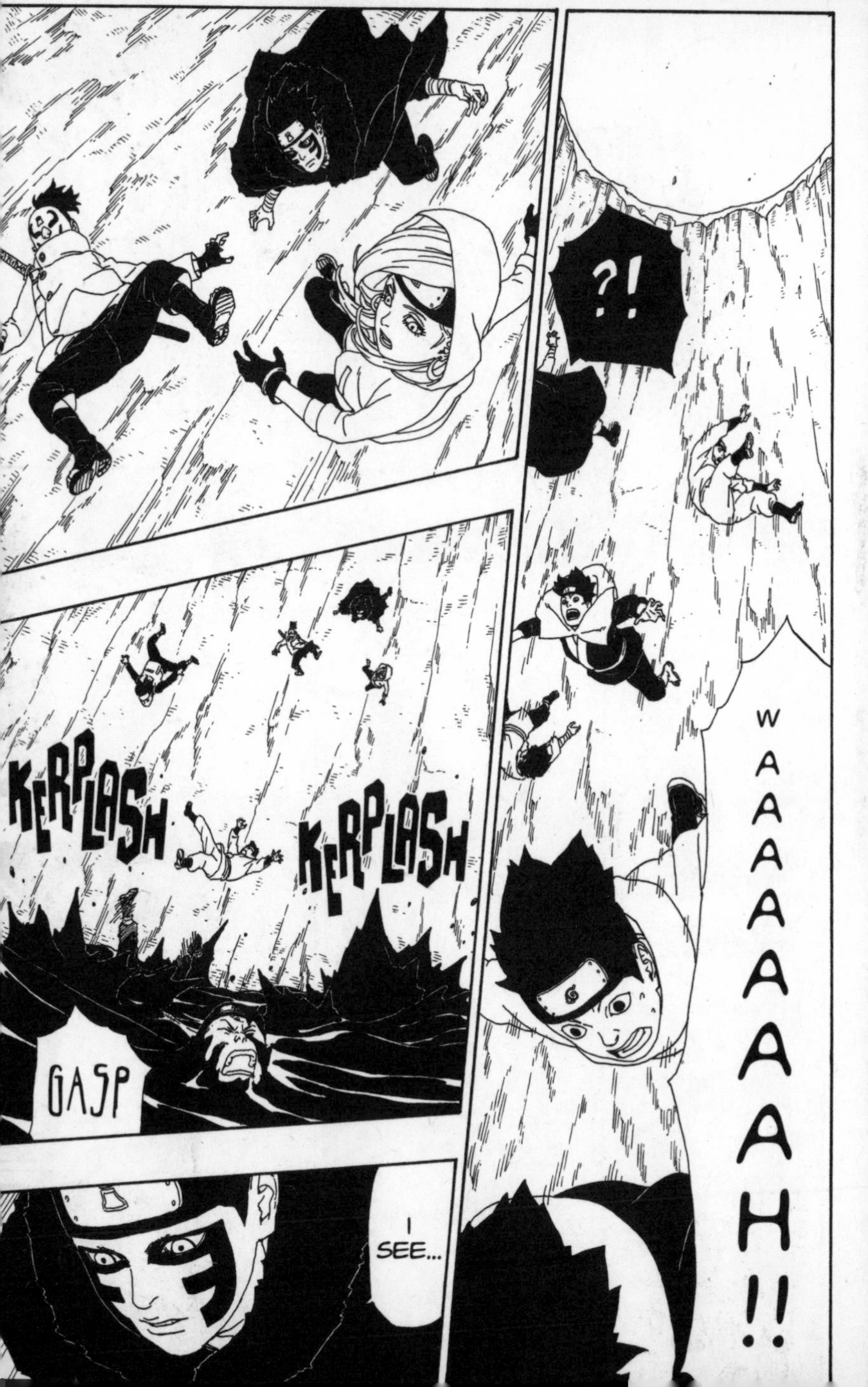

?!
WAAAAAAAH!!
KERPLASH
KERPLASH
GASP
I SEE...

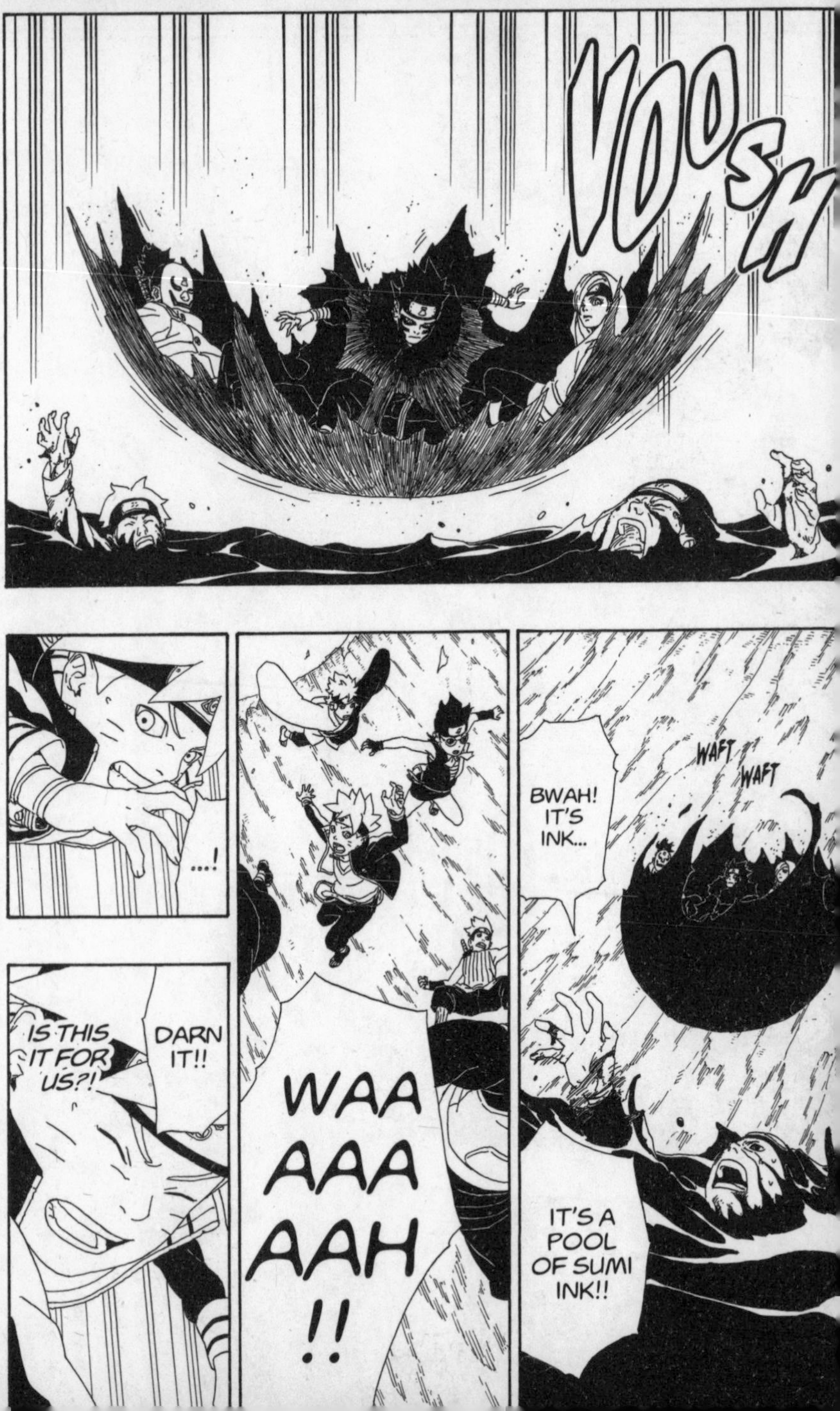
VOOSH
WAFT
WAFT
BWAH! IT'S INK...
IT'S A POOL OF SUMI INK!!
WAAAAAAAH!!
...!
DARN IT!!
IS THIS IT FOR US?!

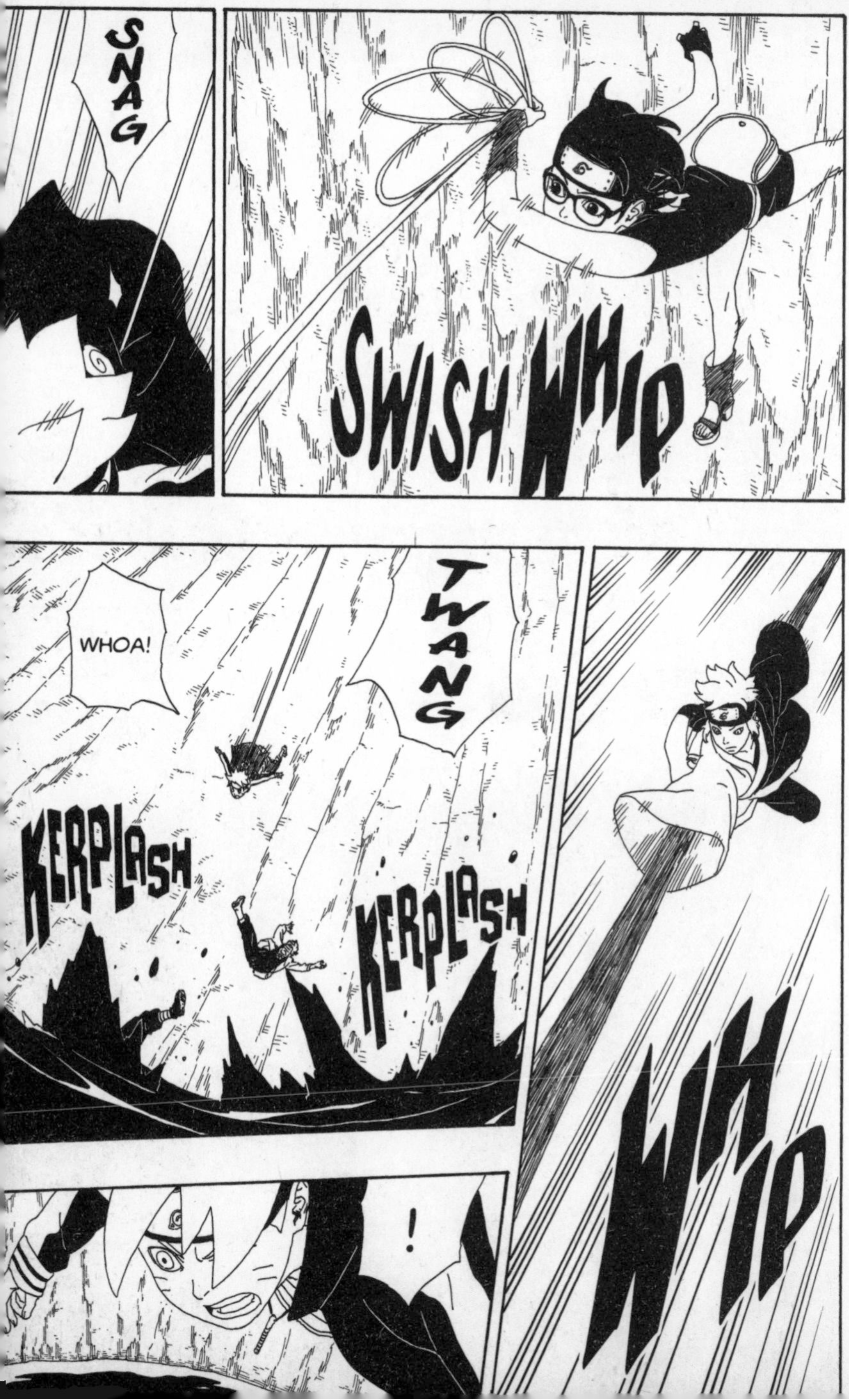
SWISH
WHIP
SNAG
WHIP
TWANG
WHOA!
KERPLASH
KERPLASH
!

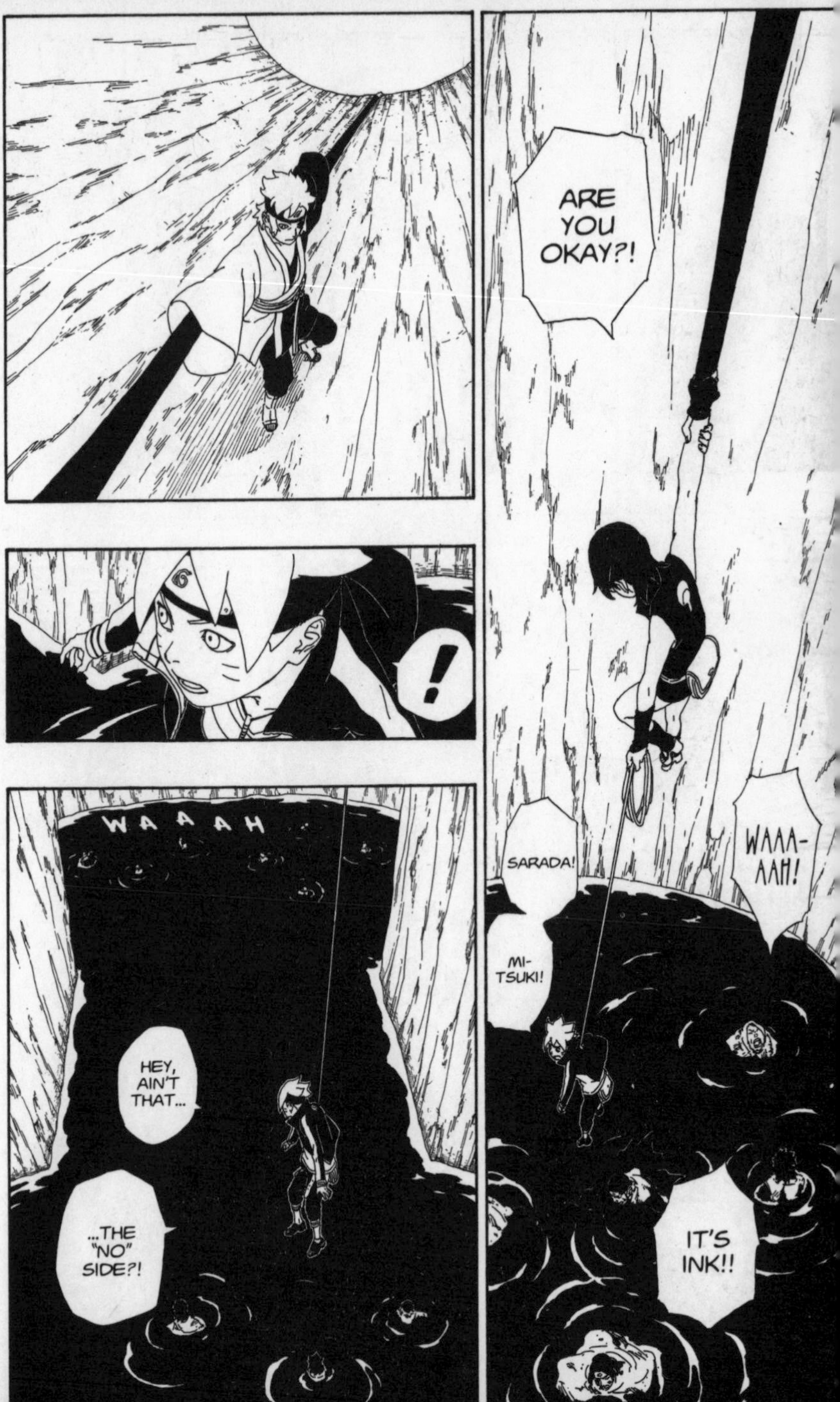
ARE YOU OKAY?!
WAAA-AAH!
SARADA!
MI-TSUKI!
IT'S INK!!
!
WAAAH
HEY, AIN'T THAT...
...THE "NO" SIDE?!

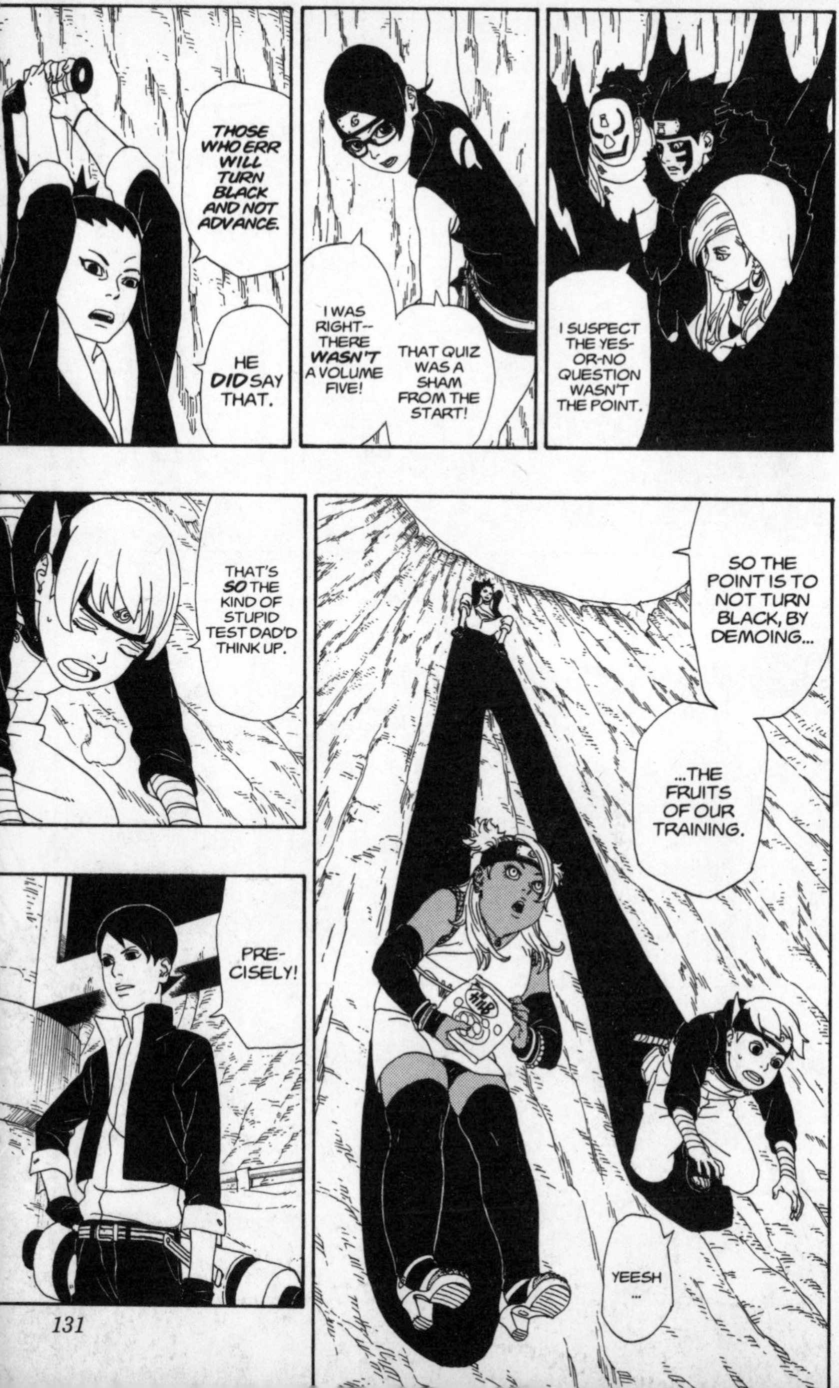
I SUSPECT THE YES-OR-NO QUESTION WASN'T THE POINT.
I WAS RIGHT-- THERE WASN'T A VOLUME FIVE!
THAT QUIZ WAS A SHAM FROM THE START!
THOSE WHO ERR WILL TURN BLACK AND NOT ADVANCE.
HE DID SAY THAT.
SO THE POINT IS TO NOT TURN BLACK, BY DEMOING...
...THE FRUITS OF OUR TRAINING.
YEESH...
THAT'S SO THE KIND OF STUPID TEST DAD'D THINK UP.
PRE-CISELY!

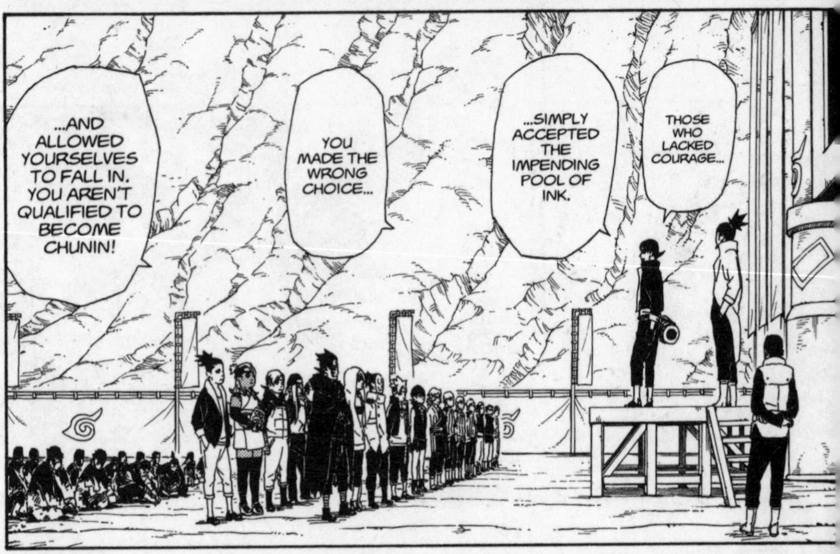
THOSE WHO LACKED COURAGE...
...SIMPLY ACCEPTED THE IMPENDING POOL OF INK.
YOU MADE THE WRONG CHOICE...
...AND ALLOWED YOURSELVES TO FALL IN. YOU AREN'T QUALIFIED TO BECOME CHUNIN!

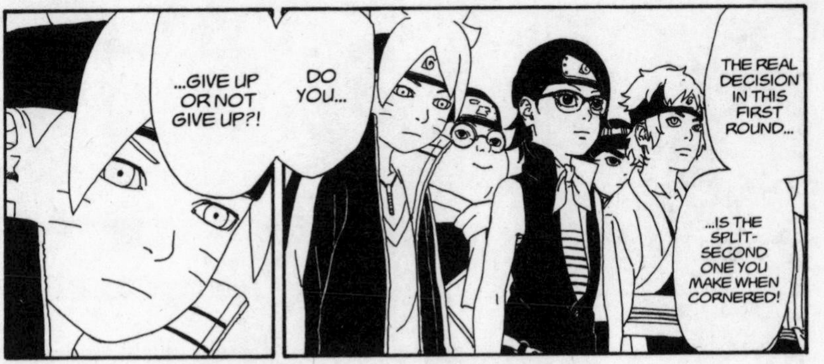
THE REAL DECISION IN THIS FIRST ROUND...
...IS THE SPLIT-SECOND ONE YOU MAKE WHEN CORNERED!
DO YOU...
...GIVE UP OR NOT GIVE UP?!

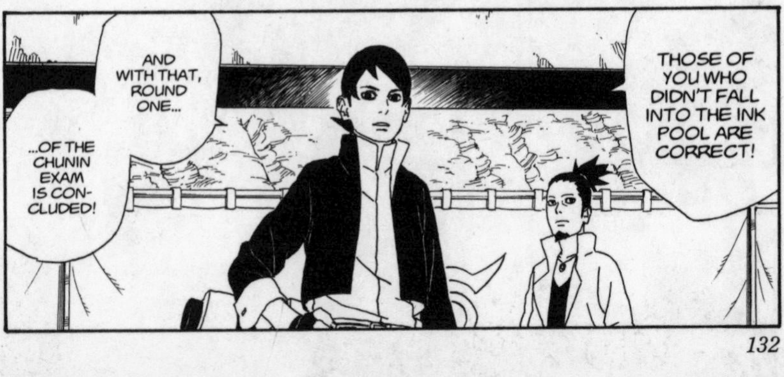
THOSE OF YOU WHO DIDN'T FALL INTO THE INK POOL ARE CORRECT!
AND WITH THAT, ROUND ONE...
...OF THE CHUNIN EXAM IS CONCLUDED!

KLENCH

...

YES!

WE MADE IT.

FSH

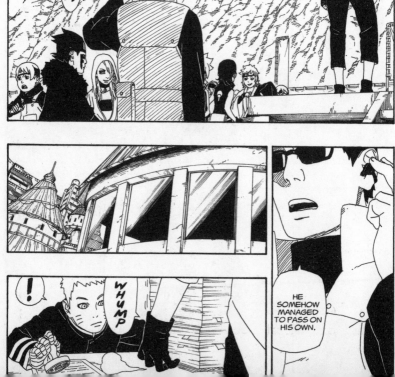

HE SOMEHOW MANAGED TO PASS ON HIS OWN.

!

WHUMP

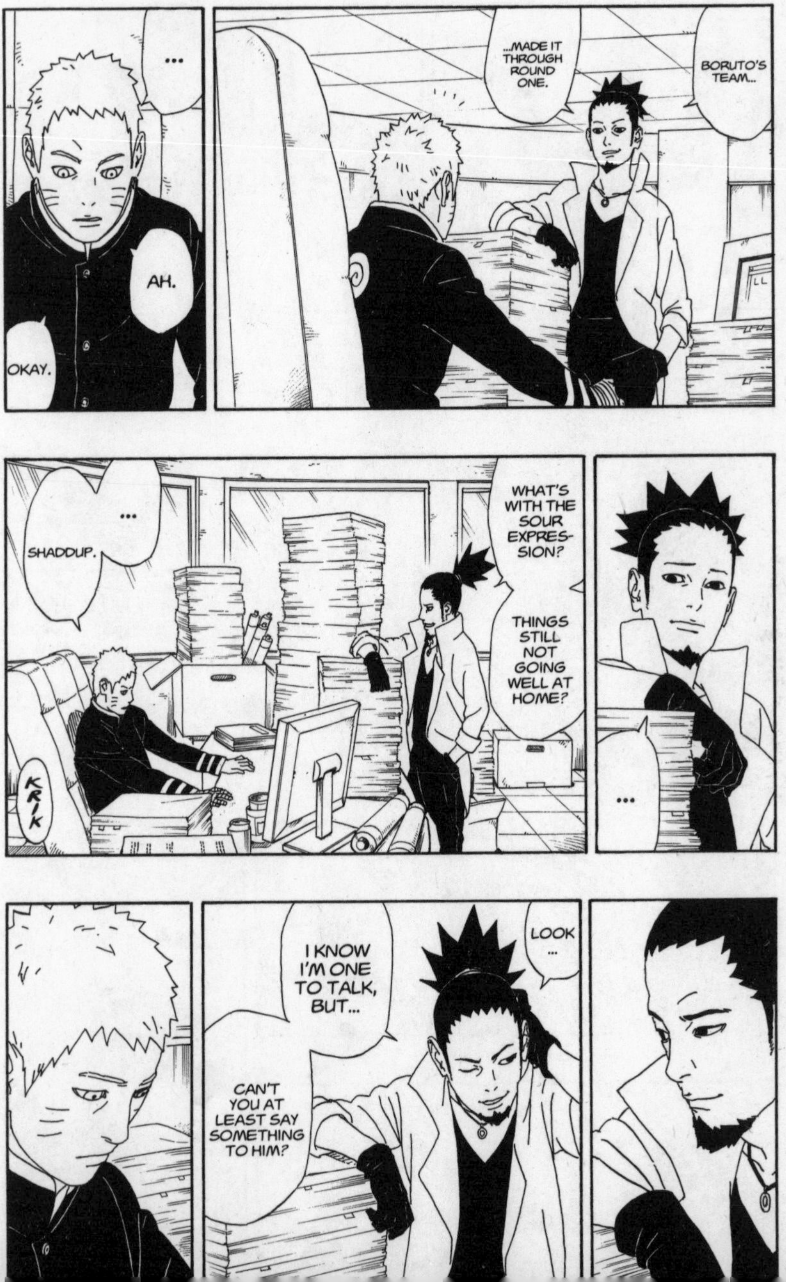
BORUTO'S TEAM...
...MADE IT THROUGH ROUND ONE.
...
AH.
OKAY.
...
WHAT'S WITH THE SOUR EXPRES-SION?
THINGS STILL NOT GOING WELL AT HOME?
...
SHADDUP.
KRIK
LOOK...
I KNOW I'M ONE TO TALK, BUT...
CAN'T YOU AT LEAST SAY SOMETHING TO HIM?

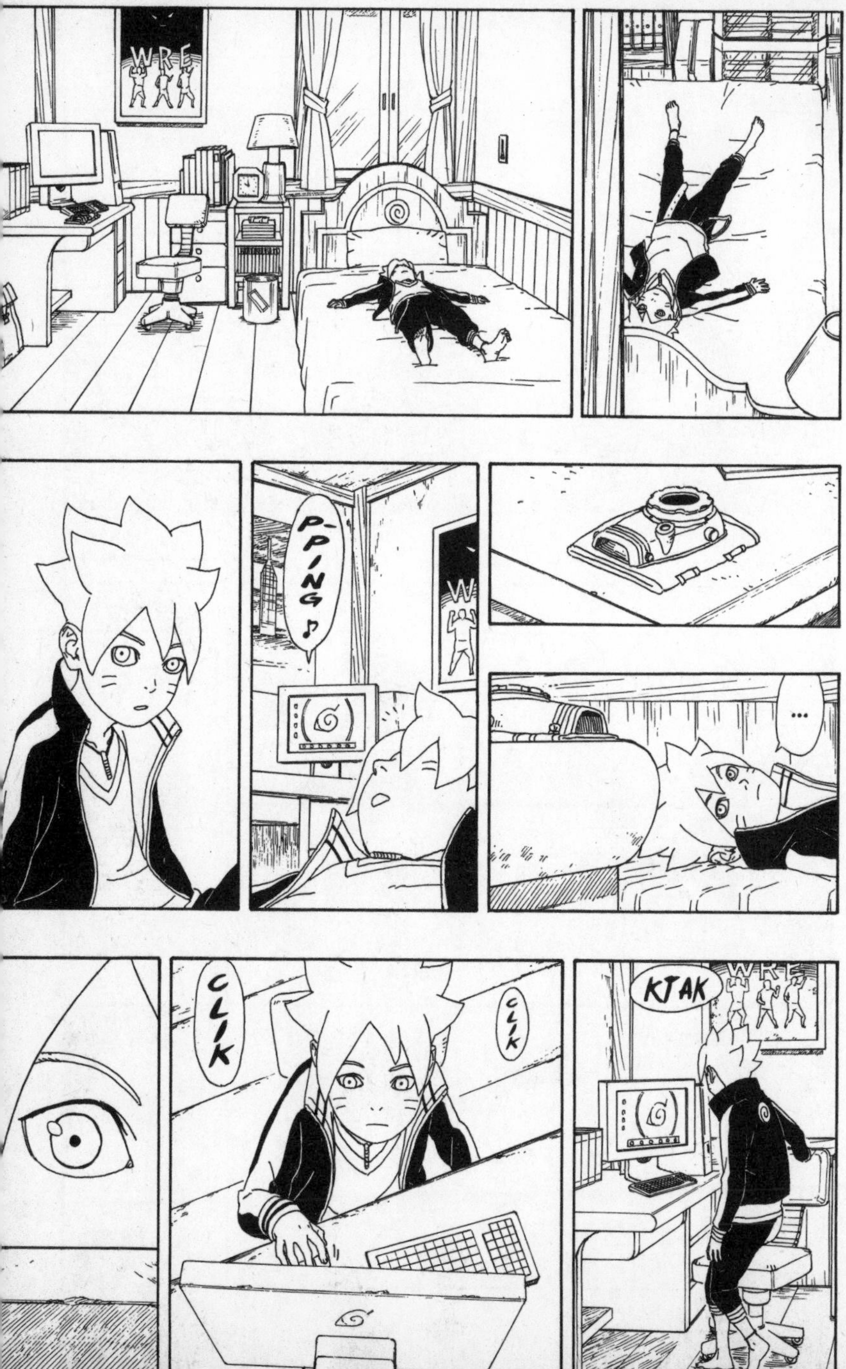
WRE
...
P-PING ♪
KJAK
CLIK
CLIK

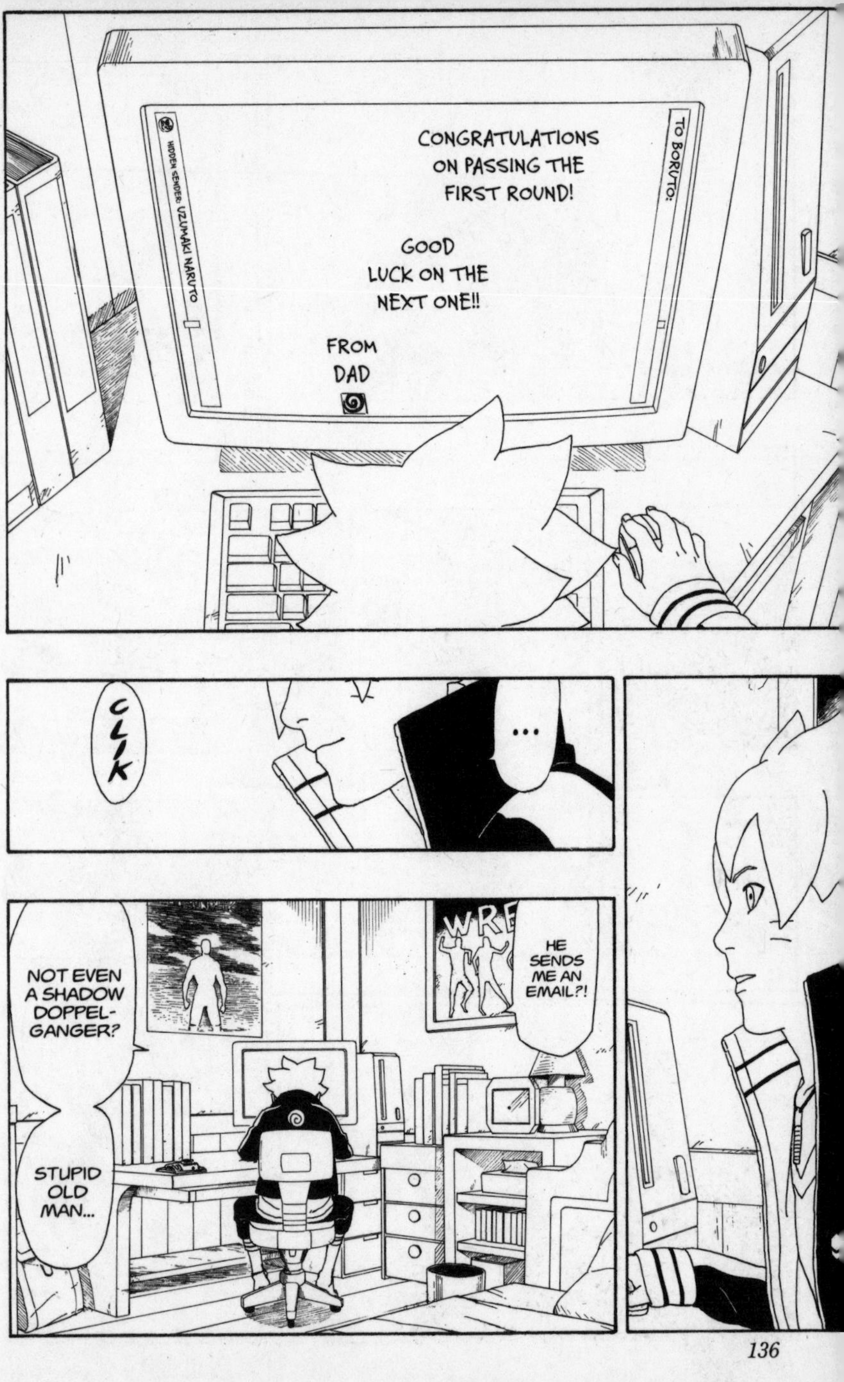
TO BORUTO:
CONGRATULATIONS ON PASSING THE FIRST ROUND!
GOOD LUCK ON THE NEXT ONE!!
FROM DAD
HIDDEN SENDER: UZUMAKI NARUTO
CLIK
...
HE SENDS ME AN EMAIL?!
NOT EVEN A SHADOW DOPPEL-GANGER?
STUPID OLD MAN...

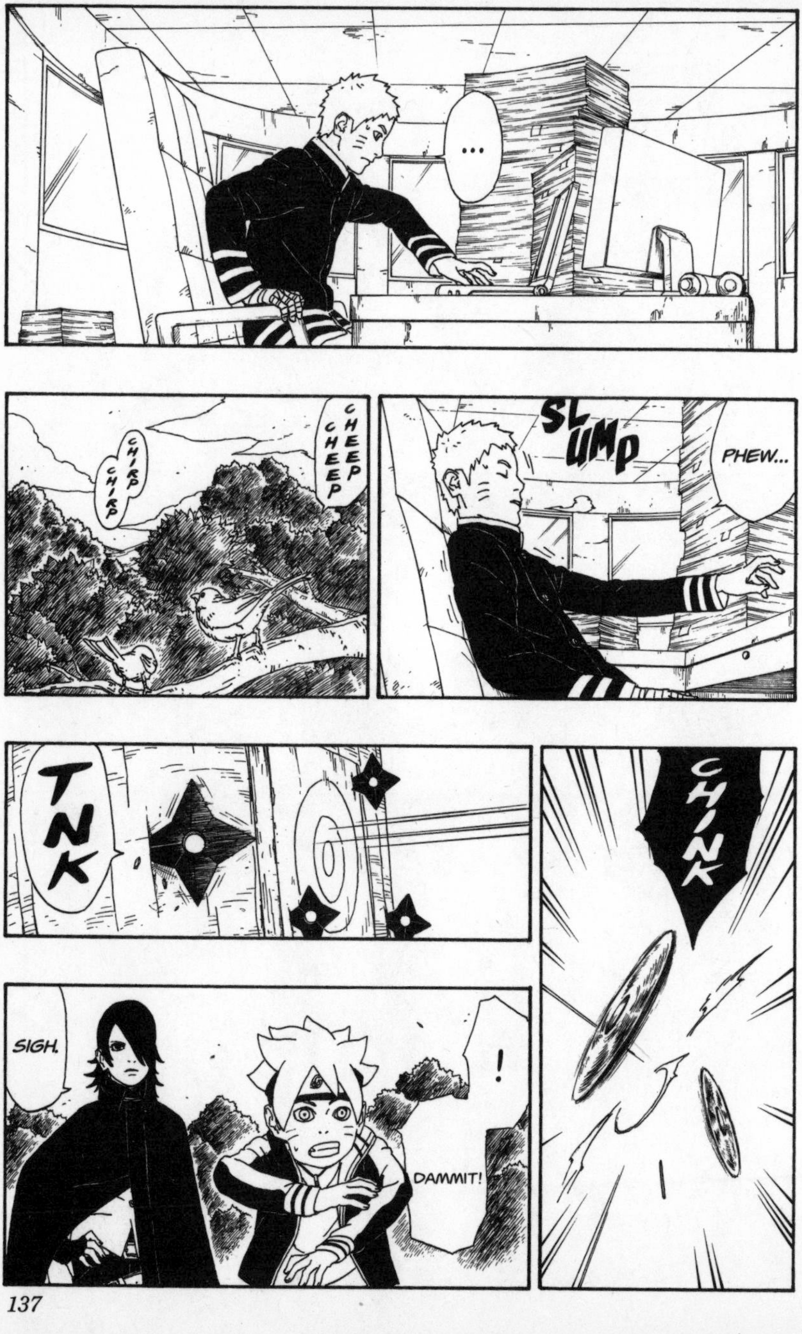
...
SLUMP
PHEW...
CHEEP CHEEP
CHIRP CHIRP
CHINK
TNK
!
DAMMIT!
SIGH.

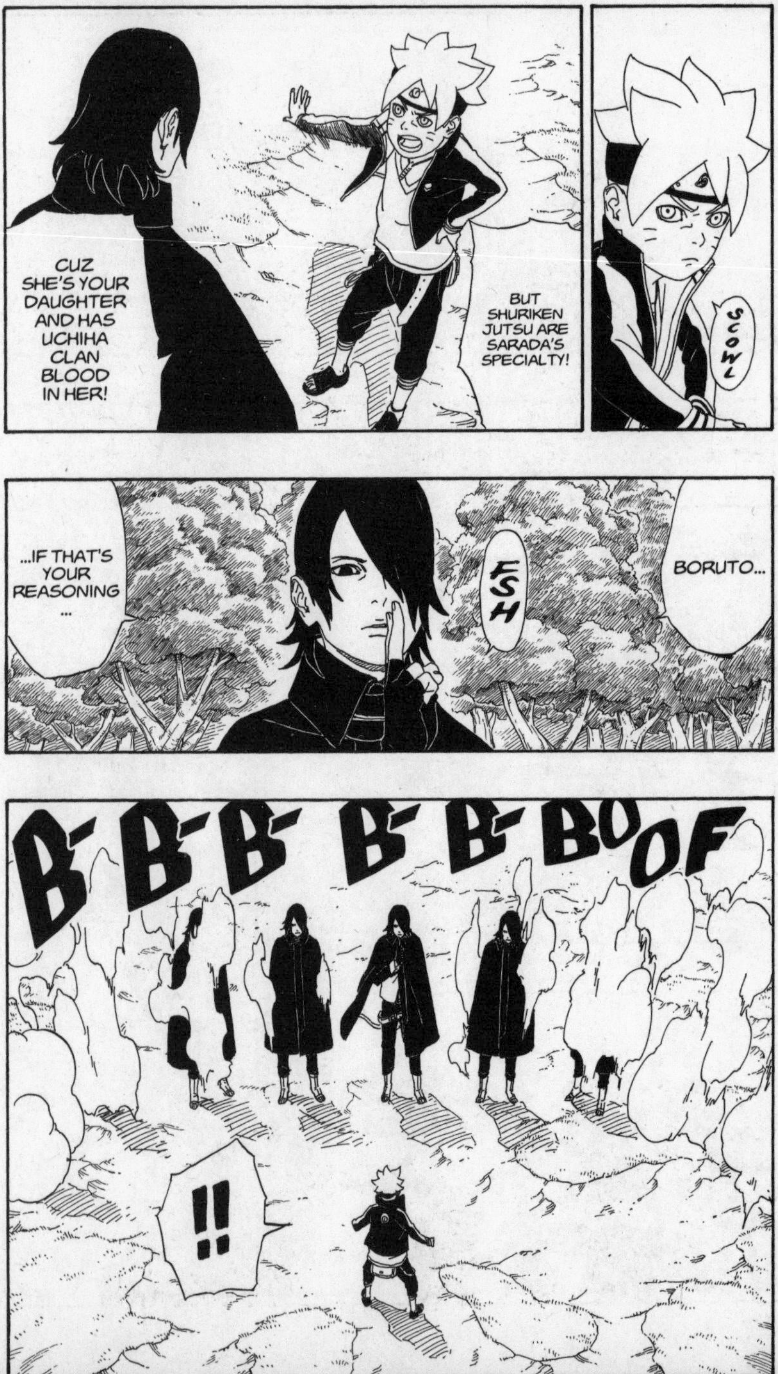
SCOWL
BUT SHURIKEN JUTSU ARE SARADA'S SPECIALTY!
CUZ SHE'S YOUR DAUGHTER AND HAS UCHIHA CLAN BLOOD IN HER!
BORUTO...
FSH
...IF THAT'S YOUR REASONING ...
B-B-B- B-B-BOOF
!!

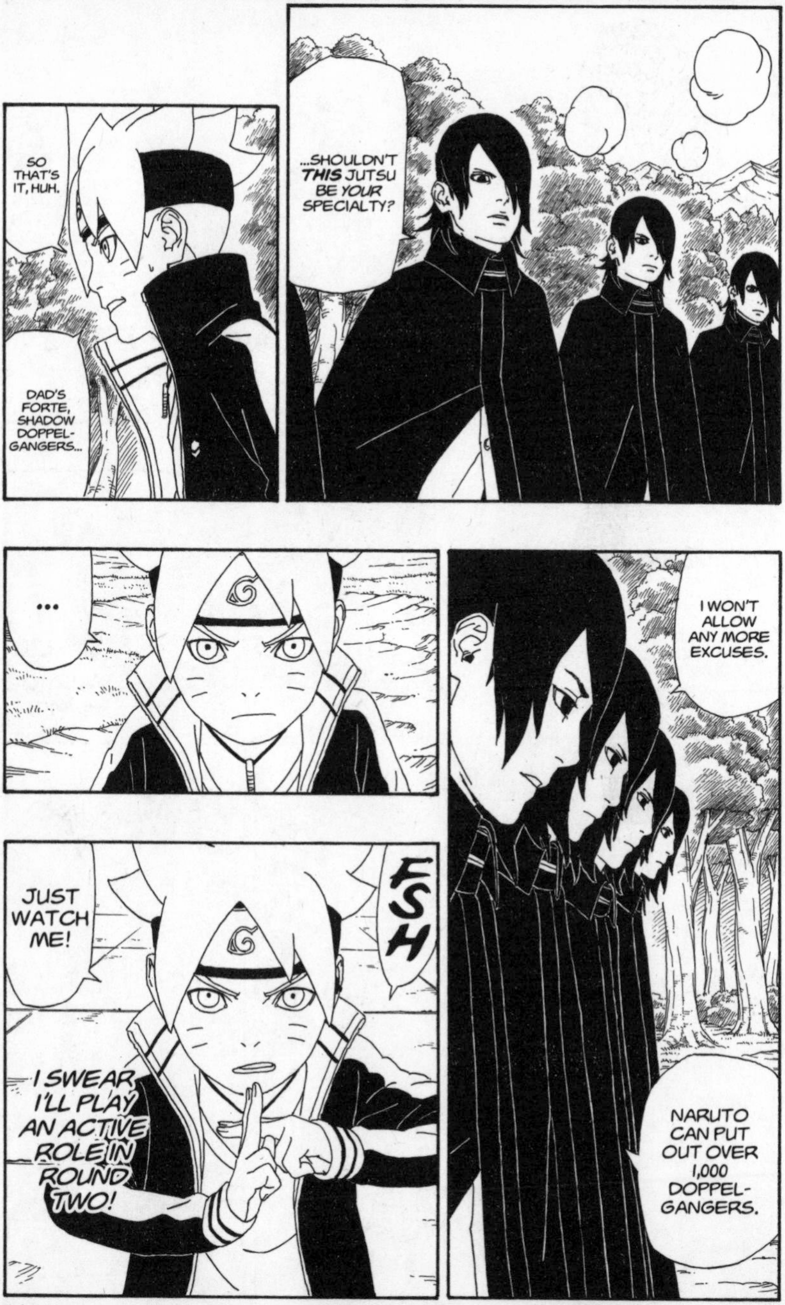
...SHOULDN'T THIS JUTSU BE YOUR SPECIALTY?
SO THAT'S IT, HUH.
DAD'S FORTE, SHADOW DOPPEL-GANGERS...
I WON'T ALLOW ANY MORE EXCUSES.
NARUTO CAN PUT OUT OVER 1,000 DOPPEL-GANGERS.
...
JUST WATCH ME!
FSH
I SWEAR I'LL PLAY AN ACTIVE ROLE IN ROUND TWO!

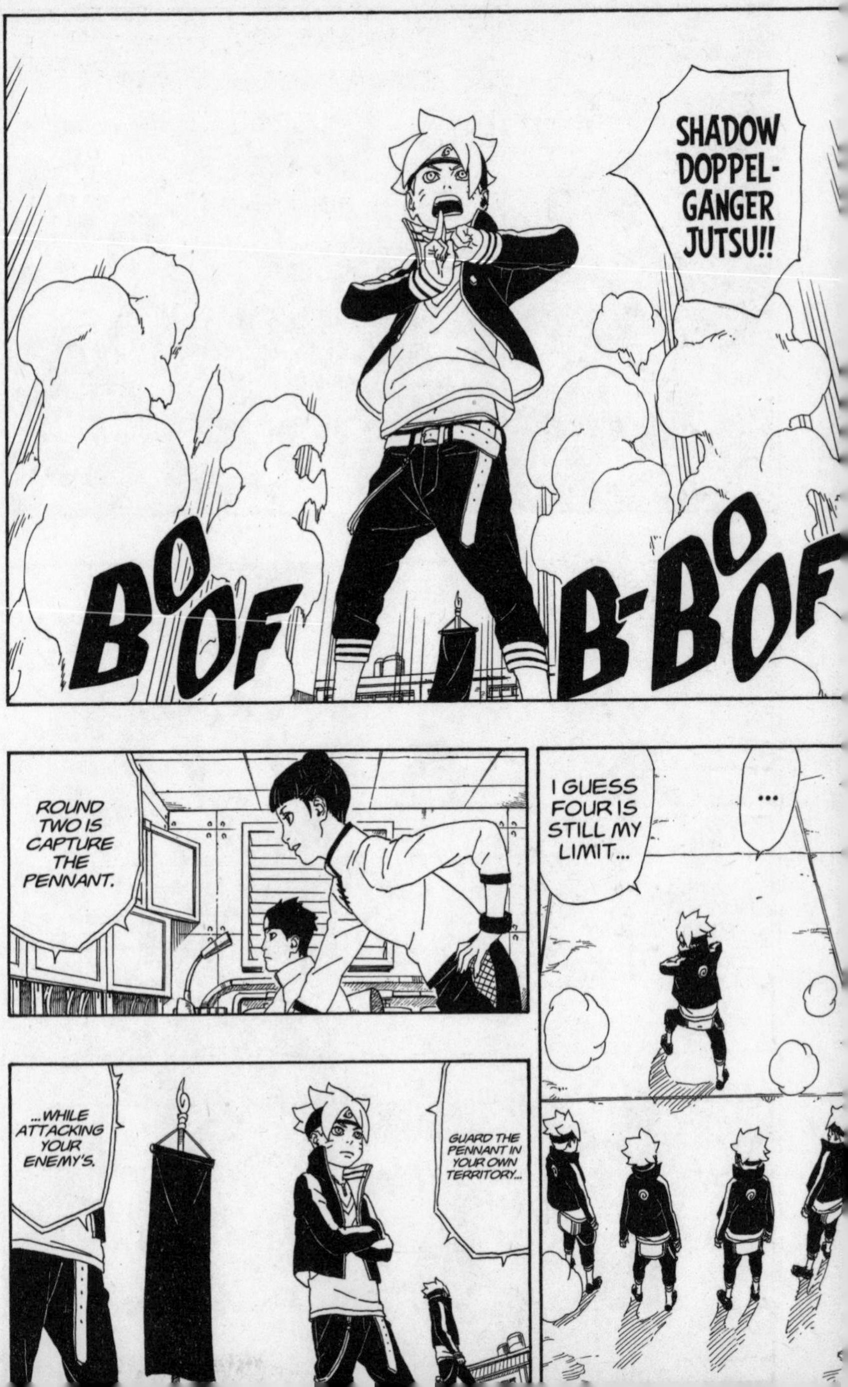
SHADOW DOPPEL-GANGER JUTSU!!
B-BOOF
BOOF
...
I GUESS FOUR IS STILL MY LIMIT...
ROUND TWO IS CAPTURE THE PENNANT.
GUARD THE PENNANT IN YOUR OWN TERRITORY...
...WHILE ATTACKING YOUR ENEMY'S.

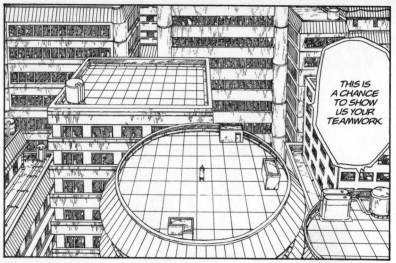

THIS IS A CHANCE TO SHOW US YOUR TEAMWORK.

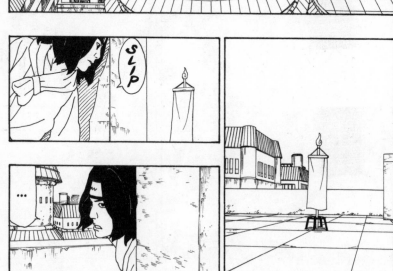

SLIP

...

TAK

GOTCHA!!

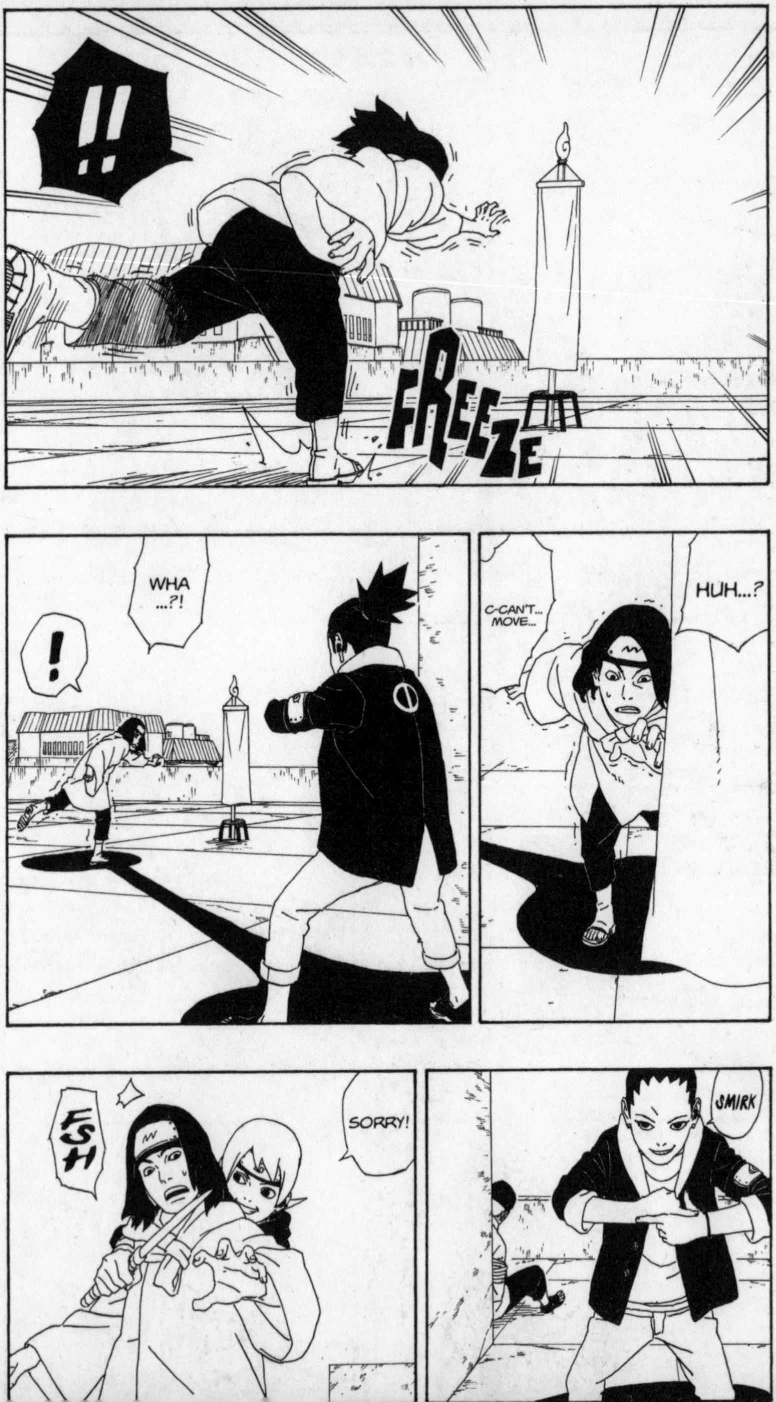
!!
FREEZE
HUH...?
C-CAN'T... MOVE...
WHA ...?!
!
SMIRK
SORRY!
FSH

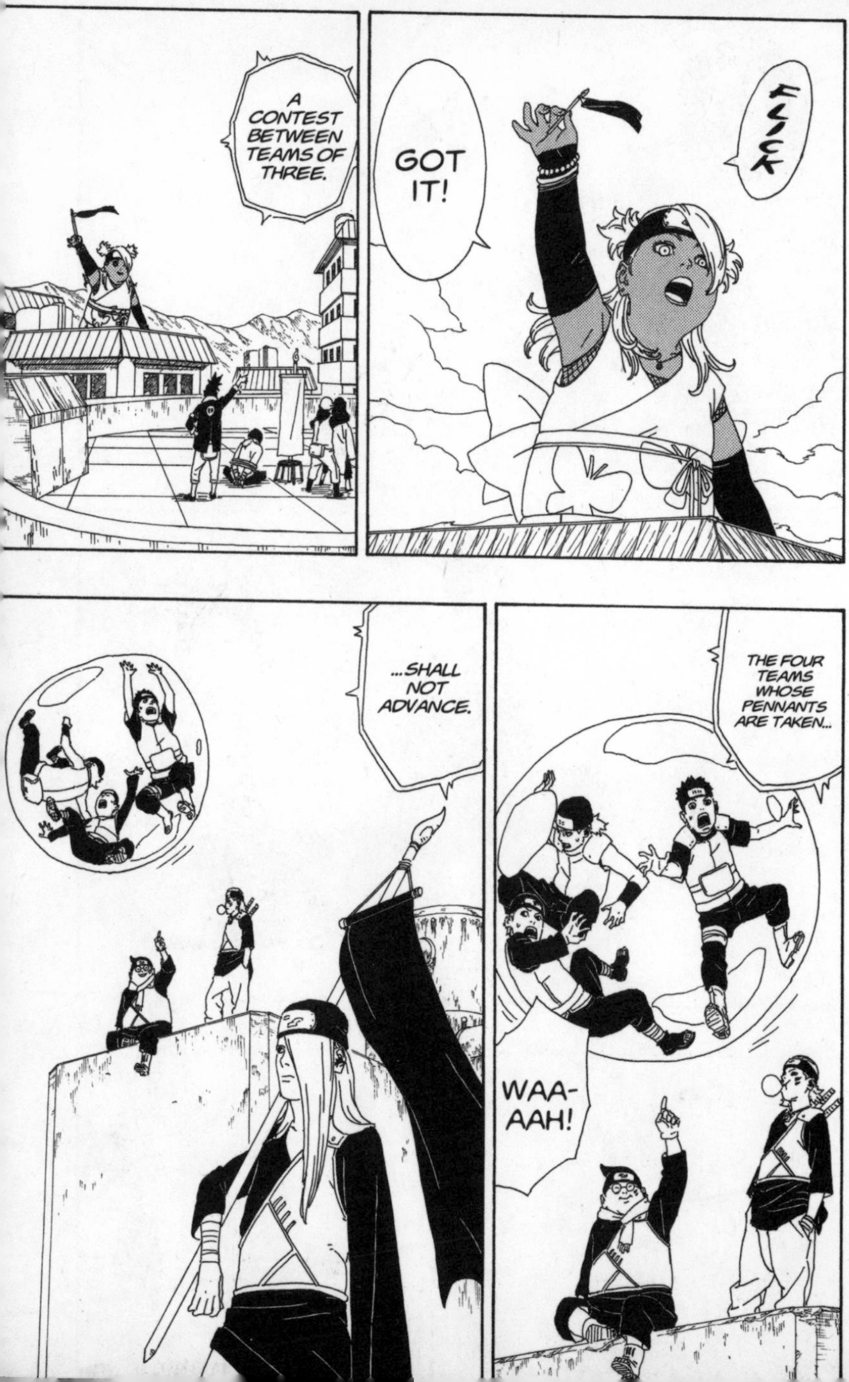
FLICK
GOT IT!
A CONTEST BETWEEN TEAMS OF THREE.
THE FOUR TEAMS WHOSE PENNANTS ARE TAKEN...
WAA-AAH!
...SHALL NOT ADVANCE.

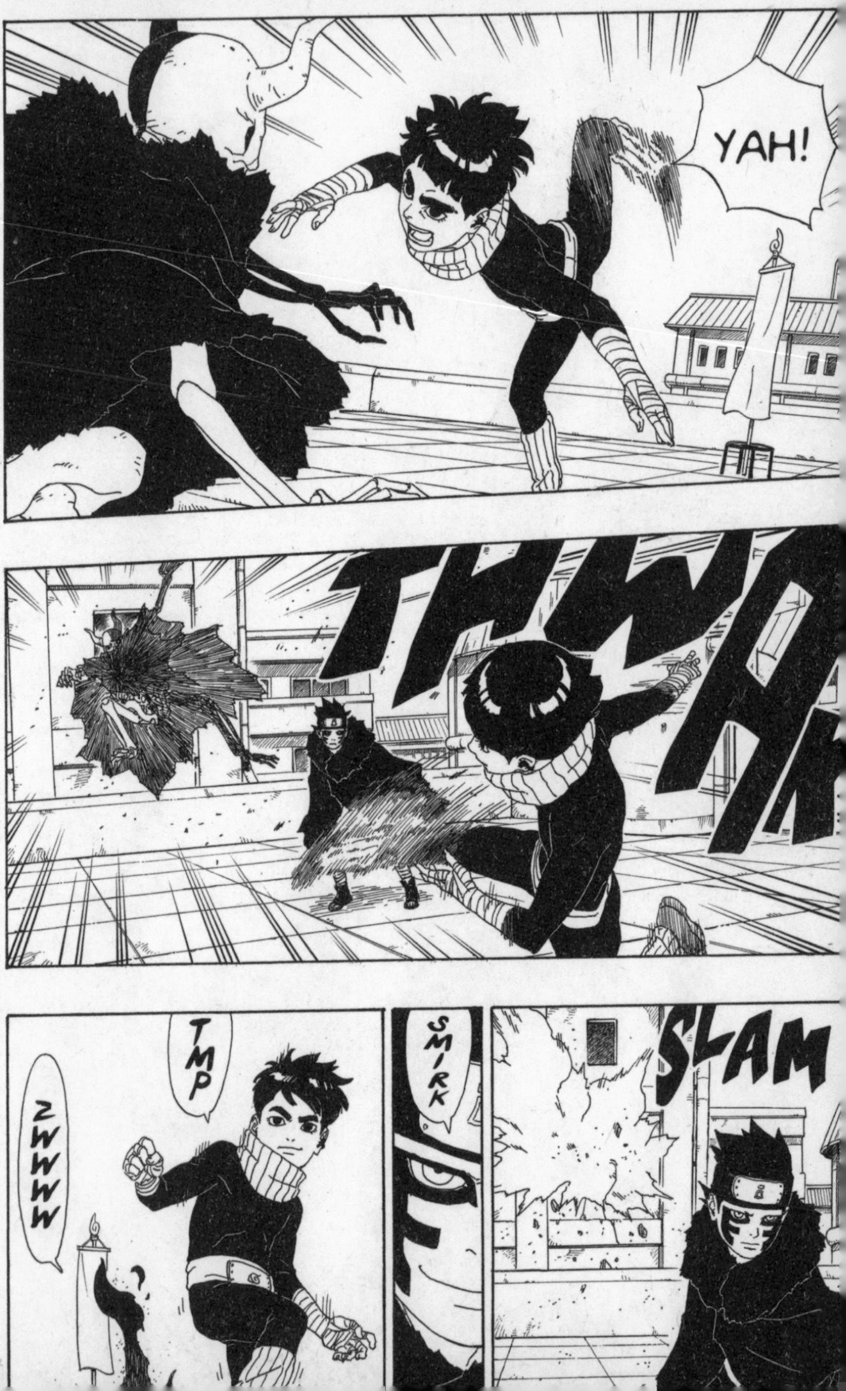
YAH!
THWA
SLAM
SMIRK
TMP
ZWWWW

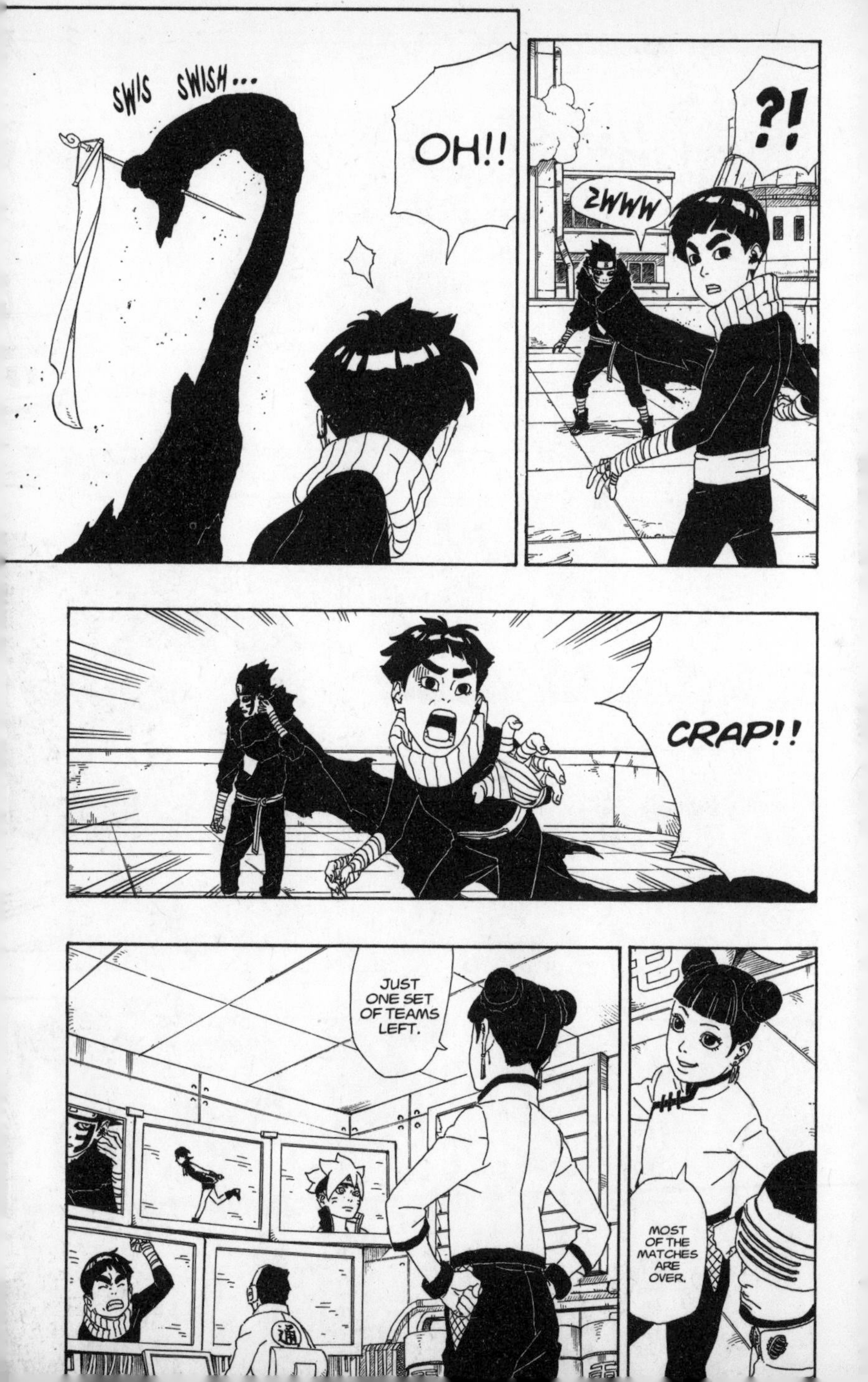
?!
ZWWW
SWIS SWISH...
OH!!
CRAP!!
MOST OF THE MATCHES ARE OVER.
JUST ONE SET OF TEAMS LEFT.

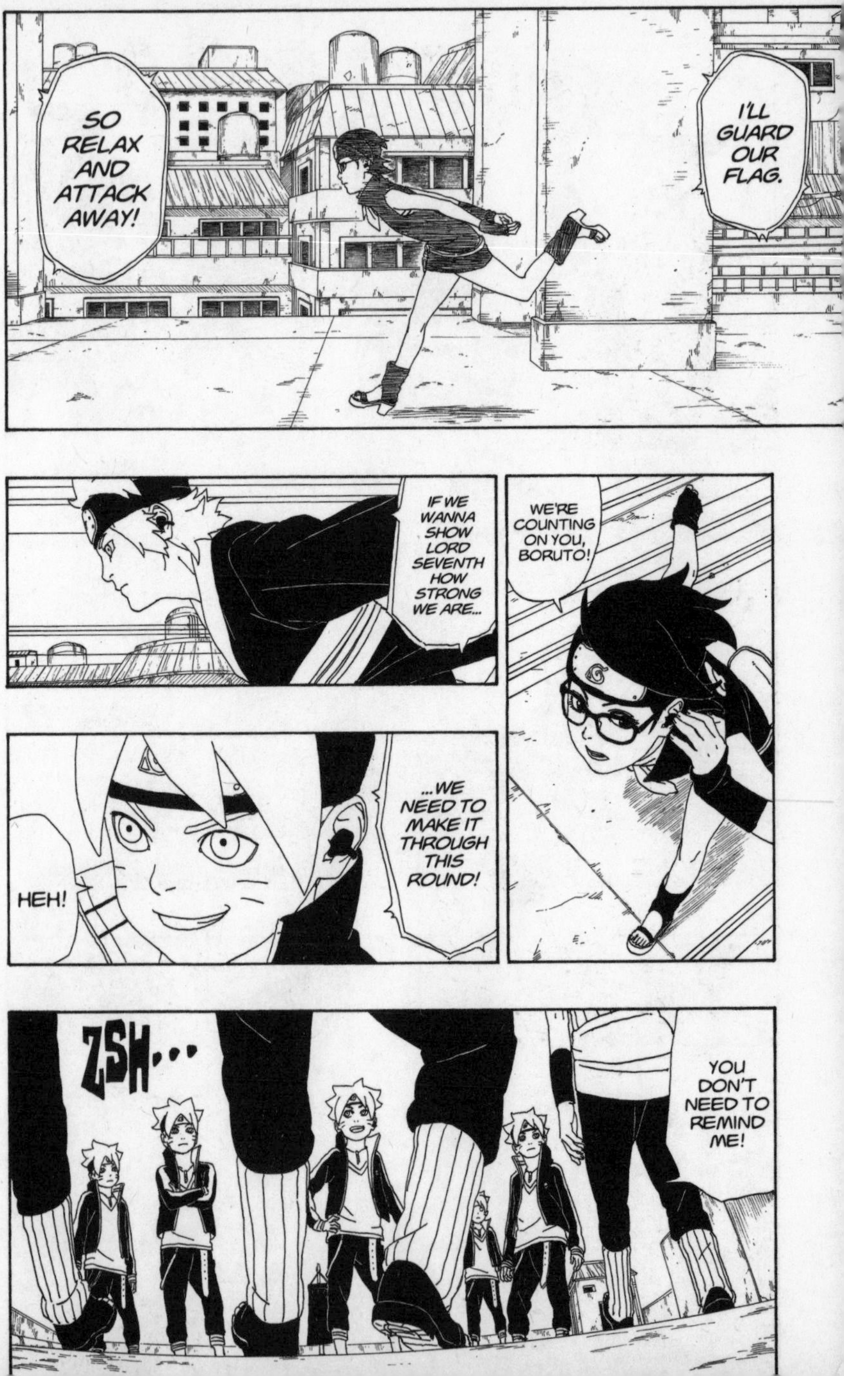
I'LL GUARD OUR FLAG.
SO RELAX AND ATTACK AWAY!
WE'RE COUNTING ON YOU, BORUTO!
IF WE WANNA SHOW LORD SEVENTH HOW STRONG WE ARE...
...WE NEED TO MAKE IT THROUGH THIS ROUND!
HEH!
YOU DON'T NEED TO REMIND ME!
ZSH...

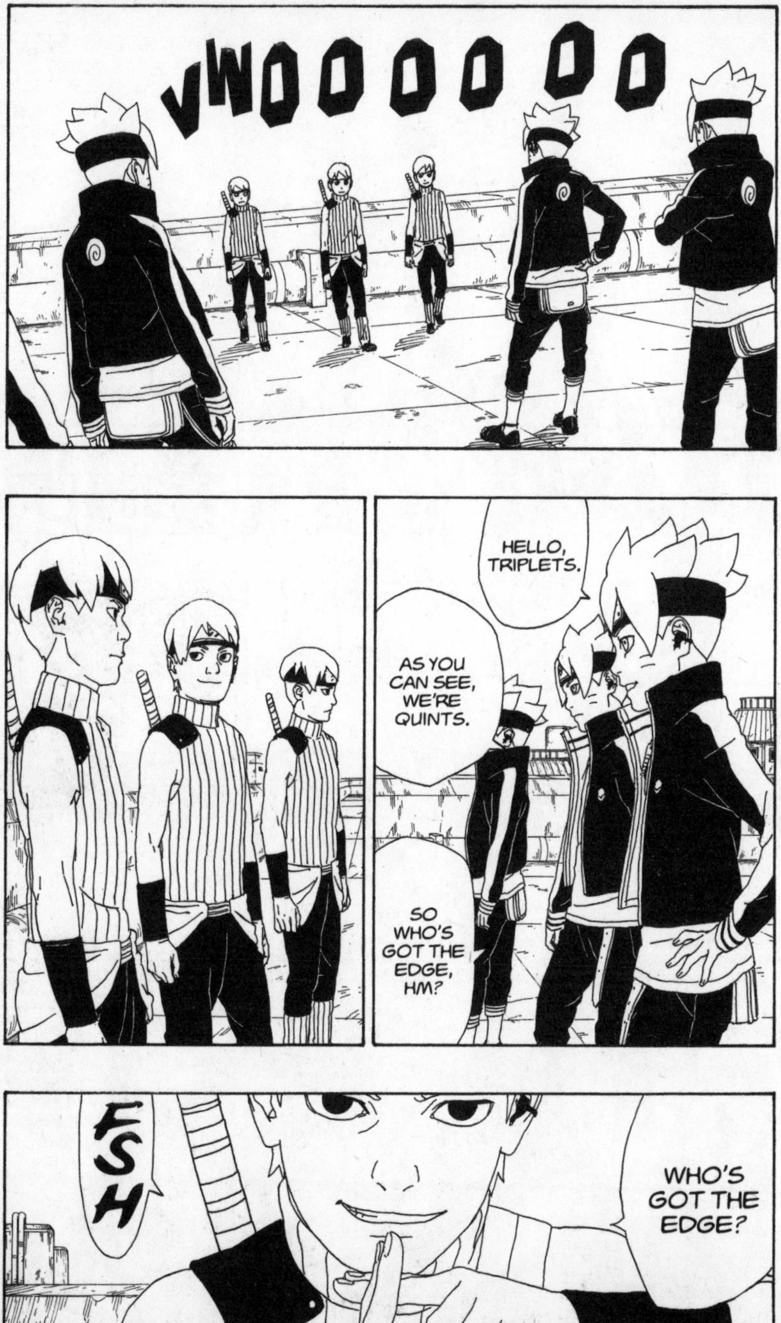
VWOOOOOO
HELLO, TRIPLETS.
AS YOU CAN SEE, WE'RE QUINTS.
SO WHO'S GOT THE EDGE, HM?
WHO'S GOT THE EDGE?
FSH

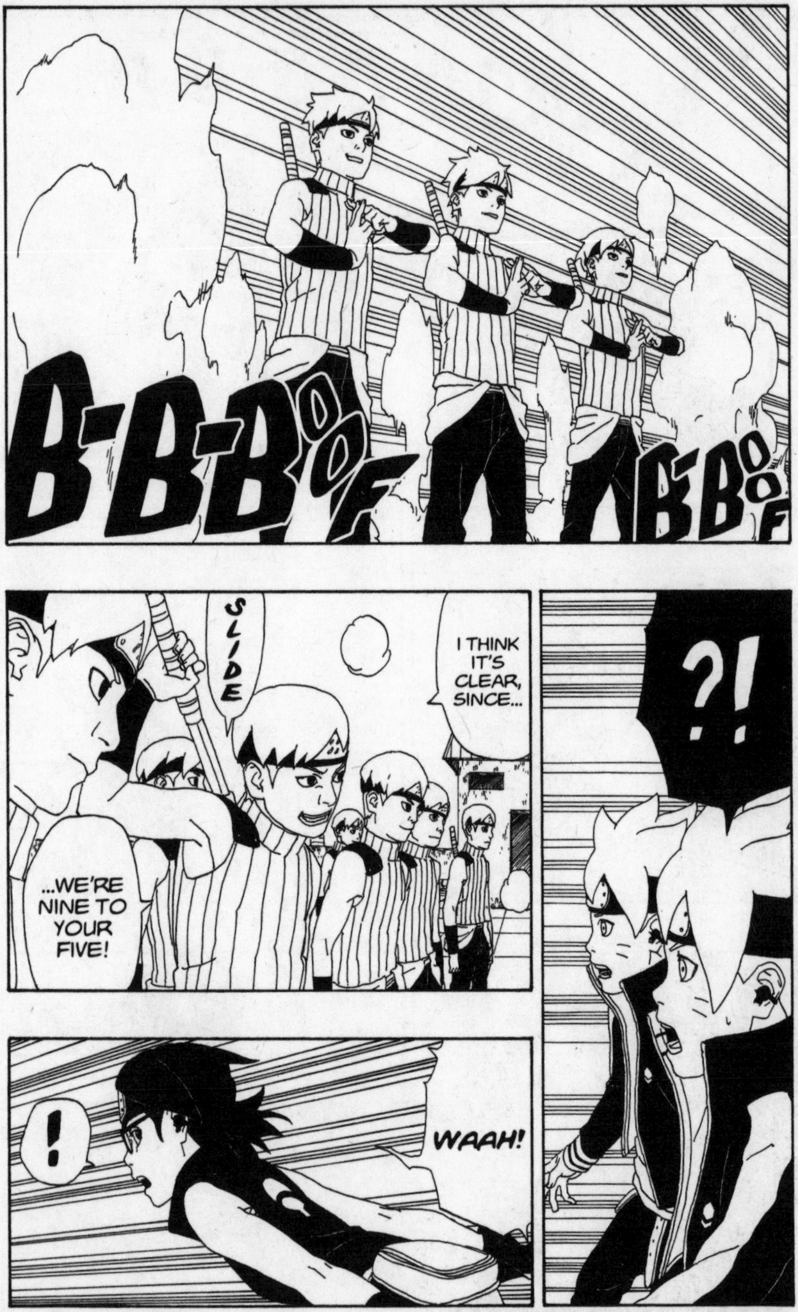
B-BOOF
B-B-BOOF
?!
I THINK IT'S CLEAR, SINCE...
SLIDE
...WE'RE NINE TO YOUR FIVE!
WAAH!
!

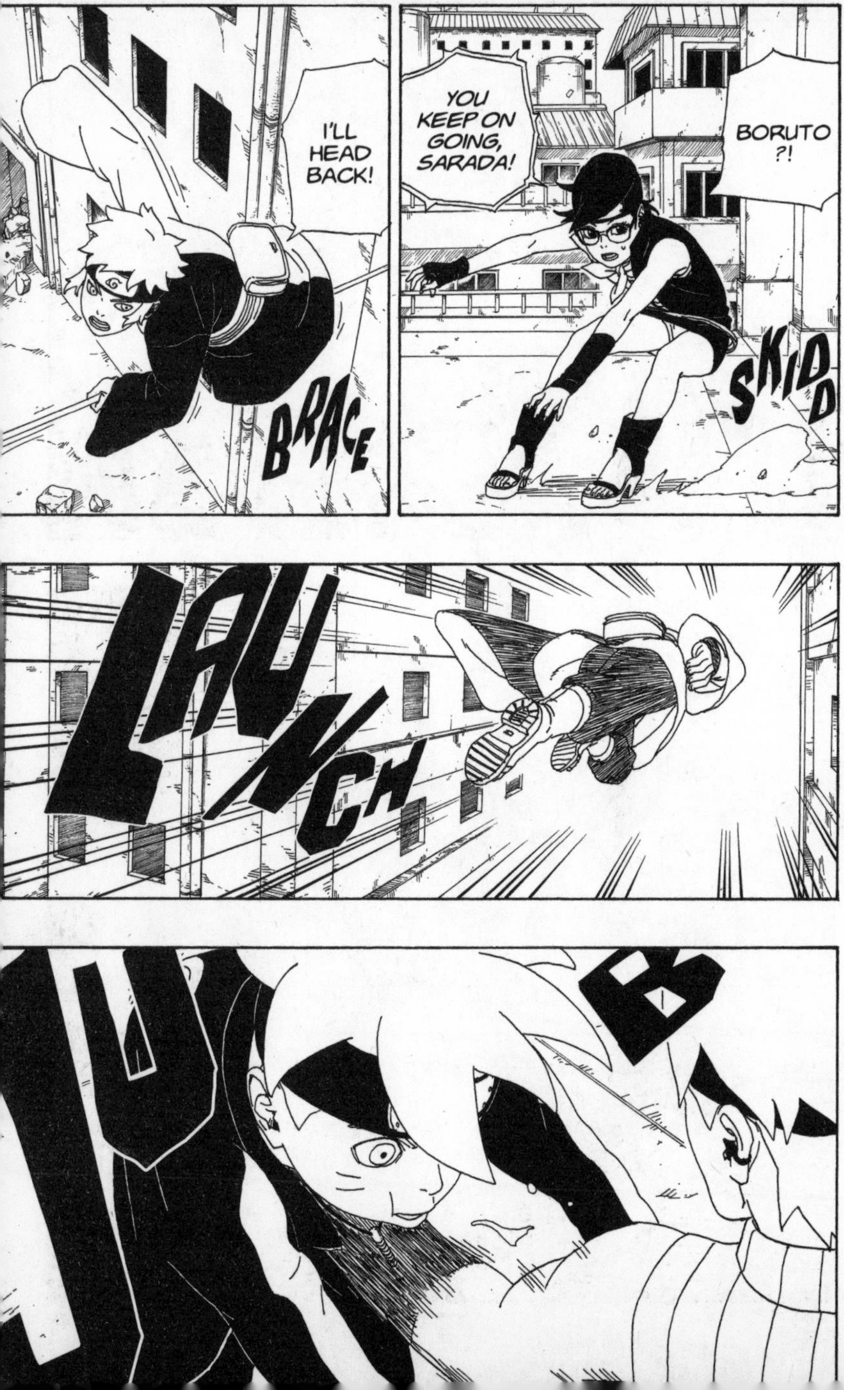
BORUTO ?!
YOU KEEP ON GOING, SARADA!
SKIDD
I'LL HEAD BACK!
BRACE
LAUNCH

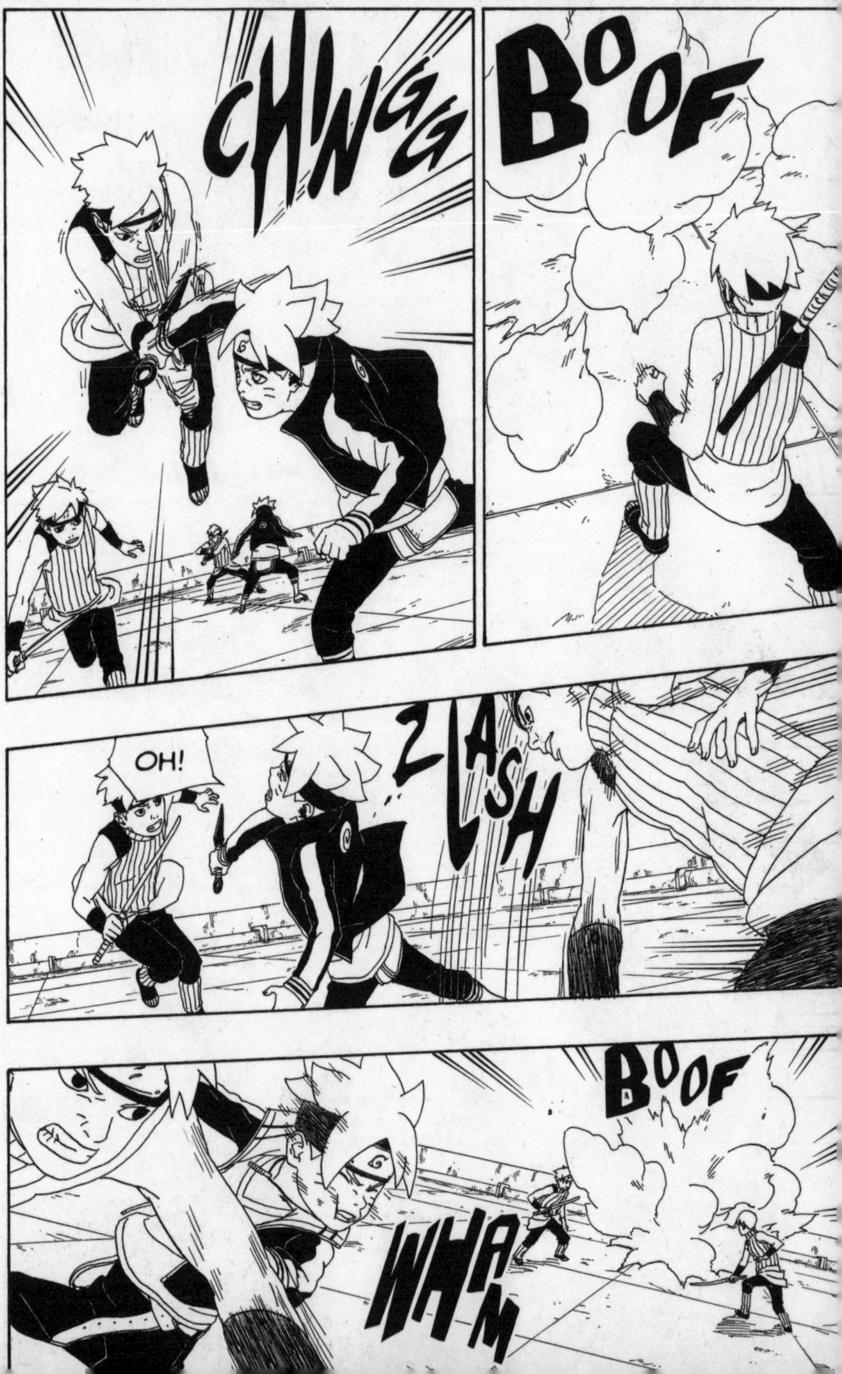
BOOF
CHINGG
ZLASH
OH!
BOOF
WHAM

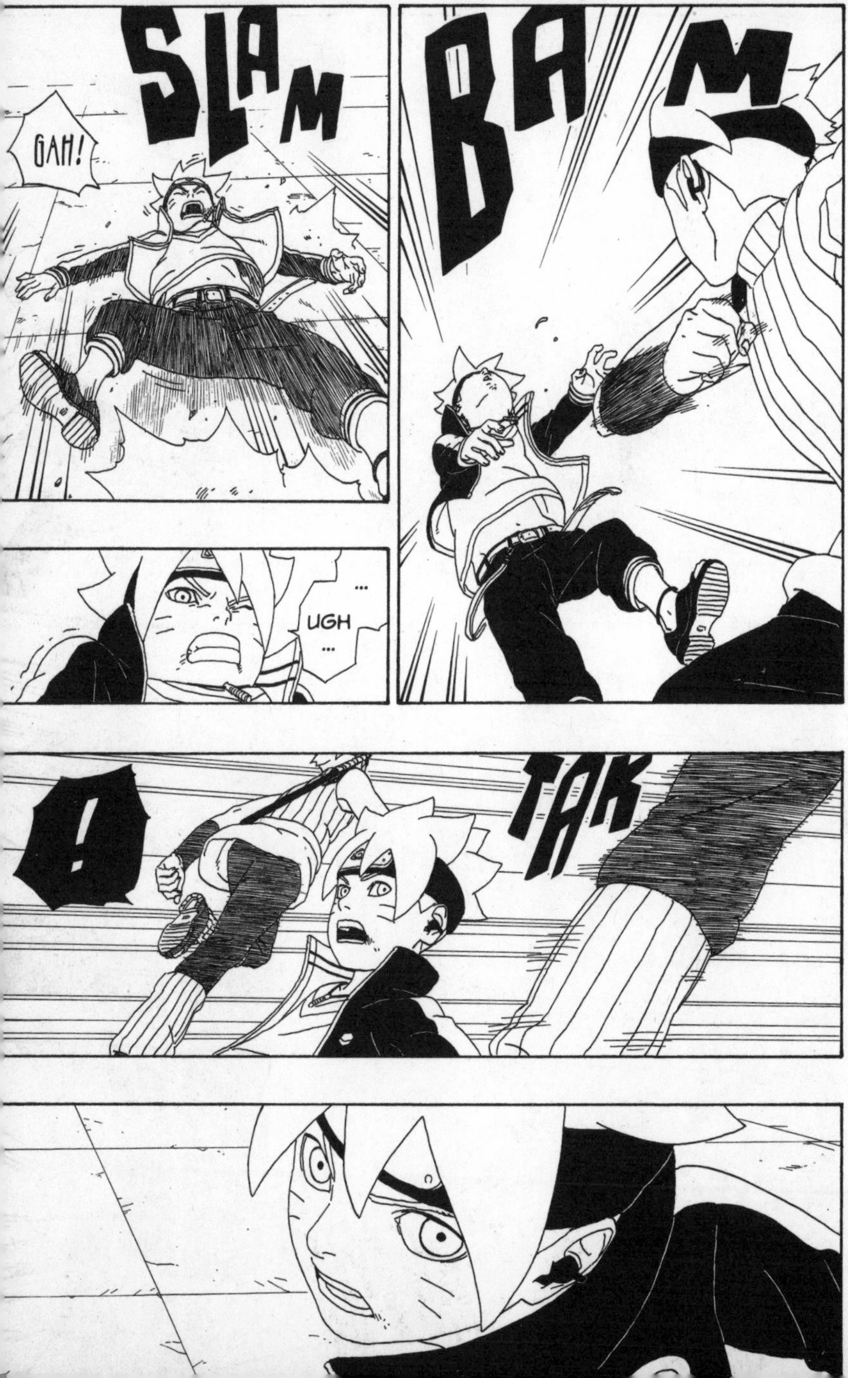
BAM
SLAM
GAH!
... UGH ...
TAK
!

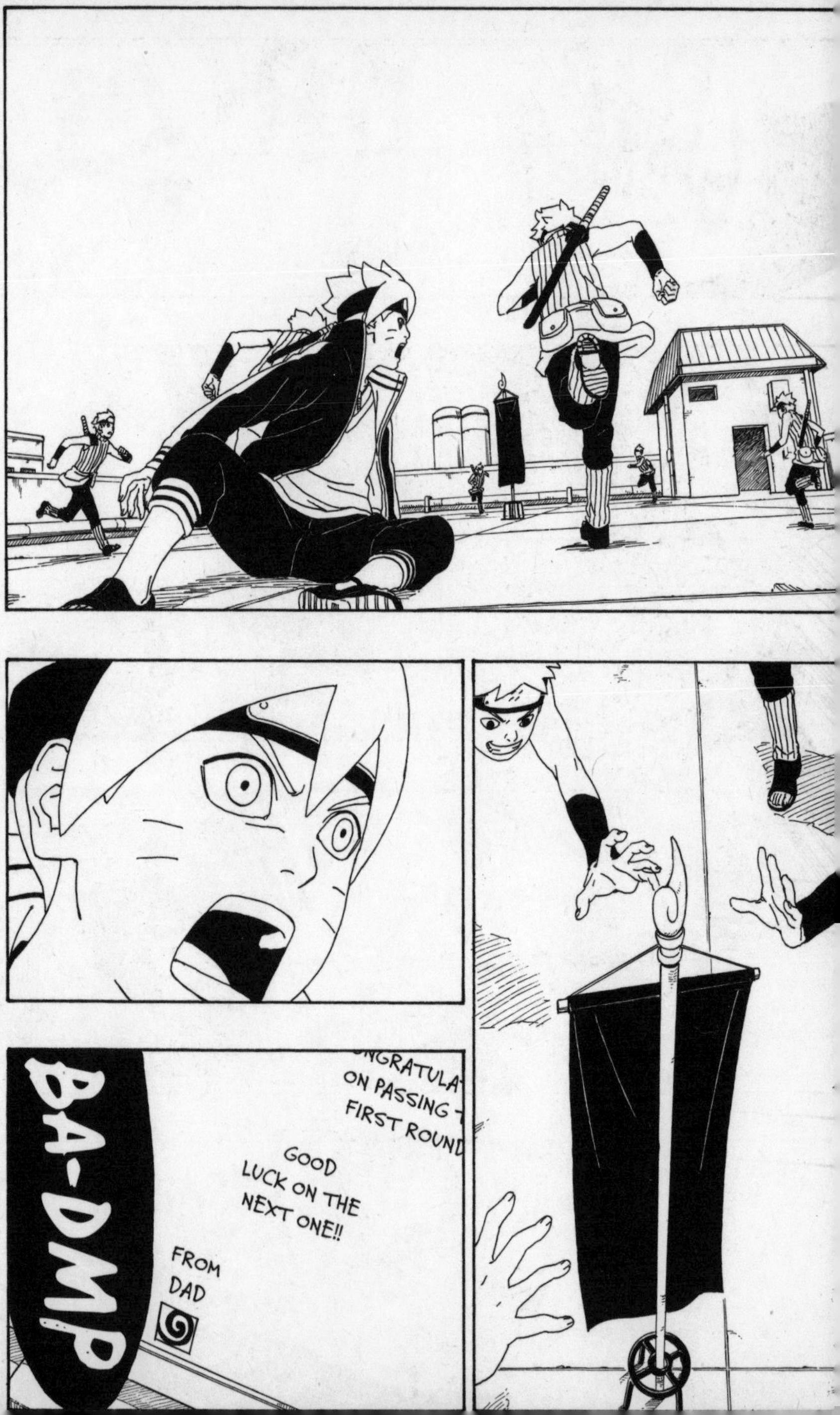
NGRATULA
ON PASSING
FIRST ROUND
GOOD LUCK ON THE NEXT ONE!!
FROM DAD
BA-DMP

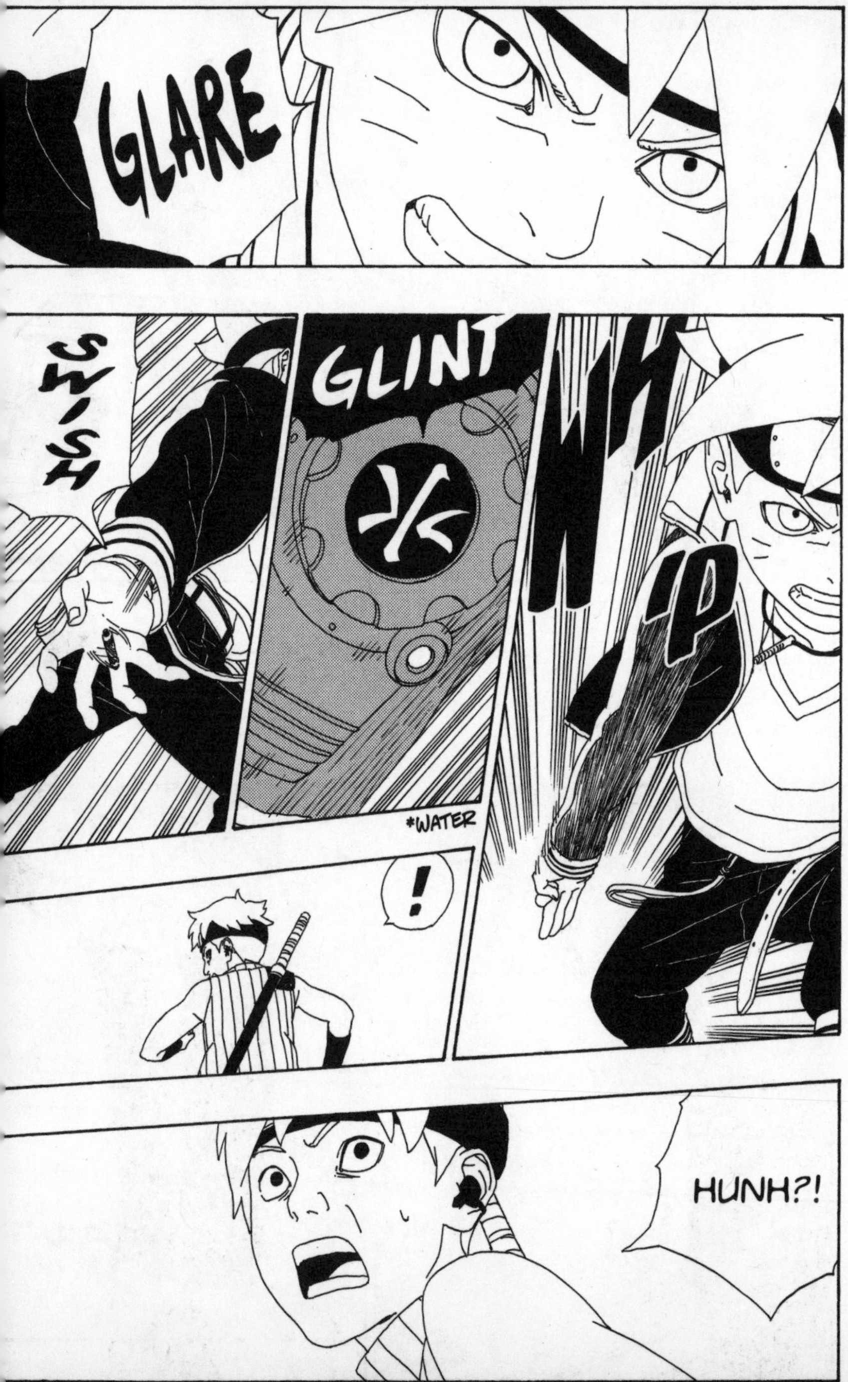
GLARE
WHIP
GLINT
*WATER
SWISH
!
HUNH?!

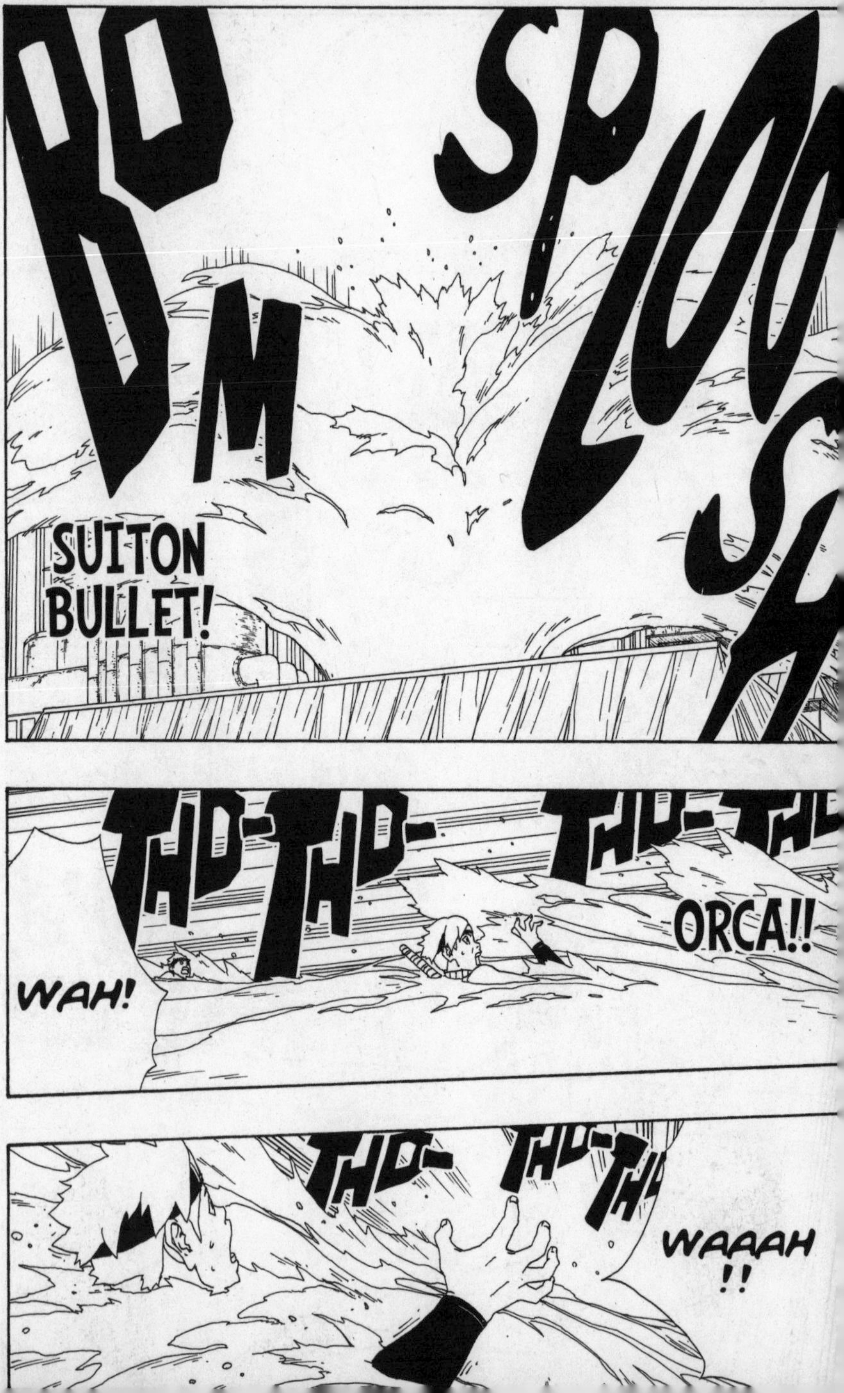
SPLOOSH
BOOM
SUITON BULLET!
THD-THD-
THD-THD-
ORCA!!
WAH!
THD-
THD-THD-
WAAAH !!

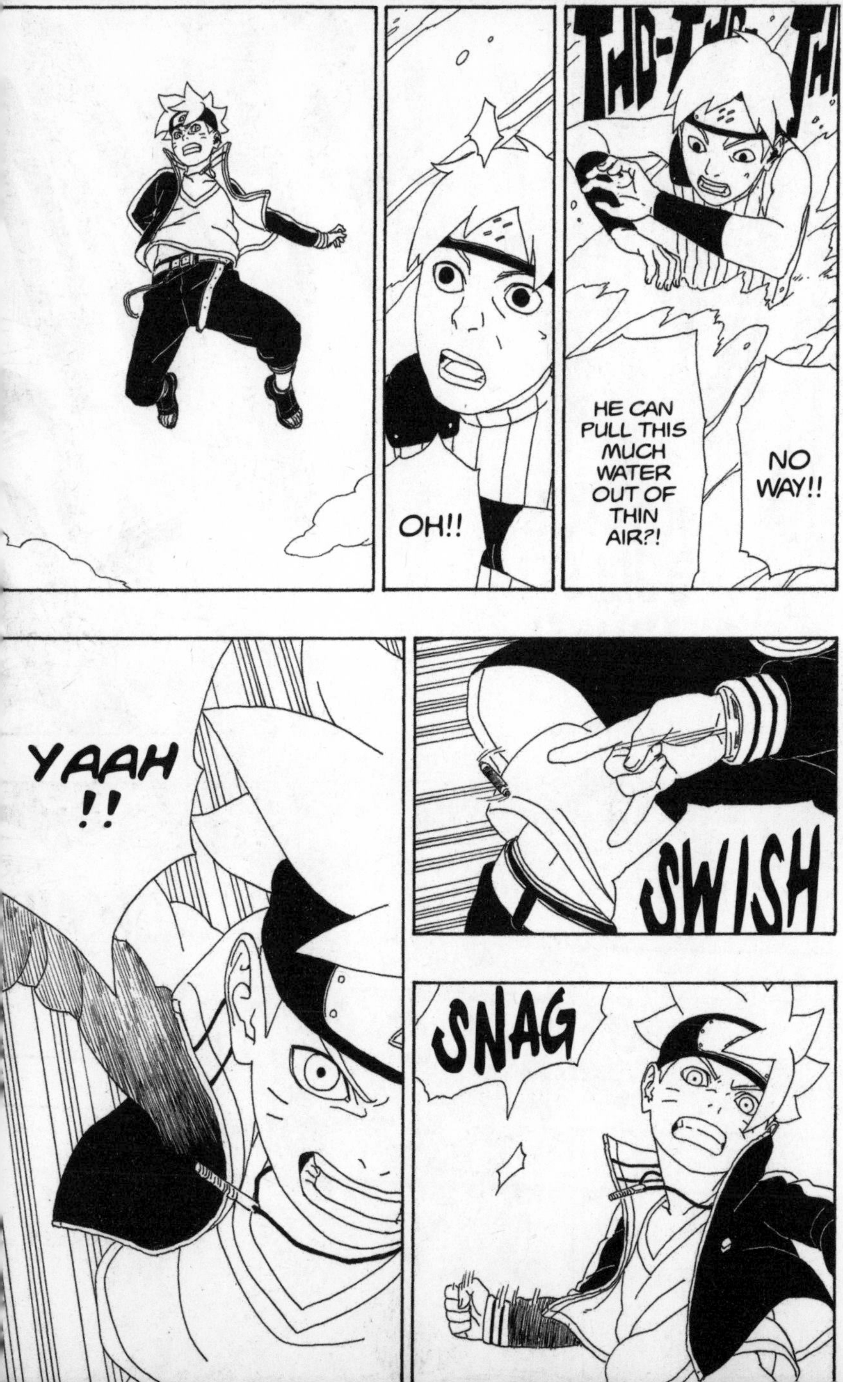
THD-THD-TH
NO WAY!!
HE CAN PULL THIS MUCH WATER OUT OF THIN AIR?!
OH!!
SWISH
SNAG
YAAH!!

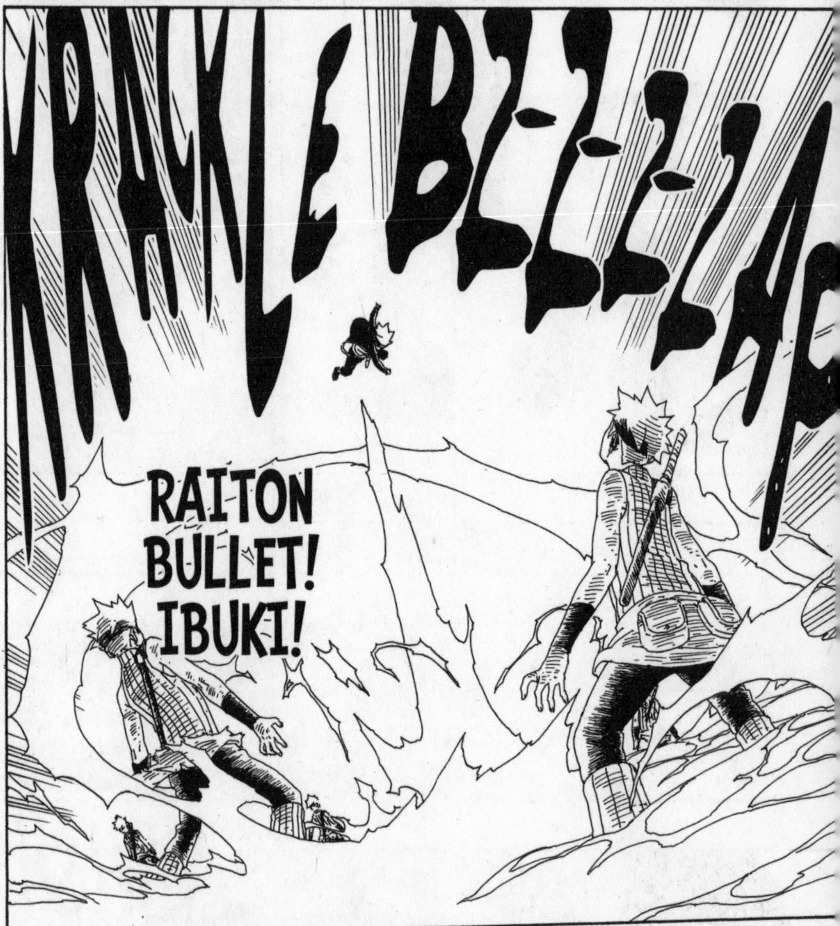
KRACKLE BZ-Z-Z-ZAP
RAITON BULLET! IBUKI!

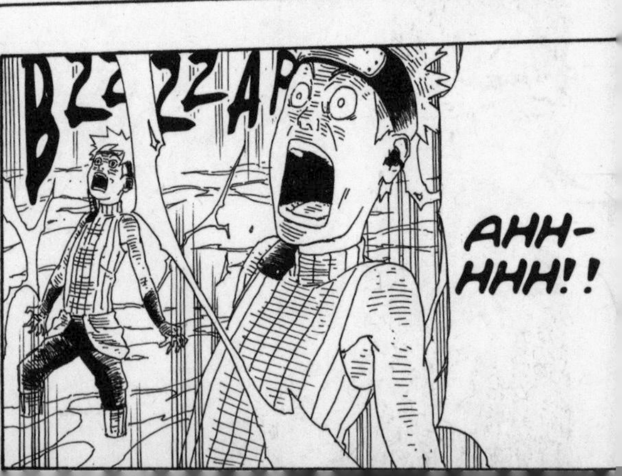
BZZZZAP
AHH-HHH!!

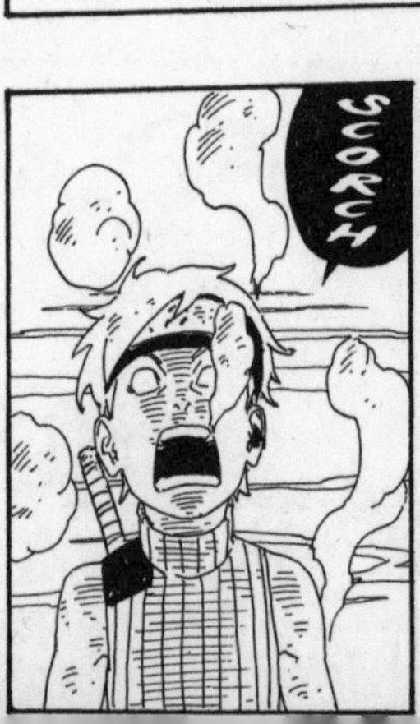
SCORCH

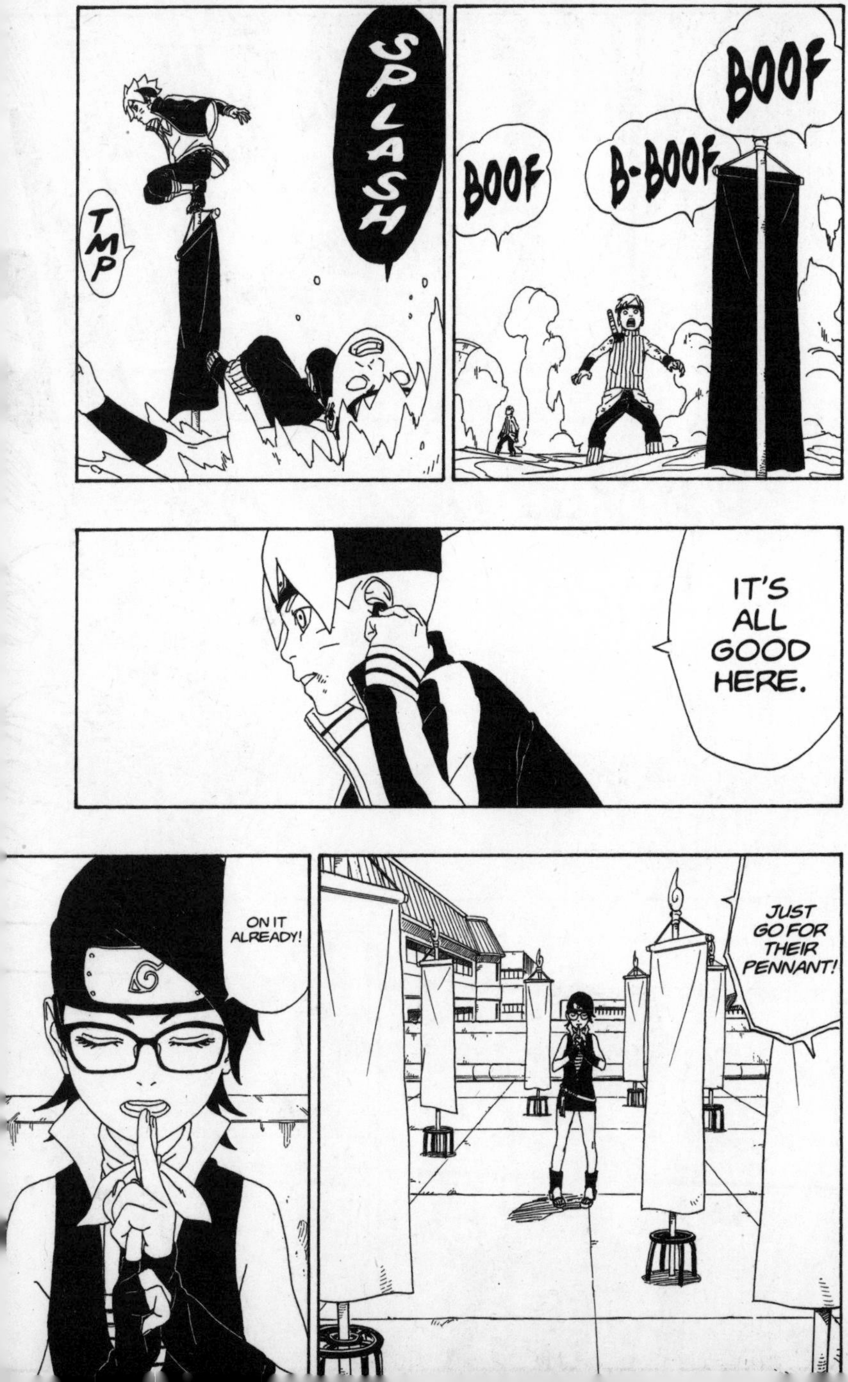
BOOF
B-BOOF
BOOF
SPLASH
TMP
IT'S ALL GOOD HERE.
JUST GO FOR THEIR PENNANT!
ON IT ALREADY!

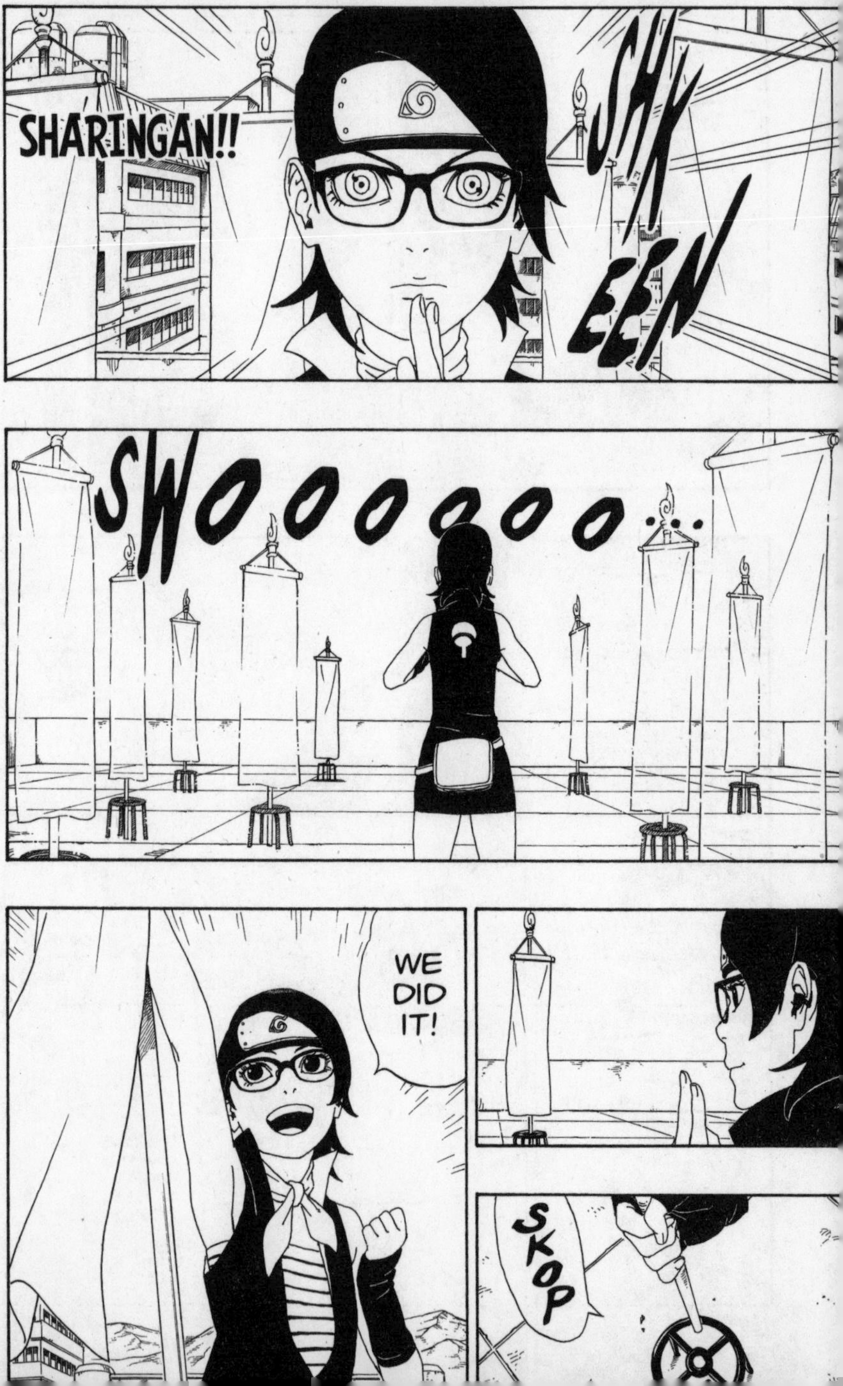
SHKEEN
SHARINGAN!!
SWOOOOOO...
SKOP
WE DID IT!

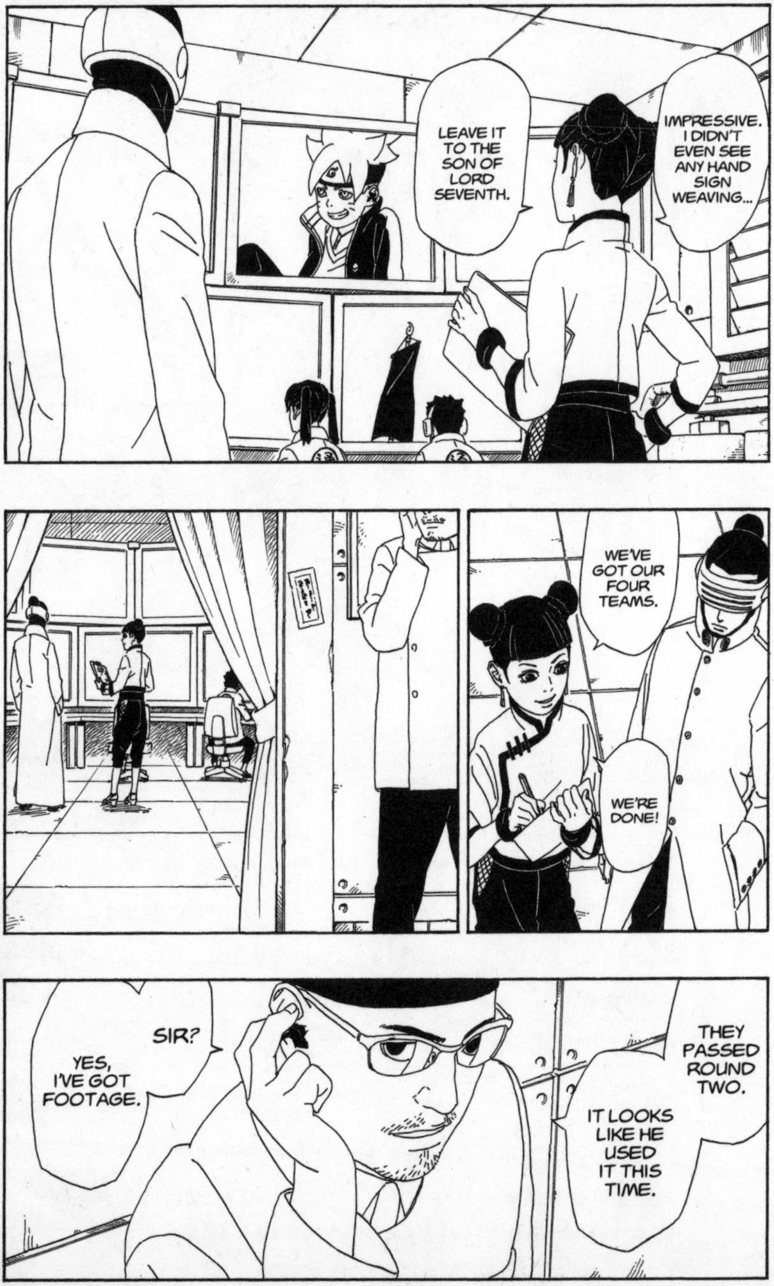
IMPRESSIVE. I DIDN'T EVEN SEE ANY HAND SIGN WEAVING...
LEAVE IT TO THE SON OF LORD SEVENTH.
WE'VE GOT OUR FOUR TEAMS.
WE'RE DONE!
THEY PASSED ROUND TWO.
IT LOOKS LIKE HE USED IT THIS TIME.
SIR?
YES, I'VE GOT FOOTAGE.

NINJA ENCYCLOPEDIA • ENTRY 3

MITSUKI

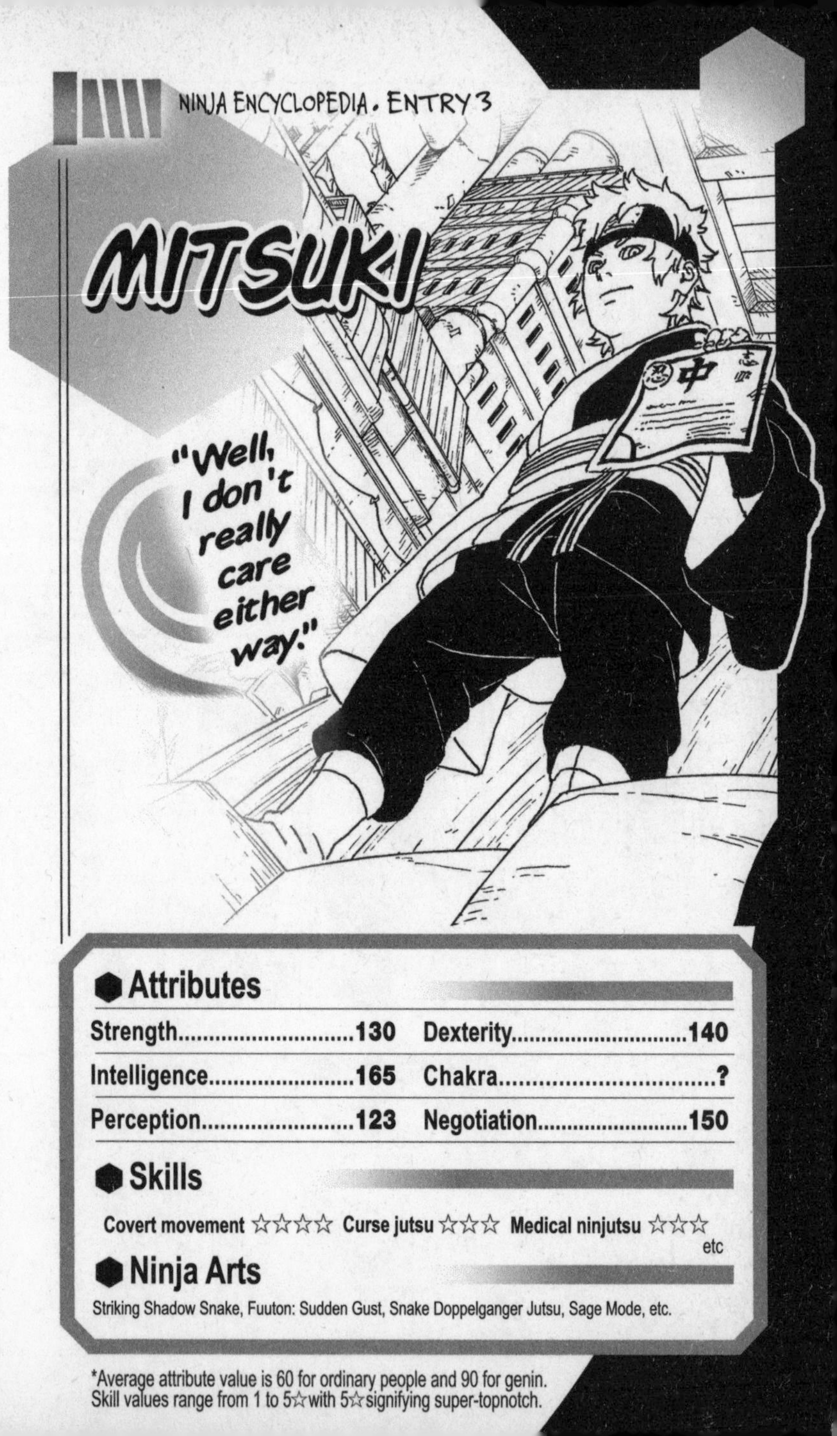
"Well, I don't really care either way."

Attributes

Strength	130	Dexterity	140
Intelligence	165	Chakra	?
Perception	123	Negotiation	150

Skills

Covert movement ☆☆☆☆ Curse jutsu ☆☆☆ Medical ninjutsu ☆☆☆ etc

Ninja Arts

Striking Shadow Snake, Fuuton: Sudden Gust, Snake Doppelganger Jutsu, Sage Mode, etc.

*Average attribute value is 60 for ordinary people and 90 for genin. Skill values range from 1 to 5☆ with 5☆ signifying super-topnotch.

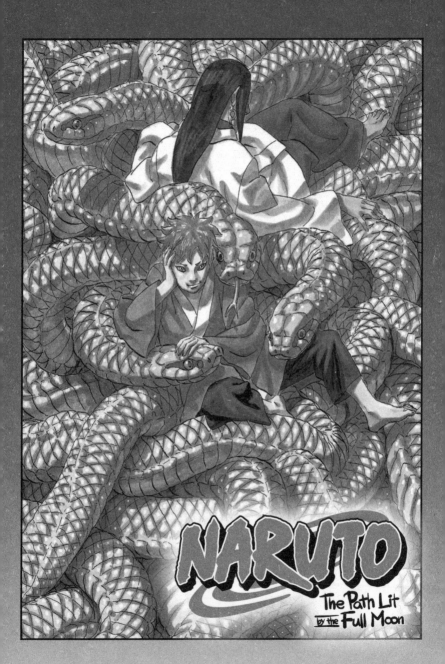

NARUTO
The Path Lit
by the Full Moon

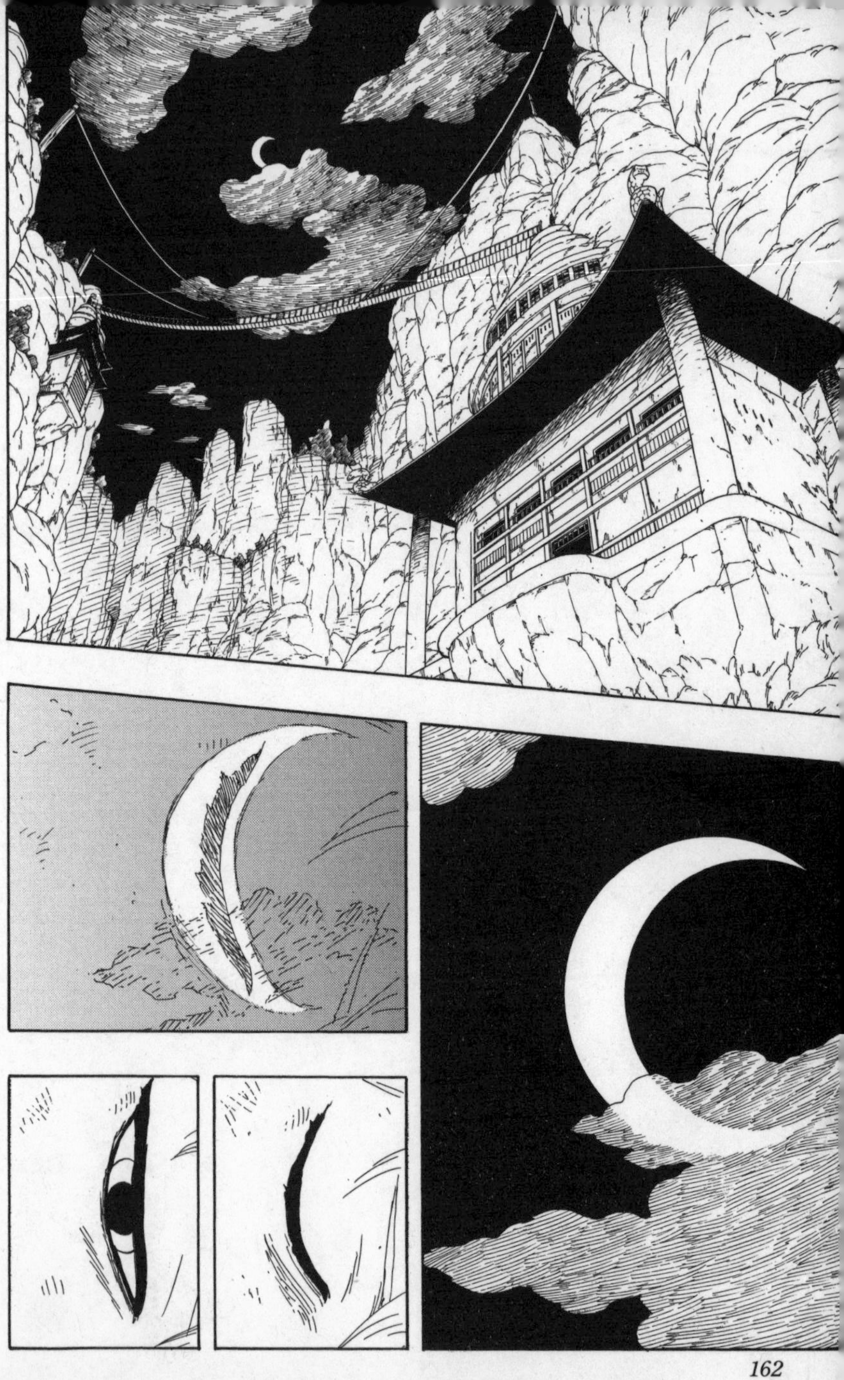

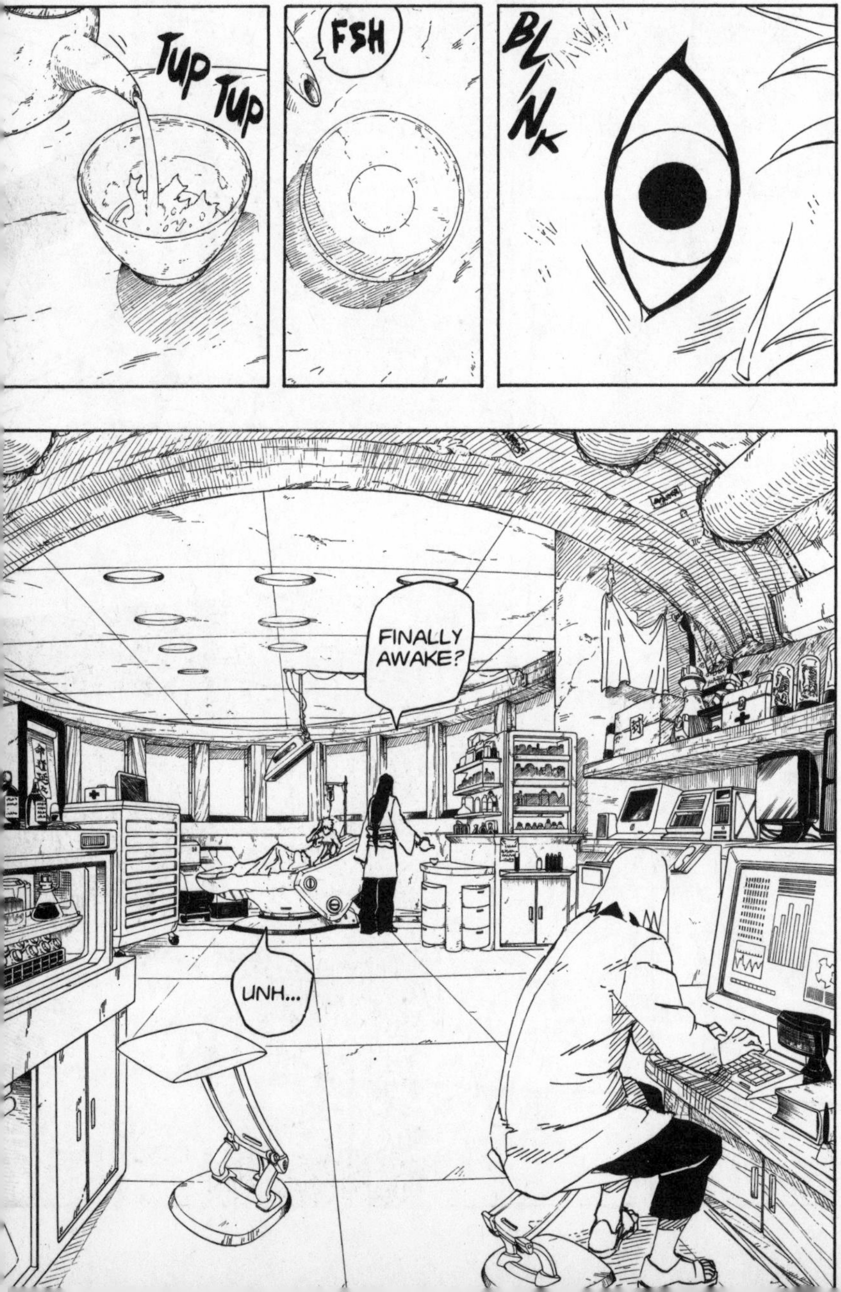
BLINK
FSH
TUP TUP
FINALLY AWAKE?
UNH...

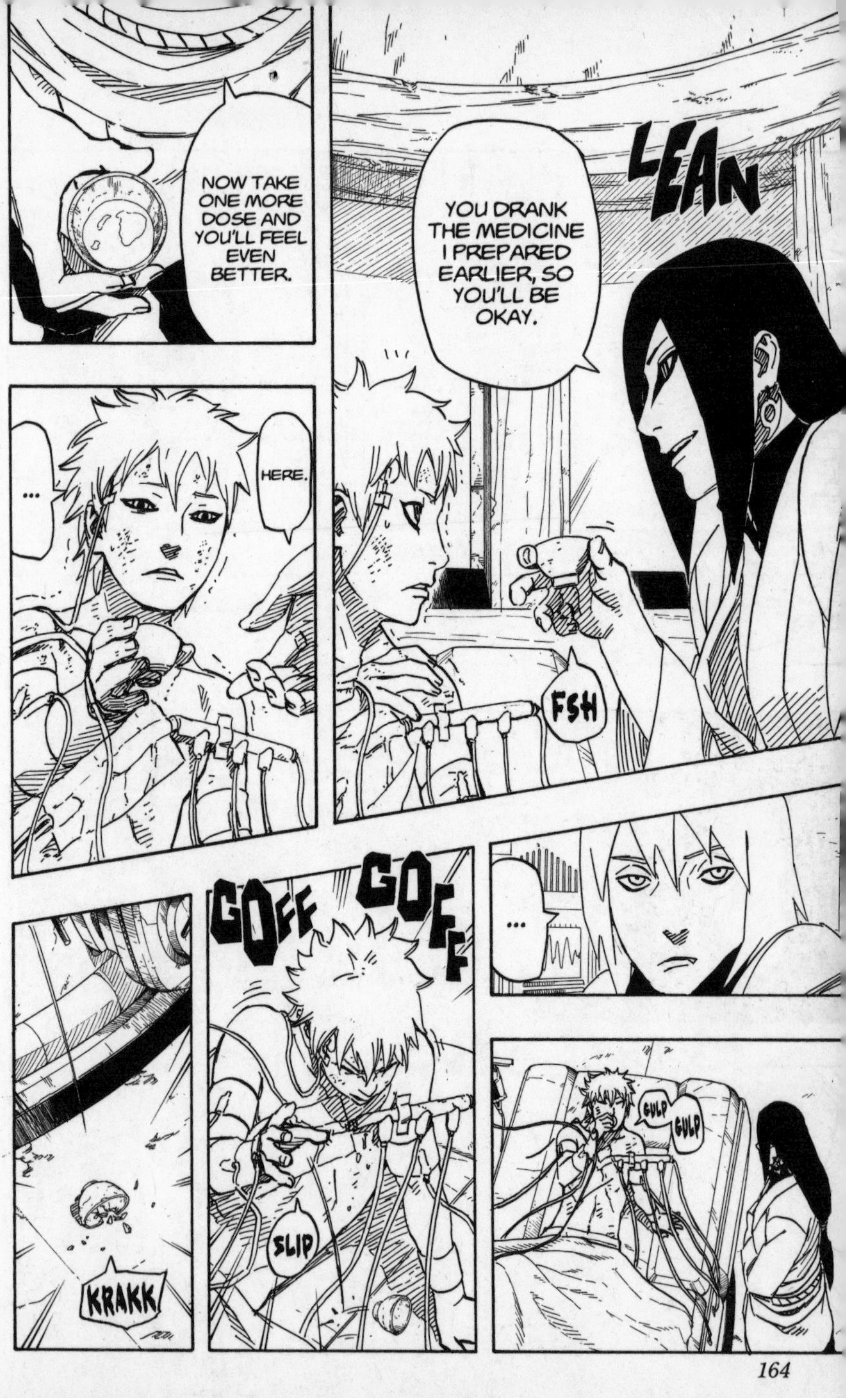

YOU DRANK THE MEDICINE I PREPARED EARLIER, SO YOU'LL BE OKAY.
LEAN
FSH
NOW TAKE ONE MORE DOSE AND YOU'LL FEEL EVEN BETTER.
HERE.
...
...
GULP
GULP
GOFF
GOFF
SLIP
KRAKK

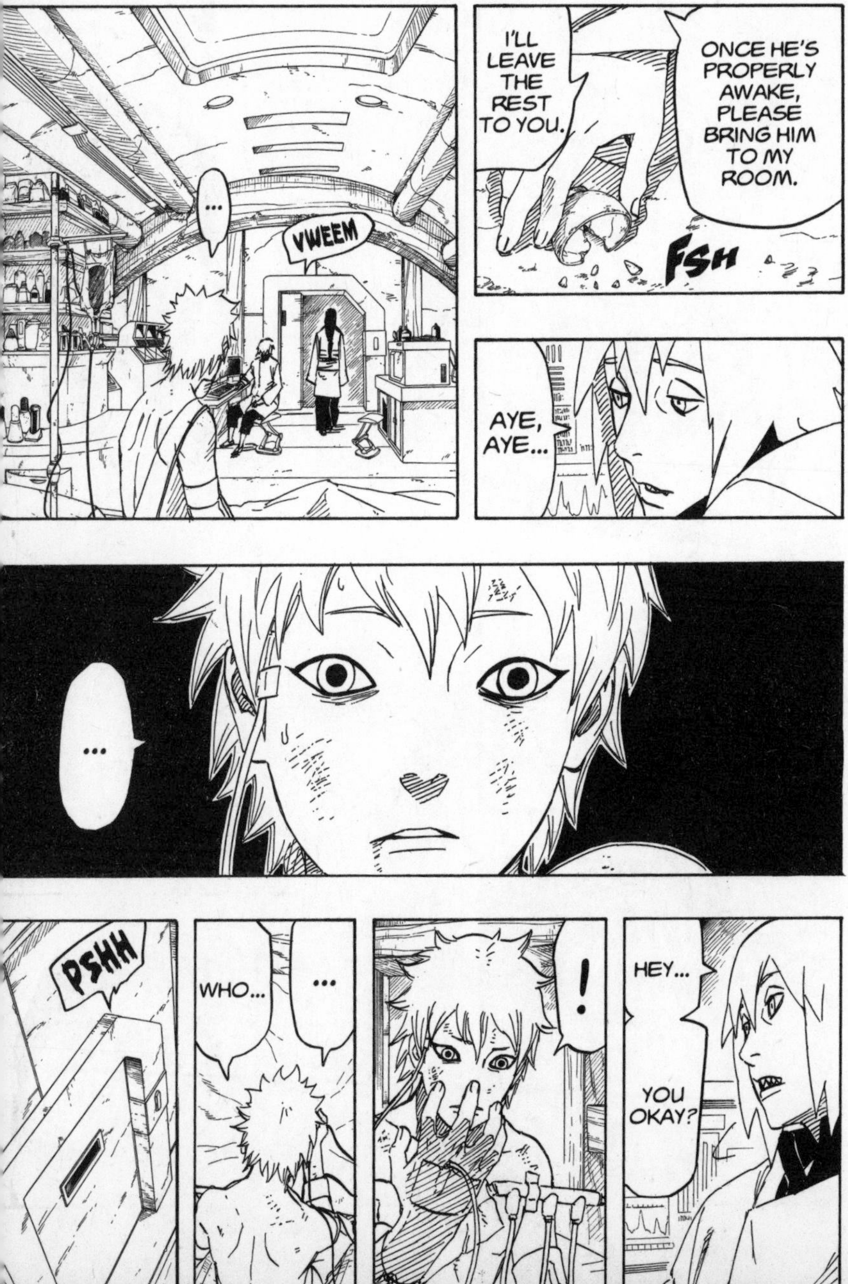
ONCE HE'S PROPERLY AWAKE, PLEASE BRING HIM TO MY ROOM.
I'LL LEAVE THE REST TO YOU.
FSH
AYE, AYE...
VWEEM
...
...
HEY... YOU OKAY?
!
...
WHO...
PSHH

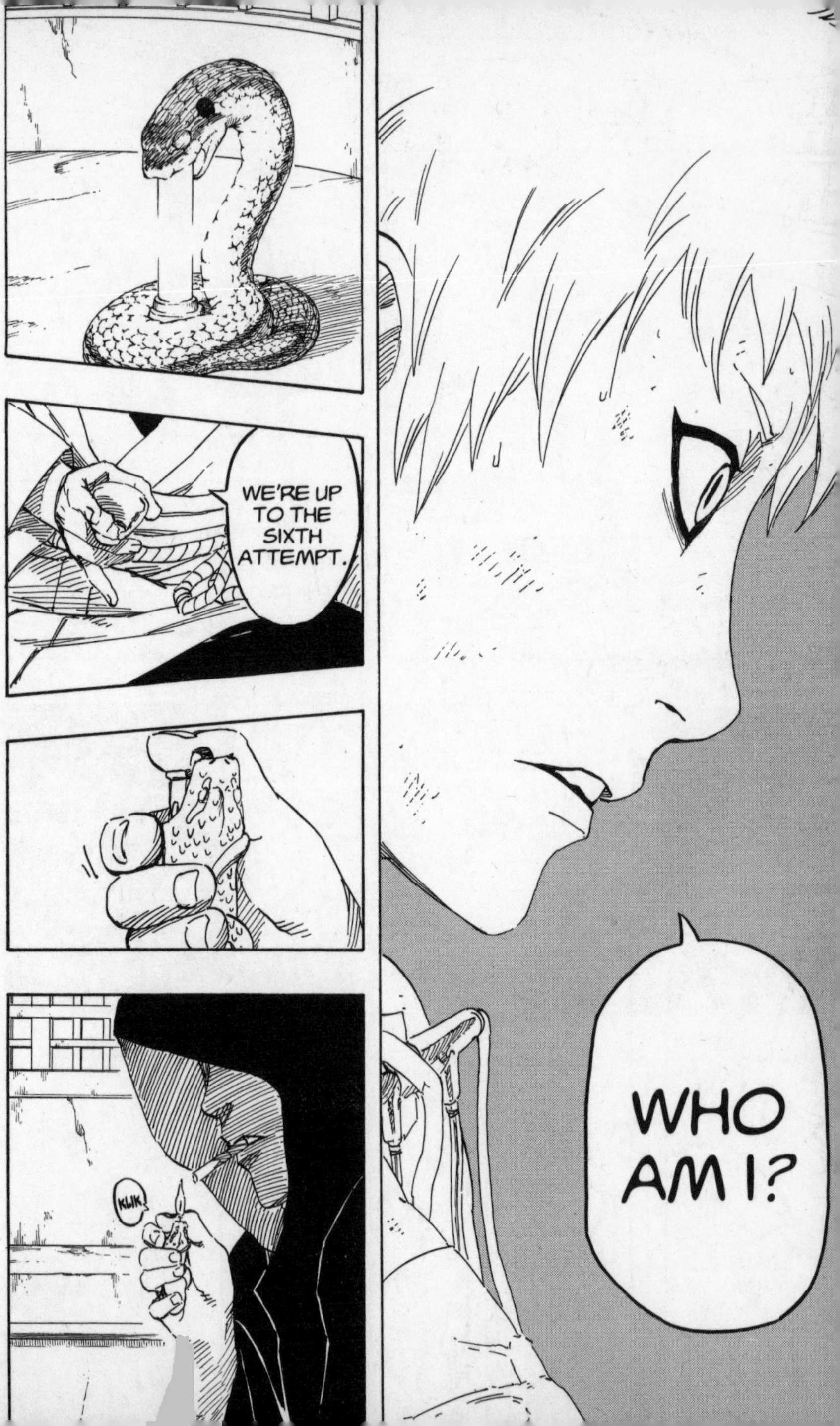
WHO AM I?
WE'RE UP TO THE SIXTH ATTEMPT.
KLIK

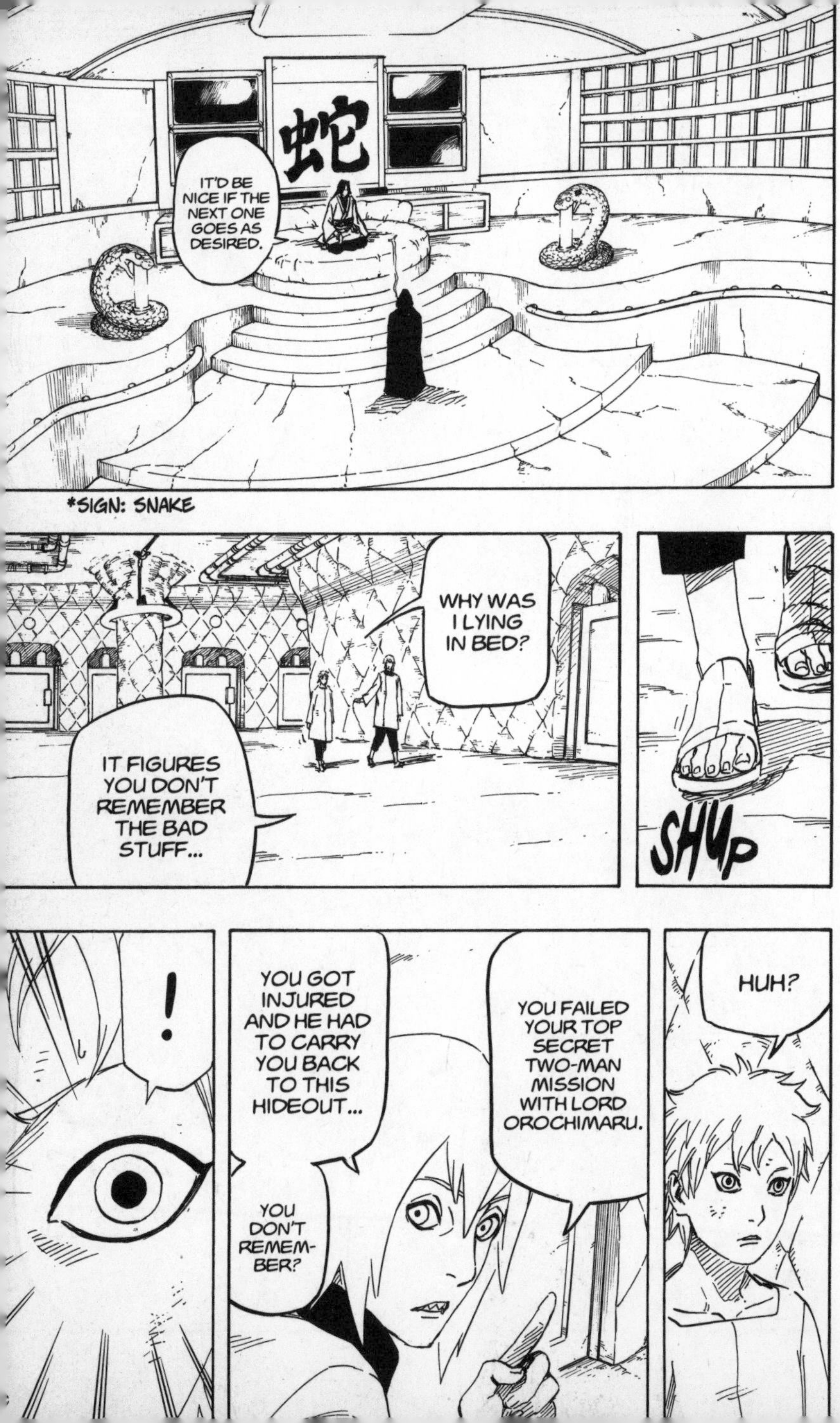
蛇
IT'D BE NICE IF THE NEXT ONE GOES AS DESIRED.
*SIGN: SNAKE
SHUP
WHY WAS I LYING IN BED?
IT FIGURES YOU DON'T REMEMBER THE BAD STUFF...
HUH?
YOU FAILED YOUR TOP SECRET TWO-MAN MISSION WITH LORD OROCHIMARU.
YOU GOT INJURED AND HE HAD TO CARRY YOU BACK TO THIS HIDEOUT...
YOU DON'T REMEM-BER?
!

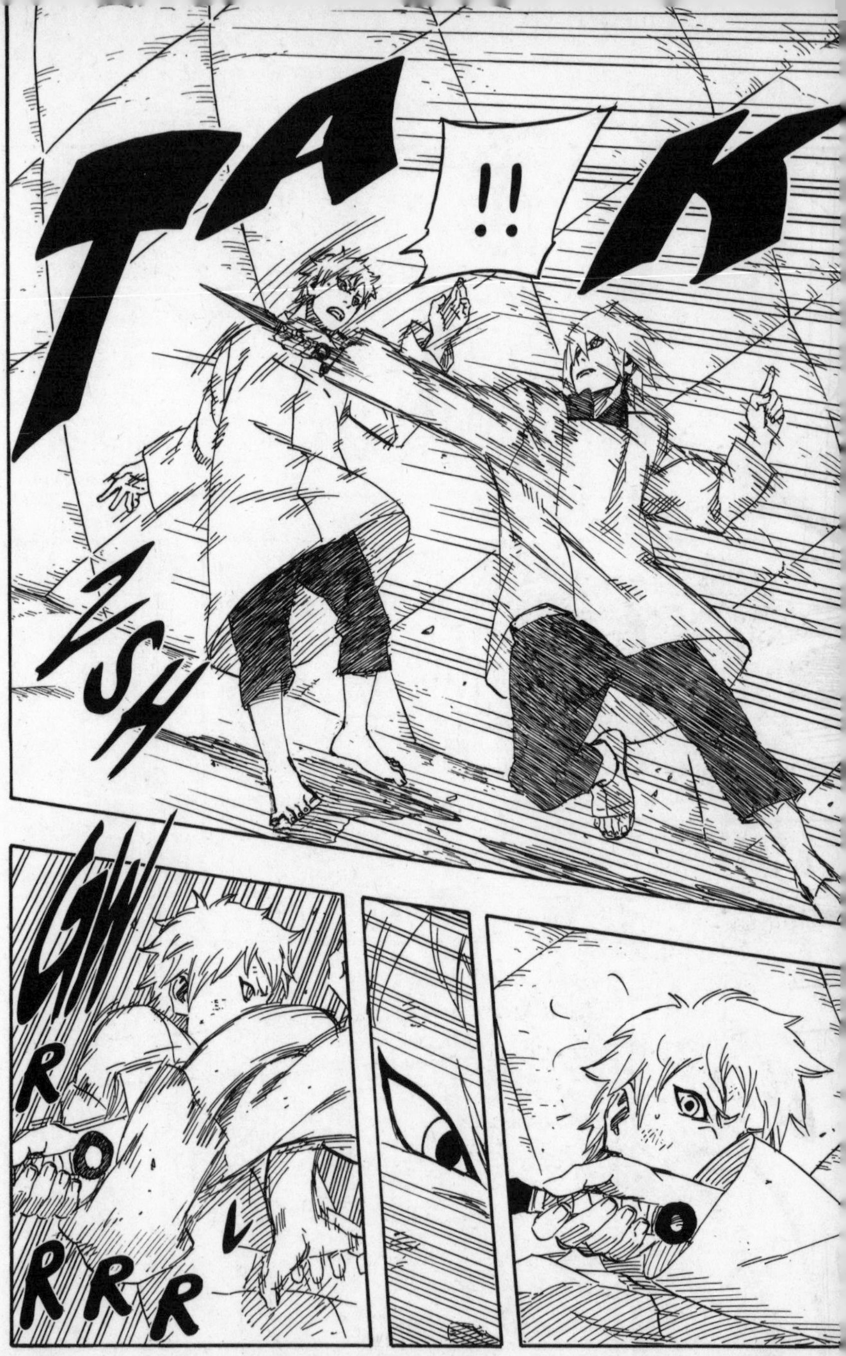
TAK
!!
ZSH
GWRRRR

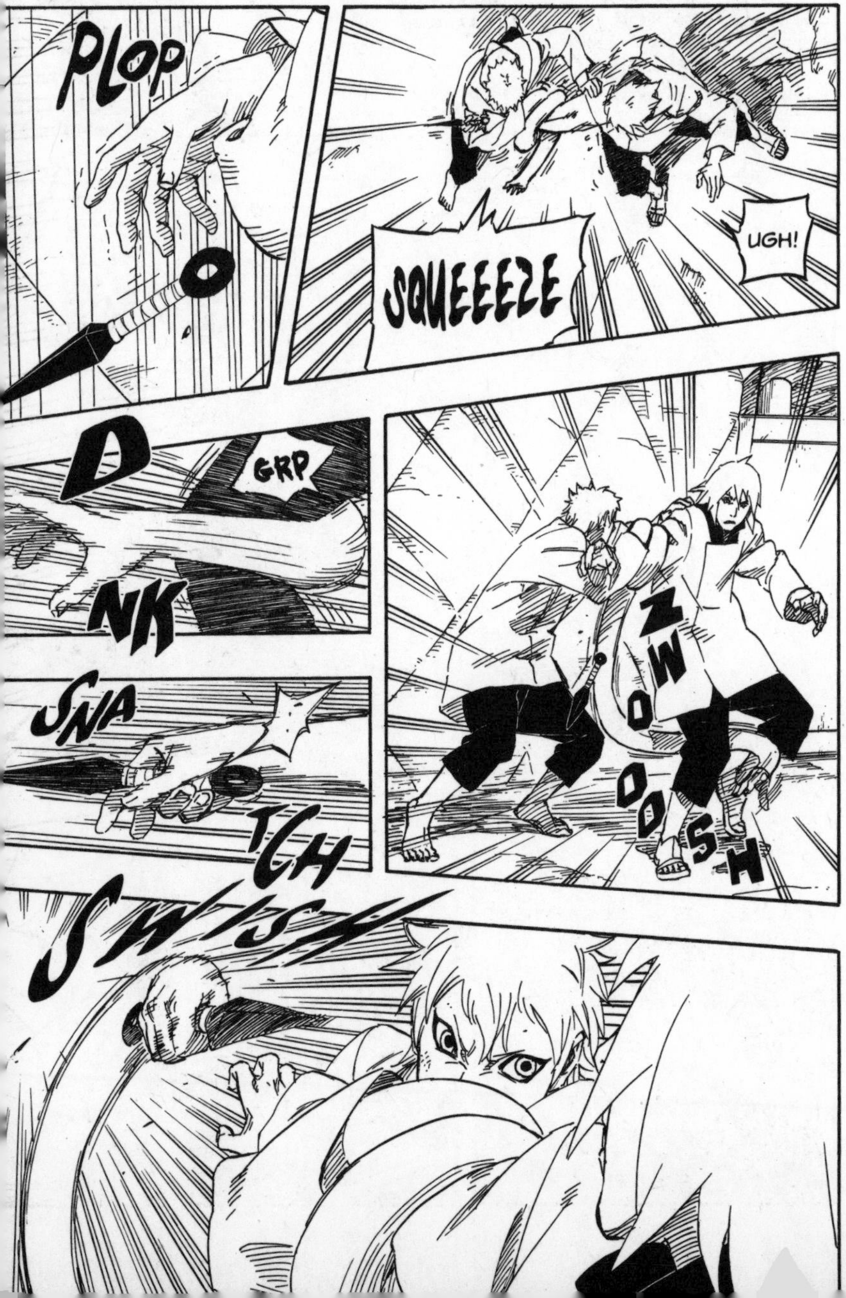
UGH!
SQUEEEZE
PLOP
ZWOOOSH
GRP
DNK
SNATCH
SWISH

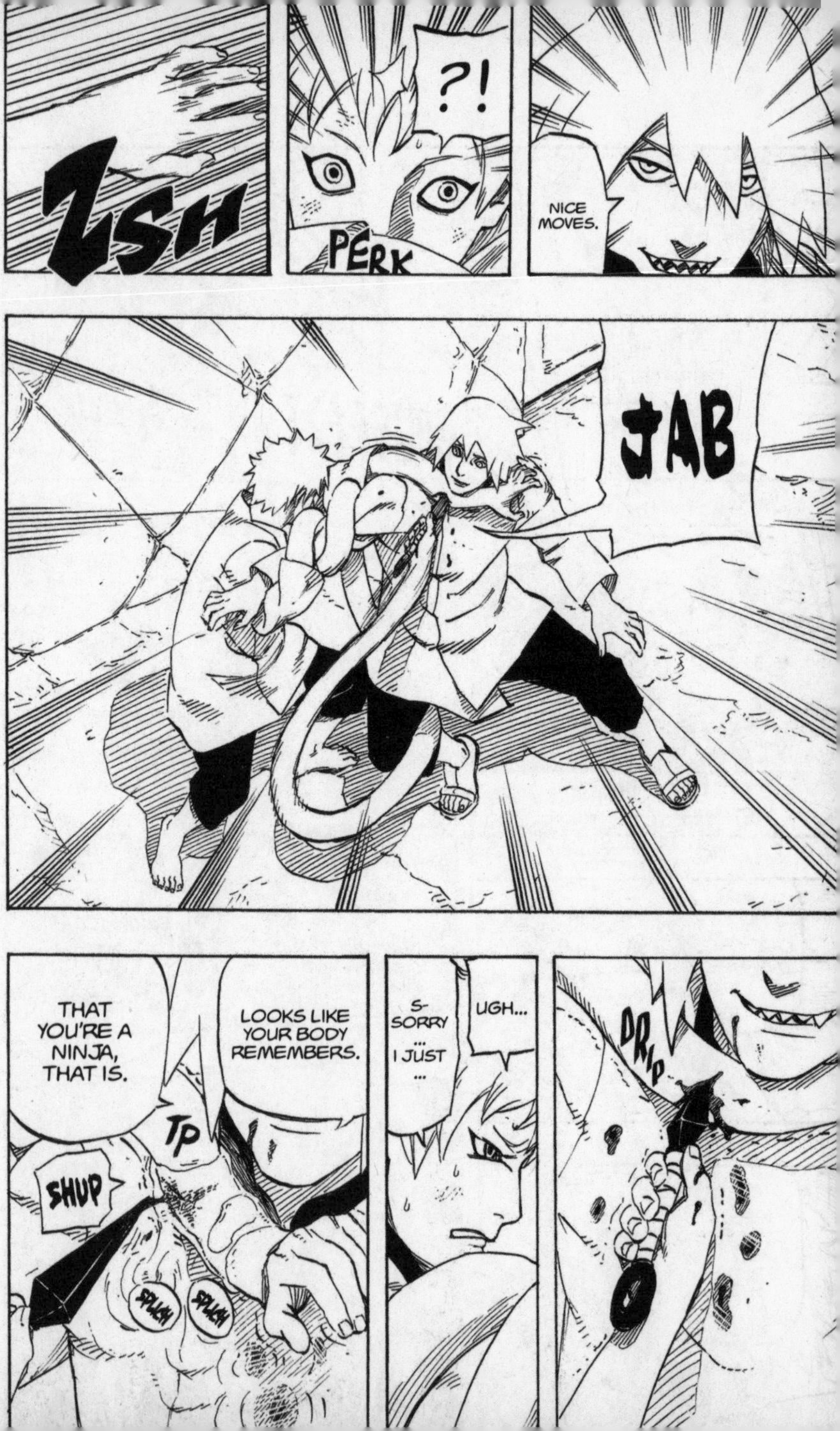
NICE MOVES.
?!
PERK
ZSH
JAB
DRIP
UGH...
S-SORRY ... I JUST ...
LOOKS LIKE YOUR BODY REMEMBERS.
THAT YOU'RE A NINJA, THAT IS.
TP
SHUP
SPLUCH
SPLUCH

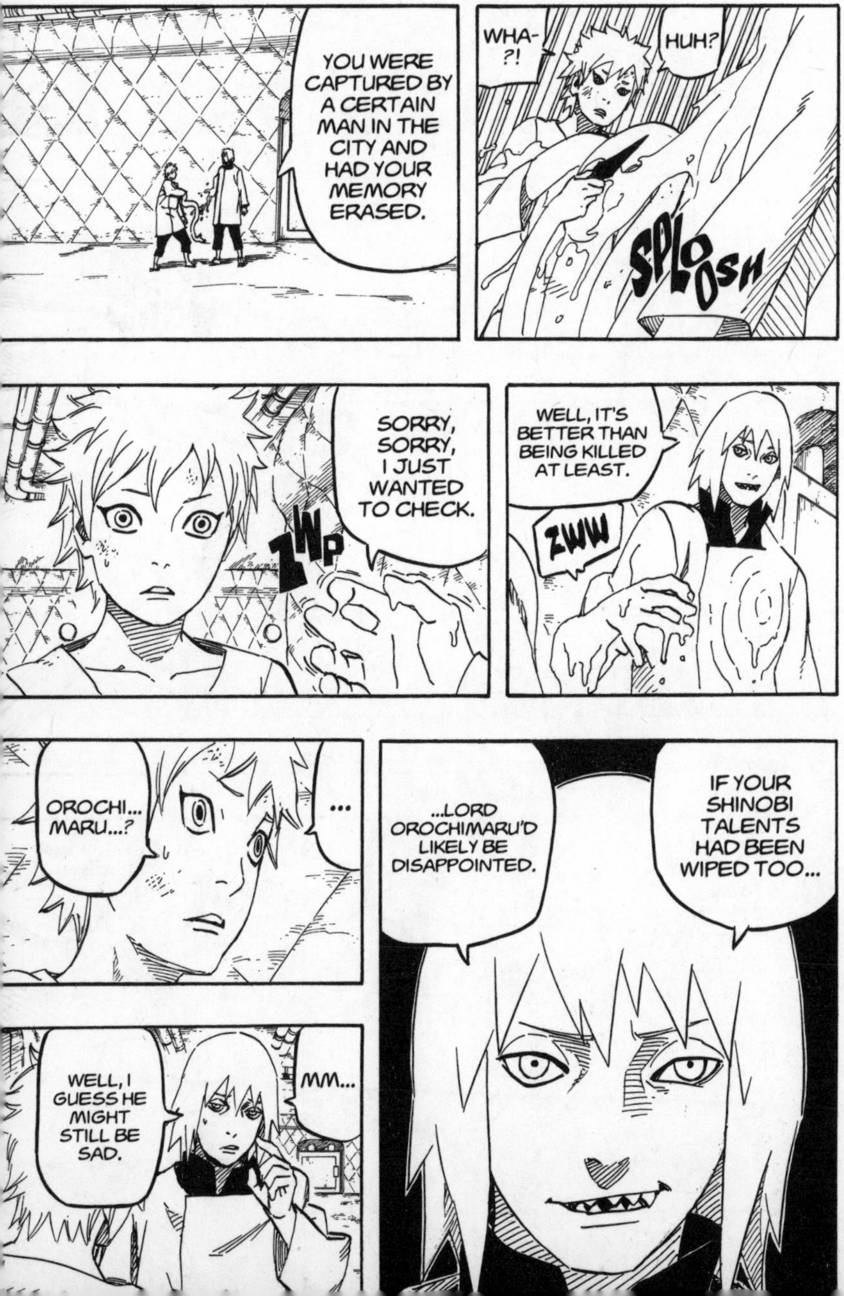
HUH?
WHA- ?!
SPLOOSH
YOU WERE CAPTURED BY A CERTAIN MAN IN THE CITY AND HAD YOUR MEMORY ERASED.
WELL, IT'S BETTER THAN BEING KILLED AT LEAST.
ZWW
SORRY, SORRY, I JUST WANTED TO CHECK.
ZWP
IF YOUR SHINOBI TALENTS HAD BEEN WIPED TOO...
...LORD OROCHIMARU'D LIKELY BE DISAPPOINTED.
...
OROCHI... MARU...?
MM...
WELL, I GUESS HE MIGHT STILL BE SAD.

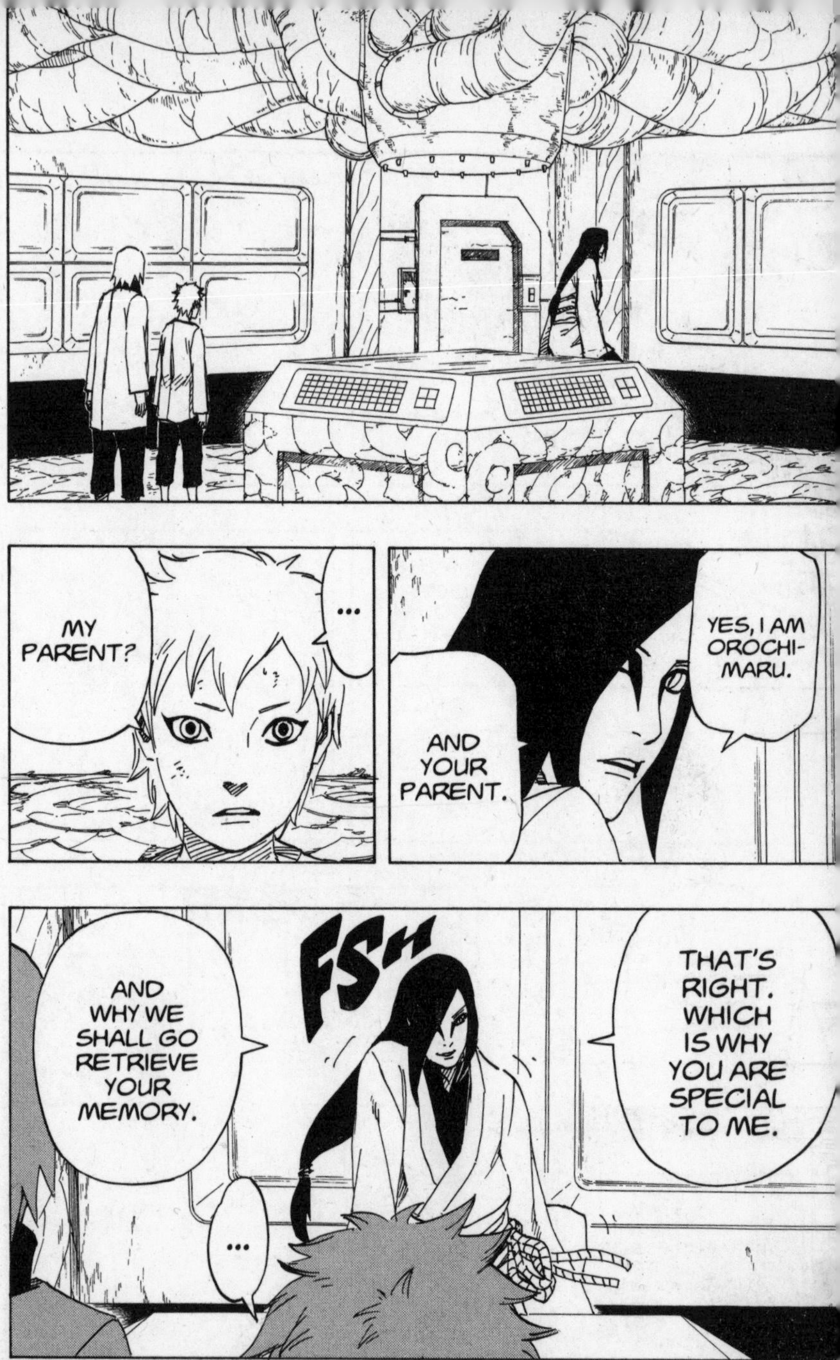
YES, I AM OROCHI-MARU.
AND YOUR PARENT.
...
MY PARENT?
THAT'S RIGHT. WHICH IS WHY YOU ARE SPECIAL TO ME.
FSH
AND WHY WE SHALL GO RETRIEVE YOUR MEMORY.
...

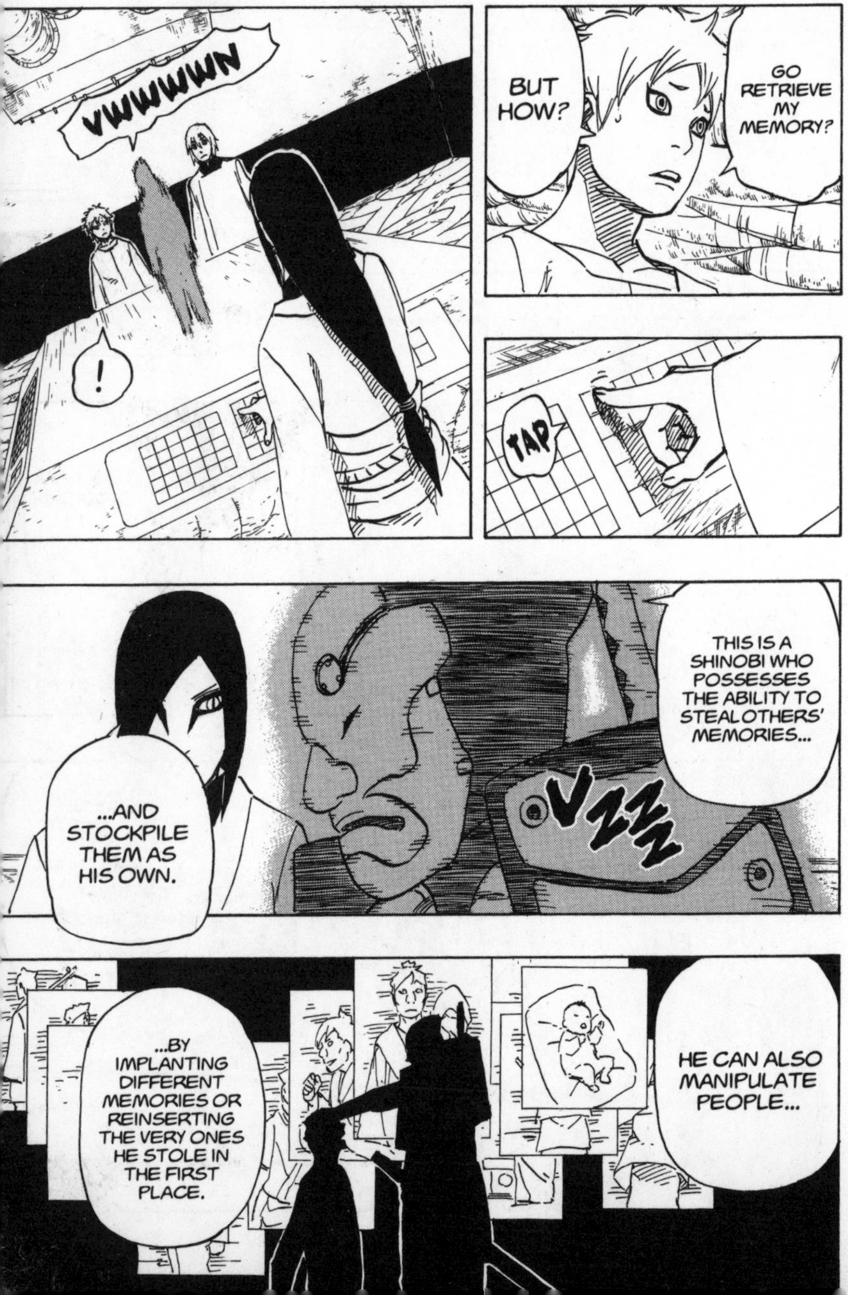
GO RETRIEVE MY MEMORY?
BUT HOW?
TAP
VWWWWN
!
THIS IS A SHINOBI WHO POSSESSES THE ABILITY TO STEAL OTHERS' MEMORIES...
VZZZ
...AND STOCKPILE THEM AS HIS OWN.
HE CAN ALSO MANIPULATE PEOPLE...
...BY IMPLANTING DIFFERENT MEMORIES OR REINSERTING THE VERY ONES HE STOLE IN THE FIRST PLACE.

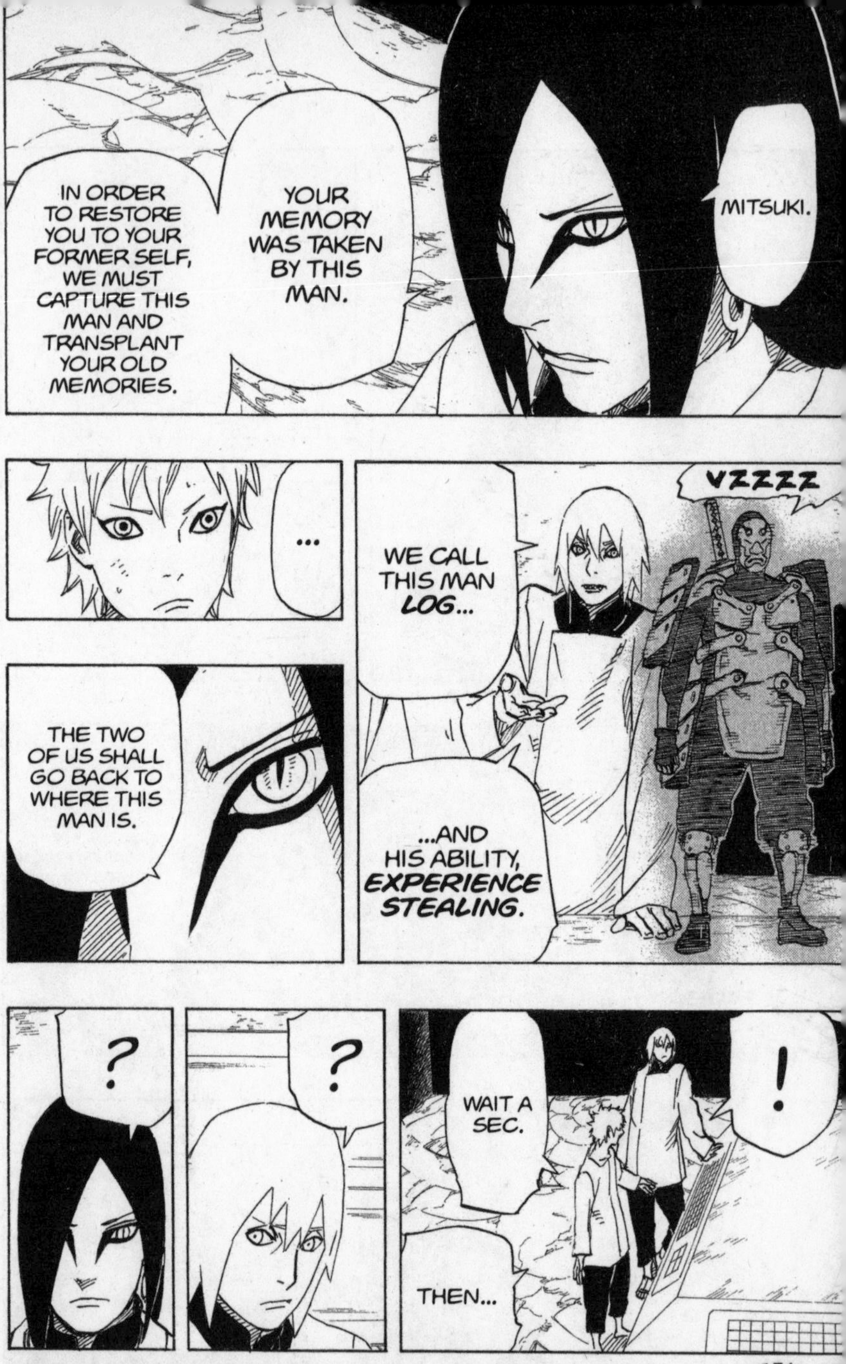
MITSUKI.
YOUR MEMORY WAS TAKEN BY THIS MAN.
IN ORDER TO RESTORE YOU TO YOUR FORMER SELF, WE MUST CAPTURE THIS MAN AND TRANSPLANT YOUR OLD MEMORIES.
VZZZZ
WE CALL THIS MAN *LOG*...
...AND HIS ABILITY, *EXPERIENCE STEALING*.
...
THE TWO OF US SHALL GO BACK TO WHERE THIS MAN IS.
!
WAIT A SEC.
THEN...
?
?

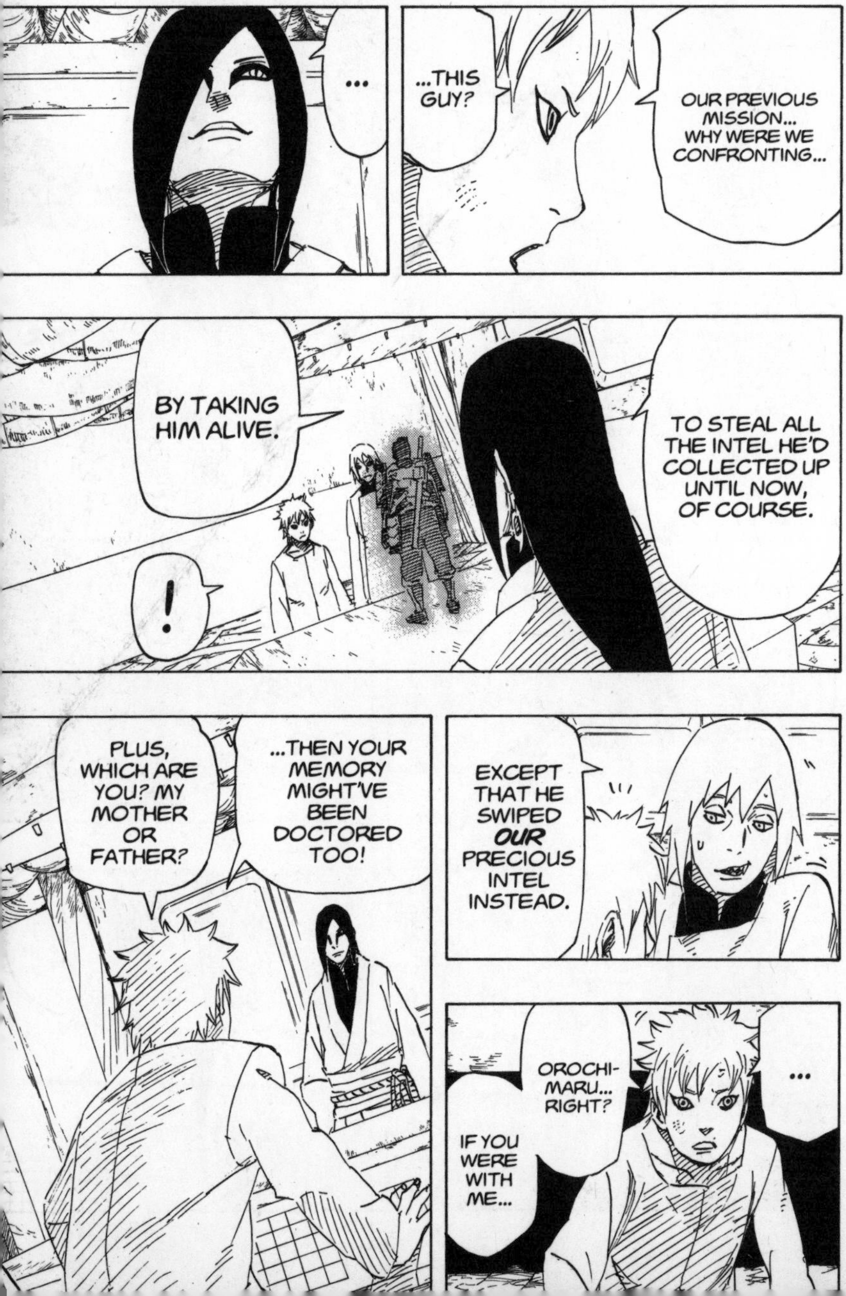
OUR PREVIOUS MISSION... WHY WERE WE CONFRONTING...
...THIS GUY?
...
TO STEAL ALL THE INTEL HE'D COLLECTED UP UNTIL NOW, OF COURSE.
BY TAKING HIM ALIVE.
!
EXCEPT THAT HE SWIPED *OUR* PRECIOUS INTEL INSTEAD.
...
OROCHIMARU... RIGHT?
IF YOU WERE WITH ME...
...THEN YOUR MEMORY MIGHT'VE BEEN DOCTORED TOO!
PLUS, WHICH ARE YOU? MY MOTHER OR FATHER?

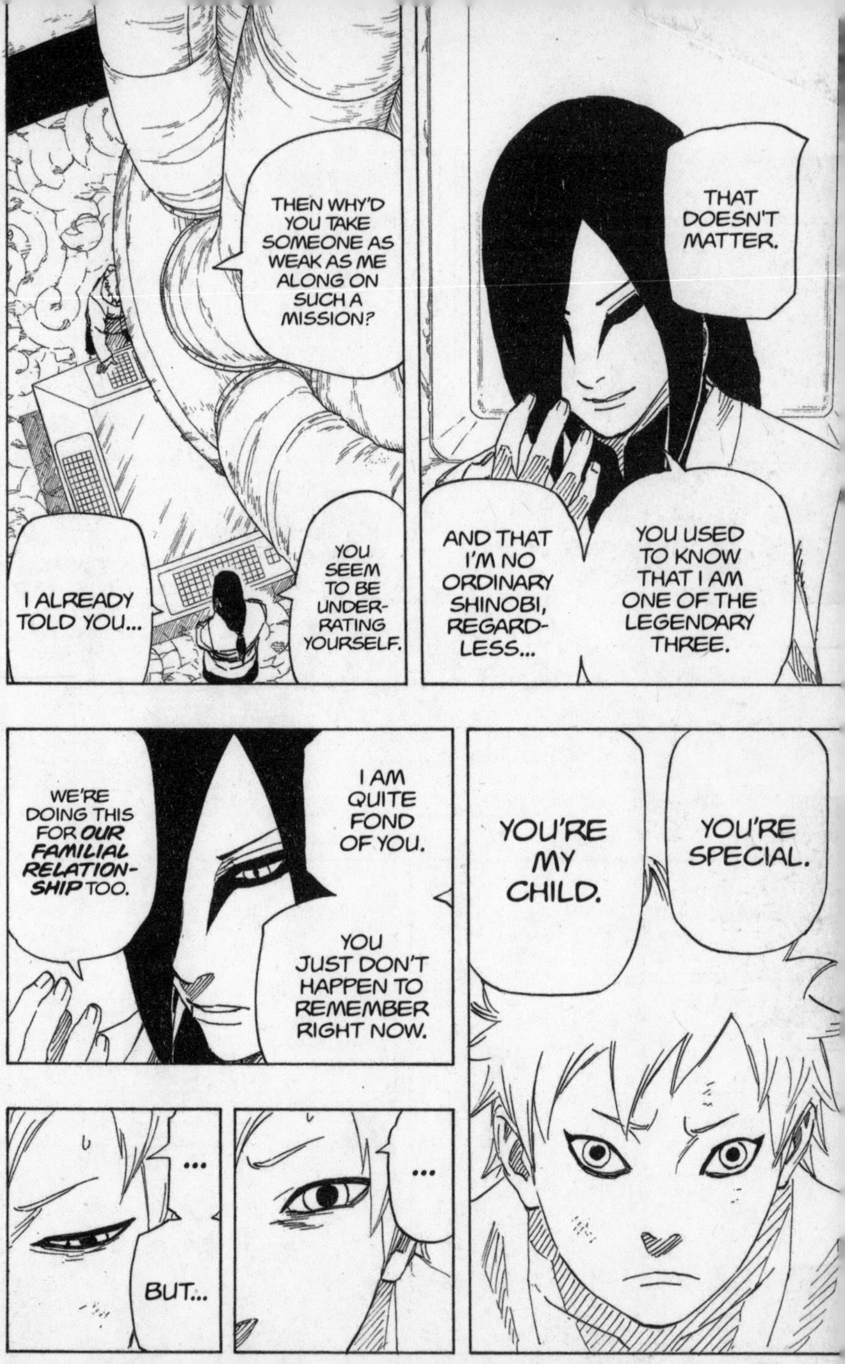
THAT DOESN'T MATTER.
YOU USED TO KNOW THAT I AM ONE OF THE LEGENDARY THREE.
AND THAT I'M NO ORDINARY SHINOBI, REGARDLESS...
THEN WHY'D YOU TAKE SOMEONE AS WEAK AS ME ALONG ON SUCH A MISSION?
YOU SEEM TO BE UNDER-RATING YOURSELF.
I ALREADY TOLD YOU...
YOU'RE SPECIAL.
YOU'RE MY CHILD.
I AM QUITE FOND OF YOU.
YOU JUST DON'T HAPPEN TO REMEMBER RIGHT NOW.
WE'RE DOING THIS FOR ***OUR FAMILIAL RELATIONSHIP*** TOO.
...
...
BUT...

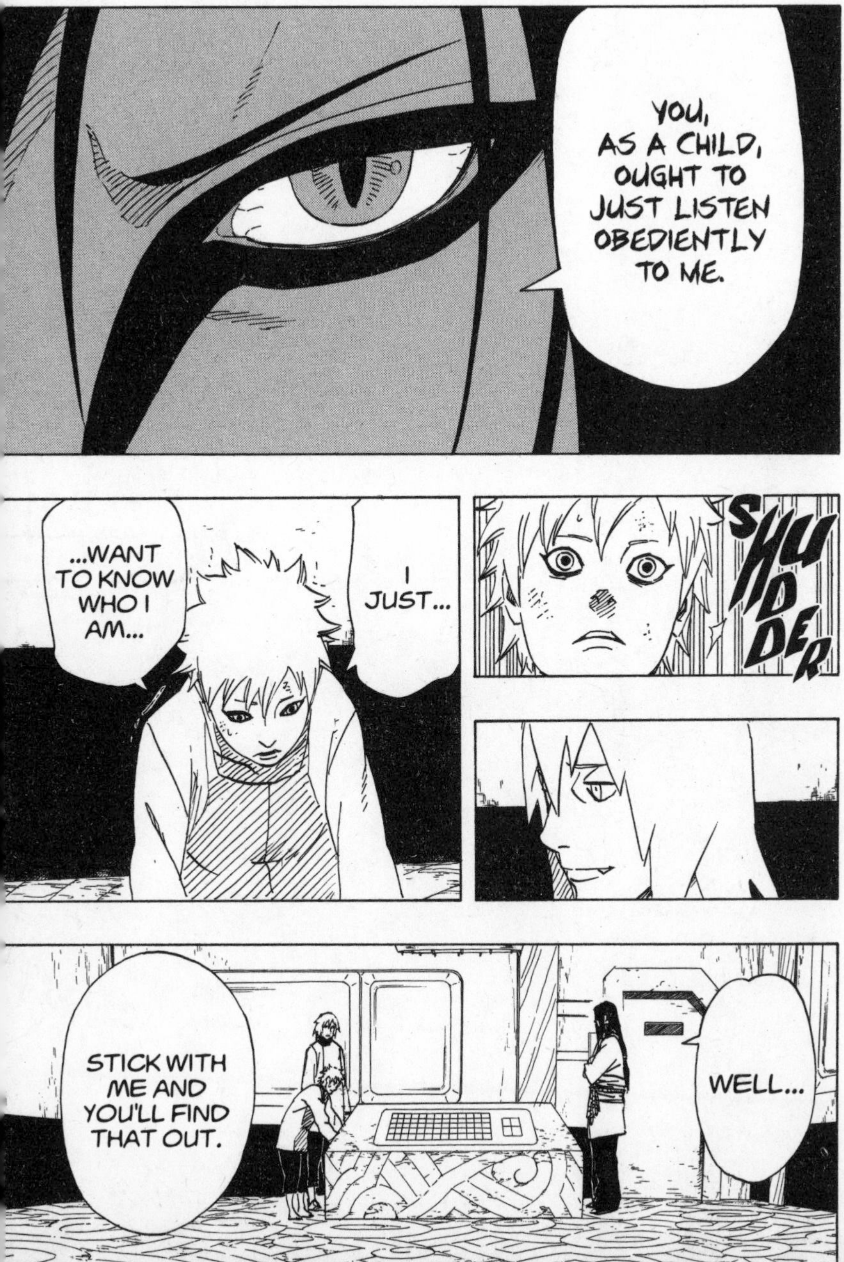
YOU, AS A CHILD, OUGHT TO JUST LISTEN OBEDIENTLY TO ME.
SHUDDER
I JUST...
...WANT TO KNOW WHO I AM...
WELL...
STICK WITH ME AND YOU'LL FIND THAT OUT.

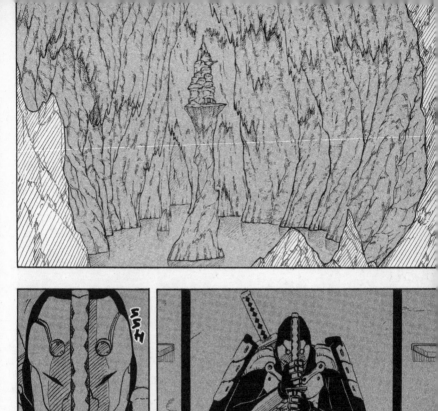

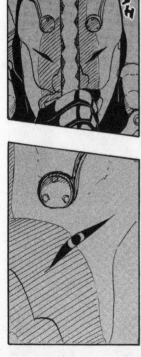

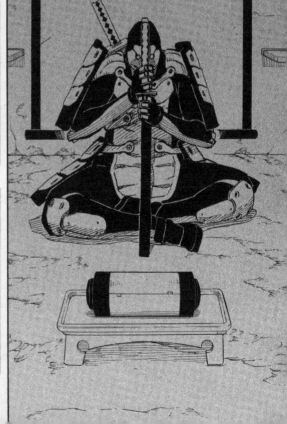

SSH

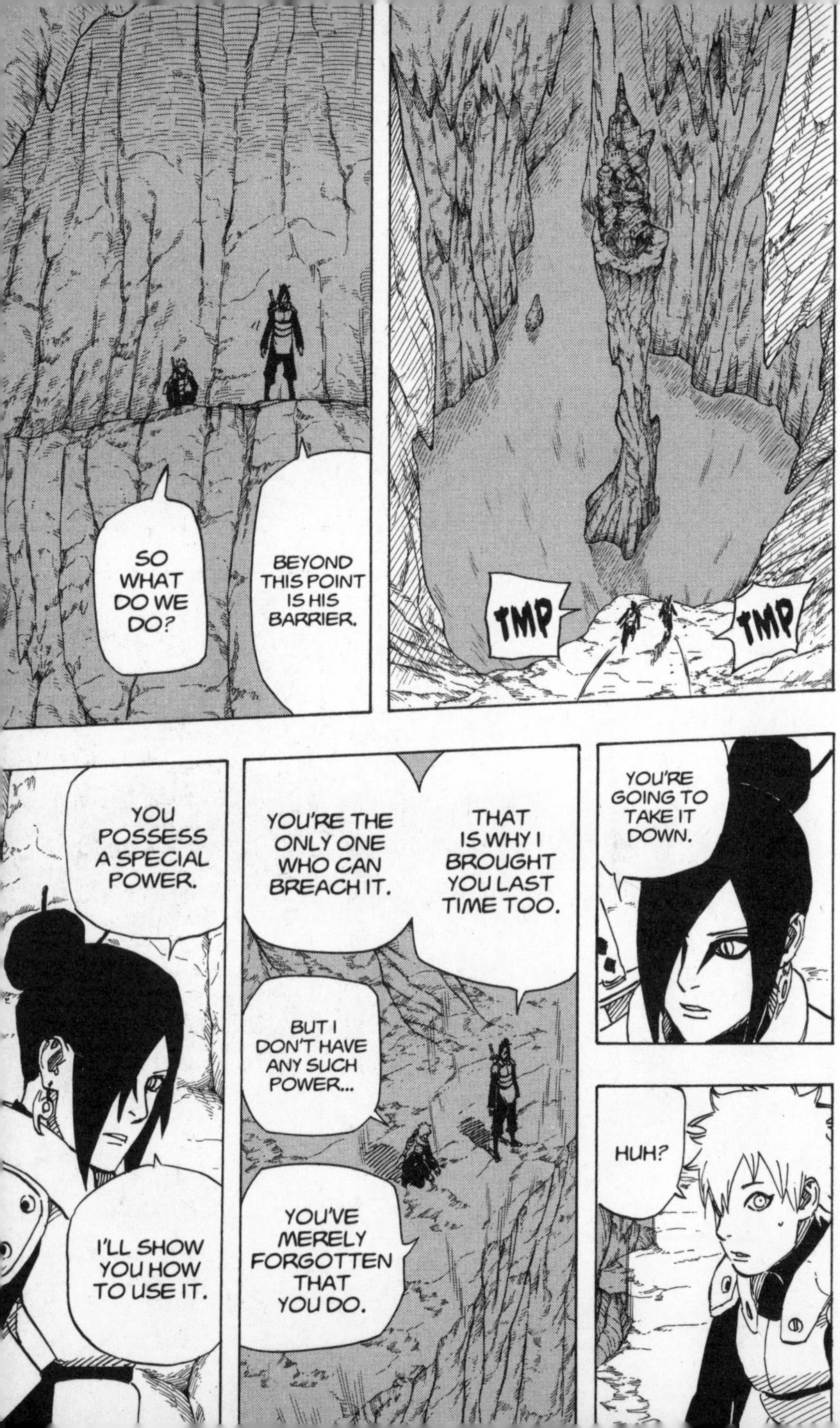
TMP
TMP
BEYOND THIS POINT IS HIS BARRIER.
SO WHAT DO WE DO?
YOU'RE GOING TO TAKE IT DOWN.
HUH?
THAT IS WHY I BROUGHT YOU LAST TIME TOO.
YOU'RE THE ONLY ONE WHO CAN BREACH IT.
BUT I DON'T HAVE ANY SUCH POWER...
YOU'VE MERELY FORGOTTEN THAT YOU DO.
YOU POSSESS A SPECIAL POWER.
I'LL SHOW YOU HOW TO USE IT.

FSH

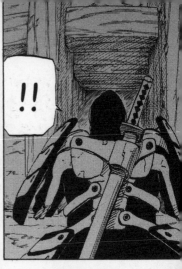

!!

KLAK

SSS

THEY'RE HERE.

MY BARRIER...

ZW OSH

BLUB
BLUB

BLUB

BL UB

BL UB
BLUB

...

180

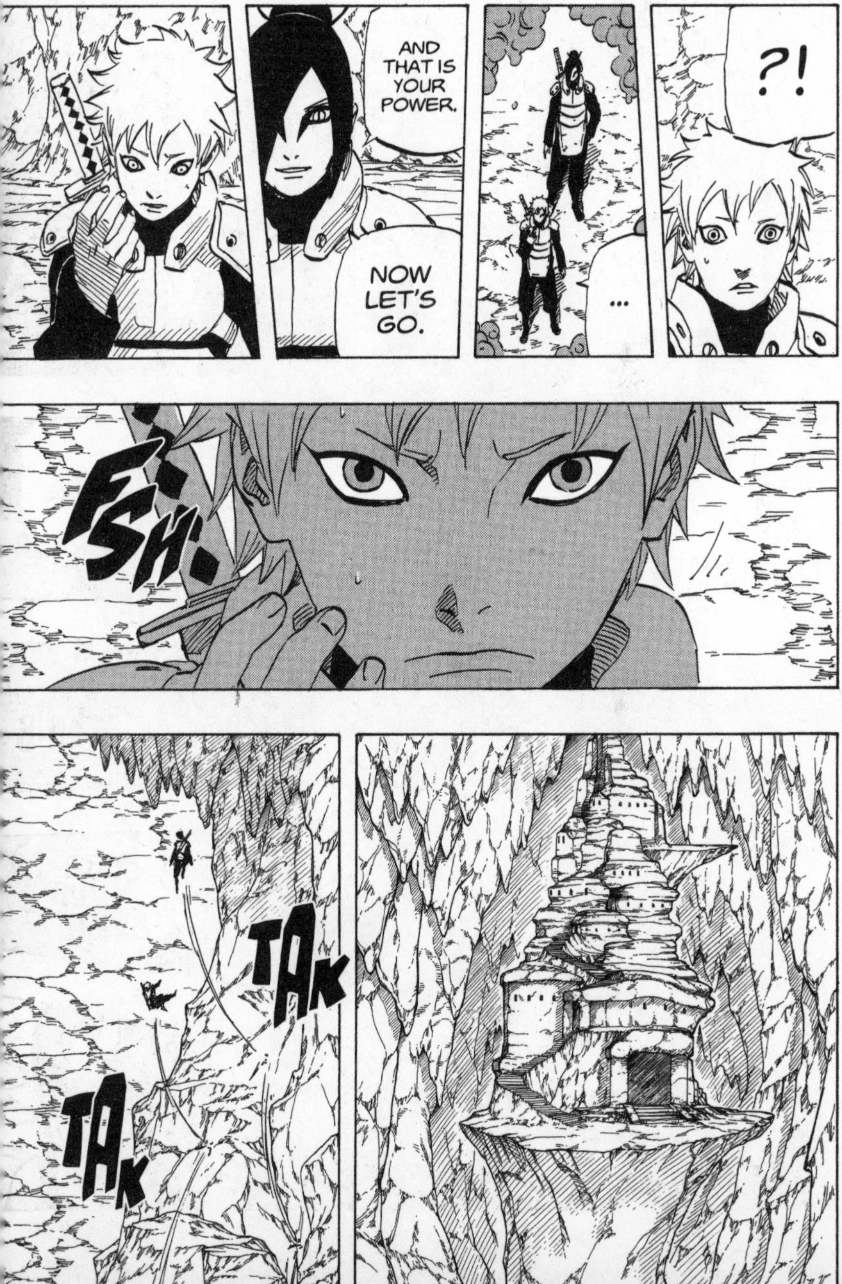
?!
...
AND THAT IS YOUR POWER.
NOW LET'S GO.
FSH
TAK
TAK

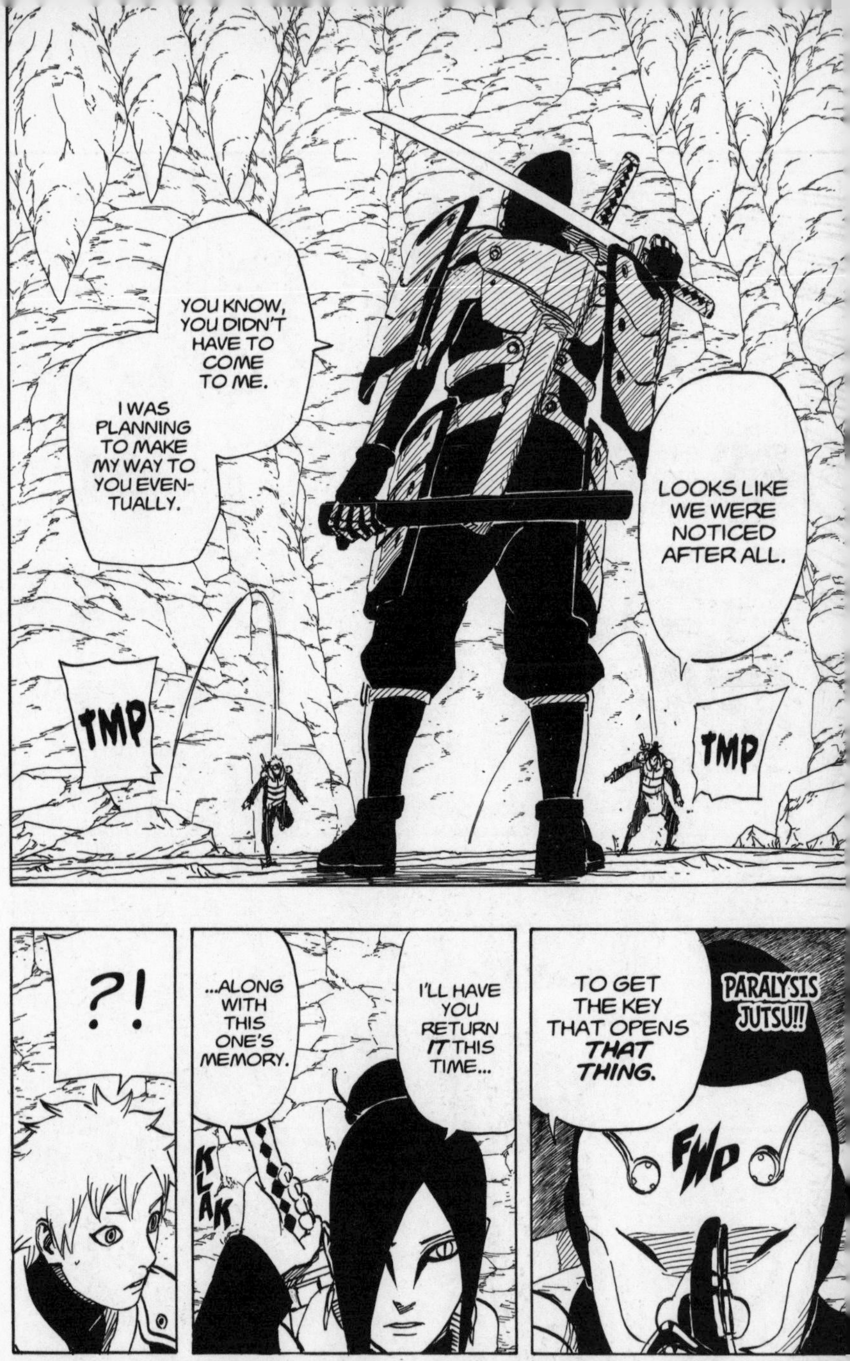
LOOKS LIKE WE WERE NOTICED AFTER ALL.
TMP
YOU KNOW, YOU DIDN'T HAVE TO COME TO ME.
I WAS PLANNING TO MAKE MY WAY TO YOU EVEN-TUALLY.
TMP
PARALYSIS JUTSU!!
TO GET THE KEY THAT OPENS *THAT THING.*
FWP
I'LL HAVE YOU RETURN *IT* THIS TIME...
...ALONG WITH THIS ONE'S MEMORY.
KLAK
?!

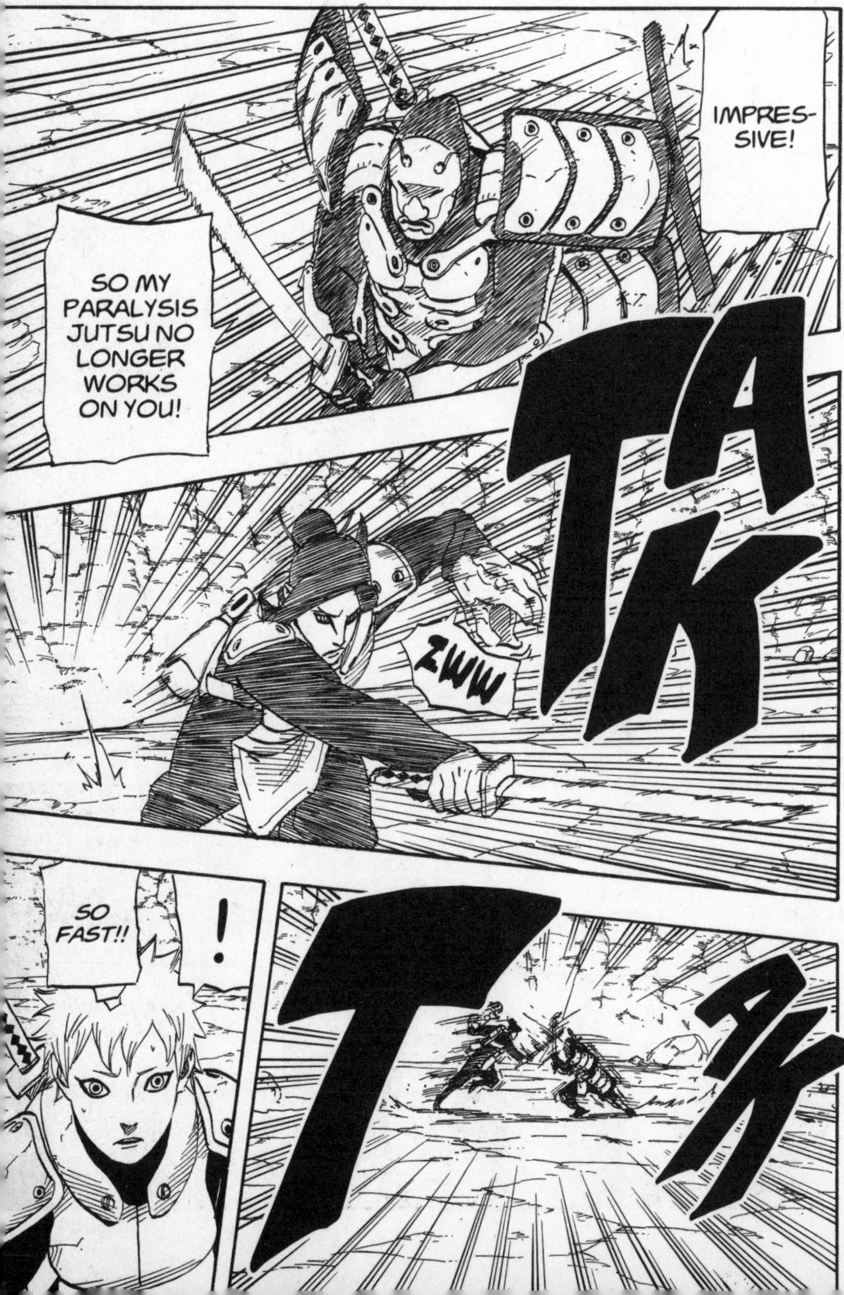
IMPRES-
SIVE!
SO MY PARALYSIS JUTSU NO LONGER WORKS ON YOU!
TAK
ZWW
TAK
!
SO FAST!!

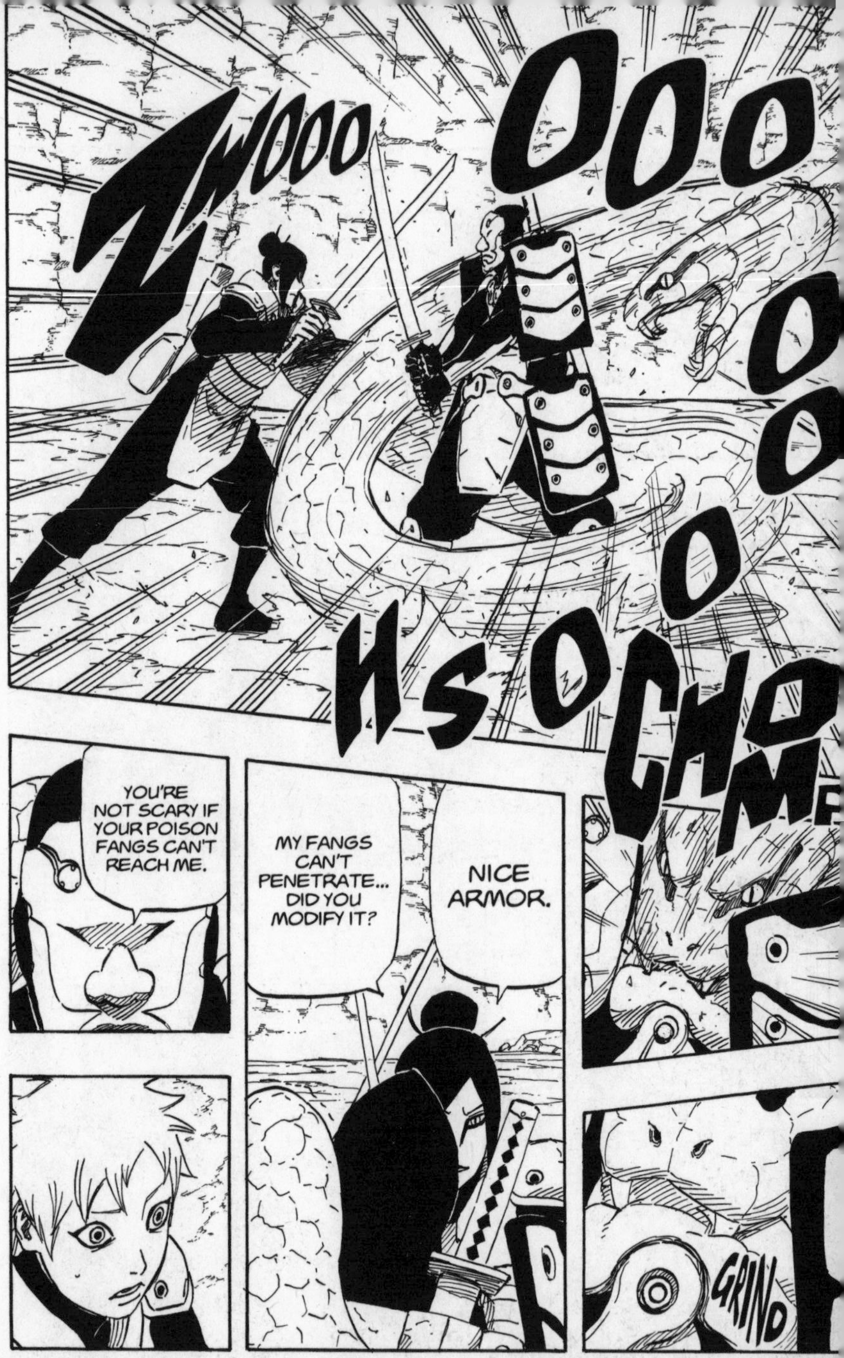
ZWOOOOOOOOOOOOOSH
CHOMP
NICE ARMOR.
MY FANGS CAN'T PENETRATE... DID YOU MODIFY IT?
YOU'RE NOT SCARY IF YOUR POISON FANGS CAN'T REACH ME.
GRIND

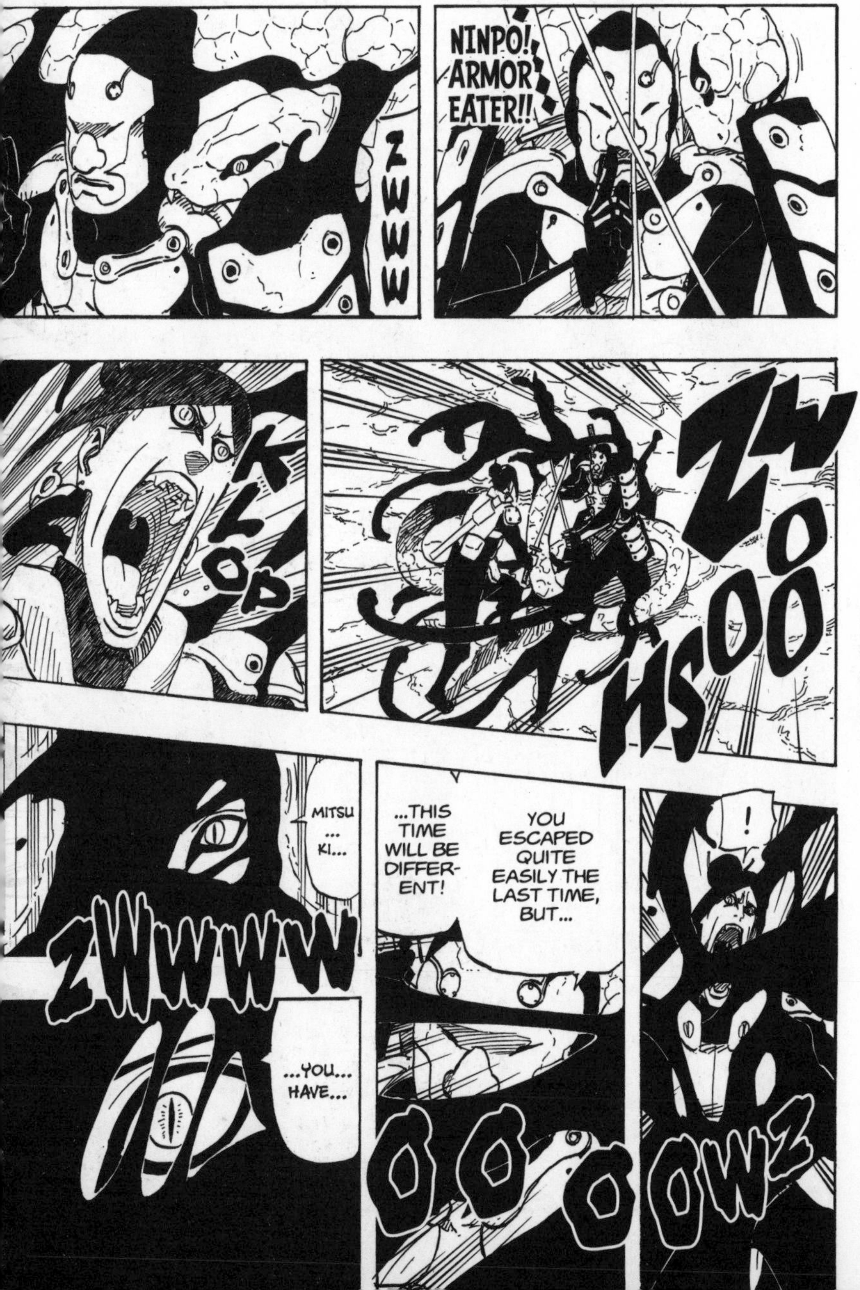
NINPO! ARMOR EATER!!
ZWWWW
ZWOOOSH
KLOP
!
YOU ESCAPED QUITE EASILY THE LAST TIME, BUT...
...THIS TIME WILL BE DIFFER-ENT!
MITSU ... KI...
ZWWWWW
...YOU... HAVE...
ZWOOOO

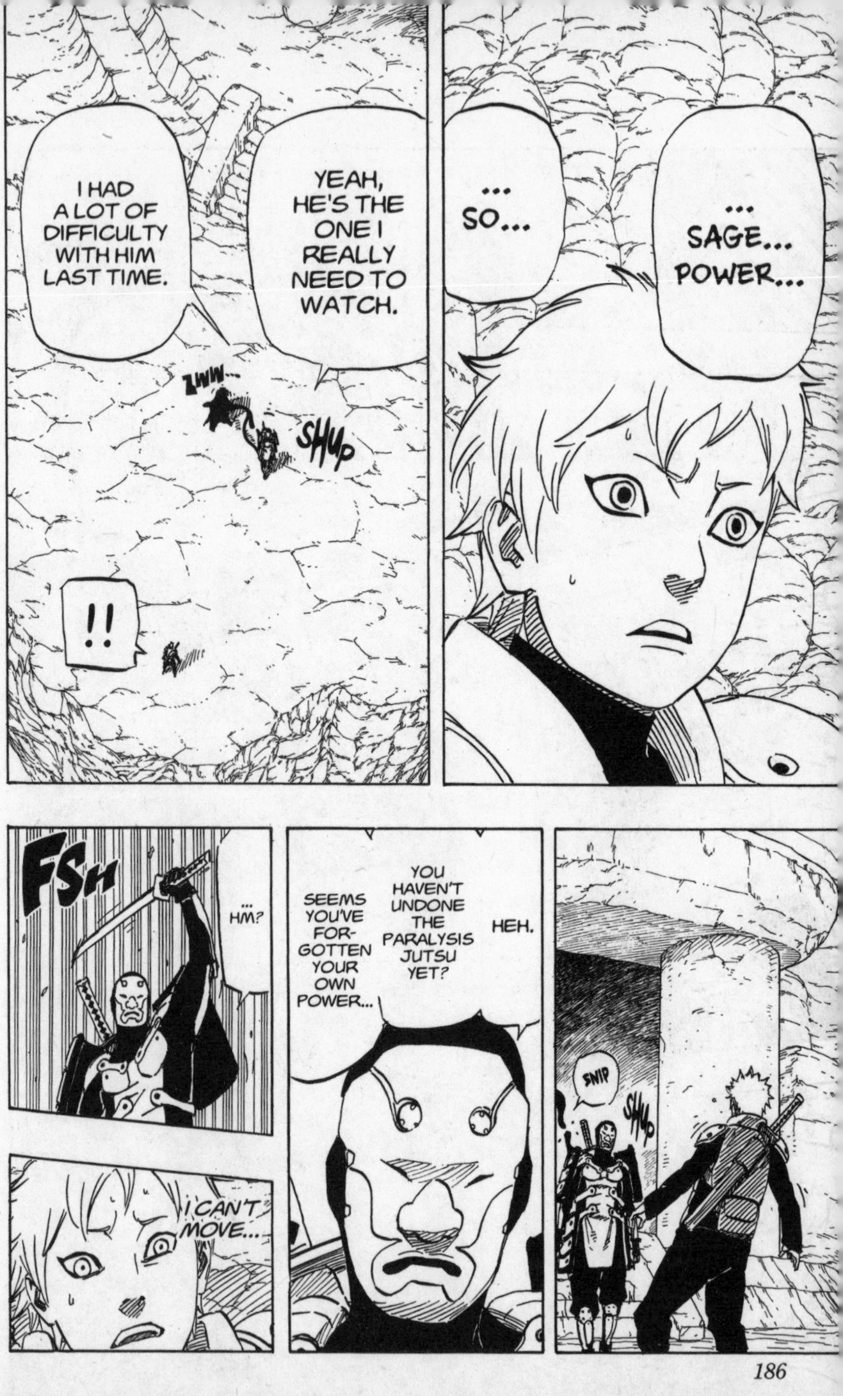
... SAGE... POWER...
... SO...
YEAH, HE'S THE ONE I REALLY NEED TO WATCH.
I HAD A LOT OF DIFFICULTY WITH HIM LAST TIME.
ZWW...
SHUP
!!
SNIP
SHUP
HEH.
YOU HAVEN'T UNDONE THE PARALYSIS JUTSU YET?
SEEMS YOU'VE FOR-GOTTEN YOUR OWN POWER...
FSH
... HM?
I CAN'T MOVE...

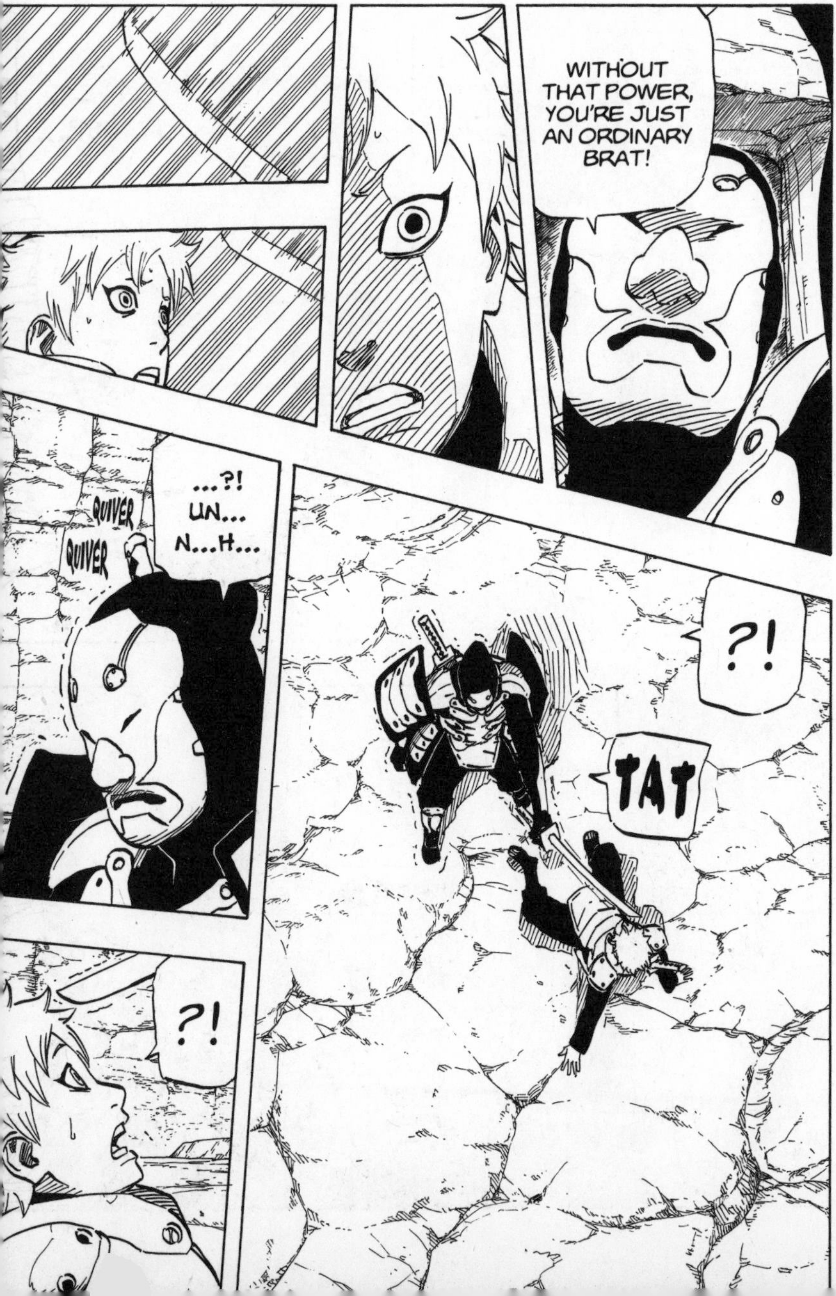
WITHOUT THAT POWER, YOU'RE JUST AN ORDINARY BRAT!
?!
TAT
...?! UN... N...H...
QUIVER
QUIVER
?!

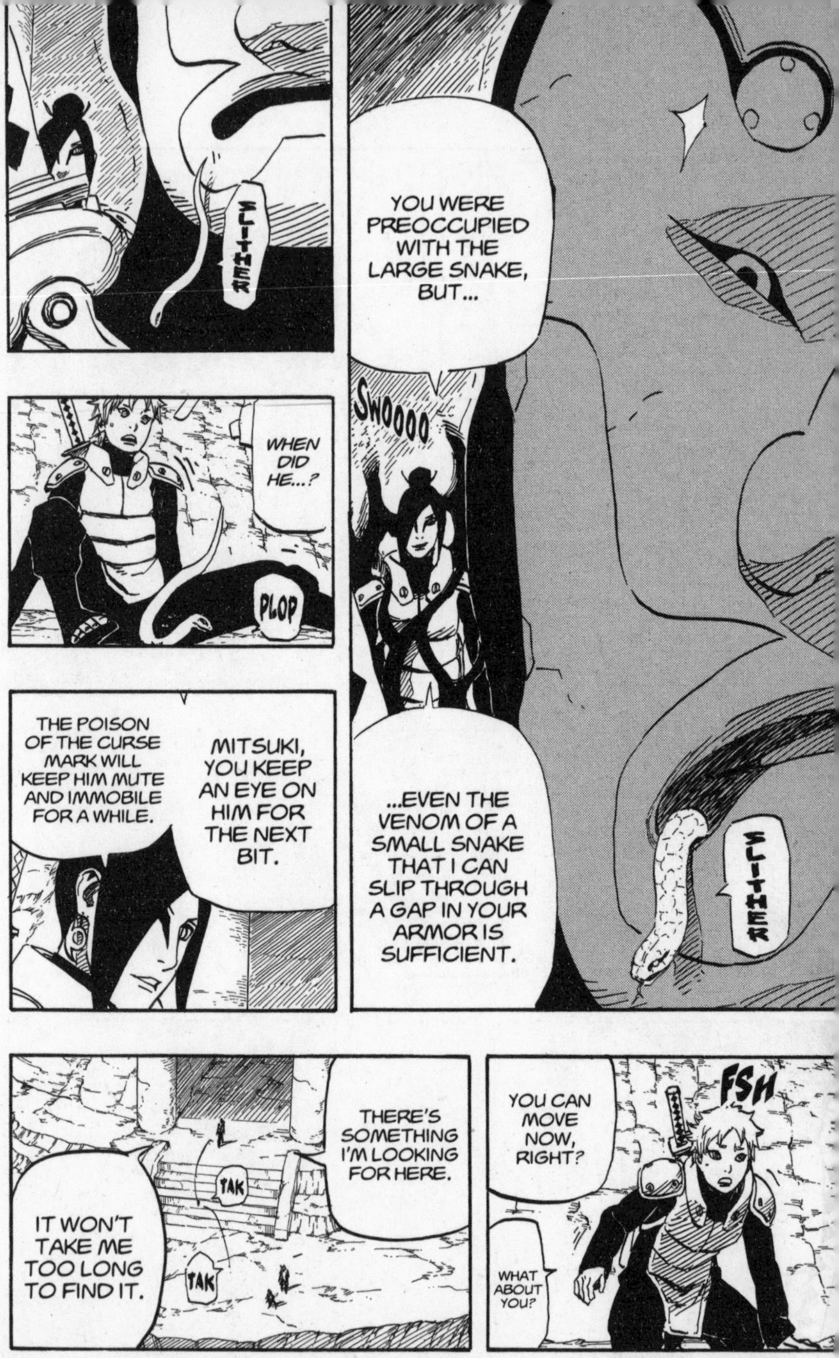
YOU WERE PREOCCUPIED WITH THE LARGE SNAKE, BUT...
SWOOOO
...EVEN THE VENOM OF A SMALL SNAKE THAT I CAN SLIP THROUGH A GAP IN YOUR ARMOR IS SUFFICIENT.
SLITHER
SLITHER
WHEN DID HE...?
PLOP
MITSUKI, YOU KEEP AN EYE ON HIM FOR THE NEXT BIT.
THE POISON OF THE CURSE MARK WILL KEEP HIM MUTE AND IMMOBILE FOR A WHILE.
FSH
YOU CAN MOVE NOW, RIGHT?
WHAT ABOUT YOU?
THERE'S SOMETHING I'M LOOKING FOR HERE.
TAK
TAK
IT WON'T TAKE ME TOO LONG TO FIND IT.

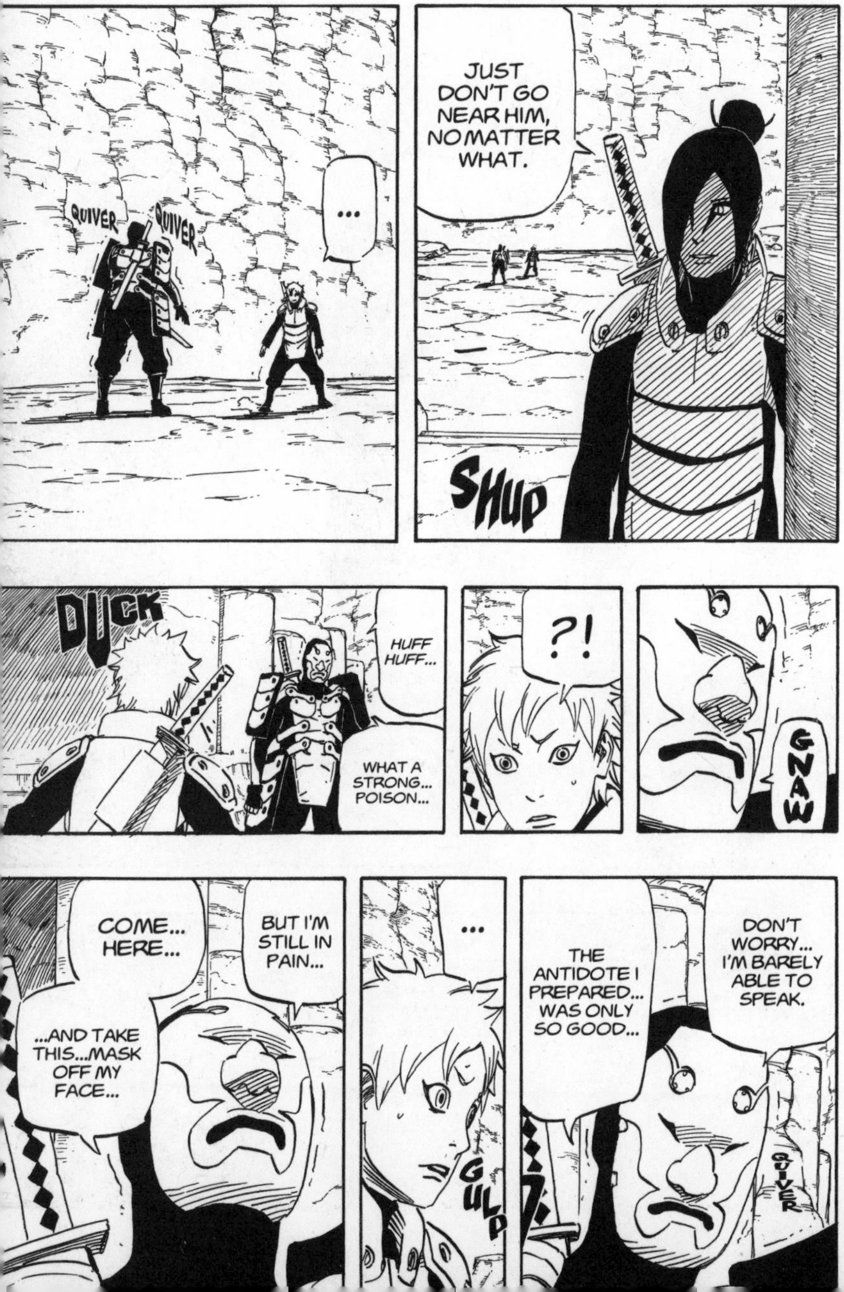
JUST DON'T GO NEAR HIM, NO MATTER WHAT.
SHUP
...
QUIVER
QUIVER
GNAW
?!
DUCK
HUFF HUFF...
WHAT A STRONG... POISON...
DON'T WORRY... I'M BARELY ABLE TO SPEAK.
THE ANTIDOTE I PREPARED... WAS ONLY SO GOOD...
QUIVER
...
GULP
BUT I'M STILL IN PAIN...
COME... HERE...
...AND TAKE THIS...MASK OFF MY FACE...

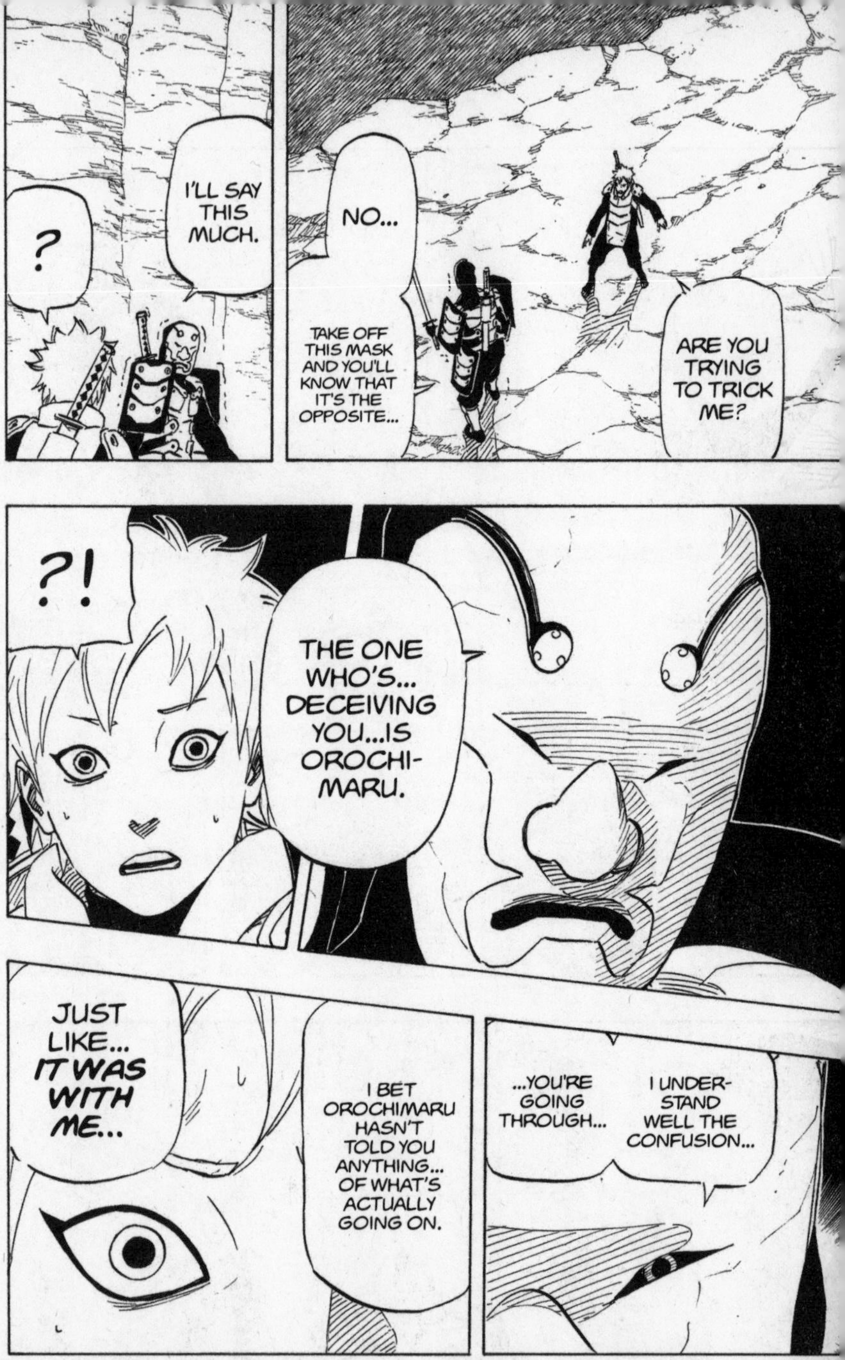
ARE YOU TRYING TO TRICK ME?
NO...
TAKE OFF THIS MASK AND YOU'LL KNOW THAT IT'S THE OPPOSITE...
I'LL SAY THIS MUCH.
?
THE ONE WHO'S... DECEIVING YOU...IS OROCHI-MARU.
?!
I UNDER-STAND WELL THE CONFUSION...
...YOU'RE GOING THROUGH...
I BET OROCHIMARU HASN'T TOLD YOU ANYTHING... OF WHAT'S ACTUALLY GOING ON.
JUST LIKE... *IT WAS WITH ME...*

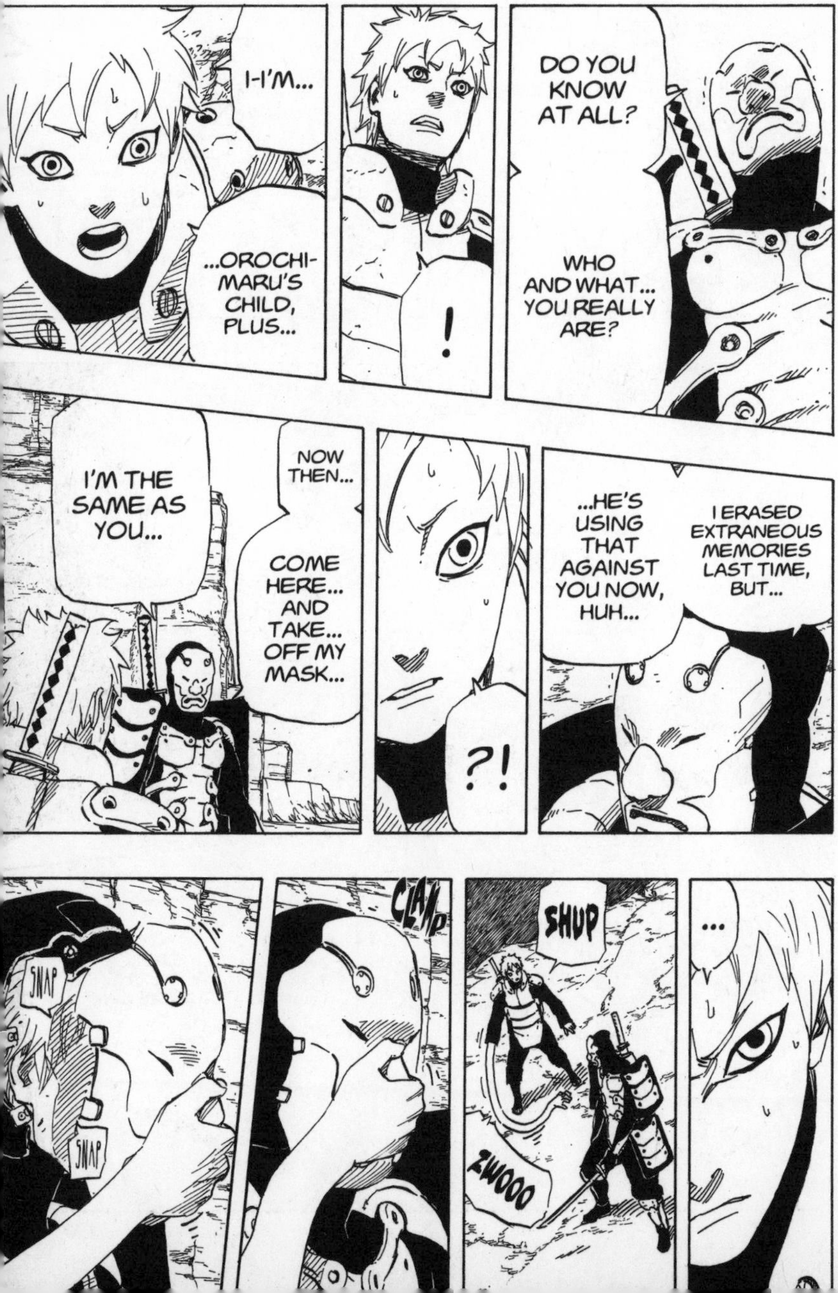
DO YOU KNOW AT ALL?
WHO AND WHAT... YOU REALLY ARE?
!
I-I'M...
...OROCHIMARU'S CHILD, PLUS...
I ERASED EXTRANEOUS MEMORIES LAST TIME, BUT...
...HE'S USING THAT AGAINST YOU NOW, HUH...
?!
NOW THEN...
COME HERE... AND TAKE... OFF MY MASK...
I'M THE SAME AS YOU...
...
SHUP
ZWOOO
CLAMP
SNAP
SNAP

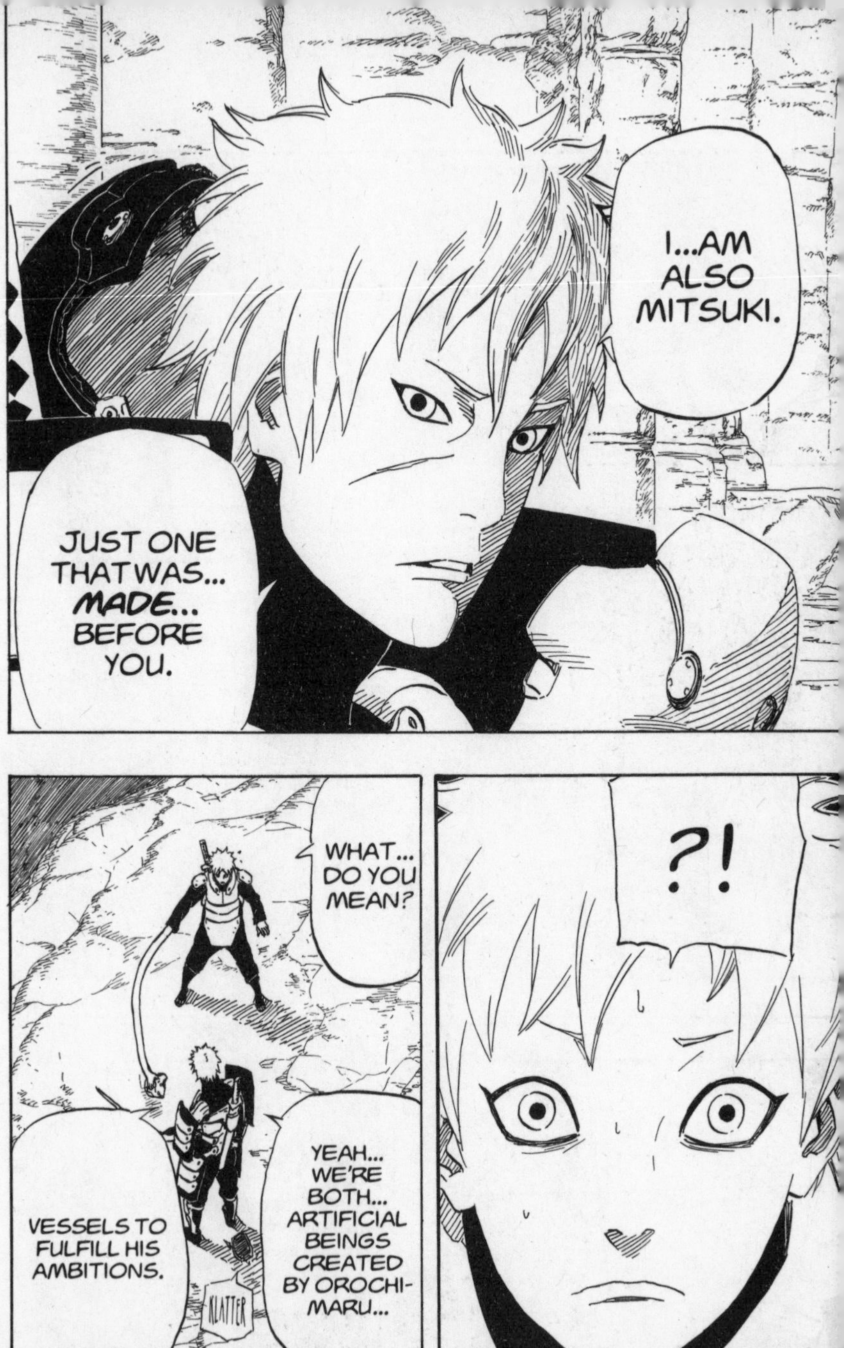
I...AM ALSO MITSUKI.
JUST ONE THAT WAS... MADE... BEFORE YOU.
?!
WHAT... DO YOU MEAN?
YEAH... WE'RE BOTH... ARTIFICIAL BEINGS CREATED BY OROCHI-MARU...
VESSELS TO FULFILL HIS AMBITIONS.
KLATTER

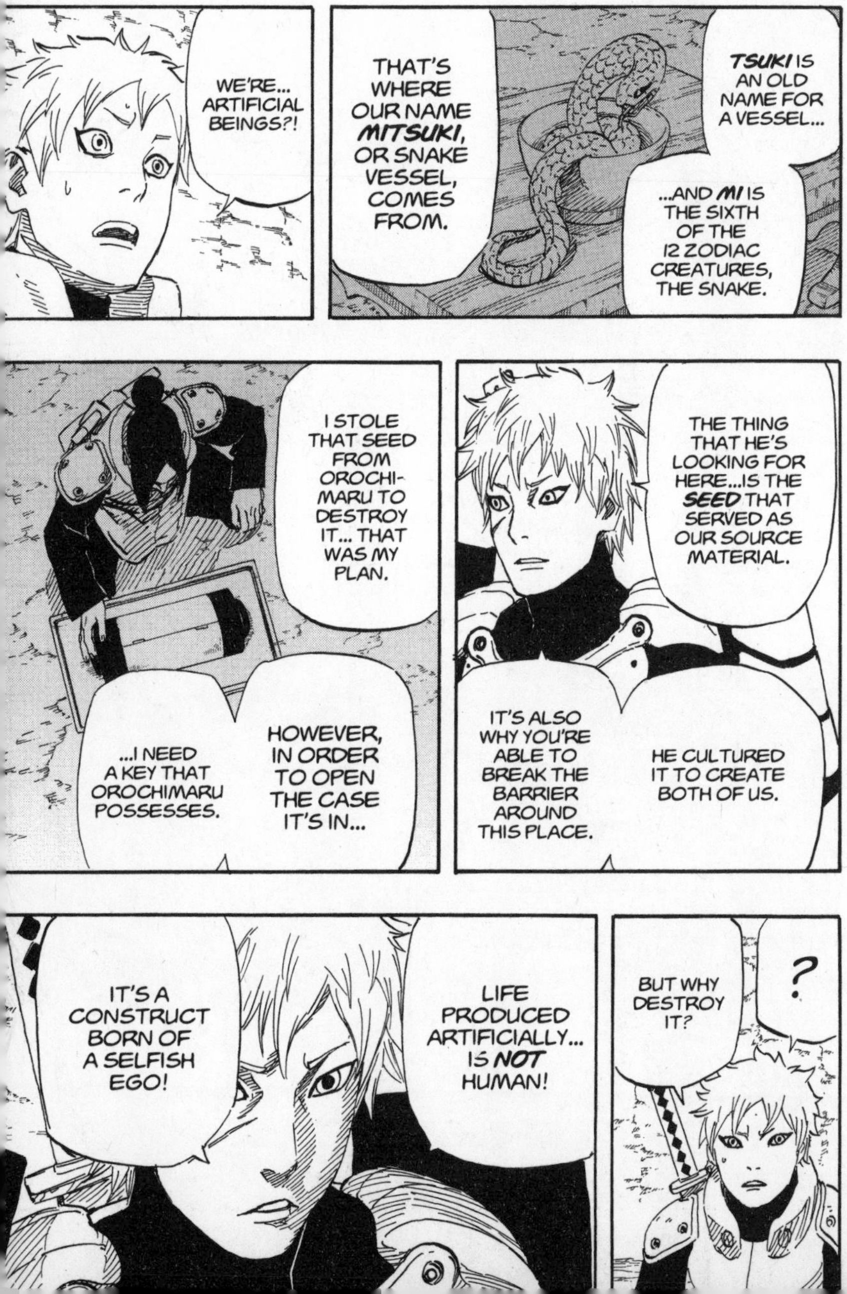
TSUKI IS AN OLD NAME FOR A VESSEL...
...AND MI IS THE SIXTH OF THE 12 ZODIAC CREATURES, THE SNAKE.
THAT'S WHERE OUR NAME MITSUKI, OR SNAKE VESSEL, COMES FROM.
WE'RE... ARTIFICIAL BEINGS?!
THE THING THAT HE'S LOOKING FOR HERE...IS THE SEED THAT SERVED AS OUR SOURCE MATERIAL.
HE CULTURED IT TO CREATE BOTH OF US.
IT'S ALSO WHY YOU'RE ABLE TO BREAK THE BARRIER AROUND THIS PLACE.
I STOLE THAT SEED FROM OROCHIMARU TO DESTROY IT... THAT WAS MY PLAN.
HOWEVER, IN ORDER TO OPEN THE CASE IT'S IN...
...I NEED A KEY THAT OROCHIMARU POSSESSES.
?
BUT WHY DESTROY IT?
LIFE PRODUCED ARTIFICIALLY... IS NOT HUMAN!
IT'S A CONSTRUCT BORN OF A SELFISH EGO!

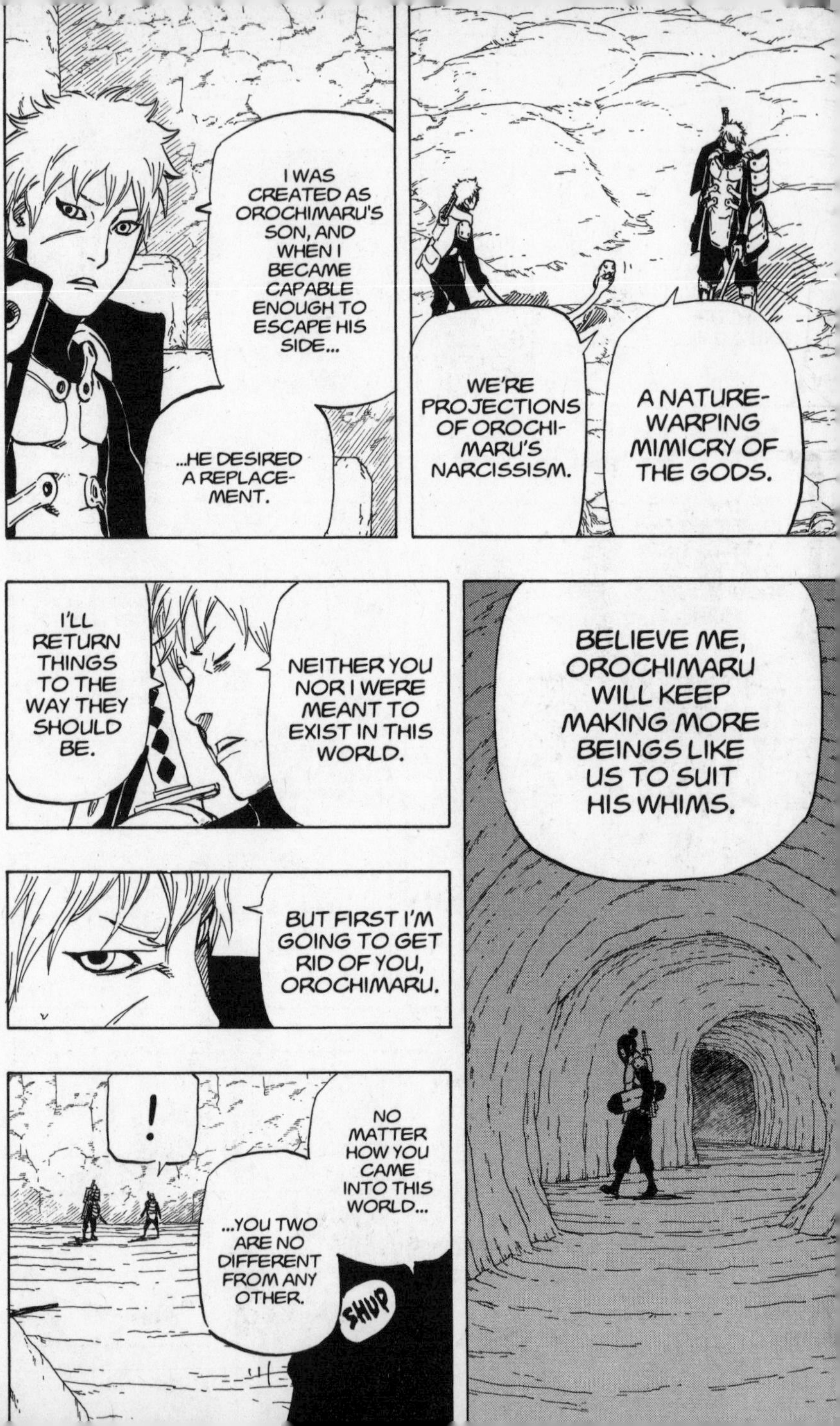
A NATURE-WARPING MIMICRY OF THE GODS.
WE'RE PROJECTIONS OF OROCHIMARU'S NARCISSISM.
I WAS CREATED AS OROCHIMARU'S SON, AND WHEN I BECAME CAPABLE ENOUGH TO ESCAPE HIS SIDE...
...HE DESIRED A REPLACEMENT.
BELIEVE ME, OROCHIMARU WILL KEEP MAKING MORE BEINGS LIKE US TO SUIT HIS WHIMS.
NEITHER YOU NOR I WERE MEANT TO EXIST IN THIS WORLD.
I'LL RETURN THINGS TO THE WAY THEY SHOULD BE.
BUT FIRST I'M GOING TO GET RID OF YOU, OROCHIMARU.
!
NO MATTER HOW YOU CAME INTO THIS WORLD...
...YOU TWO ARE NO DIFFERENT FROM ANY OTHER.
SHUP

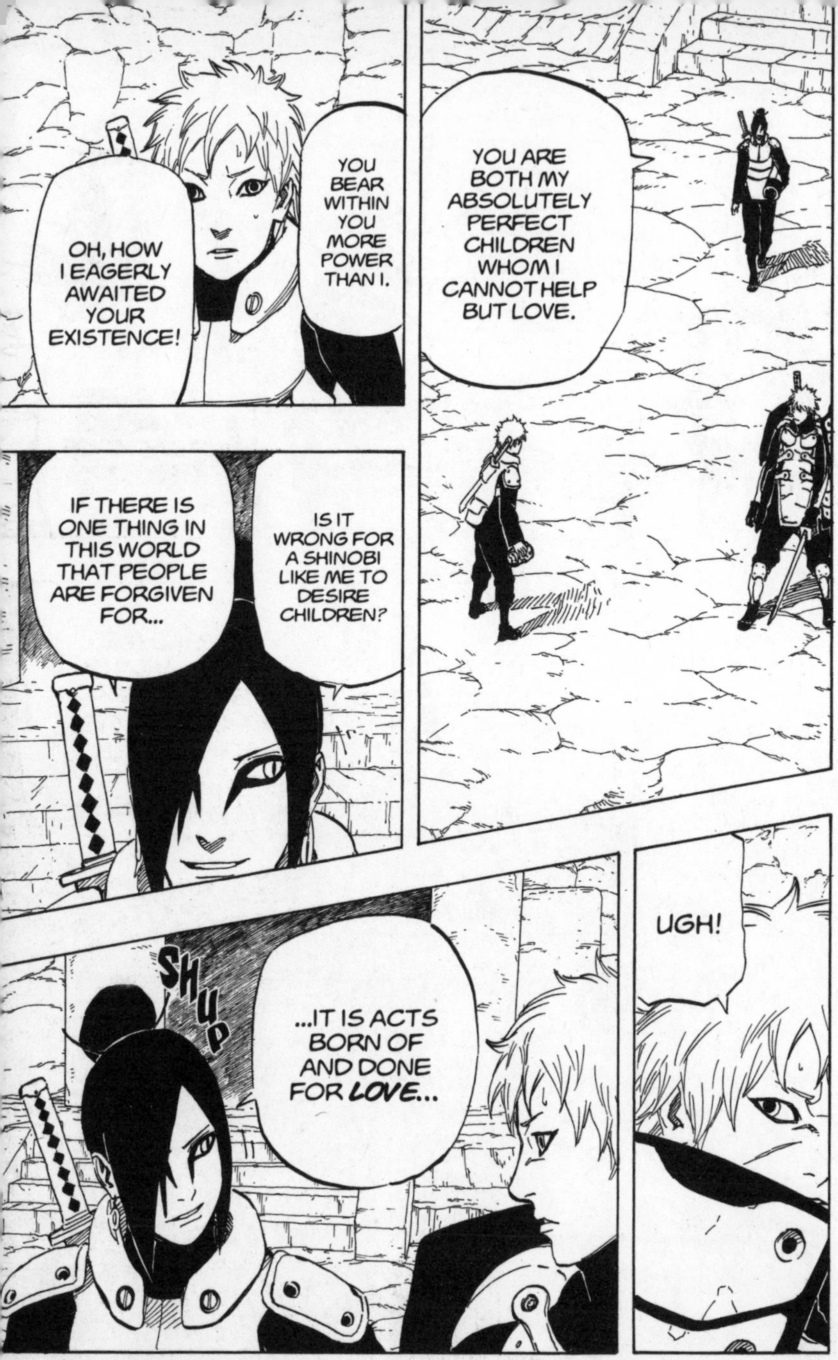
YOU ARE BOTH MY ABSOLUTELY PERFECT CHILDREN WHOM I CANNOT HELP BUT LOVE.
YOU BEAR WITHIN YOU MORE POWER THAN I.
OH, HOW I EAGERLY AWAITED YOUR EXISTENCE!
IS IT WRONG FOR A SHINOBI LIKE ME TO DESIRE CHILDREN?
IF THERE IS ONE THING IN THIS WORLD THAT PEOPLE ARE FORGIVEN FOR...
SHUP
...IT IS ACTS BORN OF AND DONE FOR *LOVE*...
UGH!

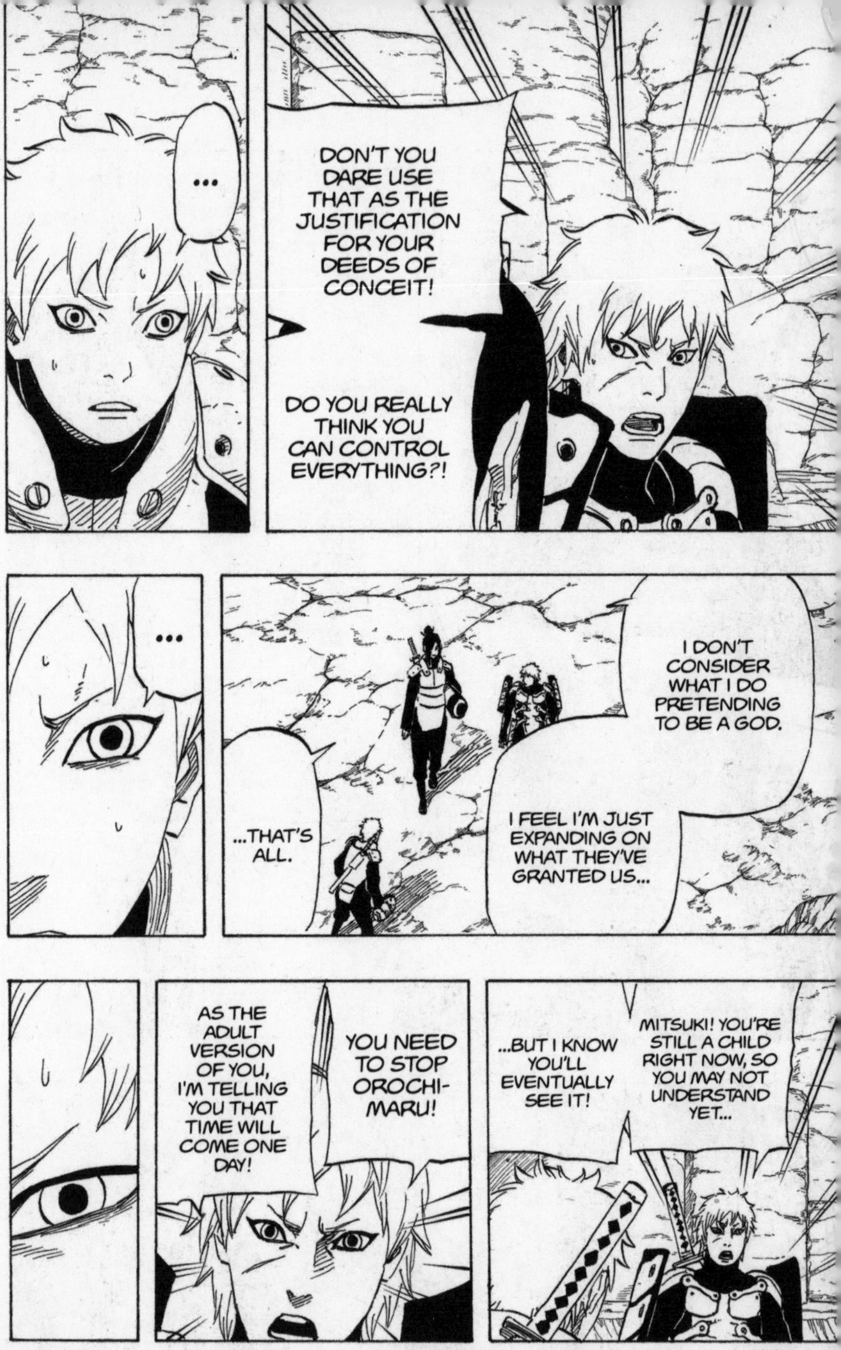
DON'T YOU DARE USE THAT AS THE JUSTIFICATION FOR YOUR DEEDS OF CONCEIT!
DO YOU REALLY THINK YOU CAN CONTROL EVERYTHING?!
...
I DON'T CONSIDER WHAT I DO PRETENDING TO BE A GOD.
I FEEL I'M JUST EXPANDING ON WHAT THEY'VE GRANTED US...
...THAT'S ALL.
...
MITSUKI! YOU'RE STILL A CHILD RIGHT NOW, SO YOU MAY NOT UNDERSTAND YET...
...BUT I KNOW YOU'LL EVENTUALLY SEE IT!
YOU NEED TO STOP OROCHI-MARU!
AS THE ADULT VERSION OF YOU, I'M TELLING YOU THAT TIME WILL COME ONE DAY!

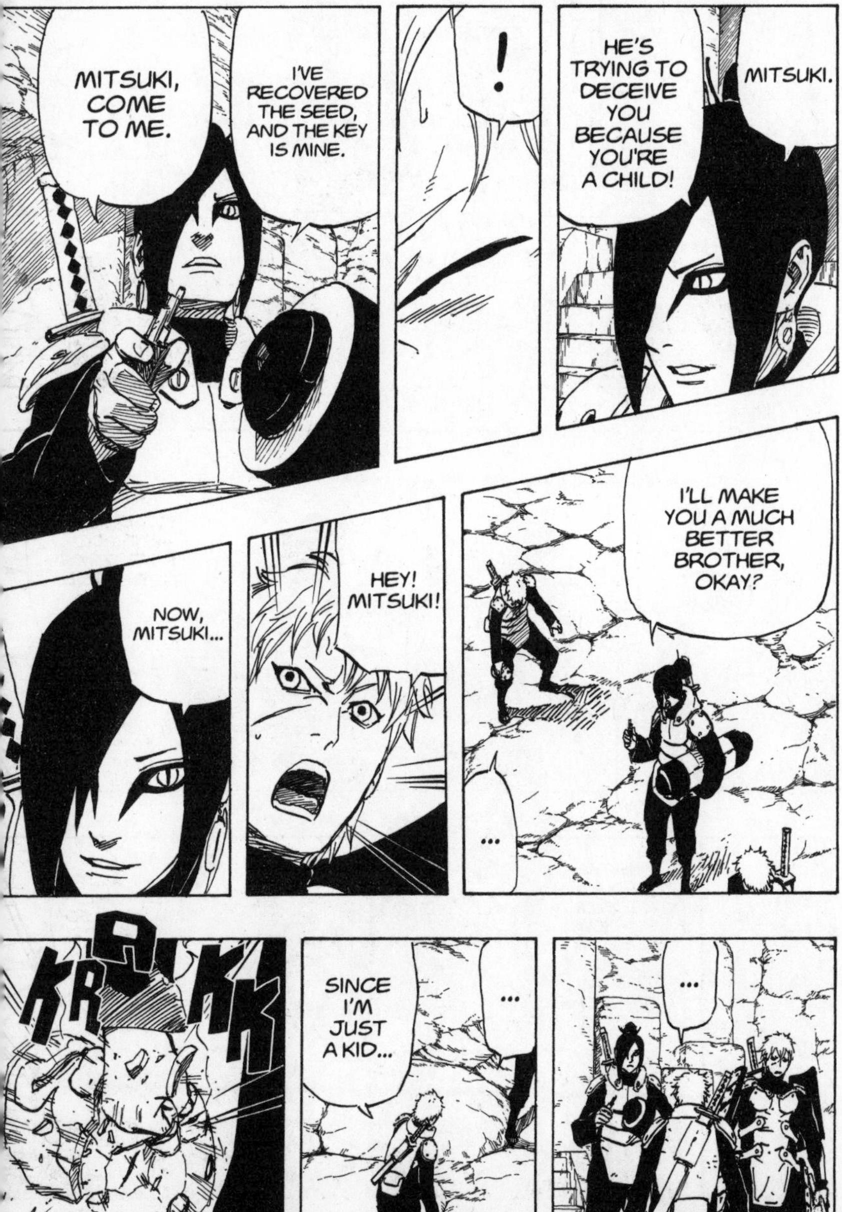
MITSUKI.
HE'S TRYING TO DECEIVE YOU BECAUSE YOU'RE A CHILD!
!
I'VE RECOVERED THE SEED, AND THE KEY IS MINE.
MITSUKI, COME TO ME.
I'LL MAKE YOU A MUCH BETTER BROTHER, OKAY?
...
HEY! MITSUKI!
NOW, MITSUKI...
...
...
SINCE I'M JUST A KID...
KRAKK

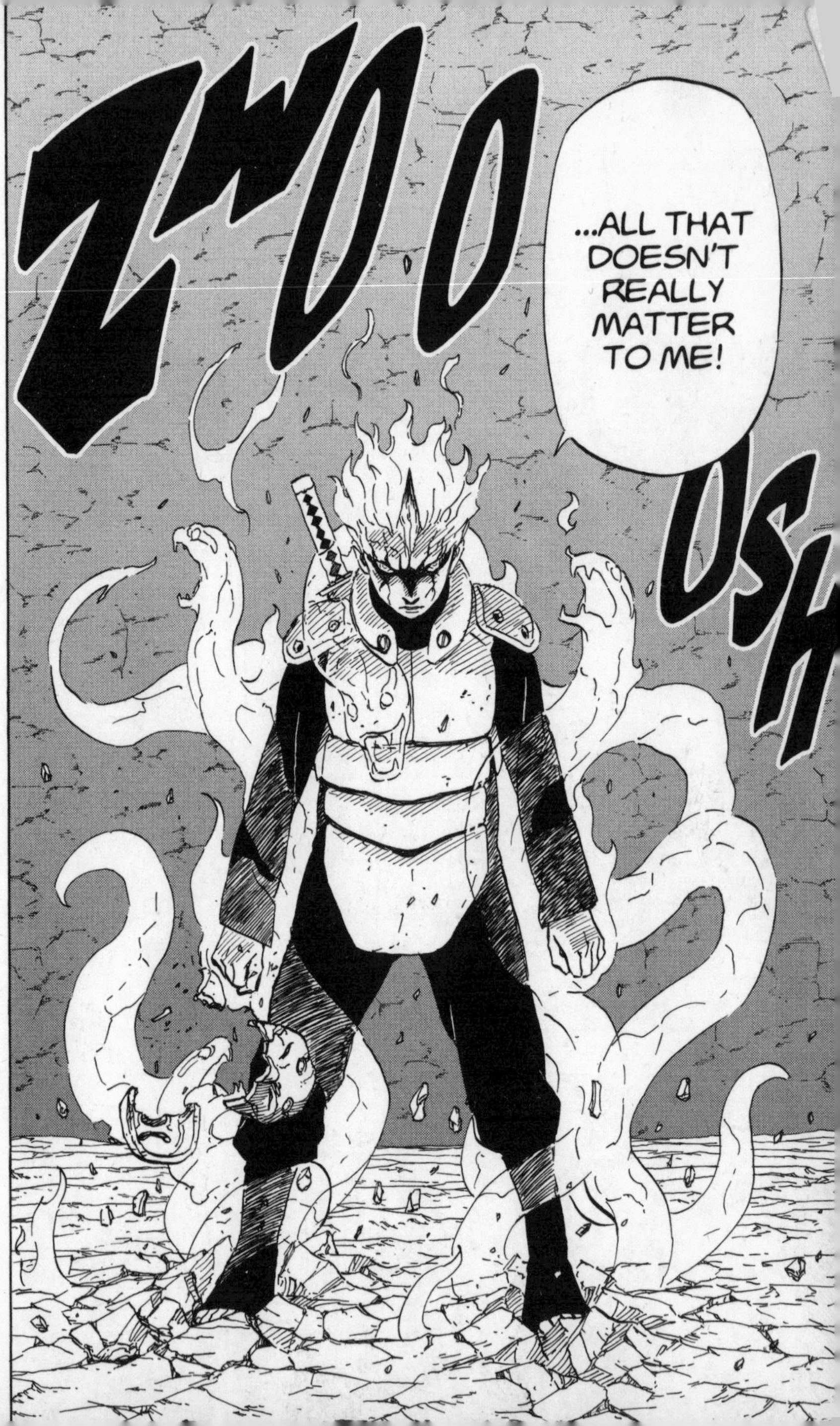

ZWOO
...ALL THAT DOESN'T REALLY MATTER TO ME!
OSH

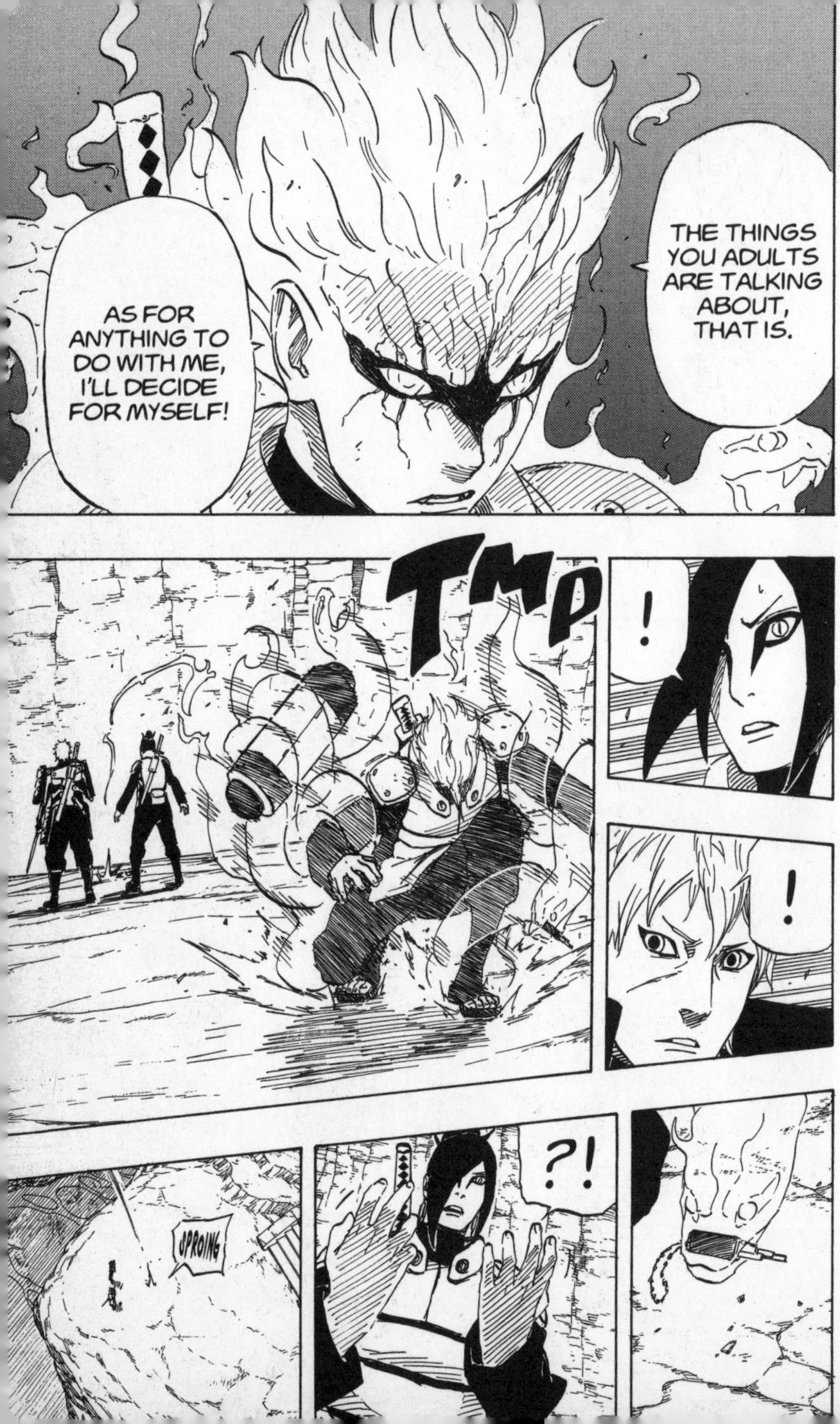
THE THINGS YOU ADULTS ARE TALKING ABOUT, THAT IS.
AS FOR ANYTHING TO DO WITH ME, I'LL DECIDE FOR MYSELF!
!
TMP
!
?!
SPROING

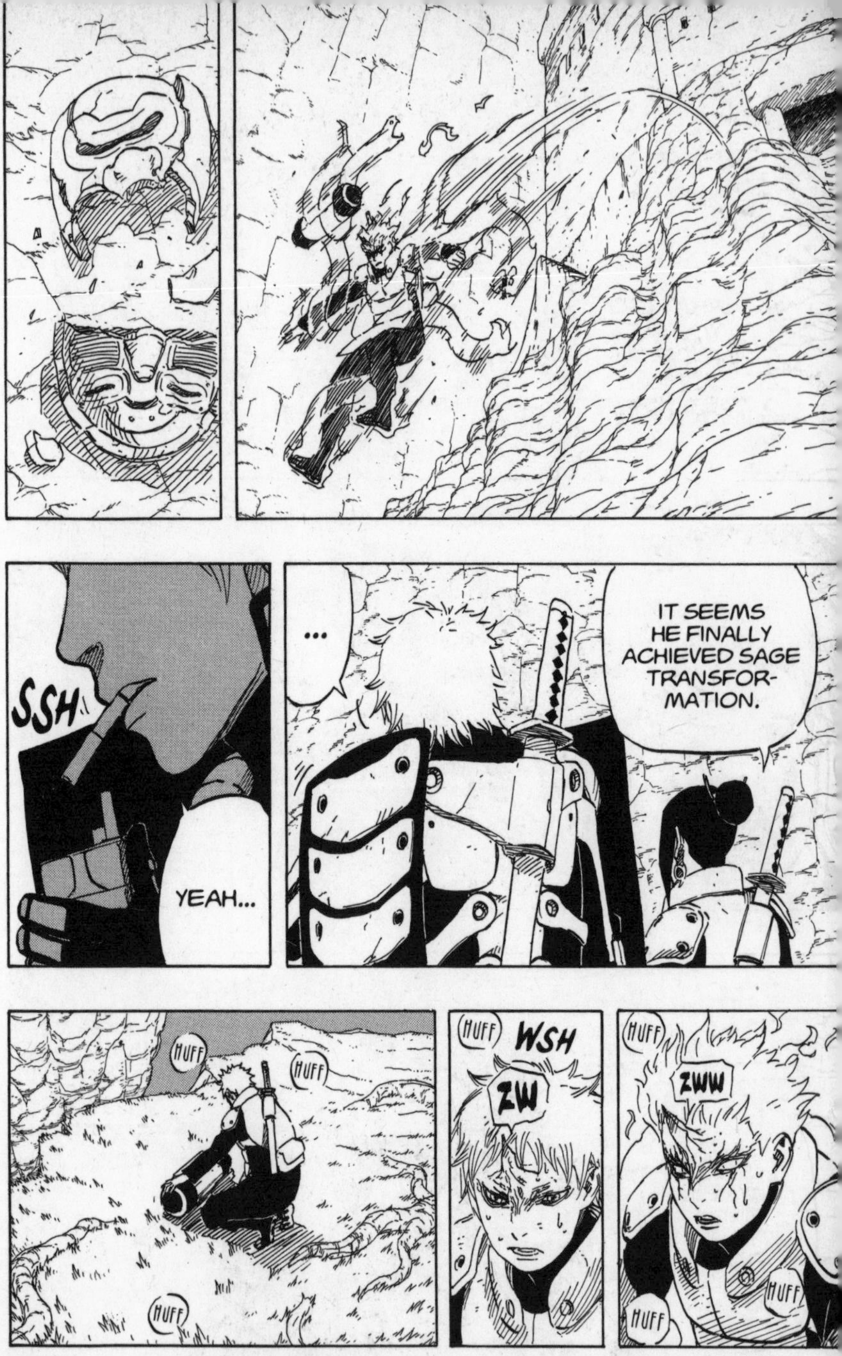
IT SEEMS HE FINALLY ACHIEVED SAGE TRANSFOR-MATION.
...
SSH
YEAH...
HUFF
ZWW
HUFF
HUFF
HUFF
WSH
ZW
HUFF
HUFF
HUFF

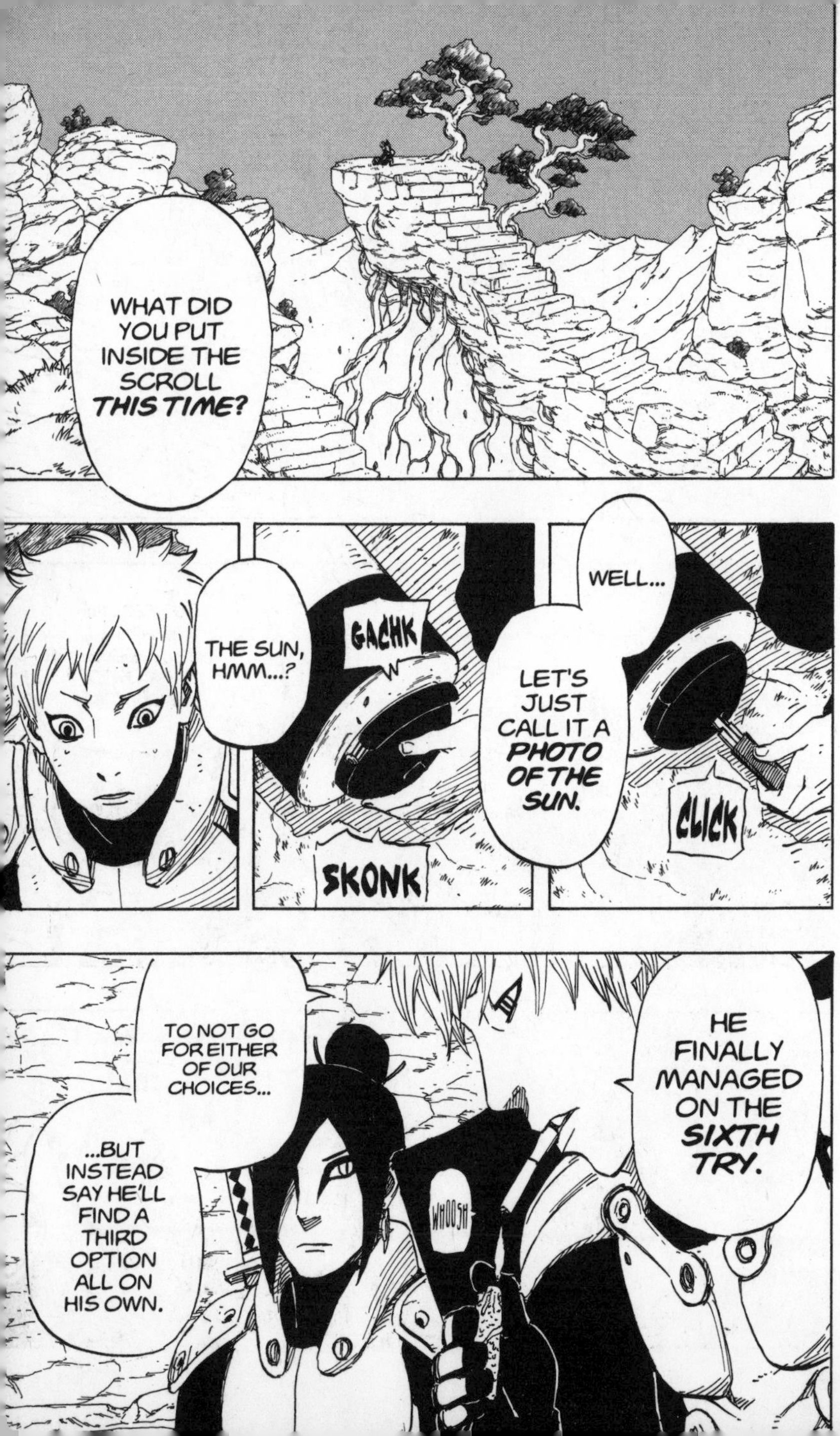
WHAT DID YOU PUT INSIDE THE SCROLL THIS TIME?
WELL...
LET'S JUST CALL IT A PHOTO OF THE SUN.
CLICK
GACHK
SKONK
THE SUN, HMM...?
HE FINALLY MANAGED ON THE SIXTH TRY.
WHOOSH
TO NOT GO FOR EITHER OF OUR CHOICES...
...BUT INSTEAD SAY HE'LL FIND A THIRD OPTION ALL ON HIS OWN.

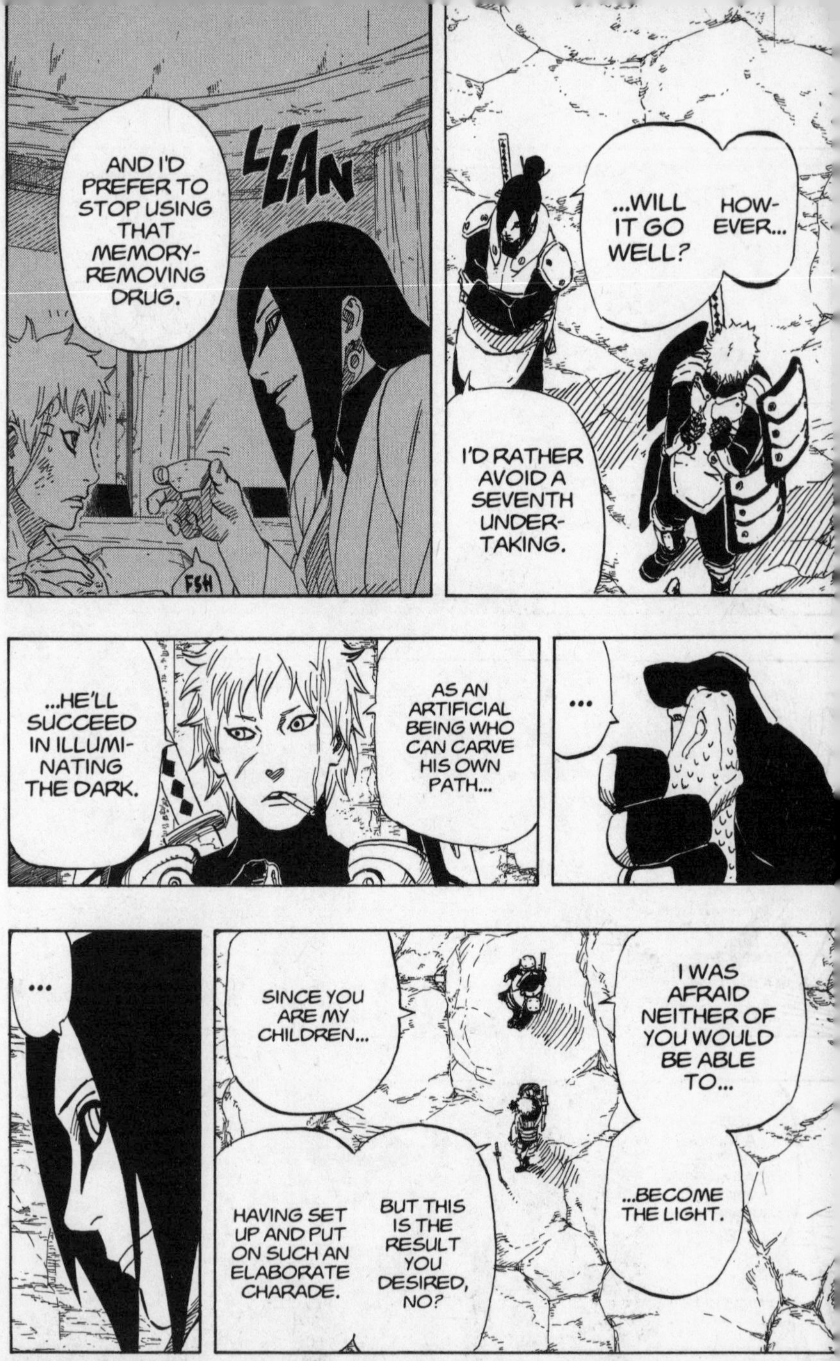
HOW-EVER...
...WILL IT GO WELL?
I'D RATHER AVOID A SEVENTH UNDER-TAKING.
LEAN
AND I'D PREFER TO STOP USING THAT MEMORY-REMOVING DRUG.
FSH
...
AS AN ARTIFICIAL BEING WHO CAN CARVE HIS OWN PATH...
...HE'LL SUCCEED IN ILLUMI-NATING THE DARK.
I WAS AFRAID NEITHER OF YOU WOULD BE ABLE TO...
SINCE YOU ARE MY CHILDREN...
...BECOME THE LIGHT.
BUT THIS IS THE RESULT YOU DESIRED, NO?
HAVING SET UP AND PUT ON SUCH AN ELABORATE CHARADE.
...

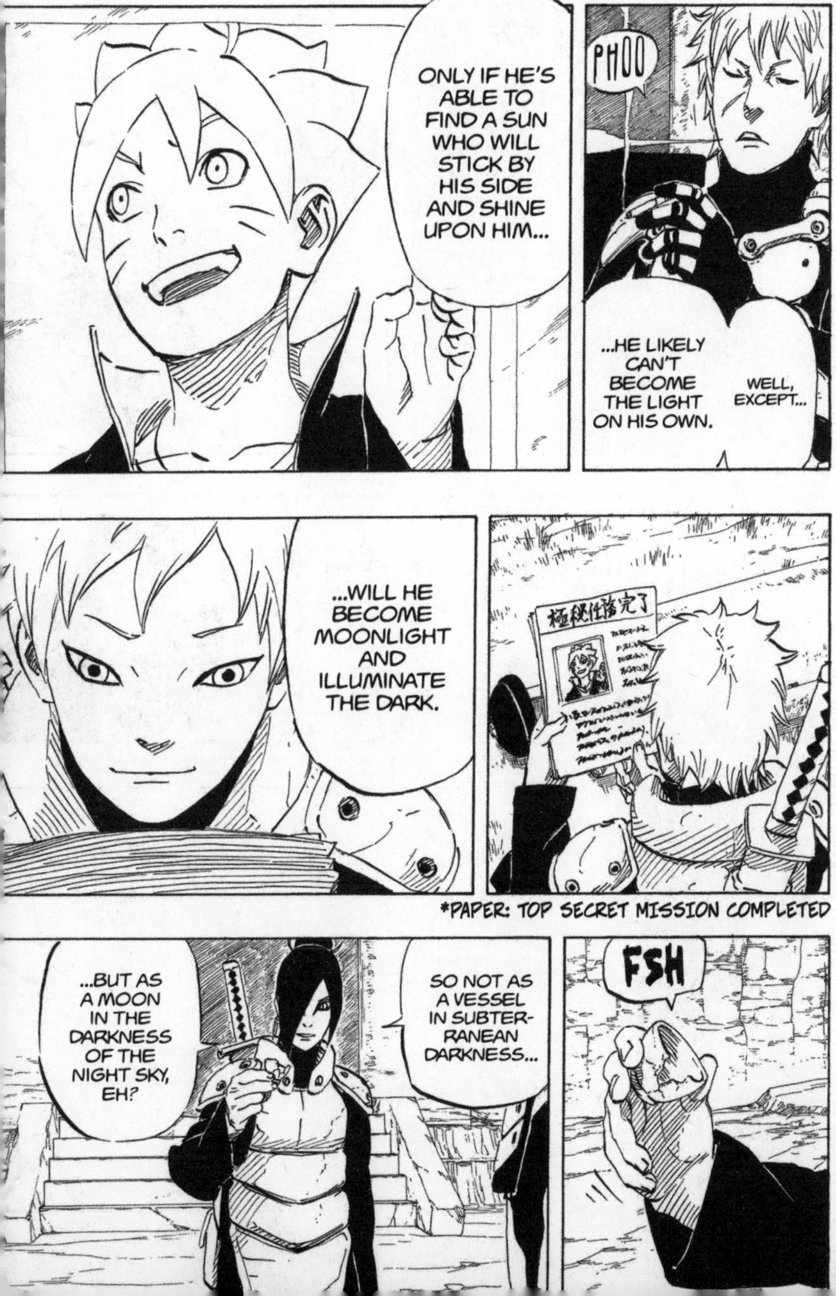
PHOO
...HE LIKELY CAN'T BECOME THE LIGHT ON HIS OWN.
WELL, EXCEPT...
ONLY IF HE'S ABLE TO FIND A SUN WHO WILL STICK BY HIS SIDE AND SHINE UPON HIM...
極秘任務完了
...WILL HE BECOME MOONLIGHT AND ILLUMINATE THE DARK.
*PAPER: TOP SECRET MISSION COMPLETED
FSH
SO NOT AS A VESSEL IN SUBTER-RANEAN DARKNESS...
...BUT AS A MOON IN THE DARKNESS OF THE NIGHT SKY, EH?

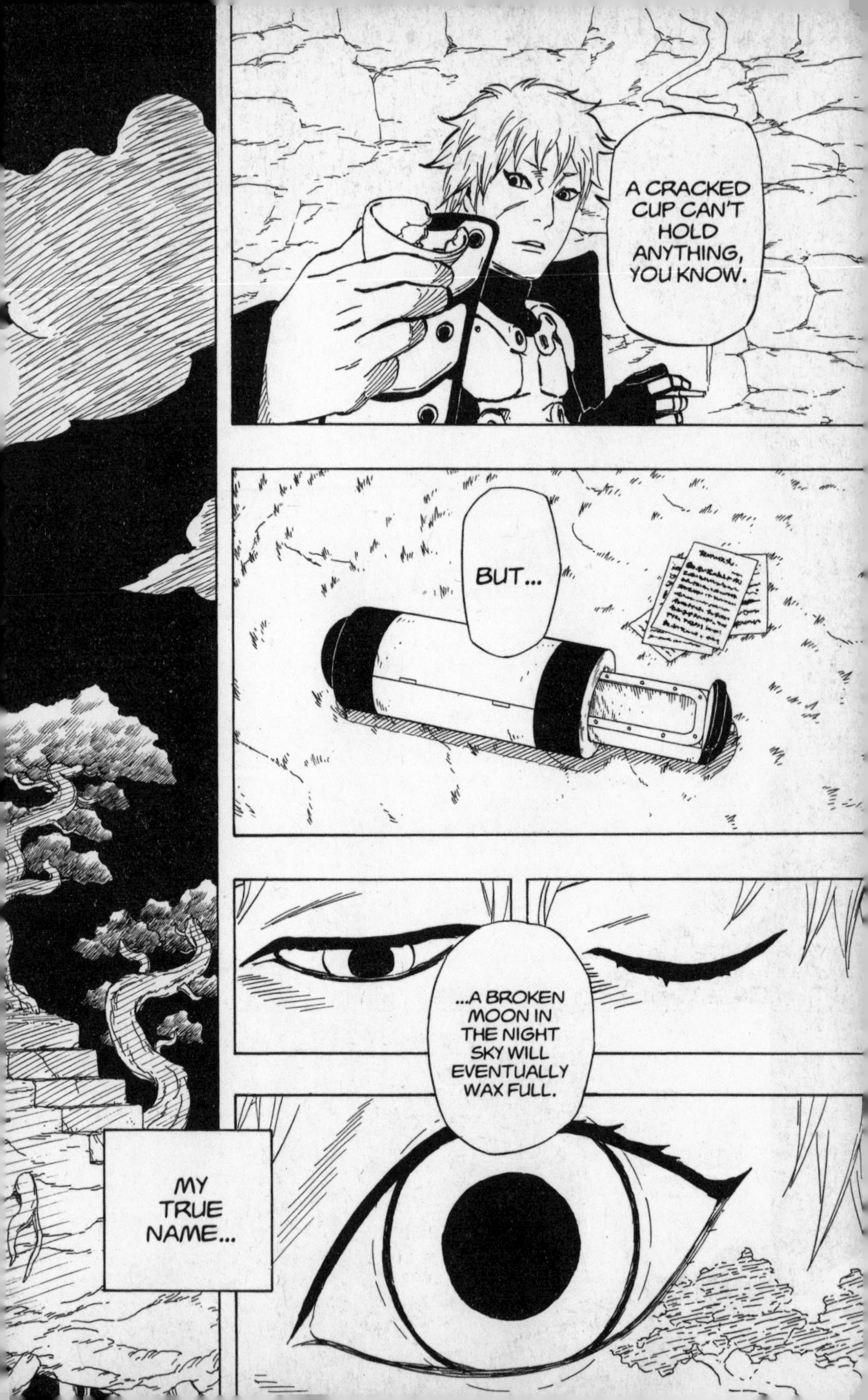
A CRACKED CUP CAN'T HOLD ANYTHING, YOU KNOW.
BUT...
...A BROKEN MOON IN THE NIGHT SKY WILL EVENTUALLY WAX FULL.
MY TRUE NAME...

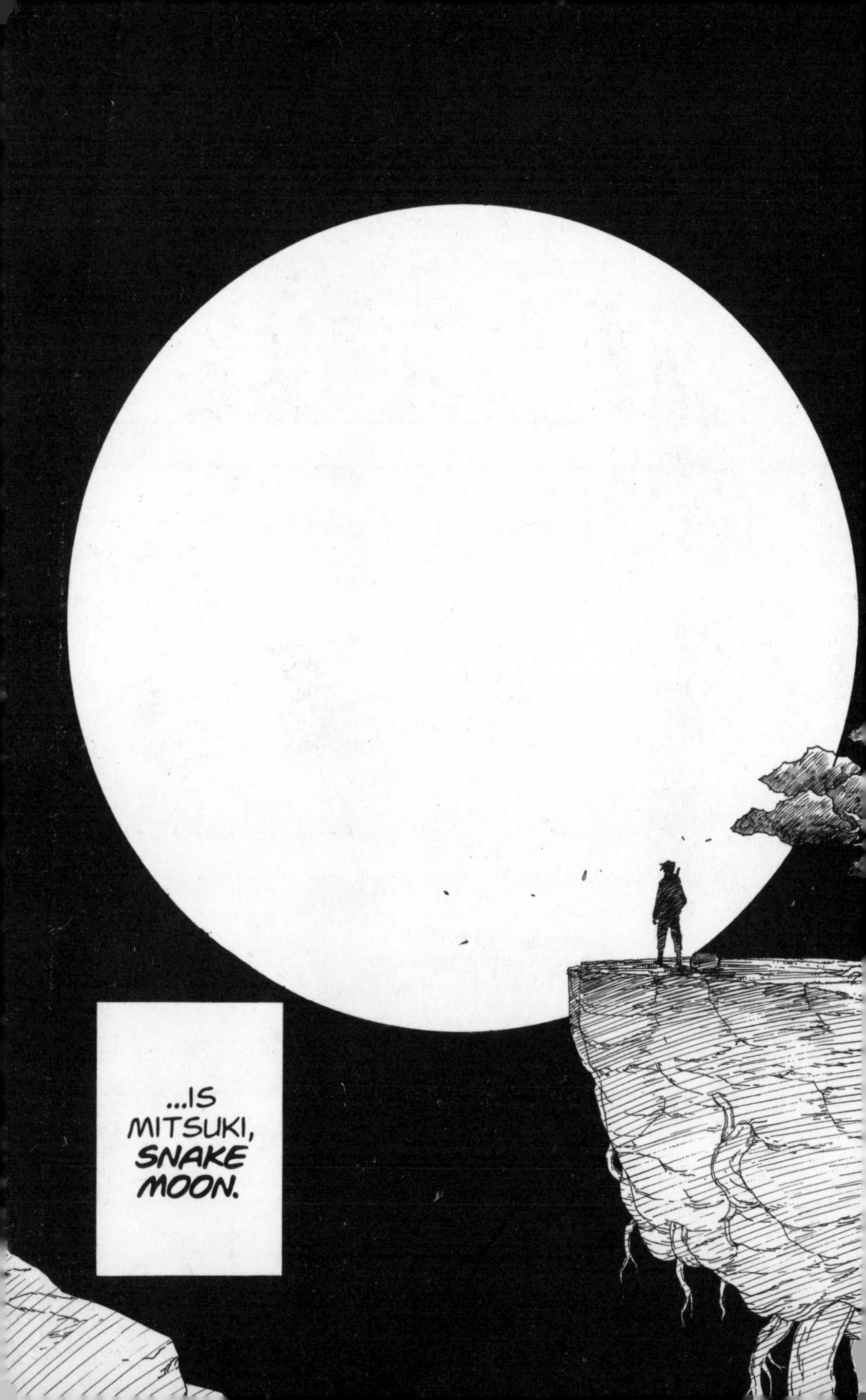
...IS MITSUKI, SNAKE MOON.

BORU-FANS!!!

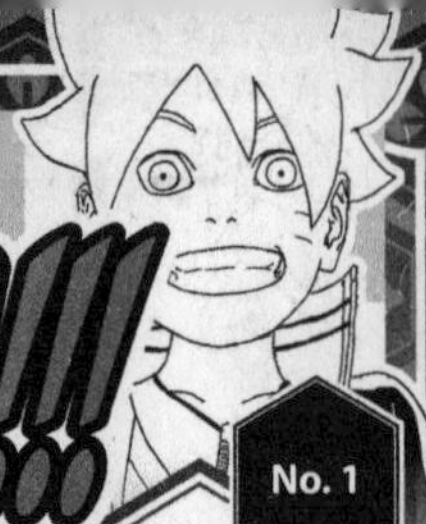

No. 1

The popular Boruto Fan Cluster page in *Weekly Shonen Jump*, abbreviated as Boru-fans!!!, will run in the graphic novels as well. This commemoration-worthy first segment will introduce Boruto's friends! A must-read for Boruto fans!!

Graphic novel version!!

Introducing Boruto's Friends
For this first segment, we're gonna introduce Boruto's classmates!!

UCHIHA SARADA

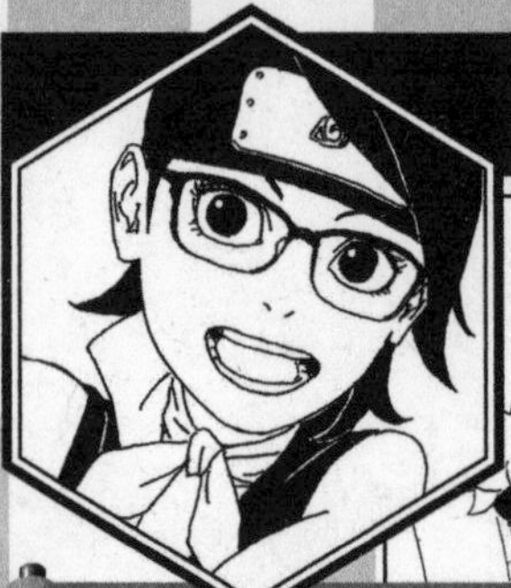

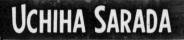

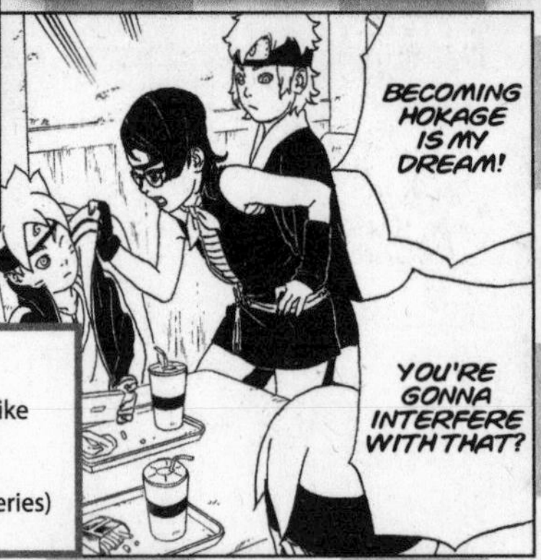
BECOMING HOKAGE IS MY DREAM!
YOU'RE GONNA INTERFERE WITH THAT?

Birthday: March 31
Favorite food: Things that taste like black tea
Food dislikes: Tomatoes
Hobbies: Reading (history, mysteries)

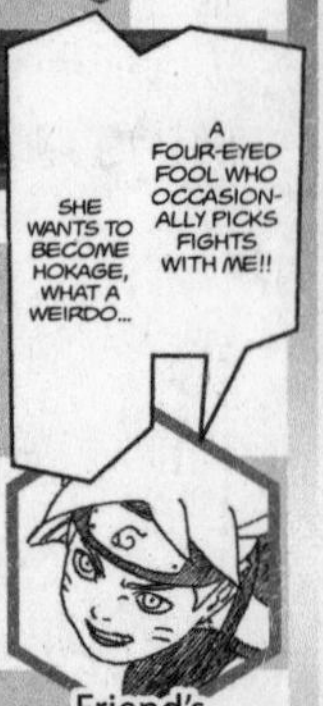
A FOUR-EYED FOOL WHO OCCASIONALLY PICKS FIGHTS WITH ME!!
SHE WANTS TO BECOME HOKAGE, WHAT A WEIRDO...

Friend's Comment

Going for her dream! She won't suffer any fools who get in her way!

MITSUKI

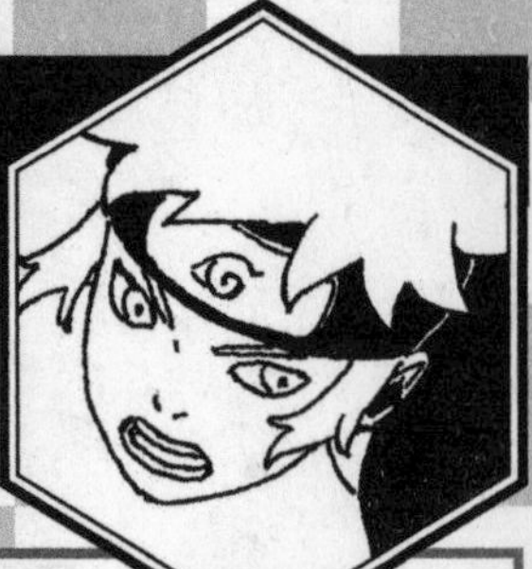

Mitsuki is always cool and collected. Makes you want to see him mad.

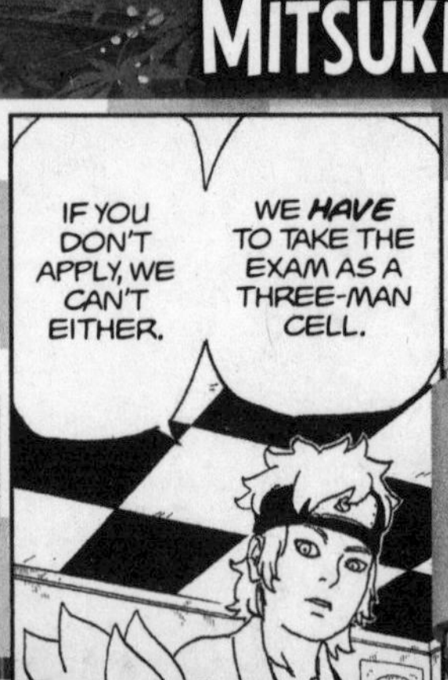
WE *HAVE* TO TAKE THE EXAM AS A THREE-MAN CELL.
IF YOU DON'T APPLY, WE CAN'T EITHER.

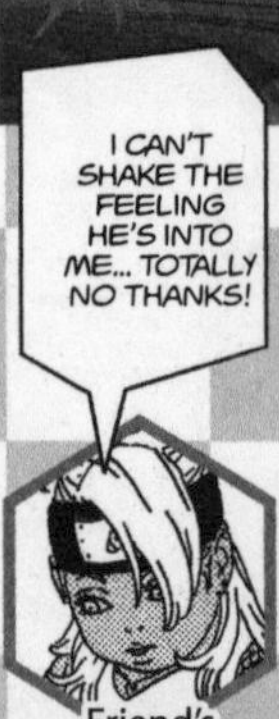
I CAN'T SHAKE THE FEELING HE'S INTO ME... TOTALLY NO THANKS!

Friend's Comment

Birthday: July 25
Favorite food: Scrambled eggs
Food dislikes: Meat from animals with scales
Hobbies: Reading data books, card games

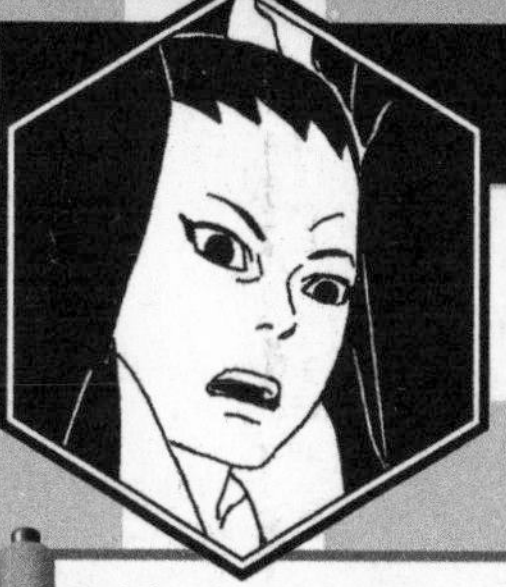

NARA SHIKADAI

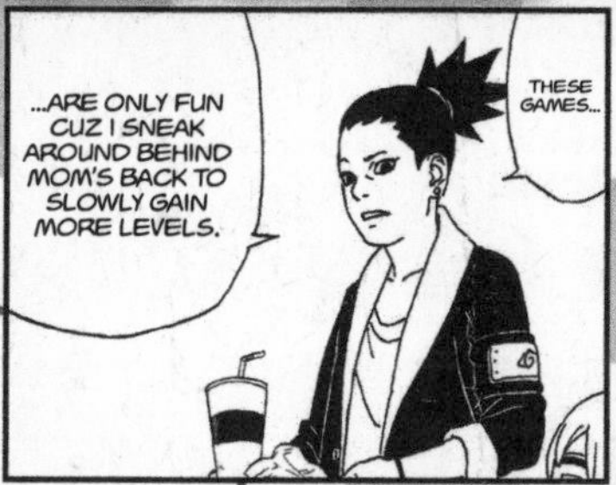
THESE GAMES...
...ARE ONLY FUN CUZ I SNEAK AROUND BEHIND MOM'S BACK TO SLOWLY GAIN MORE LEVELS.

Loves video games! Takes after his dad in hating bothersome things?!

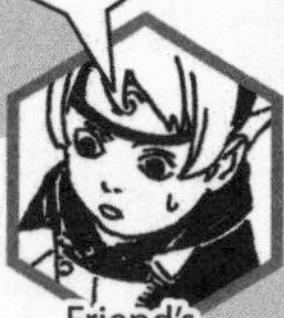
HE'S A GOOD GAMER, I CAN'T BEAT HIM... AND HE OVERSLEEPS TOO MUCH!
Friend's Comment

Birthday: September 23
Favorite food: Sashimi, eggplant
Food dislikes: Spinach
Hobbies: Simulation Games, afternoon naps

YAMANAKA INOJIN

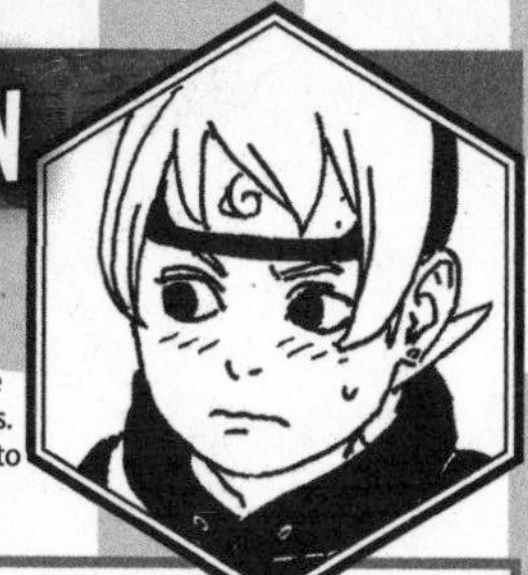

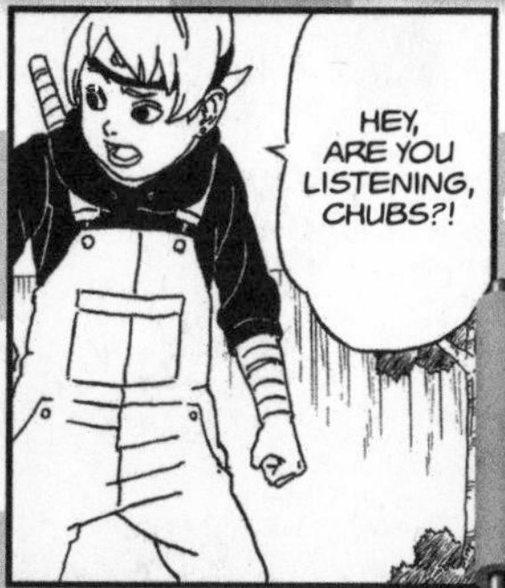
HEY, ARE YOU LISTENING, CHUBS?!

Said to have a sharp tongue, which he often uses. Someone to keep an eye on!!

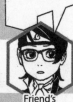

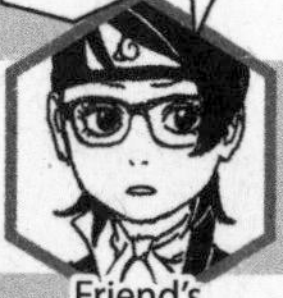
HUH? HMM... HE DRAWS WELL, AND HE'S SUPPOSED TO HAVE A SHARP TONGUE, BUT...
...HE'S NEVER USED IT ON ME...
Friend's Comment

Birthday: December 5
Favorite food: Cheese, takoyaki
Food dislikes: Fatty meat
Hobbies: Drawing, FPS games

AKIMICHI CHO-CHO

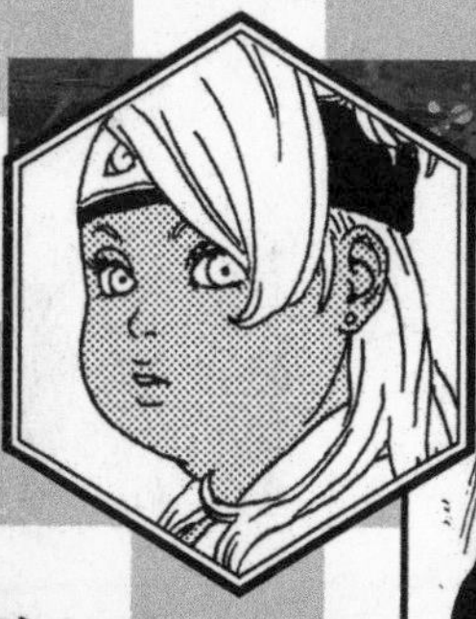

Her unique style includes munching whenever, wherever.

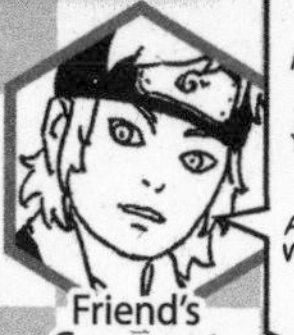
AKIMICHI STANDS OUT, SO NO MATTER WHERE SHE IS, YOU CAN TELL RIGHT AWAY! NO WORRIES !!
Friend's Comment

Birthday: August 8
Favorite food: Pretty much everything
Food dislikes: Almost nothing
Hobbies: Tastings, watching TV dramas

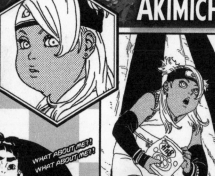

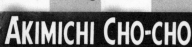

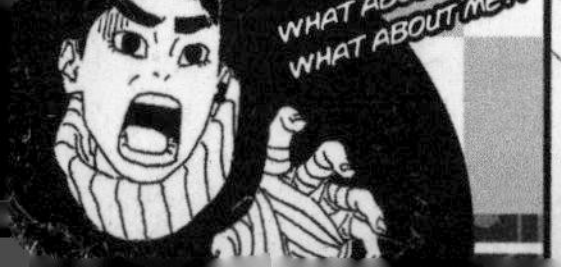
WHAT ABOUT ME?!
WHAT ABOUT ME?!

YOU'RE READING
IN THE
WRONG DIRECTION!!

WHOOPS! Guess what? You're starting at the wrong end of the comic!

...It's true! In keeping with the original Japanese format, **Boruto** is meant to be read from right to left, starting in the upper-right corner.

Unlike English, which is read from left to right, Japanese is read from right to left, meaning that action, sound effects and word-balloon order are completely reversed... something which can make readers unfamiliar with Japanese feel pretty backwards themselves. For this reason, manga or Japanese comics published in the U.S. in English have sometimes been published "flopped"—that is, printed in exact reverse order, as though seen from the other side of a mirror.

By flopping pages, U.S. publishers can avoid confusing readers, but the compromise is not without its downside. For one thing, a character in a flopped manga series who once wore in the original Japanese version a T-shirt emblazoned with "M A Y" (as in "the merry month of") now wears one which reads "Y A M"! Additionally, many manga creators in Japan are themselves unhappy with the process, as some feel the mirror-imaging of their art alters their original intentions.

We are proud to bring you **Boruto** in the original unflopped format. Turn to the other side of the book and let the ninjutsu begin...!

—Editor

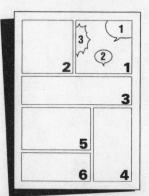